RELIGION AND THE STATE

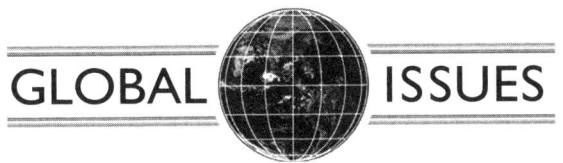

RELIGION AND THE STATE

Natalie Goldstein

Foreword by Walton Brown-Foster
Professor of Political Science
Central Connecticut State University

An imprint of Infobase Publishing

GLOBAL ISSUES: RELIGION AND THE STATE

Copyright © 2010 by Infobase Publishing

All rights reserved. No part of this book may be reproduced or utilized in any form or by any means, electronic or mechanical, including photocopying, recording, or by any information storage or retrieval systems, without permission in writing from the publisher. For information contact:

Facts On File, Inc.
An imprint of Infobase Publishing
132 West 31st Street
New York NY 10001

Library of Congress Cataloging-in-Publication Data

Goldstein, Natalie.
  Religion and the state / Natalie Goldstein; foreword by Walton Brown-Foster.
    p. cm.
  Includes bibliographical references (p.) and index.
  ISBN 978-0-8160-8090-8
  1. Religion and state. I. Title.
  BL65.S8G65 2010
  322'.1—dc22   2009043653

Facts On File books are available at special discounts when purchased in bulk quantities for businesses, associations, institutions, or sales promotions. Please call our Special Sales Department in New York at (212) 967-8800 or (800) 322-8755.

You can find Facts On File on the World Wide Web at http://www.factsonfile.com

Text design by Erika K. Arroyo
Illustrations by Dale Williams
Composition by Mary Susan Ryan Flynn
Cover printed by Art Print, Taylor, Pa.
Book printed and bound by Maple Press, York, Pa.
Date printed: April 2010
Printed in the United States of America

10 9 8 7 6 5 4 3 2 1

This book is printed on acid-free paper.

CONTENTS

List of Maps, Tables, and Graphs   ix
Foreword by Walton Brown-Foster   xi

PART I: AT ISSUE

Chapter 1:

Introduction   3
  Why Does Religion Exist?   4
  Politics and Religion   6
  Hinduism   7
  Buddhism: A Religion Without God   8
  Judaism and the Rise of Monotheism   12
  Western Christianity   14
  Islam   38

Chapter 2:

Focus on the United States   62
  The Birth of Religious Tolerance   62
  Religion and the Courts   68
  Is the United States a
    Christian or Secular Nation? 77

Chapter 3:

Global Perspectives   103
  Islamic Revolution in Iran   103
  Saudi Arabia: Theocratic Monarchy   113
  Tibet: Theocracy, Identity,
    and Autonomy   120
  Hindu Nationalism in India   127
  Western Europe: Secularism and
    the Paradox of Tolerance   133

PART II: PRIMARY SOURCES

Chapter 4:
United States Documents   **145**

Chapter 5:
International Documents   **183**
  Hinduism **183**
  Buddhism **184**
  Christianity **189**
  Islam **217**

PART III: RESEARCH TOOLS

Chapter 6:
How to Research Religion and the State **239**
  Book Research **239**
  Periodicals Research **241**
  Internet Searches **243**
  Legal Issues **248**

Chapter 7:
Facts and Figures **249**
  Introduction **249**
  United States **257**
  Global Perspectives **259**

Chapter 8:
Key Players **264**

Chapter 9:
Organizations and Agencies **276**

Chapter 10:
Annotated Bibliography **297**
  Religion and the State: General Works **297**
  Christianity: General and Early History **301**
  Christianity and Politics **303**
  Religion and the State in Europe **305**
  Religion and the State in
    the United States **307**
  Religious Fundamentalism
    in the United States **311**

    Islam: General Works and
        Early History   **314**
    Islam, Politics, and the State   **316**
    Islam: Fundamentalism and Terrorism   **319**
    Hinduism and Buddhism   **322**
    Nonprint Resources   **323**
    Web Sites and Documents   **327**

Chronology   **336**

Glossary   **345**

Index **351**

List of Maps, Tables, and Graphs

1.1	Percentage of World Population for Major Religions	249
1.2	How Select Nationalities View Religious Influence on Government	250
1.3	Religion(s) and Government of Selected World Nations	251
1.4	Holy Roman Empire, 1215–1250	253
1.5	Expansion of Islam, 632–2000	254
1.6	The Ottoman Empire, 1520	256
2.1	Religious Groups in the British Colonies, 1750	257
2.2	Biblical Worldview of American Christians	258
2.3	How Americans View Religious Influence on Government	258
3.1	Modern Iran	259
3.2	Ibn Saud's Campaigns of Conquest, 1902–1932	260
3.3	Tibet Autonomous Region and Historic Tibet	261
3.4	BJP-Ruled States in India, 2009	262
3.5	Muslim Populations in Key European Countries and the United States	263

Foreword

Several years ago I set out to develop a comparative politics course that would compare and contrast the role of the five major world religions in politics and states. The course I designed looked at the five major world religions in both global and domestic contexts of various nation-states. The course was a response to what seemed a gap in the range of courses that addressed the forces affecting politics and government throughout the world. It was also part of an emerging trend in which scholars and researchers were increasingly interested in the intersection between religion, politics, and the state, especially after the events of 9/11 and the response by the newly mobilized forces of Christian conservatism in the United States. A similar mobilization of conservative political forces occurred in India with the rise of a Hindu fundamentalist political party, the BJP (Bharatiya Janata Party, "Indian People's Party"), in the late 1990s, and in Iran during the Iranian Revolution in 1979, which led to the creation of the first modern theocracy.

Typically the study of religion, politics, and the state has been confined to the halls of academia and highly specialized academics focused on either comparative religion or political science. Their publications and research are targeted to the college- and university-level audience. In the latter part of the 20th century, the momentum toward multicultural training for secondary-level teachers and the inclusion of diversity and multicultural courses and learning opportunities for students in the United States took off in earnest. By the first decade of the 21st century, interest in cultural and diversity competency training and courses changed from merely an interest to a matter of necessity, given the rapid pace of globalization and the 9/11 attacks on the World Trade Center.

In an effort to make this area of study and inquiry accessible to students beyond the walls of higher education, Natalie Goldstein has taken a major step in writing a volume in the Global Issues series, *Religion and the State*, which is geared primarily toward high school students. However, she has

RELIGION AND THE STATE

produced a volume that not only the high school audience will appreciate but that will also be of great use at the college level. Goldstein's book presents and introduces the major religious traditions of the world to students in a style that both informs readers of the important precepts of each religious tradition and introduces them to the political and historic contexts in which each tradition developed and had its impact. Goldstein does all of this clearly, thoughtfully, and factually.

Religion and the State is an answer to the major dilemma facing anyone teaching a course in comparative religion and politics: finding a book that addresses the quintessential issues that the course is designed to investigate. Religion informs the state and politics on matters of ethics, areas of policy, and political processes while politics affects organized religions, persons of faith in politics, and the very functions of government. The relationships between religion and politics vary depending on the religious tradition and governing context. The complexity and subtlety of these relationships, and the variety of circumstances that affect them, make the topic difficult to research. These relationships are precisely what this book is written to clarify and illuminate.

Religion, state, and politics produce a powerful combination of concepts, ideas, and values that influence events in countries as well as relationships between countries. Throughout history religion has been a force in the conduct of politics and the formation and functions of most nation-states. In the modern global system, the concept of secularization has been a cause for debate, controversy, and in some cases political violence. But at the core of the secular debate is defining the parameters and degree to which religion should influence the state and politics. No political regime or state has successfully discarded the role of religion in politics and policy making. Some degree of success may have been achieved in managing the influence and reach of religious institutions and actors in matters of the state and politics, but religion by its nature manifests itself individually, personally, and communally. Thus, even where organized religions are monitored, controlled, or even eliminated, individuals will or may act on their religious convictions in the public and governing arena.

Goldstein's volume is a valuable addition to Facts On File's Global Issues series, which provides resources and guidance to students researching and inquiring into topics that are of vital and global concern today. Part I of *Religion and the State* introduces the topic of religion and state using real-world experiences and examples to which almost anyone can relate. Rarely have I found such clear and concise definitions of religion and basic explanations of the role of religion in society, especially the politics in a society. The author asks the simple and basic question, "What is the relationship between religion and politics?" Goldstein explains, "Because it is so comprehensive, religion

Foreword

encompasses politics insofar as it provides a framework on which believers collectively can understand and organize their lives and their society.... Religions and states are infinitely varied, as are the ways they affect each other. History and circumstance determine how the relationship between religion and the state evolves. The interaction between the state and religion (or its institutions) is usually fluid; it changes as religion/believers and/or the state/politics change in response to the vagaries of history and, sometimes, by how this history is interpreted by seminal thinkers."

After laying the foundation for understanding the relationship among religion, politics, and the state in general defining terms, chapter 1 is devoted to introducing the reader to the major faith traditions—Islam, Christianity, Buddhism, and Hinduism—which are the focus of the book. The historical context in which each faith tradition emerged to inform politics and the creation of states are discussed. Just enough depth and detail are given to adequately treat the important points in the histories of each religion and their relationship to politics and the state.

Chapter 2 focuses on the United States as a specific case. The case of the United States is particularly important because of its success in adopting the idea of secularization, notions of religious freedom, tolerance, and diversity. These concepts have become a standard by which to measure the level of modernization and political development for the majority of nation-states in the global system. The concept of religious tolerance as a governing principle is one area of focus in the chapter.

Chapter 3 expands the area of discussion to Iran, Saudi Arabia, India, Tibet, and Western Europe. Comparing religion and politics in these countries raises awareness and understanding of the relationship between religion and the political context—each country in this chapter being fundamentally different from the United States on some levels and like the United States on other levels. It is in this chapter that one develops an understanding of the cross-national and cultural similarities and differences in how the various traditions affect politics and the state and vice versa.

The book is also a practical guide to research tools, strategies, and resources. Chapters 4 and 5 are devoted to the presentation of various historical documents and materials important when researching the evolution of religion and state relations in the United States, Islam, Christianity, Buddhism, and Hinduism. The choices and range of resources provided in these chapters are invaluable to students and conveniently located in this book.

The last chapters provide bibliographic information, research methodologies and approaches, statistical information and maps, a glossary, and biographical data about some important individuals in the histories of each religious tradition, a list of organizations and agencies, and a chronology. The

RELIGION AND THE STATE

treasure trove of information and resources provided in these chapters will benefit students in all areas of research.

I was honored when Natalie Goldstein invited me to write the foreword for this new and exiting book. I am truly looking forward to the publication, and I am certain that those who adopt this volume will be more than pleased with it. There is no other book that I have come across that fills such a unique and important niche in the literature on the topic. It will help both intellectually and academically prepare students, high school students especially, who will inherit a world that is much more interconnected due to the forces of technology and globalization. Without the foundation and opportunities to gain greater knowledge and information about the diverse cultures, traditions, and histories in our world, the opportunities for international cooperation and finding global solutions to globally shared and common problems, challenges, and dilemmas will be harder, if not nearly impossible, to address. At the very basic level, then, an understanding of the linkages and interactions among politics, religion, and the state in the varying contexts and traditions will be fundamentally important to the common and entwined destinies of us all. Thanks to *Religion and the State* by Natalie Goldstein, we are one small step closer to that goal.

—Walton Brown-Foster
Professor of Political Science
Central Connecticut State University

PART I

At Issue

1

Introduction

Airports have always been a hassle. Nowadays, every air traveler has to submit to the indignities of searches and intrusive scans of both bags and body. Yet even before our age of enhanced security, navigating unmolested from ticket counter to departure gate was a tricky business. Not all that long ago, the harried flier dragging luggage through miles of airport corridors lived in dread of an unwanted and intensely aggravating encounter with the Hare Krishna people. The telltale clanging of metal cymbals and the caterwauling of ecstatic singers sometimes forewarned the traveler, who might then be able to take evasive action. Often, though, no warning heralded the approach of the orange-draped, beatifically smiling assailant. Once trapped, the traveler could not avoid the proffered flower and, if one was really unlucky, the reams of missionary literature intended to convert the flier to this love-filled religion. These Western devotees of the Hindu god Krishna haunted nearly every airport in the country and supported the group by requesting donations in exchange for their flowers of peace.

Although the Hare Krishnas were a huge annoyance, no one ever questioned the Hare Krishnas' right to be Hare Krishnas and to worship and live according to their chosen religion. They may have been an intolerable nuisance, and most people wished they would just go away, but everyone accepted that they had a right to believe whatever they wanted. Religious tolerance is so ingrained in the American psyche, culture, tradition, and law, no one considers prohibiting people from embracing the Hare Krishna religion or any other sincerely held religious belief that does not undermine or threaten civil law, no matter how strange it seems to be.

In the West, religious tolerance is one of the foundations of society and something everyone respects and takes for granted. Yet it was not always this way. In centuries past, Hare Krishnas might have been imprisoned, interrogated (or worse), and possibly burned at the stake for their heresy against "official" religion. The religious freedom and tolerance people in many parts of the world accept as their birthright evolved over centuries, as society's view of the relationship between religion and the state, and the individual's relationship with each, changed over time. The history of this evolution has encompassed revolutions in thought as well as in the structure of society and the state. Sometimes these transitions were fairly peaceful; at other times, the changes came only after intense social upheaval. The most important lesson taught by this history is that the principle of religious freedom we take for granted today should not be viewed as the natural order of society. Religious freedom is a hard-earned right, often paid for in blood. It is a fairly recent development in the evolution of human society, and even today it might be lost far more easily than it was won.

Religious freedom and tolerance, though occasionally found throughout history in various societies and religions, are by no means universal today. There are some modern nations in which the state enforces a particular religious observance and other states in which sectors of the populace are trying to impose their religious views on the state and its citizens. Thus, the right to religious freedom and toleration of the religious beliefs of others remain contentious. Further, religious freedom is not universally viewed as a good thing; in fact, there are a number of places where it is seen as pernicious and a threat to both religion and society.

This text attempts to show how the interaction between religion and the state has changed over time. It examines the way evolving religious institutions and beliefs have influenced states and governments, and vice versa, in different parts of the world at significant times in history. It hopes to show how the changes in this interconnection led to the current, sometimes fractious and uneasy relationship between religions and states.

Before launching into our subject, a few words must be devoted to the inevitable limitations of a project such as this. First, the text examines the interplay of religion and politics, or the state. Thus, the full scope of religious belief and practice is not included. Second, the focus of the book is on those religions that have had the most profound and dramatic effect on states and governments. For this reason, not every world religion can be covered extensively or even in passing. Their omission implies no slight to them but is due mainly to a shortage of space.

WHY DOES RELIGION EXIST?

Archaeologists have revealed that religion is probably an integral part of human existence. The grave sites of our most primeval ancestors often contain ritual objects. There are also signs of ritual burial, with all the interred

Introduction

placed in a specific position or facing the same direction. Such burials indicate that during the Middle Paleolithic period (ca. 300,000–50,000 years ago) people probably believed in some type of afterlife—a foundational element of religion. Why would our ancient ancestors conjure beliefs that must be defined as religious?

It is very likely that, like us, the earliest humans wondered at the shattering transformation of death. Once the body ceases to function, what happens to the *person,* to the essence—we may call it spirit or soul—that animated the body and made that person who he really *was?* Confronting death probably led early humans to formulate religious beliefs that gave them the assurance they sought of spiritual persistence.

When a person reaches the age of awareness, it becomes obvious that she exists in a world not made or controlled by humans. Yet people are an integral part of the world in which they must survive. This awareness raises simple but momentous questions that underlie religion. Why does the Earth exist? Where did it come from? Where did I come from? Why am I here? Societies have developed various types of religions to answer these questions. Most early religions responded by formulating creation myths about how and why the Earth began and what humanity's place and purpose are in this creation. In animistic religions, the divine is immanent in the world because natural objects and forces are endowed with spirit. In recognizing their intimate commonality with all of creation, animals, plants, and virtually all parts of the natural environment are viewed as being instilled with spirit. In polytheistic religions, natural objects or forces may or may not have souls, but they are controlled by more remote, external deities of some sort. The deities are propitiated during religious ceremonies. In both cases, worshipping or appeasing spirits gave early humans a greater sense of control over their environment. In monotheistic religions (Judaism, Christianity, Islam), the one supreme god is viewed as wholly remote and transcendent.

Religion, then, represents humans' attempts to answer fundamental questions that encompass all dimensions of experience. Religions address cosmology (creation) and eschatology (end-times) and explain nature, birth, death, suffering, and morality within a holistic framework. Many religions address the concept of salvation of the soul, its transcendence of worldly suffering, and its persistence after death. Some religions focus more on how to live a moral life in accordance with guidelines set out in scripture or enunciated by a prophet. All religions require devotees to have faith in the divinity and its power. Because it is so comprehensive, religion encompasses politics insofar as it provides a framework on which believers collectively can understand and organize their lives and their society.

RELIGION AND THE STATE

POLITICS AND RELIGION

Although religion helps order a society, it does not necessarily specify a particular type of governance even if the religion and culture are inseparably intertwined and religion informs every aspect of life. Such a religion might function in a society ruled by a god-king, chief, clan, group of elders, or the purest form of democracy in which decisions are made by the consensus of all adults. Ancient Greece provides a good example. Sparta and Athens were two Greek city-states only 95 miles (153 km) apart, and both Athenians and Spartans worshipped the same Greek gods. Yet Sparta was a severe, militarist state ruled by a warrior elite, while Athens was the birthplace of Western democracy and philosophy. Although the people worshipped the same gods, they produced totally different political and social systems.

Politics and religion intersect in humanity's search for order and for predictable results arising from human actions. Earthly and cosmic events (e.g., the seasons, the phases of the Moon) are also orderly and predictable. It follows that the two might be analogous: that there is "someone"—an immensely powerful being—who acts to control the earthly and cosmic order within which humans exist. What or who controls these phenomena? For what purpose? People sought to understand this powerful being (God) by forming a "theological image in which God, man, and world form an indissoluble divine nexus. . . . The believer has reasons for believing that he lives in this divine nexus, just as he has reasons for thinking that it offers authoritative guidance for political life."[1] The divine becomes political because, as creator and controller of the world, the divine is imbued with an ultimate power and authority. Thus, "if we conceive of God as the shaper of our cosmos, which displays his purposes, then the legitimate exercise of political authority might very well depend on understanding these purposes."[2] It follows that whoever reveals God's purpose and is recognized as a true vehicle for communicating God's will is also one who may legitimately exercise authority over others. This bestowal of authority on God and, from there, on his earthly representative creates the intersection where religion and politics meet. It also raises crucial questions about who on Earth interprets divine will as found in religion. Who, in other words, has the authority to speak for God to humans living in the world? This question is answered by a religion's political theology, which bestows authority on some person or entity based on divine revelation. This answer, however, raises issues about the relationship between those claiming God's authority and those claiming political authority. Political power can compel certain actions, but it is religion that gives these actions moral legitimacy.

Religions and states are infinitely varied, as are the ways they affect each other. History and circumstance determine how the relationship between

Introduction

religion and the state evolves. The interaction between the state and religion (or its institutions) is usually fluid; it changes as religion/believers and/or the state/politics change in response to the vagaries of history and, sometimes, by how this history is interpreted by seminal thinkers.

As civilizations developed, religion evolved. In India, polytheism matured to become the highly sophisticated and spiritual Hindu religion. There also arose new types of religion that contrasted starkly with the religions of ancient times. These were primarily Buddhism, which is atheistic, and monotheism, in which only one transcendent god is worshipped.

HINDUISM

Hinduism, a religion of great complexity and beauty, arose from the teachings found in the Vedas, ancient scriptures based on even older oral traditions, that were recorded in India about 1200 B.C.E. Some of the early Vedas, such as the Rig Veda, view kings as almost godlike and infallible, even as incarnations of a god whose power is absolute. The early Vedas emphasized ritual sacrifice, and the priests who performed these rituals, called Brahmins, became the highest order in the developing caste system, or rigid social hierarchy. As the caste system evolved, the support of Brahmins bestowed legitimacy on kings, whose authority rested on priestly approval. The Brahmins lorded it over those in lower castes: the Kshatriyas, the lordly or warrior caste; the Vaishyas, or householders, farmers, and merchants; and the Shudras, or peasants and laborers. The untouchables (Dalits) were the lowest of the low, did the most menial jobs, and were generally shunned by all other castes. The caste system had a religious basis in the Vedas, but it also served as an ironclad structure for maintaining an orderly society. Social mobility was nonexistent; one remained in the caste into which one was born. (Remnants of the rigid and unjust caste system are still being dismantled by Indian social and political activists today.)

The Upanishads, written between 800 and 300 B.C.E., evolved from the Vedas. Along with the Bhagavad Gita (ca. 200 B.C.E.), these scriptures shaped yogic and devotional Hinduism. To the Vedic teaching that a good religious life involved doing one's duty within one's caste was added the spiritual goal of devotion to the divine that might lead the worshipper's atman (god-soul) to become one with the transcendent and absolute god, Brahman. Though aspects of the one absolute god could take many forms—the major ones being Shiva (the destroyer), Brahma (the creator), and Vishnu (the sustainer)—all are subsumed within the supreme Brahman. A unique aspect of Hinduism is that all Hindus may not be devotees of the same god, or form of god. Some Hindus worship primarily Vishnu, others Shiva, and so on. Yet all are Hindus and all ascribe to the fundamental teaching of Hinduism: that one should seek release from rebirth and reincarnation.

There are, supposedly, more than a billion gods (most of them minor local deities) worshipped under the umbrella of Hinduism. This makes Hinduism the champion polytheistic religion of all time. Yet Hinduism has evolved into a sophisticated religion that allows for aspects of the one God (Brahman) to be worshipped along with or through God's many forms. Achieving spiritual enlightenment and release from rebirth are accomplished by practicing one or more forms of yoga (bhakti [devotion], karma [good works], *jnana* [knowledge], etc.). The concept of dharma, or living in harmony with the world, nature, and god, arose in the Hindu tradition and was later adopted, with the concept of karma, by Buddhists.

Hinduism is not organized into an institutional church, has no one central religious authority, such as a pope, and allows devotees to follow different scriptures and worship different aspects of god. Its longevity and resilience are an outgrowth of this flexibility and of its deep and ancient roots as the organizing principle and foundation of Indian social structure. The caste system maintained kingly and princely power throughout the Muslim conquest of much of India in the second millennium C.E., though this is due partly to the similarities in Hindu and Muslim concepts of kingship and ideal kingly rule. The British raj undermined Hindu kingship and the age-old structure of Hindu society, though the colonial power did engage with cooperative regional princes who were allowed to retain their titles (if not their power). However, the British conquest of India led inevitably to an independence movement that was, at least to some degree, intent on reestablishing traditional Hindu society.

BUDDHISM: A RELIGION WITHOUT GOD

Most experts would call Buddhism a religion while admitting that it does not fit neatly into any religious definition. For one thing, Buddhism denies the existence of a creator; there is no god either engaged with or disengaged from the world. God, as creator or guide, is irrelevant. Despite its emphasis on disengagement, Buddhism has influenced statecraft throughout its history.

Siddhartha Gautama

Buddhism was founded by a prince, or raja, called Siddhartha Gautama, who was born around 563 B.C.E. in northern India. Legend has it that this prince led a sheltered and luxurious life until, one day, he left his palace. What he saw—an old man, a sick man, a dead man, and a serene monk—shook him to

Introduction

his core. He was struck by the conviction that life contains much suffering, but that it may be possible to free oneself from it. So, at age 29, Siddhartha shaved his head, dressed in the rags of a mendicant, and left his palace and family to attain release from suffering.

Siddhartha studied with holy men, or yogis, of the highest rank. But they did not provide what he was looking for. He then spent years as an ascetic, purifying his body through long fasts and other mortifications. After six years of punishing asceticism, Siddhartha was nearer to death than he was to the truth. He rejected asceticism as a path to enlightenment.

Siddhartha determined to find another, middle way to ultimate truth. Upon arrival in Bodhgaya, Gautama sat down beneath a tree and vowed to meditate until the truth was revealed to him. On the 49th day of meditation, Siddhartha became the Buddha, or the Enlightened One. In his meditation he saw all of his past lives, or incarnations. He also experienced the supreme, blissful insight called nirvana, the profound realization of the truth of impermanence. It is the indescribable bliss one experiences when one "lets go" of ignorant identification with an insubstantial, craving ego. Buddha became a teacher of enlightenment.

Buddha stated, "I teach one thing and one thing only: suffering and the end of suffering." Buddha realized that craving was the cause of most suffering, and craving is fueled by the three poisons of greed, hatred, and delusion. Buddha taught his disciples the Four Noble Truths: (1) there is suffering in life; (2) suffering arises from ignorant craving; (3) suffering may be ended by abolishing ignorant craving; through (4) the Eightfold Path (of right living and understanding). Before anyone can begin to seek enlightenment, one must live a life based on the dharma, or in harmony with the moral order of the cosmos. Buddha also taught Ten Precepts, such as never harming or killing any living thing, not stealing or lying, and other rules for living a righteous and conscious life. What Buddha taught, then, was not a belief system, but a practice, or type of mental training, in which ethical living leads to meditative insight.

Buddhism and the State

The core of Buddha's teaching is nonattachment to worldly things, a practice embraced by monks and nuns, or members of the Buddhist *sangha* (community), who dedicate their lives to achieving nirvana. Of course, not everyone can renounce the world or is suited to the ascetic life of a monk. As Buddhism spread, the vast majority of adherents remained householders and went on with their normal lives. As ever-larger regions adopted Buddhism, it naturally affected the social order. It may seem odd that a religion that teaches nonattachment to an illusory world would be applicable to governance, but Buddhist precepts shaped some of the world's most enlightened forms of government.

Within a few centuries after Buddha's death, Buddhism had taken hold in what are today India, China, Mongolia, Korea, Japan, Nepal, and Afghanistan, and throughout Southeast Asia. Different forms of Buddhism evolved as Buddhism spread. Three aspects of Buddhism, in particular, influenced governance. The first was Buddhism's great flexibility. Just as Buddhism recognized that individuals vary in their level of spiritual awareness, it accepted that the same was true for societies. So Buddhism could be widely adapted to suit the political needs of different cultures. The second factor was Buddhism's embrace of the concept of kingship, which was likely an outgrowth of the existing political landscape in Asia at the time. The third important influence on politics was the organization of the *sangha*, in which many decisions were made collectively.

Buddha insisted that society be organized by the spiritual bond between the *sangha* and householders, who support the *sangha* with donations and thereby earn spiritual merit (good karma). A similar, mutually beneficial relationship exists between the *sangha* and the ruler. In both cases, the centrality of the *sangha* keeps the society in the path of the Buddha. Scripture recounts that the Buddha praised the people of the small Vajjian state. The Vajjian government was a republican democracy based on an ideology of social equality. Buddha lauded the justice and social cohesion of the Vajjians and proposed their social organization as a model for the *sangha*. (Despite recent political struggles, some modern Buddhist states, such as Sri Lanka and Nepal, base their republican democracies on the Vajjian model.)

In Buddha's time, the example of the Vajjians was extremely rare. Most societies were ruled by kings. Though Buddha did not openly denounce hereditary monarchy, he voiced his preference for an elected monarch. Buddha taught that kingship should be conferred only on someone of great virtue who would rule according to the dharma, in which case his people would prosper both spiritually and materially. If a king used his power badly, both he and his people would suffer. The king should support the *sangha* both personally and with his dharmic policies, earning him and the society merit. Most important, this would earn the king the support of the *sangha*, which would give his rule legitimacy in the eyes of the people. The *sangha* was expected to maintain the highest spiritual discipline and virtue.

Ashoka: The Ideal Buddhist King

Buddha taught that it is ignorance and craving transitory worldly things that lead people to commit "unskillful," or non-dharmic, acts. Therefore, someone

Introduction

who is attuned to the dharma does not lay blame but has compassion for those who do evil, for evil acts arise out of ignorance. Buddha also taught that all life is precious and should never be harmed or destroyed. These teachings put compassion at the center of Buddhist teaching, life, and governance. Ashoka (274–236 B.C.E.), a ruler of the Maurya Empire of India, made compassion the guiding principle of society during his reign. After being converted to Buddhism by a monk, Ashoka is believed to have turned his kingdom into a living example of the dharma. Ashoka's rule probably never achieved the Buddhist perfection ascribed to it. Its idealization comes from the stone pillars Ashoka had erected all over his kingdom. Wise and compassionate teachings about the dharma are engraved on these pillars, and it is these sayings that have shaped our understanding of Ashoka's legendary rule.

Ashoka's emissaries taught the dharma throughout his realm. His renown as a great and just ruler was crucial to the rapid spread of Buddhism during his lifetime, when Buddhism became established from the Bay of Bengal to Afghanistan and from Sri Lanka to the Himalayas.

Ashoka embraced the Buddhist view that "the state [was] an agency for the moral transformation of man."[3] According to legend, Ashoka disallowed the killing of animals and established nature preserves to protect wildlife. Compassion's constituent, forgiveness, led to the abolition of capital punishment. Ashoka established schools and water systems, promoted the practice of medicine, and protected farmers. Justice was a universal right for every individual, regardless of one's station in society. Ashoka's ideal Buddhist state promoted religious freedom and tolerance. Because dharma is universal, all people are viewed as being on the path of spiritual growth no matter what teachings they follow. Buddhists view non-Buddhists as deserving of the same compassion and justice as everyone else. A good Buddhist ruler therefore treats all people alike and affords them all the benefits of his just policies, which include allowing them to freely practice their own religion.

Although ideal states like that ruled by Ashoka may never have actually existed, some Buddhist nations today (e.g., Bhutan, Thailand) have tried to incorporate the tenets of Buddhism to create a hybrid state ruled by a constitutional monarchy. Tibetans continue their struggle to retain their Buddhist identity in the face of Communist oppression; Tibet has not been ruled by its spiritual leader, the Dalai Lama, since the Chinese Communists took over in the early 1950s. Many Buddhist nations have been rent by political strife as "good kings" become increasingly rare and the modern world makes such rulers seem quaint. "How can a Buddhist society following its classical political ideals hope to survive in the modern world where nations' 'civil religions' require universal loyalty, where violent retribution is often regarded as virtuous, and where showing compassion is regarded as political weakness?"[4] As with so many other exemplary and principled traditions, perhaps political Buddhism is too idealistic for our 21st-century world. Still, the yearning for a dharmic life remains powerful. In Bhutan, for example, the king has created a measure of gross national happiness (in direct contrast to other nations' economic gross national product) to ensure that government policies enhance dharmic values of compassion, peace of mind, and happiness among his people.

JUDAISM AND THE RISE OF MONOTHEISM

Judaism traces its lineage to Abraham and the descendants of Jacob, who led the nomadic Israelites into Egypt. In biblical times, the main unit of social organization was the extended family, headed by a strong, polygamous patriarch who acted as ruler, judge, and priest. The patriarch's authority was limited only by a council of elders who had final say in serious interfamily or tribal disputes. During their sojourn in Egypt, the Jews were enslaved by the pharaoh. Led by their great leader, Moses, they made their exodus from Egypt around 1290 B.C.E. and eventually settled in Palestine.

It was Moses who, atop Mount Sinai, received the Ten Commandments from God and gave them to the Israelites. The Ten Commandments reveal much about the ancient Israelites. The commandment "Thou shall have no other gods before me" (Exodus, 20:3) implies that the early Jews had, at least at times, adopted the worship of one or more gods of other cultures, occasionally lapsing into idol worship (e.g., the golden calf). The Commandments are unequivocal that the Israelites must adhere to the monotheistic worship of the one true God.

In many ways, Judaic monotheism represents a unique way of conceiving God. Unlike some ancient religions in which God, people, and the cosmos form a unified whole, Jewish monotheism delineates a clear division between a transcendent God and his creation. The creation is fallen because although it was created by God it is not a part of God. God made humans in his image but put them in a kind of limbo between heaven and earth. God communicates to people through his laws, and people worship God by obeying them. However, this God has given humans free will. When humans flout God's laws, they incur his wrath. Such a God is neither arbitrary nor knowable, and he is difficult to relate to: He cannot be reached through his creation, nor can he be known in his transcendence. This puts believers in an awkward position, having "the temptation . . . to draw God closer to the world or cut him free from it."[5] Historically, there has been a tug of war in the political theologies derived from Judaism, including Christianity, between God in the world and the remote, transcendent God.

Introduction

In the Book of the Covenant (Exodus, Chapters 20–23), God explicitly prescribes how the Jews are to live, worship, and maintain order. The laws in these chapters (and in Exodus 34 and Deuteronomy 12–26) refer to nearly every aspect of life, including marriage, diet, dispute resolution, judgment and punishment, and so on. The ultimate goal of obedience to the law is to re-create God's kingdom on Earth. Scripture accepts the rule of kings, of prophets, or the tripartite leadership of king-priest-sage as a means of achieving this goal. Because Jews lived under the domination of foreign political powers during most of the biblical period (and thereafter), whatever political ideas are found in scripture describe more of a utopian ideal state than a blueprint for exercising real political power.

Life for the Jews in Palestine was difficult, and they were under frequent siege by other peoples, such as the Philistines, who subjugated them. The Jews longed for unity and strength, and they sought it in a wise and powerful king. Saul was the first Israelite king elected by a popular assembly (though some accounts have him anointed by Samuel). Saul defeated the Philistines, but he made the very impolitic move of alienating the revered Samuel, who then shifted his allegiance to David. At the end of Saul's reign (1000 B.C.E.), King David ascended to the throne of Judea. Eventually, through effort and luck, David united all the tribes of Israel. David's reign (ca. 1000–961 B.C.E.) is considered the golden age of the Israelites. However, toward the end of his rule, David began to swerve from the path God prescribed for Israel's kings. His family life was a shambles: He took up with Bathsheba, conspired to kill her husband, and generally scandalized the populace. After King David's death, his son Solomon, begat by Bathsheba, won a bloody struggle for the throne. King Solomon built the original Temple in Jerusalem that became the sacred and revered center of the Jewish faith. Though he is also remembered for his wisdom and subtle understanding of justice, according to John Hutchinson, professor of philosophy and religion, Solomon ruled like "an Oriental despot."[6] He did build temples but mainly constructed palaces for himself, his favorite wife (one of 300), and his 600 concubines. His lavish lifestyle was partly funded by expanded trade, but the lion's share came from taxation. When Solomon's reign ended (922 B.C.E.), the Israelites petitioned the elders for redress. Solomon's son, Rehoboam, would have none of it. The upshot was that the northern tribes seceded, and the short-lived unity of the Israelites ended. The tribal divisions and a series of weak kings led to greater disunity, and eventually the tribes were scattered by the conquering Assyrians.

After a period of exile, some Jews were permitted to return to Jerusalem to rebuild the Temple that had been destroyed in 586 B.C.E. The new Temple, dedicated in 516 B.C.E., became the center of Jewish life. The official temple priests led the people in worship and also served as scholars, lawyers, and judges. Lacking other rulers, the temple priests essentially became the governors of the Jewish people.

And so things remained until the death of Alexander the Great in 322 B.C.E. Alexander had conquered most of the Near East, including Jerusalem. Alexander's successors attempted to coerce the Jews into worshipping the Greek pantheon. When Antiochus IV outlawed their religion, the Jews resisted, organizing a successful rebellion under the leadership of the Maccabees. In 164 B.C.E., they rededicated the Temple in Jerusalem and set up their own ministate in Palestine under Maccabean leadership. Initially, the community prospered, but outbreaks of civil war destroyed it. By the end of the biblical period (63 B.C.E.), the Israelites were so weak and disorganized they were easily overcome by Rome. Palestine became a province of the Roman Empire.

Though many believe that in the Old Testament God promises the Jews a homeland in Palestine, Judaic scripture has little to say about governance primarily because Jews have almost always been stateless, subjugated people. Jews had no nation of their own from biblical times to the formation of the state of Israel in 1948. Israel does not "define its political institutions by opening Scripture . . . and replicating its plan . . . for a government," mainly because there really is no plan.[7] Some laws, such as observance of the Sabbath and Jewish religious holidays, derive from scripture. For the most part, the Israeli government is modern, democratic, and secular.

WESTERN CHRISTIANITY
Judaism in the Roman Empire

Under Roman rule, Jews were permitted to practice their religion. The Romans ruled a vast empire and so had a policy of religious tolerance. For the Romans, religious tolerance was not so much a matter of principle as a matter of practicality. The Romans knew they would face far more resistance if they tried to force worship of the Roman pantheon upon the heterogeneous cultures under their control. To ensure the greatest stability and least bother, all the Romans asked is that their subject peoples pay their taxes and maintain the peace.

For a while, the Jews lived peaceably under the Romans, who even granted the Maccabees limited governance over their own land and people. But when Augustus Caesar placed a statue of a Roman eagle over the entrance to the Temple in Jerusalem, the Jews revolted and were violently suppressed by Roman forces. Thus began a period of almost continuous rebellion, which was met with ever-increasing violence. Some Jewish sects, such as the Sad-

Introduction

ducees, urged the Jews to compromise with the Romans. Others, such as the Pharisees and Zealots, violently opposed capitulation. The destruction of the Temple by the Romans led to a general diaspora, or dispersion, of the Jews out of Palestine. It was early in this period of violence and upheaval that Jesus was born.

The story of Jesus' life and his teachings are well known and can be found in the New Testament, especially the Gospels. After his crucifixion and resurrection, some Jews believed that Jesus was the Messiah (he who would bring the kingdom of God), or Christ (the Anointed One). For at least a century after his death, Jesus' followers were viewed, and viewed themselves, as Jews, or a Jewish sect. As such, they did not attract much attention from their Roman overlords. Yet there was a limit to the degree of tolerance the Romans could safely indulge and still maintain the semblance of a unified empire. When Augustus Caesar was proclaimed a god, the imperial government mandated some form of emperor worship among all the empire's peoples. For the most part, Rome was satisfied with subjects' lip service and acceptance of Roman symbols. Most people preferred peace and pretended to worship Jove and the god Augustus. The new Jewish sect, however, was adamant in its refusal to bend a knee to either of them.

The obstinacy of this Jewish sect drew the attention and the wrath of Roman officials. After Augustus, a series of increasingly megalomaniacal emperors ruled Rome, and they were unforgiving toward those who refused their form of worship. Such refusal was seen as seditious and was severely punished. Thus began the era of the Christian martyrs, who were put to death for their religion. For two centuries, until the end of the reign of Marcus Aurelius in 180 C.E., the nascent Christian sect suffered persecution. This is also the period when believers began to think of themselves as Christians. Christianity was evolving into a religion and spreading widely, due largely to the Jewish diaspora that had begun so long before.

Political Theology among Early Christians

Christianity arose from Judaism, but crucial differences made it inevitable that Christians would break away from their original faith. Jews believe in a Messiah, a fully human being who will be born on Earth, create a perfect Jewish state based on Jewish law, and redeem the Jewish people and unite them with God by establishing the kingdom of God on Earth. In contrast, early Christians believed that Jesus was the Messiah, but one who was an incarnation of God, not a mere human. Further, Jesus was incarnated to save all humankind, not just the nation of Israel. Most important, Christians believe that Jesus will return at the Second Coming, and this will usher in the end-times, when all will be judged and the world and time will end. These two very different eschatological (end-times) views made Judaism and Christianity irreconcilable.

Christians also broke with the Jewish view of an unbroken, linear history stretching from the creation to the kingdom of God on Earth. Judaism teaches that throughout time humankind's relationship with God remains the same via divine law. In Christianity, the relationship between humankind and God since the creation has been severed by the incarnation of God in Jesus. After Jesus, humans' relationship to God comes not through the law but through divine grace and love. This era of divine love will end with the Second Coming, when "all things will be made new" (Rev. 21:5), time itself will end, and the righteous are gathered up into heaven after the Last Judgment.

What Christianity and Judaism have in common is that both developed their relationship to politics while they were dominated by a foreign political power. This tended to make both religions wary of direct engagement with politics. For Jews, the law was paramount whether it was implemented by a priest, sage, or king. Involvement in politics was essential only to the degree that it brought forth leaders who ensured that the Jewish people obeyed divine law. Early Christians cited Jesus' directive to "render unto Caesar that which is Caesar's and to God that which is God's" (Matthew 22:21) to diminish (though not eliminate) the importance of the political realm relative to that of the spirit. Earthly powers had to be acknowledged and dealt with, but early followers of Jesus were essentially apolitical. They were also generally unconcerned with the law. As Christianity developed, the biblical description of a religion without politics would haunt church-state relations for centuries, but it also made the distinction between religion and the state a hallmark of Western civilization.

The first Christians were (and many Christians still are) obsessed with the end-days and the Second Coming of Christ, which is one reason most rejected political involvement. The drive to live a life as pure as Christ's and to welcome martyrdom rather than contaminate one's soul with falsehood was an outgrowth of the conviction that the Second Coming was imminent. Yet three centuries passed and still there was no sign of Jesus' return. During this period, Christianity was gaining adherents throughout the Near East and North Africa. Christian leaders, such as bishops, arose everywhere to interpret the scriptures and perform religious rituals. (Until the end of the second century, women could lead as well.) During this period, converts were clandestinely baptized into the faith, and Christians attended secret weekly religious ceremonies where the New Testament was read aloud (the only way ordinary people could hear it) and communion was taken as part of a communal meal.

Introduction

Early Christians were heartened by the growing popularity of the new religion. Yet without a central religious authority, people could interpret the New Testament in any way they saw fit. What would soon be deemed heresies were widely believed and practiced. The burgeoning faith needed a central authority to define heresy by first establishing a core creed of acceptable beliefs and practices. Although the far-flung Christian sects had a great deal of autonomy, the highest authority came to be granted to the bishop of Rome. According to the New Testament, Jesus had chosen the apostle Peter as the rock upon whom he would build his church; since Peter was martyred in Rome and Rome was the center of the Roman Empire, the city became the apostolic center of the new religion.

Constantine and Official Acceptance

After a centuries-long parade of caesars who persecuted Christians, the throne of imperial Rome was won by Constantine (ca. 288–337), ruler of Gaul (France). To gain his prize, Constantine had to gather an army and defeat several rivals who, as rulers of other parts of the empire, also coveted imperial power. Historians assert that Constantine had a dream instructing him to inscribe a Christian cross on his soldiers' shields to ensure victory. It worked. Constantine was so impressed and grateful that he converted to Christianity and, in the Edict of Milan (313), prohibited persecution of Christians. This was a vital turning point in the history of Christianity: The emperor who ruled the entire western half of the Roman Empire now officially adopted Christianity as the religion of the realm.

Constantine's adoption of Christianity in 325 was more a pragmatic move than a true religious conversion; he was only baptized on his deathbed. His acceptance of the religion, however, allowed it to be practiced openly. This was joyous news for many Christians. For some, aligning the faith with temporal power was a sign that God intended Christianity to span the world. Other Christians were far more wary. They felt that the spiritual church would be transformed into a tool for wielding earthly power, and they were sure this was not what Jesus intended. A number of early Christians broke with the church and fled to the deserts of Egypt and Syria to live a life of ascetic simplicity and contemplation—a life that imitated Jesus' own. These ascetics established the great monastic movement of the Desert Fathers, which would infuse the religion with profound mysticism and love of God.

For those Christians who welcomed recognition and acceptance, it quickly became obvious that an official religion had to have a uniform creed that applied to all Christians everywhere. With Constantine's approval, in 325 the First Ecumenical Council of bishops convened in Nicea (Greece) to hash out a religious doctrine. This would prove to be more difficult than it at first seemed.

The primary problem the bishops had to grapple with arose from the concept of the Trinity, the triune divinity of Father, Son, and Holy Spirit. The Christian God, or Father, is a transcendent (remote) god, but one who sent his Son into the world as a flesh-and-blood man—an immanent god. Yet the immanent Jesus did not stay in the world: He left with a promise to return at the end of time, date uncertain. In this, he is like a totally remote god because the time of his return cannot be known. This absence is mitigated only by the loving presence of the Holy Spirit, which represents another form of immanence.

It was the bishops' task to reconcile these seemingly irreconcilable aspects of the divinity and to come up with a religious doctrine that made sense. Is the Trinity three divine persons or just three aspects of one divine person? If God is infinite and timeless, how could he send part of himself into the temporal world? How much of Jesus was divine and how much was human? Can the divine be transcendent, immanent, and remote all at the same time? The answers to these questions would have a profound impact on Christian religion and political theology. (A disagreement over Christ's humanity caused the Eastern Orthodox Church to break with the Church of Rome.)

The bishops finally agreed on a statement that would serve as the central doctrine of Christianity. The Nicene Creed, which was amended at later ecumenical councils, states:

> *We believe in one God, the Father Almighty, maker of heaven and earth, and of all things visible and invisible. And in one Lord Jesus Christ, the only begotten Son of God, and born of the Father before all ages, light of light, true God of true God. Begotten not made, of one substance with the Father, through whom all things were made. Who for us men and for our salvation came down from heaven. And was incarnate of the Holy Spirit and the Virgin Mary and was made man; was crucified also for us, suffered and was buried, and the third day rose again according to the Scriptures. And ascended into heaven, sits at the right hand of the Father, and shall come again with glory to judge the living and the dead, of whose Kingdom there shall be no end. And in the Holy Spirit, the Lord and Giver of life, who proceeds from the Father and the Son, who together with the Father and the Son is to be adored and glorified, who spoke through the Prophets. And one holy, catholic, and apostolic Church. We confess one baptism for the remission of sins. And we look for the resurrection of the dead and the life of the world to come. Amen.*[8]

Introduction

The creed gave little guidance to rulers about how a Christian state should be governed. On one hand, some Christians interpreted the creed as confirming the goodness of the world created by an immanent God. In this view, the world is not abandoned and corrupt but filled with God's grace. This view encourages a political theology of engagement with a world so infused with grace and the Holy Spirit that involvement with it helps the believer come to God. A polar opposite view also arose. Some theologians feared that Christians might interpret the creed to mean that since creation is essentially good, people are too; therefore they do not need divine grace—or the church—to realize God. These theologians stressed the remoteness of God; that Jesus' departure left the world corrupted, and the only way to rise above the corruption was via the church and the Holy Spirit. In this view, engagement with the corrupted world is discouraged because it cannot bring one closer to God; only God's grace will accomplish that. The lack of clarity in the creed created tensions, both religious and political, that would persist for centuries. The church would, however, find ways to turn this confusion to its own advantage. "[W]hen the church was oppressed it held the political world in contempt, then changed its tune once it succeeded in seizing or influencing power."[9]

The fourth-century church attempted to develop some type of political philosophy that would help consolidate its vast membership. The bishop of Rome assumed increasing authority and became known as the pope (father). The pope's authority, however, was not based on any political theology; nothing in the religion explained why the pope should exercise power over the faithful. In his *Church History* (ca. 326), Eusebius of Caesarea attempted to justify the Roman church's authority by describing it as the will of God, who intended that the singular authority of the pope would help the church acquire earthly political power and spread Christianity throughout the world.

The favor the church enjoyed under Constantine was short lived. After his death, Constantine was replaced by the pagan Julian, who reinstituted policies of Christian persecution. Not all later emperors persecuted Christians, but few were friendly. A more subdued Christian community produced some great thinkers and saints, but political power eluded the church. Then a period of great destruction ensued. Rome was sacked by the Goths in 410 and again by the Vandals 45 years later. Over the next several centuries, invaders from the east and north, including the Visigoths, Franks, Lombards, Vikings, Magyars, and others, brought ruin and disunity to the western Roman Empire, with each group setting up its own fiefdom. The eastern empire persisted in some form at Constantinople, with an official bishop, for several centuries. Although it retained the illusion of unity, this vestige of the Roman Empire was eventually fatally weakened by invasions.

The sack of Rome in 410 prompted St. Augustine of Hippo (in North Africa) to write his monumental, 23-volume defense of Christianity, *The City of God*. Although it was never used as a real-world model of state governance, the book was the first Christian explication of how the secular world interacts with divine will. Augustine describes the City of God existing within the earthly city because it is in the hearts of Christians. The difference between the two cities is that those of the City of God place love of God before all else, even themselves, while those who are of the earthly city place love of self above love of God. Only those of the City of God will be redeemed on Judgment Day. Augustine wrote that rulers of the earthly city are driven by a "lust for power," while in the City of God "all serve each other in charity; governors by taking thought for all and subjects by obeying."[10]

Although the political philosophy of the Christian church was ostensibly to partner with and sustain a political system that promoted the "good" and created a political and social space in which Christians could come to God, in fact the church was eventually seduced by wealth and power. As Christianity expanded, church leaders resided almost exclusively in the earthly city.

The Dark Ages and Medieval Period

Once the "barbarian" (i.e., non-Roman) invaders established their own little kingdoms, Christians were left more or less in peace. Some European rulers converted to Christianity. In the sixth century, Charles Martel, a leader of the converted Franks, conquered surrounding fiefdoms and brought a semblance of unity to the region around modern France. In 751, his son, Pepin the Short, was anointed king of the Franks by a local bishop acting under orders from the pope in Rome. Pepin was the first monarch to receive Christian blessing for his reign. This marked a turning point in the political history of the church.

Pepin's son was the great Charlemagne. Invasions and political strife in Italy impelled the pope to seek a defensive alliance with the Franks. For his part, Charlemagne wanted the historical glory of empire and the divine sanction represented by Rome. On Christmas Day in the year 800, Pope Leo III crowned Charlemagne, not king of the Franks, but Holy Roman Emperor. This alliance brought the church broader political influence and an avenue for expansion, as well as a military force to defend its political control of Rome. In his conquests of other tribes, Charlemagne not only expanded his empire, but he forcibly converted conquered peoples to Christianity, vastly expanding the religion's range.

Introduction

Charlemagne benefited hugely from the alliance. Barbarian invasions were seen as an attack on Christianity itself, so Charlemagne became the savior of Christendom. Further, biblical prophecy endowed Rome with immense power: Daniel had prophesied four kingdoms, the last of which—Rome—would endure until the Second Coming. By accepting the pope's coronation, Charlemagne associated himself with both the sacred church and a vast and united earthly kingdom that would endure until the end of time. For centuries afterward, the Holy Roman Empire was intimately associated with the Roman church. Thus Christianity, which was integral to every aspect of medieval life, became an inseparable part of politics.

During the coronation, the pope cited scripture in anointing Charlemagne "with this holy oil of unction whence thou has anointed priests, kings, and prophets."[11] In this act, Charlemagne was given tacit approval to anoint priests. Charlemagne wrote to the pope, instructing, "Your part is to aid our efforts with your prayers," an overt claim that kings, not popes, had the power to appoint clerics.[12] Investiture, the appointment of church officials, became a vital right of monarchs and, inevitably, a source of centuries-long conflict with the church.

In Charlemagne's time, nearly every layperson was illiterate. The emperor had to seek literate and competent government officials among churchmen, who therefore became an indispensable part of the political system. At the same time, the monarch used his investiture power to promote his most loyal and favored vassals to powerful and lucrative positions within the church. In no time, the upper rungs of church hierarchy were peopled by nobles appointed by the emperor. Some of these aristocrats-turned-bishops were then recruited into the king's service as political officials. This incestuous relationship had unfortunate consequences: Many clergy had no religious calling, and the purportedly spiritual interests of the church were corrupted by secular political power.

This situation persisted primarily because nothing in Christian theology granted political authority to a pope, and popes anointed monarchs in the same way and with the same words as they anointed priests, giving kings the aura of religious authority. As feudal monarchy was the unquestioned political organization in medieval society, church power became subordinated to that of the state, whose kings were viewed as anointed by God. Thus did the divine right of kings come to prevail in medieval Europe. It must be remembered, however, that church and state remained two parts of a spiritually based, authoritative whole.

With the waning of Charlemagne's kingdom, power shifted eastward to today's Germany. In 961, Otto, then a German prince, booted the Lombards out of Italy. Proclaimed savior of Christendom, Otto was crowned Holy Roman Emperor by Pope John XII. It was under Otto's rule that royal control of the church reached its height. Otto appointed loyal nobles to high church office, where they enriched themselves and the emperor with the church lands and church treasure they controlled. After more than a century of this unholy intermingling of church and monarchy, ecclesiastical corruption led to widespread protests among the faithful. Simony, the practice of selling ecclesiastical positions, was rampant; it created a clergy that had little or no interest in spiritual matters, and devout peasants feared for the salvation of their souls.

The papacy was the most coveted office, for it was the richest. It was not long before the papacy was being bought and sold by rival princes. Occasionally, if there was no papal vacancy one was created. Sitting popes were strangled, poisoned, stabbed, walled up in dungeons, and starved to death, or otherwise disposed of. The situation got so out of hand that there were at various times two or even three popes simultaneously, each invested by a different prince. The rival popes were constantly excommunicating each other in the vain hope that one of them would emerge as the sole head of the church.

Finally in 1046, Holy Roman Emperor Henry III took matters in hand. He convened a meeting with three competing popes and fired them all. He named Clement II pope. Clement was a competent pope, as were his immediate successors. Although the papacy achieved a modicum of stability, lower-ranking clergy still served at the whim of local aristocrats, who were constantly firing serving clergy to install their favorites. The situation became intolerable. In 1059, Pope Nicholas II convened a council that decided that henceforth popes would be elected by cardinals. It was a revolutionary act and a direct challenge to kingly authority. The battle over investiture was joined in earnest.

In 1073, Cardinal Hildebrand was elected Pope Gregory VII, one of the church's greatest and most ambitious leaders. While the future emperor Henry IV, the German king, was putting down a revolt in Saxony, he inadvertently conceded to the pope the power of investiture for a particular church appointment. Henry soon regretted this political gaffe and demanded reinstatement of his investiture power. Gregory refused to return it. Incensed, Henry declared Gregory's papacy invalid. Gregory responded by excommunicating the king. In these times, people took excommunication very seriously, as they truly believed the fate of their eternal soul was at stake. Yet Henry could lose more than his soul; he might forfeit his empire if the pope who anointed him expelled him from the church. Henry tried to ignore the incident. Then, in a decisive move, Gregory issued his *Dictatus Papae* (1075), a ferocious and unequivocal document returning investiture power to the church.

Introduction

After his excommunication, Henry's power waned as ambitious vassals sought to unseat him. Henry had no choice but to capitulate. He traveled to Canossa, Italy, to meet with Gregory. A penitential King Henry was forced to stand barefoot in the snow for three days before Gregory would see him. Only then did the pope lift the sentence of excommunication. The clear symbolism of this incident signaled the church's intent to take back the power of investiture.

The right of investiture was so vital because it came to involve more than wealth and alliances within the church, though these were important. It became an issue of law and governance. The church had been granting its clergy immunity from secular law. Clerics freely flouted the law as they pleased, a situation no self-respecting monarch could tolerate. The church also conducted ecclesiastical courts in which it could try and punish the king's men. This too was an intolerable usurpation of state power.

The most famous jurisdictional conflict occurred between the church and King Henry II of England (1133–89). When Henry decided he had had enough of ecclesiastical meddling in the running of his kingdom, he named as archbishop of Canterbury his good friend and chancellor, Thomas Becket (1118–70). In Becket, Henry thought he had an ally who would support him and oppose the church. Henry was livid when Becket began to take his religious office seriously and to oppose the king. Henry had Becket assassinated in Canterbury Cathedral. Becket was later canonized for his ultimate sacrifice for the church, but Henry continued to battle Rome to uphold the supremacy of secular over church law.

The church never relinquished its right to be the ultimate judge of the moral and spiritual behavior of all Christians, regardless of station. Church doctrine and liturgy became more aggressively rigid, and adherence to church law was monitored closely. At the same time, clerical corruption in pursuit of riches became epidemic. (As one pope supposedly said, "Since God has given us the papacy, let's enjoy it."[13]) The faithful were bled dry by the selling of indulgences, paying for absolution from sin. Some priests even denied the sacraments to Christians who refused to pony up. Many believers felt that the church had lost its way, and they in turn lost faith in it. There arose in Europe a host of heretical Christian sects whose wide membership exposed Rome's spiritual bankruptcy and threatened its hegemony. Refusing reform, or even a nod to Christ's exaltation of poverty, the church responded with the implementation of the most wide-ranging and comprehensive judicial effort in its history: the Inquisition. While it was in force (from 1184 to the 1800s), the Inquisition reportedly executed thousands of Europeans.

The conspicuous wealth, lavish lifestyle, and depraved morals of most clergymen began to turn secular powers, and even some bishops, against the church. Despite evident abuses, Boniface VIII issued his *Unam Sanctam*, a brazen declaration that the absolute supremacy of the pope was necessary for human salvation. The kings, nobles, and high clerics in France and England had had enough, and they openly rejected church authority. Disgruntled Italian nobles supported the rebellion, and in 1303 they captured the pope and dragged him out of Rome. This marked another turning point in the history of church power. For the first time, the legitimacy of the church was challenged by educated leaders. This would evolve, in later centuries, into a rejection of the church by many European intellectuals. Eventually, it would lead to the separation of church and state. This first break was initiated not only by conflicts between church and state over power and jurisdiction. The church was largely undone by its corruption. "Spiritual failure was now increasingly to draw fire; in the near future the papacy was to be condemned more for standing in the way of religious reform than for claiming too much of kings."[14]

The Reformation

By the 15th century, the church was in a desperate and despicable situation. After Boniface VIII was deposed, his successor, Clement V, seeking the protection of the French, established a papal court in Avignon, France. Clement was subservient to the French king, and papal political power was severely curtailed. Clement's residence in Avignon began the period of the Great Schism (1378–1414), in which church authority was claimed by two rival popes: one in Rome, one in Avignon. Both popes wooed Europe's princes to gain legitimacy. In jockeying for position, both popes took simony and corruption to unheard-of levels. A meeting convened in Pisa, Italy, in 1409 officially deposed the two rival popes and then elected another official pope. Alas, the rivals refused to be dismissed, and so there were again three popes conniving against one another. The schism ended in 1414 when a church council elected Pope Martin V.

Many Christians had blamed God's wrath at the opulence of Clement's court for the ravages of the Black Plague that swept through Europe in 1348. Reformers of the 14th and 15th centuries, such as John Wycliffe in England, Jan Hus in Bohemia, and Girolamo Savonarola in Florence, railed against the Roman church as the "whore of Babylon" that betrayed Christianity. Numerous reform religious sects arose; all were viewed by the church as heretical.

MARTIN LUTHER AND THE RISE OF PROTESTANTISM

While preparing a lecture on the Bible in 1515, Martin Luther, an Augustinian monk, had a religious epiphany that revealed to him that righteousness and faith are not earned but rather are gifts from God. That both saints and

Introduction

sinners might receive this gift contradicted the penitential system central to Roman Christian theology. For Luther, God was forgiving, not punitive. Luther was so persuasive, and disillusion with the church was so ubiquitous, many of his colleagues and students accepted his teaching.

To clarify his ideas, Luther spent evenings writing them down in a list of "theses," which included his condemnation of church corruption, particularly the sale of indulgences. On October 31, 1517 (All Saints' Day), Luther nailed his Ninety-five Theses to the door of the castle church in Wittenberg. That date heralded the beginning of the Reformation.

The pope and the German Holy Roman Emperor demanded that Luther be arrested and silenced. Luther lived a rather adventurous life, narrowly escaping capture, living in hiding, and always a hair's breadth away from the Inquisition and the stake. However, Luther had powerful protectors in Germany and even in Catholic France. Kings and princes throughout Europe were, like their subjects, sick of Rome's corruption, and they overtly or secretly supported and protected Luther. More important, his ideas could be disseminated by a truly revolutionary invention—the printing press. Before 1450, books were laboriously copied by hand; by 1500, hundreds of printing presses throughout Europe had produced more than 6 million books, roughly equivalent to the total number of books produced in the prior 15 centuries. With the princes' protection, Luther's writings and ideas were disseminated throughout Europe, giving voice and order to the sometimes inchoate longing for true religion among the populace.

Luther's theology taught that the word of God as found in scripture was the ultimate source of salvation and the model for living a truly Christian life. For him, the Bible was the embodiment of Jesus Christ and had authority over the church, the pope, and liturgical practice; thus he translated the Bible into German (1534), following others who had translated the Bible into vernacular languages as part of the reform movement. As literacy increased and more people read the vernacular Bible, Luther's belief that an individual could gain salvation through faith and a personal relationship with God through the Bible gained currency. Thus, one of the church's greatest sources of power, the sacraments (e.g., Holy Communion, a church ceremony that imbues one with Christ's grace; Confession, in which the church assumes the power to absolve sin) came to be seen by some as unnecessary. Church power was also undermined by the idea that individuals could seek and find salvation in the Bible on their own instead of through the mediation of a priest.

Luther taught that there were the "two kingdoms" established by God to address the relationship between church and state. For Luther, God's secular world was ruled by secular law, whose purpose was to limit sinful behavior. God's second, spiritual kingdom, Christianity, was governed by the gospels.

RELIGION AND THE STATE

The Reformation thus advanced the notion that the state may not need an institutional church to legitimize it. The state cannot be expected to govern via the gospels, nor does it have the authority to support one religious view over another. The ruler of a state may therefore hold any religious belief as long as he upholds secular law. It follows that civic leaders have no authority over believers' adherence to the gospel, and believers are bound to follow only secular laws that do not impinge on their faith. Here again, Luther's ideas tended toward the separation of church and state: "... [T]rue faith should not seek to impose itself by means of civil authority, but only through the power of the Word."[15]

Luther's theology embodied religious tolerance: "Luther was more ready to live under a just and intelligent non-Christian ruler than he would be under a fellow Christian who was unjust and unwise."[16] Luther's concept of the "two kingdoms" discouraged believers from engagement with politics, either civic or religious. Lutherans traditionally left control of their church to electors and their state to a remote secular authority.

This approach is in direct contrast to that taken by the other great reformer, John Calvin (1509–64). In Geneva, Switzerland, Calvin strove mightily to create a civic authority guided by Reformation principles. No separation of church and state for him. Calvin's teachings were rigid and uncompromising. He did not tolerate dissenters or laws that were not based on God's laws as found in the Bible. For Calvin, believers were required to engage with politics to ensure that the polity adhered to and upheld scripture. It was Christians' duty to scour the sin and evil from civic life and to mold the state along strict Calvinist lines. In effect, Calvin created a theocratic state governed only by believers.

Luther had sought to reform the church, and he would likely have been appalled at the new political reality he helped create. Princes used religious plurality as a political weapon against the church and other princes. By 1519, most German princes had broken with Rome. Princes saw upholding the true faith as their primary duty, and those with a gripe against Rome and the Holy Roman Empire upheld Lutheranism. Their incessant arguments with the emperor led German princes to be dubbed Protestants. By 1555, greater Germany was religiously pluralistic, with both Catholic and Protestant citizens. The religion of each German principality was that of its prince, so some were Roman Catholic and others Protestant.

NATIONALISM AND STATE RELIGION

Luther's religious tolerance notwithstanding, the establishment and enforcement of a state religion was pretty much the rule throughout Europe and would remain so for years. Usually, the monarch's religion was imposed

Introduction

on the entire population; nonbelievers might be persecuted, ghettoized, or expelled. This practice only added to already tense relationships among many European nations. Catholic nations, such as France and Spain, sought to gain heavenly reward and papal approval by warring against majority Protestant countries (Britain, the Netherlands) to bring them back into the fold of the "one true faith." Since both Roman Catholics and Protestants existed in most nations, the quest for religious freedom often added internal strife to ongoing external religious conflicts. The tradition of a national religion made matters worse: Each group of believers strove to make theirs the national faith to accrue power to themselves and to delegitimize the belief system of the other group.

Religious strife in Tudor England provides an excellent example. Henry VIII (r. 1509–47) famously sought to divorce his first wife, Catharine, because she had not borne him a son and heir. For years, Henry tried to persuade the Roman pontiff to grant him a divorce, but the pope was adamant in his opposition. Henry pleaded and cajoled to no avail. At his wits' end and panting to marry Anne Boleyn, Henry finally took the drastic measure of breaking with the Roman church. He issued the revolutionary Act of Supremacy (1534), making the monarch the head of the church in England. He replaced the Roman Church with the Anglican Church, which he and clergymen he appointed would control. His handpicked clerics granted him a quick divorce and an even quicker marriage.

Although at first the Anglican Church was almost identical to the Roman one in all but name, the break with Rome permitted English monarchs to easily adapt it to the more acceptable Protestant faith. Queen Elizabeth I (r. 1558–1603), daughter of Henry and Anne Boleyn, was a Protestant but also a tolerant ruler who permitted Roman Catholic worship. Unfortunately, Rome could not tolerate a heretical head of state in England. Plots were hatched; assassinations attempted. Elizabeth's cousin, Mary, Queen of Scots, was among the conspirators who sought to murder Elizabeth in order to establish the "one true faith" in England. (Mary was beheaded for treason.) Urged on by the pope, in 1588 the Spanish king Philip II sent an armada of warships to conquer England, kill its heretics, and ally it once more with Rome. The Spanish Armada was soundly defeated by the far fewer but much nimbler ships of the English.

Prior to Elizabeth I's reign, Henry's daughter by the Spanish Catharine had ruled for a time. Mary I (r. 1553–58), or Bloody Mary as she was called, was a devout, even fanatical, Roman Catholic. She earned her nickname because of the hundreds of English Protestants her church councils tried, condemned for heresy, and then burned alive. Mary's bloodthirsty rule was typical of what went on in many European nations at that time. For example,

Catholics slaughtered about 2,000 Protestants in Paris during the St. Bartholomew's Day massacre (August 24, 1522). Catholic Spain let loose rivers of blood in the Netherlands in their persecution of that country's Protestants. Everywhere, Christians were slaughtering Christians in a fanatical effort to impose one brand of Christianity over another.

Violence begat violence until, exhausted by all the bloodletting, a modicum of peace and tolerance was established. Upon reflection, most Catholics and Protestants were horrified at the religious violence that had been unleashed. Thinkers and clerics in both camps tried to make sense of what had happened and to formulate a political theology that all Christendom could live with. Most reformers believed that changes in the ecclesiastical hierarchy, ritual, and doctrine, along with greater religious tolerance and an emphasis on humanism and classical rational thought, would create a church and political institutions that would promote stability and peace. It was never to be, mainly because, by the 17th century, most Christians had given up on the possibility of finding any political theology within Christianity. The Christian attempt to situate humanity within the nexus of the divine and the world was abandoned. What replaced it was "a new approach to politics focused exclusively on human nature and human needs. A Great Separation took place, severing Western political philosophy decisively from cosmology and theology. It remains the most distinctive feature of the modern West to this day."[17]

Philosophers as Reformers
THOMAS HOBBES

By the mid-17th century, the idea of Christendom as a powerful political entity was defunct. As national identities solidified, the authority of the sovereign state grew. Monarchs, increasingly associated with the more identifiably bounded states they ruled, became the ultimate source of all law.

The notion of the absolute authority of secular power was forcefully expounded in the truly revolutionary ideas of the English philosopher Thomas Hobbes (1588–1679), particularly in his *Leviathan* (1651). Hobbes's ideas were likely influenced by the Thirty Years' War (1618–48), a conflict between the Holy Roman Emperor and dissenting German princes that was thus a battle between Catholics and Protestants. The noted historian Veronica C. Wedgwood wrote, "Almost all [combatants] were actuated by fear rather than by lust of conquest or passion of faith. They wanted peace and they fought for thirty years to be sure of it. They did not learn then, and have not learned since, that war only breeds war."[18]

The war was resolved by the Treaty of Westphalia (1648), which granted equal rights to Catholics and Protestants. Pope Innocent X (r. 1644–55) saw

Introduction

the writing on the wall and made one last effort to restore church dignity and power by declaring the treaty "null, void, invalid, iniquitous, unjust, damnable, reprobate, inane, and devoid of meaning for all time."[19] No parade of adjectives could repair the damage; henceforth people spoke not of Christendom but of Europe.

Hobbes was deeply affected by the English Civil Wars (1642–46; 1648–51) between Royalist forces loyal to Catholic king Charles I and the Protestant rebels who fought for Oliver Cromwell. This was a time of turmoil and fear in Britain, where society was fractured along economic, regional, and religious lines. Caught among factions, Hobbes feared for his life; he escaped to France, where he lived from 1640 to 1651. Even after his return and the Restoration of the monarchy in 1660, Hobbes's security in his home country was uncertain. The Civil Wars left an estimated 618,000 dead (mostly Catholic); England lost 3.7 percent of its population, Scotland 6 percent, and Catholic Ireland about 41 percent.[20]

Reflecting on the death and disorder in his native country, Hobbes reinvented human nature and its relationship to the state and religion. Hobbes's revolutionary aim was nothing less than to destroy Christian political theology and the notion that the souls of sinful humans can be saved by God's grace. Hobbes argued that the "soul" is nothing more than the human mind, which is matter governed by aversion to pain and craving for pleasure. As the mind only vaguely comprehends its own experience, it is totally ignorant of anything beyond itself. Thus, when people speak of God, they are speaking of a construct created out of their own ignorant minds.

People strive to fulfill their worldly desires, but nature often thwarts them. They cannot control nature to get what they want, so they fear nature, including the pain and death it will bring. From this fear humans create God, a being who can control nature to make it fulfill human desires. Religion exploits this God born out of fear and desire by teaching that God will exercise his power in humans' interest only if he is strictly obeyed and appeased. Inevitably, people begin to fear the all-powerful God they created, especially the Christian God who threatens imperfect souls with eternal damnation. Humans now fear both nature and the God they devised to help them overcome it. Religious leaders pretend to speak for God, instilling more fear with their power and capricious demands.

Priests claim that their material minds understand God, but of course they are as ignorant as everyone else. Priestly claims confer power, but power is always contested—most often by priests with another set of beliefs who offer identical guarantees for spiritual salvation. The result is a war over souls, which leads to fanaticism and violence. Since princes are protectors of the "one true faith," those with different beliefs battle each other to "prove" that only their belief gains humans entry into heaven (and freedom from the fear of death).

Fear is also the bedrock of society. People fear competition from other humans who have identical desires and who would kill them to get what they want. Given the fearful nature of man and society, and the competition of all against all for fulfillment of desire, the natural human condition is one of war, or of perpetual anxiety that conflict is imminent. When the fear at the heart of religion and society merge, fanaticism and violence are inevitable. In such conditions, without an omnipotent ruler to control them, humans live in "continual fear and danger of violent death, and the life of man [is] solitary, poor, nasty, brutish, and short."[21]

Hobbes proposed a radical solution to this horror of perpetual war: People enter into a "social contract" with an absolute ruler who is given unlimited power to maintain the peace. Hobbes asserted that people must live under an absolute sovereign who rules by fear and ensures that his subjects fear no other, neither God nor other princes. Hobbes called this absolute ruler "an earthly God" who would control Christianity and subsume it under his rule.[22]

Hobbes's contemporaries were scandalized by his ideas. Yet modern notions of religion and the state owe a tremendous debt to him. Hobbes recast religious questions about the one true faith and God's law into questions about human behavior and psychology and how these have created the artifact we call religion. Hobbes undermined religion while setting Christians free from the tangled web of political theology and the violence and fanaticism it engendered. Religious concepts cannot be proven empirically. After Hobbes, anyone who argued for a particular political system based on revealed truth would have to prove that this truth was not simply a construct of the human mind and/or a grab for power. It could not be done. In time, Hobbes's ideas would destroy the long-cherished traditions of the divine right of kings and any pretensions to political power by the church.

When Hobbes's argument is taken to its logical conclusion, people who have freed their minds and no longer need religiously sanctioned politics would no longer need to subjugate themselves to a fearsome autocrat. Thus, despite his pessimism about human nature, religion, and government, Hobbes opened the door to the theology of tolerance and separation of church and state that would emerge from the Enlightenment.

JOHN LOCKE AND RELIGIOUS TOLERANCE

Hobbes freed the state from the bonds of religion. Before Hobbes, reform meant tinkering endlessly with the structure of religion to adapt political theology to the needs of the state. Hobbes simply "changed the subject" from theology to psychology and severed religion from politics altogether.[23] Once theology was

Introduction

divorced from the state, religion and worship became a personal matter over which the state had, or should have, no control.

Hobbes's ideas were transformed and expanded by the great thinkers of the Enlightenment, particularly the British philosopher John Locke (1632–1704). Locke agreed with Hobbes that the human mind has its limitations, but he gave people credit for having curiosity and an ability to learn new things, and he did not see fear as the driving force in the human psyche. Locke thought that the tendency to cling to familiar and comfortable ideas was probably the primary characteristic of the human mind. If complacency gives people so little control over their own beliefs, they cannot impose belief in the minds of others. It follows that they must respect the beliefs of others as they would have others respect theirs.

Locke expounded his convictions about religious tolerance and the separation of church and state in his great *Letter Concerning Toleration* (1689), the most influential masterwork of 18th-century liberal philosophy. (In this context, liberal means tolerant, questioning orthodoxy, and believing in human moral progress.) Here, Locke uses a question-and-response style to present an irrefutable argument for religious tolerance and for the noninterference of civil authority in religion. Locke argues that intolerance is an outgrowth of muddled thinking, as when people confuse judgments about faith with empirical certainty based on reason. He demonstrates how sectarian churches can and must embrace tolerance of other beliefs. Churches are, after all, "voluntary associations" whose members could and should embrace the same tolerance for others that they seek for themselves. As citizens of a state, Christian churchgoers do not want government interfering in their worship. It follows that, as citizens, they could see to it that civil authorities do not meddle in the affairs of *any* church.

Locke questioned Hobbes's notion that war was the natural state of humans and societies. He thought that peace could be maintained so long as a state was able to protect citizens' life, liberty, and property. Any state that could guarantee these protections and individual rights, while steering clear of religious entanglements, would be a peaceful and prosperous one. If such a state had legally limited power, separate branches of government, and elected representatives, it would no longer be the target of power-hungry clerics who sought to control it either for the salvation of souls or for their own aggrandizement. If this sounds familiar, it should. Locke's philosophy helped launch the American Revolution and greatly influenced the U.S. Constitution.

After Locke, when it came to political systems and political thought, references and appeals to theology were generally considered illegitimate. Christianity was certainly not abolished in the West, but for the most part it was kept distinct from politics. Yet religion remained a powerful force in human life. The human mind may be weak and imperfect, but there might be something about religion that is innate in humans seeking to understand their place in the world and the cosmos. Locke attributed religious tendencies largely to habit and complacency. The German philosopher Immanuel Kant (1724–1804) saw religion as a necessary construct to help individuals overcome their innate corruption. Although he agreed with Locke about the separation of church and state, he insisted that the church had an important role to play in society. Through religion, people could strive collectively to overcome their inherent corruption and create a truly moral society. For Kant, only Christianity could accomplish this.

THE FRENCH REVOLUTION

The French Revolution was an outgrowth of extreme economic hardship among France's poor due primarily to the punishing taxes imposed by King Louis XVI to support his lavish court. (The American Revolution also inspired the uprising.) The king convened a meeting of the national representative body, the Estates General, whose members represented the clergy, nobility, and third estate, to try to wheedle more money out of its members. Instead, the Estates General reorganized itself into a National Assembly and began debating the creation of a national constitution. When the king tried to disband the Assembly, there was an uprising. On July 14, 1789, the poor of Paris stormed the Bastille prison and liberated its inmates, initiating the revolution.

The history of the French Revolution cannot be detailed here.[24] Its influence on the relationship between church and state was profound. The Assembly immediately began issuing declarations to guide the creation of its constitution. Among these was the famous Declaration of the Rights of Man, which included one clause related to religion: "No one shall be disturbed for his opinions, even religious, provided their manifestation does not disturb the public order established by law."[25] However in 1790, the Assembly issued a Civil Constitution of the Clergy to set legal limits on the church. Its stipulations included forbidding French clergy to appeal to the pope to overturn state laws and giving the state total power of investiture.

France had always been a Catholic nation with close ties to Rome. As elsewhere, many French clerics were mired in corruption. Most of the laws issuing from the Civil Constitution of the Clergy were intended to reform the church. In reality, the secular revolutionary government was de facto taking control of, if not nationalizing, the church. State authority was reinforced when all clergy were required to swear an oath of allegiance to the civil constitution. Those who refused would be defrocked, deported, or (later) decapitated. The oath issue immediately split the church into two camps: those who agreed to it in order to maintain their churches and those who refused to

Introduction

place allegiance to the state above their allegiance to God and the pope. Nonjuring clergy, those who refused the oath, were persecuted as counterrevolutionaries. An alarmed and outraged Pope Pius VI issued repeated, though ineffectual, condemnations of these laws. The pope prevailed upon the king to openly denounce them, but, fearing for his life, Louis did nothing.

As the revolution went into high gear, the pope threatened to excommunicate the juring priests. The Assembly accused nonjuring priests of treason and threatened to execute those who did not immediately leave the country. In August 1792, the king and his family were arrested. During the Reign of Terror, the king, most of the royal family, and many aristocrats were beheaded on the guillotine. A movement began to eliminate the Christian church completely.

On November 10, 1793, in what came to be seen as a travesty of Enlightenment principles, a ceremony was held in Paris's Notre Dame Cathedral to celebrate the goddesses of Reason and Liberty. At the same time, Catholic worship was prohibited in churches throughout France. The Cult of Reason and Liberty became, for a time, the state religion. When the revolutionary leader Maximilien Robespierre (1758–94) decided that the French people "recognize the immortality of the soul," he instituted a new state religion, the Cult of Supreme Being, wholly unrelated to Christianity.[26] Envisioned as a nature god who would be controlled by and thus benefit the state, the new French Supreme Being was first worshipped on June 8, 1794, which was declared a national religious holiday. Temples to Reason and the Supreme Being were built across France.

By this time, the revolution had become more than slightly unhinged. Its leaders on the Committee for Public Safety created a new calendar in which a week contained 10 newly named days (months were renamed after seasons). The Supreme Being was to be worshipped on the 10th day of the week; anyone caught at Christian services on old-fashioned Sundays was punished as a counterrevolutionary. The whole episode might seem merely silly if it were not for the bloodthirsty zeal of the revolutionaries. As many as 5,000 people were dispatched by "Madame Guillotine," including, finally, Robespierre. The Reign of Terror abated somewhat by 1795. In 1798, the French invaded Italy, captured Pope Pius VI, and hauled him back to a French prison, where he died.

The papacy was restored somewhat once Napoléon Bonaparte declared himself emperor in 1804. In a ritual reminiscent of Charlemagne, Napoléon had himself crowned by Pope Pius VII (r. 1800–23). However, Napoléon immediately thereafter infuriated the pontiff by granting religious freedom to Protestants. Napoléon gave the pope a modicum of authority, which he could exercise as long as it did not impinge on imperial policies. The pope bristled at these restrictions. His complaints and invective led to another French invasion of Italy, the pope's capture, and a long stint in jail. There he remained until Napoléon was defeated by allied forces in 1814, when the pope returned to Rome.

The Roman church's intransigent conservatism made it irrelevant to mainstream intellectual and theological thought. As church power declined in the secular world, Pope Pius IX (r. 1846–78) exerted his influence in the only sphere left open to him—theology. In 1854, Pius proclaimed the dogma of the Immaculate Conception of Mary (that she was born free of original sin), which greatly boosted devotion to her among the faithful. A decade later, Pius issued an encyclical that proclaimed papal infallibility. The decree was accompanied by a list of 80 "errors" that Catholics had to reject if they wanted to get into heaven.

Liberal Protestant Theology

With Roman Catholic theology apparently ossified, innovative theological thought arose out of Protestantism. Much of the new theology emerged from the dense, seemingly impenetrable works of the German philosopher Georg Wilhelm Friedrich Hegel (1770–1831). Hegel taught that history is an evolution toward an end point, or ultimate form of perfection in government, religion, etc. He also wrote that religion was a fundamental expression of a deep and sublime truth about humankind, and a people's religion was a vital foundation of their identity. Hegel put these ideas together to formulate his notion that Protestantism, particularly German Protestantism, was the historical end point of religious evolution. Because German Protestants are the embodiments of this ultimate religion, their society is the most ethical expression of religion acting through humans in the world.

Hegel's ideas were advanced by the German liberal theologians who followed him. According to the new liberal theology, as developed by Friedrich Schleiermacher (1768–1834), Ernst Troeltsch (1865–1923), and others, religion no longer rested on divine revelation; instead, it emerged from and was based exclusively on human experience. German liberal theologians dispensed with the Protestant teaching that individuals found God in the Bible and argued instead that God was found in the feelings and experiences of Christian people. Humans became the measure of religious truth. It followed that human society and the cultural Protestantism it created were the collective expression of this divine truth. (This philosophy had significant social ramifications. Not only did it deify bourgeois values [and prejudices], it also elevated middle-class acquisitiveness to a divine attribute.) In this theology, the historical and cultural evolution of Protestantism was the engine of human progress, which reached its zenith in Germany. According to the political theorist Mark Lilla, "For these liberal theologians, there could be

Introduction

no contradiction between Christianity and modern German life because the latter was the historical offspring of the former, . . . their consciousness of Christian history and their faith in progress made it difficult for them to imagine a standpoint superior to the one modern society currently occupied."[27] This philosophy provided a longed-for justification of Germany's place in history and an exaltation of its culture.

Forming a unified German nation was an on-again off-again process, begun in 1813 but beset by problems and setbacks. In 1871, Otto von Bismarck (1815–98) finally united the German principalities under the rule of Emperor Wilhelm I (r. 1871–88). During the early years of the 20th century, competition for trade increased tensions among European nations, which entered into defensive alliances. Most nations began spending heavily on armaments and the military. It is impossible to describe here the entanglements and events that led to the outbreak of World War I in 1914.[28] Yet the principles of German liberal theology and exceptionalism were a contributing factor to Germany's role in starting the war.

Liberal theologians defended Germany's aggression in shocking theological terms. In a speech given at Heidelberg, Ernst Troeltsch proclaimed: ". . . To arms, to arms! . . . [I]n these hours, when we feel and have . . . the living breath of God, when out of a mix of reverence and hope, care and faith, the feeling of God's omnipotence flows through us . . . [W]e pray this deep, serious, passionate, and firm vow: with God, for Kaiser and Reich."[29] This unimaginably awful war destroyed Germany and discredited the liberal theologians' optimistic view of human history and progress. Noted Protestant theologians, particularly Karl Barth (1886–1968), blasted the new liberal theology. Barth's theology stripped humans of their divine status and situated the divine in a transcendence that is beyond time and place. Barth argued that the relationship of humans to God is outside of time, and he reiterated biblical eschatology that reconciliation comes only at the end-times, a moment outside worldly time. Barth was particularly ferocious in his critique of the liberal theologians' support of German militarism. As Barth acidly described them, "They have wished to experience the known god of this world. Well! They have experienced him."[30]

The war was so horrific, so bloody, and fought over such flimsy, barely comprehensible issues, it transformed European society from one of smug complacency to one of doubt and cynicism. No longer could most Europeans believe in anything; faith in nationhood, government, religion, and civilization itself was shattered. The American theologian H. Richard Niebuhr later explained that the war was an outgrowth of a theology in which "a God without wrath brought men without sin into a Kingdom without judgment through ministration without the cross."[31]

RELIGION AND THE STATE

NEW OPTIONS, NEW STATES

By the end of World War I (1918), European civilization had been shattered, and people sought new ways of being in the world. Liberal theology and the culture it championed were discredited; writers, artists, and intellectuals looked for ways to create a new society diametrically opposed to the pieties of theological liberalism. Cynicism reigned even among ordinary people as they tried to find another type of meaning in the devastation of their societies. Some turned back to the transcendent, wholly other God of the Bible. Others strove for a decisive, world-changing event that would give life new meaning and direction. Some in this latter group would find this new meaning later in Nazism. Others found it in a revolution that had transformed a nation just a few years before.

In 1917, the Bolshevik revolution in Russia had overthrown the czar and instituted a communist government based on Karl Marx's *Capital* (1867–94) and *Communist Manifesto* (1848, with Friedrich Engels). Marx viewed religion as an opiate that distracted human beings from truly caring about their material and social well-being and saw both the monarchy and the church as equal oppressors of peasants and workers. Russian communist leaders destroyed the nation's churches, and the practice of religion was prohibited. Atheism (the denial of the existence of a deity) became the state religion, and it was strictly enforced. The Russian Revolution gave hope to many disillusioned Europeans. State-enforced atheism was viewed as a reasonable alternative to the moral and religious vacuum that Europeans were left with after the war. Communist parties sprouted across the continent, and many members became atheists. Virulent opposition to this new worldview by the powers that be would result in violent conflicts and a political backlash.

OUT OF THE ASHES: ANOTHER WAR

In his work, Barth had attempted to avoid any political theology. He viewed politics as a game that should never be hitched to theology. Barth wrote that no form of government is more legitimate than any other in terms of its relationship to religion. What Barth did not recognize was people's need for a messianic leader. This temporal political idol would relieve their despair, unite them in messianic fervor, and perhaps catapult them to new heights of greatness. This is what happened in Germany in 1933, with the election of Adolf Hitler (1889–1945) and the National Socialist German Worker's Party (NSDAP, or Nazi Party). To his utter dismay, people interpreted Barth's work to justify the new tyranny. In protest, Barth and other German Protestant theologians formed the Confessing Church to oppose the Reich Church established by the Nazis. They issued the Barmen Declaration in 1934 to denounce this church and the political system that supported it.

Introduction

Germany's obsession with its destiny reemerged with Hitler's election, in which some saw the hand of God. The theologian Friedrich Gogarten (1887–1968), in *Religion and Volkstum*, wrote, "Christ has come to us through Adolf Hitler ... [T]hrough his power ... the Redeemer found us.[...] The *Volk* (people) and everything connected with it, including the state, is completely permeated with religious thoughts and feelings, and is for us the bearer not only of earthly but of eternal life.... German history is ... God's revelation."[32] German exceptionalism (again) justified World War II.[33]

THE NEW SECULARISM

By the end of World War I, Western civilization as people had known it was gone forever. By the time World War II ended (1945) and many European cities were rubble-strewn wastelands, most people had had enough of political theology. The pope and the Roman Catholic Church were alleged to have collaborated with the Nazis. As Germany showed, Protestantism was hardly a viable alternative. Many Europeans embraced atheism and/or Locke's views on the total separation of church and state. The despair and devastation in the wake of World War II created the majority secular humanist outlook of Europeans today.

Even the Christian churches accepted their new role as just one institution within the civil, secular society. They gave up any pretensions to political power, while gaining a new type of independent influence that people could accept or reject. Religion became wholly a personal matter. European nations today maintain a sense of unity sufficiently strong to permit tolerance of a wide diversity of communities, both religious and secular. Beginning in the 1960s, European nations began to decouple church law from civil law. So, for example, adultery was no longer a civil crime (though it continued to be condemned by the church). Once church law was stricken from the civil code, many other aspects of morality followed. A wide range of human behavior became a matter of personal morality beyond the reach of both state and church. The archbishop of Canterbury, Dr. Rowan Williams, referred to this new freedom as the "privatization of the ten commandments."[34]

The church still weighed in on important issues that it saw as within its purview, particularly relating to scientific advances such as in vitro fertilization and stem cell research. To a large extent, the church's recalcitrance regarding these significant scientific advances further alienated Europeans from religion. As the church became increasingly irrelevant to modern Europeans, their societies became increasingly secular. Yet religious freedom and tolerance continued to be the cornerstone of European culture. This freedom and tolerance prevailed unchallenged in Europe until it was confronted by the wholly different worldview of its immigrant Muslim population.

RELIGION AND THE STATE

ISLAM
The Prophet and His Teachings

Muhammad ibn Abdullah (son of Abdulluh) (570–632) was born in Mecca (Arabia) to the fairly poor, peripheral tribe of the Quraysh, Meccan traders. His father died before he was born, and his mother died when he was only six years old. As a young man, he managed the caravan of the rich widow Khadija, whom he later married.

Muhammad was a respected trader in Mecca, but he was also a contemplative. He frequently climbed nearby Mt. Hira to sit in a cave in quiet meditation. According to the Quran, the holy book of Islam, when Muhammad was 40 years old, on "The Night of Power and Excellence," he was visited by the Angel Gabriel, who commanded simply, "Recite." The astonished Muhammad responded, understandably, that he had nothing to recite. Gabriel kept repeating the command as Muhammad became increasingly bewildered. Muhammad implored the angel, repeating that he knew no recitations. Finally, words entered Muhammad, and he uttered: "Recite in the name of your Lord who has created . . . Recite, for your Lord is the Most Generous One Who has taught by the pen, Taught man what he did not know!"[35] As these words flowed through him, Muhammad became a Prophet of God. For the next 22 years, Muhammad wrote down the divine messages he received. These teachings are collected in the Quran (the Recitation), the sacred scripture of Islam (submission [to Allah]). It must be emphasized that Muhammad was not divine but was a human conduit for the literal word of God (Allah) that he set down in the Quran.

His first decade of preaching was disappointing. Muhammad gained a few converts, particularly his cousin Ali and his father-in-law Abu Bakr, but most people rejected his teachings. As with most reformers, Muhammad's teachings, which stressed social justice and equality, threatened the rich and powerful who he exhorted to aid the poor. He also taught that traditional Arabian polytheism must give way to monotheistic worship of Allah. The Umayyad clan, the most powerful in Mecca, organized opposition to him.

In 620, Muhammad was invited to be a judge in Medina. From July to September 622, the Prophet and his 200 converts journeyed to Medina. This migration, or Hijra, marked a turning point in Islam and was later adopted as the beginning of the Islamic calendar. As ruler in Medina, Muhammad wrote a charter setting out the duties and rights of its citizens and delineating the relationship of Muslims (those who submit [to Allah]) to non-Muslims (whose religious practices were permitted) in the city. The community of Muslims *(umma)* in Medina grew, and Muhammad's teachings gained wider acceptance.

Introduction

Meanwhile in Mecca, powerful clans were organizing against Muhammad. The stage was set for the great Battle of Badr in 624. Although his troops were greatly outnumbered, Muhammad's force of holy warriors (mujahideen) gained a decisive victory over the Meccan army. This wondrous success was attributed to Allah's intervention, earning Muhammad great renown and many more followers. After some setbacks, Muhammad vanquished Meccan opposition in 627, earning him enormous prestige.

The Prophet formed alliances with many tribes and negotiated peace with many others. In 629, he and his followers went on pilgrimage to Mecca, where they emptied the Kaaba ("black box," also known as "the sacred house") of its pagan idols and resanctified it as a pilgrimage site for worshippers of Allah. By 631, Mecca and most of the Arabian Peninsula were converted to Islam. After a pilgrimage to Mecca in 632, Muhammad gave his last sermon, instructing all Muslims to be brothers and to live in a society based on equality and justice. In June 632, Muhammad died.

The life of Muhammad is seen as the ultimate sunna (example) of the good and holy life. Muhammad is revered as the "living Quran," and his actions and sayings were written down for future generations (the body of these sayings is known as the Hadith). The Sunna (Quran and the Hadith) has scriptural authority for Muslims, and the laws and civil practices the Prophet instituted in Medina became the ideal form of Islamic governance.

In the Medina charter, Muhammad in some cases amended existing customs; for example, the pilgrimage (hajj) to Mecca was now to honor Allah, not a pantheon of deities. For the most part, the Quran eliminates pre-Islamic mores and replaces them with strict codes of conduct based on divine revelation. Thus, Muhammad initiated a revolution in Arabian life. No longer was the tribe or clan the center of one's identity; instead, one was a member of and loyal to the *umma*. Vendetta was replaced by a belief in a just and merciful God. The Quran speaks of a Last Day when all are judged. Those who obey God's law enter a paradise of earthlike pleasure and bliss. The disobedient are cast into hell, where they suffer eternal physical torment.

The Quran contains the literal word of God as transmitted from heaven to Muhammad. For Muslims, the Quran is God's original and final revelation to humankind, superseding the "corrupted" revelations in the Bible's Old and New Testaments (e.g., "The Christians say 'The Messiah is the Son of God' . . . How they are perverted! . . . There is no God but He").[36] It then goes on to "correct" the "falsifications" in the previous scriptures. Because it is the direct word of God, Muslims believe that the Quran is "perfect, eternal, and unchangeable."[37] The core Islamic doctrine is belief in absolute monotheism *(tawhid)* and acceptance that God is merciful and just. Although Allah can engage with humanity, he is so totally remote and transcendent, it is forbidden *(haram)* to create an image relating to him or even to the Prophet.

The Quran and Hadith contain statements about how God's law (sharia) should be observed by God's people. Sharia is also an ethical guide for a moral life, though it does not confer political or social "rights" (such as freedom of speech and religion). Obedience to sharia is a Muslim's highest duty. The individual's responsibility to obey Allah's law is amplified in the *umma*, which should be a living example of godly life to all nations. As stated in the Quran, "You are the best community evolved for mankind, enjoining what is right and forbidding what is wrong."[38] Muslim governance and law follow from this directive. Sharia law, when defined as the revealed law of God, is divine and uncontestable. However, some Muslims have for centuries seen the more "mundane" aspects of sharia, which deal with everyday life, as being open to interpretation and debate by jurists and judges, who may attempt to adapt revelation to all areas of human conduct. Thus, sharia may be viewed as containing both the infallible and unchangeable revealed law of God in its religious and spiritual teachings, as well as more malleable suras (verses), which deal with everyday matters and may be subject to human jurisprudence.

Islamic Political Theology

The prophet Muhammad, as the first governor in Islam, saw the primary role of the state as ensuring social equality and justice. Muhammad placed great emphasis on the state's responsibility for looking after the welfare of widows, orphans, and the poor. He instituted an alms tax *(zakat)* to redistribute wealth. Muhammad also described those situations in which armed conflict, or struggle (jihad), was justified: to defend the state against an aggressor and to fight for justice for those who are oppressed.

There is much confusion about jihad among non-Muslims. Two types of jihad are mentioned in the Sunna. The greater jihad is internal: It is the personal struggle to live a virtuous life according to God's law. The lesser jihad is external: It is the struggle to defend Islam and the *umma*, either with diplomacy or arms. Jihad is so important, it is sometimes referred to as the "sixth pillar of Islam." The main Five Pillars of Islam are obligatory for all Muslims. They are: (1) professing faith in Allah ("There is no god but God") and his prophet, Muhammad; (2) prayer: saying a particular prayer to Allah (beginning "Allahu Akbar" [God is great]) at five specified times per day while facing Mecca; (3) almsgiving: paying the *zakat*; (4) fasting during Ramadan: observing a monthlong fast once a year when neither food nor drink may be taken from sunup to sunset. Ramadan is observed during the ninth month of

Introduction

the Islamic calendar; (5) pilgrimage: All Muslims are required, if possible, to make a pilgrimage (hajj) to Mecca at least once during their lifetime.

In Islam, Allah is the ultimate source of authority, and all power comes from him. Allah can be known only through divine law, and its sovereignty is absolute. Thus, political authority is embodied, not in a ruler or cleric, but in sharia. Islamic scripture does not specify an ideal political organization for the Islamic state. The role of the state in Islam is to provide the security and order needed for the *umma* to follow sharia and thereby establish Allah's earthly rule. Because of their special relationship to Allah, Muslims are enjoined to carry out God's will on Earth, and they are judged on the Last Day by the degree to which they obeyed God's law during life. Islam has no conception of original sin; the only sin is disobedience.

Islam is more than a religion: It is a way of life that encompasses both personal life and the public arena. Islam demands not just belief but specific practices in both the private and public sphere that are in accord with sharia. Ideally, the caliph (leader) is the guardian of the faith and the *umma*; the *ulama* (religious scholars) advise on religious matters that pertain to the state and community; *qadis* (judges) settle disputes based on Islamic law. The state exists only as an instrument to facilitate and promote sharia. Therefore, the Islamic state does not legislate; the sharia laws it upholds preceded it in the Sunna. Instead, it interprets the law to ensure that political and social actions are in accord with sharia. Unfortunately, the ideal religiopolitical Islamic state has been largely unattainable in the real world.

THE IDEAL V. THE REAL

Throughout their history, Muslims have viewed the period when the Prophet ruled as the perfect model of an Islamic state, a political ideal to be re-created in the world. By acting in total obedience to sharia, Muslims help bring about this ideal state. During Muhammad's rule, there was no separation of religion and the state; religion was the state, just as religion was and is the Muslim way of life. "Politics is central to the Muslim faith because it represents the means by which Islam is to be carried out in the public sphere."[39] Although politics is vital in incorporating sharia into the public arena, there is no such thing as an independent political space that has its own rules and laws. Nor is there any hierarchical clergy or organized church existing as a counterbalance to or check on political institutions.

Since Allah is the ultimate, unquestioned authority in all spheres, including politics, in the orthodox view, laws, judgments, and mores that arise from human reason must be superseded by God's law. Under the strictest form of Muslim jurisprudence, using reason to solve problems is discouraged because reason may contradict sharia. Applying reason above sharia compromises the

RELIGION AND THE STATE

purity of society, which depends on the *umma*'s moral, social, and political adherence to God's law. Thus, if the *umma* does not realize an ideal state, it must be because Muslims have failed in their perfect obedience to sharia.

It is clear that tensions might arise from this orthodoxy as social and historical conditions change and the Muslim community attempts to adapt to them. As desirable and sublime as the ideal state would be, since Muhammad's death it has generally proven to be extremely difficult to realize. Over time, invasions, imperfect rulers, contact with diverse cultures and systems of thought, and other vagaries of history made the possibility of re-creating the ideal polity of the Prophet increasingly remote. Political life and government bore less and less resemblance to the ideal. Although every Islamic government acknowledged the desirability of modeling the state on the Prophet's perfect rule, none could quite figure out how to do that. The *umma* came to terms with this by compartmentalizing political life and setting it apart from both their reverence for the ideal state and their religious practice. (This attitude was also an outgrowth of political organization in the Muslim world, in which citizens had little connection to power in the vast empires that ruled them.) By compartmentalizing politics and the state, the *umma* could continue to idealize the ancient, ideal model and keep it untainted by real-world political problems, while being resigned to imperfect governance.

The result of this dichotomy was a general public disengagement with politics. As long as rulers did not interfere with citizens' pursuit of a good and pious life, they were largely ignored. The rulers' laws were obeyed as long as they did not contradict sharia. The Quran and Hadith recognize the need for government to maintain an orderly society. But when asked "Shouldn't we fight against [bad rulers]?" Muhammad replied, "No, not so long as they say their prayers."[40] Thus, Muslims were enjoined to obey, not rebel against, bad rulers. In response, Muslims cherished the ideal state as an abstract ideal unrelated to the real, corrupt world. This attitude had several perceived advantages. First, it kept the notional ideal state from being corrupted by less than ideal leaders. Second, by withdrawing from the state, the *umma* stripped the government of authority to pronounce on religious practice or theological doctrine. In a sense, Muslims followed Christ's directive to render unto Caesar that which is Caesar's, and to pursue their religious life in the private sphere. Yet the gulf between political reality and political ideal was immense, and it led both to political pessimism among Muslims and to arbitrary governments that had little real legitimacy in the eyes of the governed. Disengagement with politics and submission to the ruler limited Muslims' ability to actively transform their political system either into a model of the Prophet's ideal state or into a state that was more attuned to its times.

Introduction

As religious, political, social, and military leader, Muhammad embodied the state and the law that Muslims revere and idealize. One reason this ideal state has been unattainable arose from what some Muslims perceive as the Sunna's ambiguous instructions about how succeeding caliphs were to be chosen and legitimized. This ambiguity would lead to strife and irreconcilable rifts in the Islamic world. Within decades of Muhammad's death, any hope for an acceptable, let alone ideal, Islamic state would be, for the most part, beyond reach.

THE FOUR RIGHTLY GUIDED CALIPHS

The four caliphs elected by consensus *(ijmaa)* and consultation *(shura)* after Muhammad's death are known as the Rightly Guided Caliphs (Rashidun), even though the period ended with serious divisions within the Islamic community. All were Companions of the Prophet. The first Rightly Guided Caliph was Abu Bakr (r. 632–634), Muhammad's father-in-law. Almost immediately, Abu Bakr faced withdrawal from the *umma* of a number of key Arab tribes that declared, as per custom, that their pact with Muhammad ended at his death. There followed the Wars of Apostasy, in which Abu Bakr's forces crushed the revolt and brought the tribes back into the Islamic fold. Abu Bakr's actions showed that membership in the *umma* was a political commitment that could not be easily broken. Abu Bakr also used military force to expand Islam into Yemen, Iraq, and Syria.

Umar succeeded Abu Bakr as caliph (r. 634–644), and he further consolidated the *umma* in a single political entity. Umar expanded the reach of Islam into Mesopotamia and North Africa. He also codified much sharia law, created the Islamic calendar, and generally set the foundation for a holistic Islam that ordered every aspect of personal and political life.

Umar was murdered, some say by a slave or captive, but no one really knows who did the deed. He was succeeded by Uthman who, unlike his two predecessors and Muhammad, was from the powerful Meccan Umayyad clan. Uthman amassed wealth through war, and he used it to install his kinsmen in positions of authority within the state. His nepotism and the elevation of his clan angered many, as did the growing decadence and corruption of his "court." The last straw was naming his nephew Muawiya governor of Syria. The Medina faction of the *umma* saw their power disappearing, and they rebelled, murdering Uthman.

The issue of the succession now became critical. In each election, the Prophet's son-in-law (husband of Muhammad's daughter Fatima) and cousin by blood, Ali, had vied for the position of caliph. In each case, the *shura* had chosen someone else. Supporters of Ali understood only too well how an election can be corrupted. Although the system was widely accepted, there were no guidelines to ensure that the *shura* was unbiased; thus, electors might be of one clan and support their clansman, not the man most suited to be caliph. After Muhammad's death, some Muslims thought the succession should go to the Prophet's blood relatives. Ali's supporters were adamant about this and furious that Ali had been repeatedly passed over.

Finally, after the rebellion and the murder of Uthman, Ali (r. 656–661) was chosen to be the fourth (and last) caliph. Ali's caliphate was plagued by rumors that he had murdered Uthman to gain power. Rumor became scandal when Ali refused to investigate the murder. In Syria, Muawiya seethed for revenge, as did Aisha, Abu Bakr's daughter and one of Muhammad's wives. A major civil war ensued. Ali defeated Aisha's forces, but he then had to face Muawiya, who used psychological warfare to his advantage. Muawiya had all his soldiers spear one page from the Quran on the tips of their lances. Ali's forces wavered, unable to attack the holy book. The armies separated, and the matter was settled by arbitration in Muawiya's favor. Muawiya declared himself caliph, though Ali remained the officially chosen caliph. In a situation reminiscent of the medieval papacy, there were for a time two caliphs. When Ali died, Muawiya became the self-proclaimed caliph. The *shura* system of selecting a caliph became discredited.

Muawiya's reign as the fifth caliph began the Umayyad Empire (661–750), a time of nepotism, decadence, corruption, and the sacrifice of Islamic doctrine to dynastic tyranny. The Umayyad dynasty built mosques, made Arabic the universal Muslim language, and expanded Islam into Byzantium and, in 719, into Andalusia in Spain. (Their ambitions in Europe were stopped only in 732 when they were defeated at Poitiers by Charles Martel.) But the empire's accomplishments are overshadowed by intense internal strife and power conflicts. The Umayyads are best remembered for the irreparable rift they caused in Islam.

SHIA ISLAM

Supporters of Ali, known as the Shiat Ali (Party of Ali), or Shia, broke with the main body of Islam, the Sunnis (from sunna), over the issue of succession. Sunnis believe that the succession should go to the most pious and qualified candidate, as determined by the *shura*. Shia believe only blood relatives should succeed the Prophet. The aged Muawiya named his son Yazid as successor. Until Yazid took power, Ali's second son, Husayn, had lived a quiet life. Now, with the promised backing of the Iraqi army, he and his supporters determined to fight an Umayyad dynasty. The Iraqi forces never showed up, and at the battle of Karbala (Iraq, 680) the Umayyad army made quick work of Husayn's small force. Husayn retreated, wrapped himself in the Prophet's

Introduction

shawl (which he had inherited from his father, Ali), and rode out to meet the Umayyads. He was killed by a rain of arrows. His death was not enough for the Umayyads. They hacked the head off Husayn's dead body and then dispatched it to Damascus, their capital, where it was put on public display.

The enormity of this desecration of a blood relative of Muhammad's began to dawn on the Muslim community. Some left the Sunni fold in disgust and joined the Shia. To this day, Shia commemorate the martyrdom of Husayn in Karbala, one of the major sites of pilgrimage for Shia Muslims.

The Shia-Sunni rift resulted in two divergent religious entities. Unlike the Sunni, the Shia no longer recognized the authority of the caliphate. Instead, they recognize a lineage of Imams (Shiite religious leaders) directly descended from Muhammad and possessing divine inspiration and infallibility. Most Shia attest to 12 Imams during their history. The 12th and last Imam is believed to have disappeared in 874, when he was a young boy. Since then, Shia believe that this last Imam is in hiding but will return as a Mahdi (Messiah) at the end of days, when he will vindicate the Shia and restore justice to the Islamic community. Until the Mahdi arrives, the Shiite community is guided by ayatollahs ("sign of God"), who are the most highly regarded religious leaders, and by *mujtahids*, who interpret divine law.

Shia Islam is vastly different from the majority Sunni beliefs, both religiously and politically. Sunnis view early Islamic history as a guide and a validation of Islam, and they are confident that the caliphate reflects God's will. Shia see history as a struggle to restore true Islam ruled by an Imam related by blood to the Prophet. Shia Islam is concerned with martyrdom, sacrifice, atonement, and redemption, none of which are found in Sunnism. Unlike Sunni Islam, the Shia belief in the return of the Hidden Imam puts eschatology at the center of their religion and places it in an earthly historical context. Most Islamic experts concur that there is little likelihood of resolution between Shia and Sunni Muslims.

Empires of the Golden Age
THE ABBASID EMPIRE

The Umayyad reign came to a bloody end in 750, when the dynasty was overcome by the Abbasids. The Abbasids moved their capital from Damascus to Baghdad and proceeded to create an Islamic civilization second to none. The Abassid Empire (750–1258) shunned ostentation and embraced sharia. The dynasty's caliphs ruled by divine mandate, a system adopted from the Persians, and were called Deputies of the Prophet.

This first flowering of Islam emerged from expanded trade rather than conquest. Openness to the ideas and cultures of converted, previously oppressed peoples invigorated Islamic culture. Great art and architecture, magnificent literature, and subtle philosophy were hallmarks of the era. The Abbasids built academies and great libraries for the training of *ulama*, who were free to study, translate, and comment upon Greek, Latin, Sanskrit, Persian, and Coptic classical texts. Great and influential artists, mathematicians, scientists, and philosophers flourished in this culturally stimulating environment. Islam also owes a great debt to the Abbasid law schools whose graduates codified and clarified most sharia law.

This was truly an Islamic renaissance created from a dynamic and creative civilization. It came about because of "... a sense of mission, power, and superiority. Muslims were the dominant force—masters, not victims.... The new ideas were Arabized and Islamized [in a] process of change characterized by continuity with the faith and practice of Muhammad. Unlike the modern period, Muslims controlled the process of assimilation and acculturation."[41]

In the end, governing a vast empire that stretched from the Atlantic Ocean to Asia proved too much for the Abbasids. Internal power struggles and secessionist movements in North Africa, Iran, and Syria weakened the empire. In 945, the Buyids of western Persia (Iran) took over Baghdad and ruled the empire, leaving an Abbasid caliph in place as titular leader. Soon after, more power was ceded to the Seljuks (Turks) and their sultan. Missionaries from the Shiite Fatimids, who had taken control of Egypt, further undermined the Sunni Abbasid state. The Shiite challenge impelled the Abbasid *ulama* to consolidate and strengthen Sunni sharia law. The Abbasid Empire could not survive this onslaught of challenges. They would succumb, finally, to greater and more destructive onslaughts—crusaders and Mongols.

THE CRUSADES

In 1095, Pope Urban II (r. 1088–99) urged a large gathering of Christians to unite in a "War of the Cross" to deliver the holy city of Jerusalem from the infidels (Muslims) who controlled it. The campaign was instigated by the Byzantine emperor who urgently needed help keeping the encroaching Seljuks at bay.

When the First Crusade (1096–99) embarked in September 1096, the pope proclaimed, "Anyone who sets out on that journey, not out of lust for worldly advantage but only for the salvation of his soul and for the liberation of the Church, is remitted in entirety all penance for his sins ... ," a statement that echoes a sura in the Quran about the blessings of jihad.[42] Christians considered the First Crusade the most "successful," though it was certainly the bloodiest. After slaughtering thousands of Jews en route through Europe, the crusaders captured Jerusalem on July 15, 1099, killing every man, woman, and child they found (including some Christians). This Crusade is notorious for its extreme brutality.

Introduction

Three major Crusades followed, all in response to Muslims recapturing formerly won land. The Second Crusade (1147–49) attempted but failed to capture Damascus. The Third Crusade (1189–93) attempted to recapture Jerusalem from the Abbasid Saracen leader Saladin (r. 1174–93), but the city remained in Muslim hands (as it would for the next 700 years). The Fourth Crusade (1202–04) was an unmitigated disaster for the Christians, who in their frustration turned on the Christians in Constantinople.

There is no reliable record of how many Muslims died during these Crusades, but the bloodletting described by witnesses indicates the slaughter of tens of thousands. The Crusades instilled in Muslims an indelible image of Christians as bloodthirsty savages. Where Muslim leaders in the Holy Land were generally tolerant of citizens of other faiths, the Christians insulted Islam and the prophet Muhammad and deliberately demolished Muslim holy sites in Jerusalem. Muslim distrust and antagonism engendered by the Crusades colors Christian-Muslim relations to this day.

Although the Abbasid Empire was weakened and destabilized by the Crusades, it was destroyed by Mongol invaders from Central Asia. After Genghis (Chinggis) Khan (r. 1206–27) overran Syria, Turkey, and Persia, his grandson Hulagu (1217–65) attacked Iraq. In 1258, after two years of intense warfare, the Abbasid capital of Baghdad fell to the Mongols. This great cultural empire was lost, but in the years following its fall the Mongols converted to Islam and adapted it to their own culture.

EMPIRES OF THE SIXTEENTH CENTURY

The Abbasid Empire was the forerunner of several Muslim empires that flourished during the 16th century. The Safavid Empire (1501–1722) controlled Persia. The Savafids arose in the 13th century from a revivalist Sufi (mystical Islamic) sect that sought to purify Islam. By the 15th century, a large number of Shia had joined the movement, giving it a definite messianic bent. After conquering Tabriz, the Safavid leader proclaimed himself shah (king) of Iran. Shia Islam became the official state religion and was imposed by persuasion or force on the Sunni population. Non-Shiite beliefs were suppressed. The greatest Savafid leader, Shah Abbas, lavished the empire's wealth on the building of mosques, schools, hospitals, and other public works.

The Mughal Empire arose in northern India around the same time. Muslims had moved into the area as early as the 13th century, establishing a sultanate in Delhi. Akbar (r. 1565–1605) was the greatest Mughal emperor, extending Islam throughout much of the subcontinent. Akbar is revered for his tolerance of Hinduism and other Indian religions. His enlightened efforts at melding Islam and Hinduism into a single "true" religion were never realized, as he was vehemently opposed by the Muslim *ulama*. Akbar was later succeeded by Aurangzeb (r. 1658–1707), who reinstated the primacy of "uncorrupted" Islam. The Mughals are world famous for the magnificence of their art and architecture. The Taj Mahal is the epitome of the grandeur and grace of Mughal design.

THE OTTOMAN EMPIRE

The Ottomans rose to power out of a great warrior tradition. As a Turkish Muslim tribe from Anatolia, the Ottomans blocked Mongol threats from the east and pushed the Byzantines farther west. In 1453, they captured Constantinople (pronounced in Turkish "Costan-pull," which became Istanbul in 1924) and established it as their capital and launching pad for invasions into eastern Europe (particularly the Balkans), North Africa, and parts of the Arabian Peninsula, all of which they came to rule. The Ottomans reigned over much of the *dar al-Islam* (abode or heartland of Islam) for nearly 500 years.

The Ottoman Empire was known for its religious tolerance of the *dhimmi*, or non-Muslims, throughout the empire. Most Islamic states had been fairly tolerant of non-Muslims. In contrast to most previous empires, the Ottomans did not exact a special tax on nonbelievers, who were free to build and operate their own places of worship. In fact, many religious groups enjoyed a limited autonomy as long as they sent their taxes to Istanbul.

Ottoman government absorbed the *ulama*, which became part of its elaborate bureaucracy. Although the *ulama* was integrated into the state, Ottoman leaders, or sultans, never attempted to institute a state religion. The Ottomans tried to expand the sultan's role by also calling him caliph in an attempt to invest him with greater religious power, but they never quite pulled it off. Religious authority remained with the *ulama*, while secular bureaucrats and the sultan controlled the political affairs of empire. At one point, the office of *shayk-al-Islam* was created as the premier arbiter of Islamic law, or chief mufti (legal specialist). There were a few instances in which this official weighed in on political matters, issuing the occasional fatwa (legal opinion), but no one grasped this opportunity to create a judiciary independent of both religious and state power.

Suleyman the Magnificent (r. 1520–66) was the greatest sultan, and Ottoman expansion and culture reached their height during his reign. Istanbul was a thriving cultural and trade city of more than half a million people. Yet within a decade of Suleyman's death, Ottoman expansion was blocked by a significant defeat at the Battle of Lepanto, Greece (1571), and the failure of the siege of Vienna (1683), which marked the end of Ottoman expansion in Europe. Though limited to its existing boundaries, the Ottoman Empire would persist until the end of World War I (1918), at which time the Muslim world would be turned upside down.

Introduction

DISSOLUTION AND COLONIZATION

For centuries, the Ottoman Empire had been threatened by Russia, which wanted to wrest control of the Bosporus Strait, a narrow but vital water link between the Black Sea and the Mediterranean. When World War I began and the Central Powers (Germany and Austria) faced off against the Entente (Britain, France, and Russia), the Ottomans sided with the former against Russia. It was an understandable though ultimately disastrous decision. The end of the war spelled the end of the Ottoman Empire. The Ottomans were limited to Anatolia (Turkey), and the rest of the empire was parceled out among the victorious nations of the Entente.

The 18th and 19th centuries were the age of imperialism, when European powers colonized (by force or trade) a considerable portion of the Muslim world. (Lack of space limits this discussion mainly to the Middle East, although Asian Muslim nations, such as Indonesia, were also colonized.) After World War I, most of the Middle East and North Africa was divvied up among Britain, France, Italy, and Russia into regions of direct control or spheres of influence, as prescribed by the Sykes-Picot Agreement of 1915–17. (Interestingly, no one bothered to claim Arabia, a desert wasteland thought to have nothing of value.) In later decades, some of these areas under foreign control were lassoed into "nations" circumscribed by arbitrary boundaries drawn by their European overlords. Some remained protectorates or wholly owned subsidiaries of their imperialist masters. Others achieved a semblance of nationhood based on generally recognized commonalities of culture, language, etc. (e.g., Egypt, Iran [Persia]). Yet even those ostensibly free nations had leaders who were under the thumb of an imperial power.

Whether subjugated or "free," for the next few decades the citizens of these "entities" engaged in repeated rebellion. Every nation in this part of the Muslim world experienced uprisings in response to its unique political and economic circumstances. It is impossible here even to outline the political upheavals that occurred throughout this region during this period. However, it must be emphasized that the nationalist feelings that led to these uprisings gained massive popular support because they were fed by universal and overwhelming resentment of the European interloper. Ridding the nation of imperialism unified the populace, but that unity would unravel once independence was achieved. Then, the fierce debate about how the newly autonomous Muslim nations should be governed would begin. Then, decisions made about religion's role in state governance would become critical and ultimately defining. The conflicts that resulted from diametrically opposed and passionately held views on these issues frequently threatened to tear nations apart. They would lead to the divisive and sometimes violent struggles that persist today.

RELIGION AND THE STATE

The Struggle over Religion and the State
ESTABLISHMENT WESTERNIZATION

For more than a millennium, the Muslim community's positive view of itself in history was validated by reality. It had created empires that were powerful, self-governing, and culturally sophisticated. All this was accomplished by an Islamic society guided by Islamic law. Then everything changed. The *dar al-Islam* was no longer triumphant; it was divided, oppressed, and humiliated. The Muslim worldview and its political and religious identity were shattered, and Muslims searched for explanations. Why had Muslim greatness vanished? Had Muslims caused this debacle by failing to live according to Islam, or had Islam itself failed? Colonialism created crises in politics and religion: "The fundamental spiritual crisis in Islam in the twentieth century stems from an awareness that something is awry between the religion which God has appointed and the historical development of the world which He controls."[43] How should Muslims respond to these crises to regain their identity and respect?

There were several ways Muslims could respond to this change in their fortunes. First, they might reject all things Western and withdraw into their own closed society. Second, they might adopt Western secularism or adapt it and aspects of Western society to their own societies. Third, they might actively modernize or Westernize Islamic society. The first option was adopted by those who refused to deal with the world as it was and who sought to remake the world the way they imagined it should be (traditionally Islamic). The second and third options were embraced by those who to some extent admired the accomplishments of Western society and thought that Islamic society would benefit by learning from the West and emulating it to a greater or lesser extent.

Versions of the latter approach had been promulgated by several Muslim intellectuals, particularly Jamal al-Din al-Afghani (1838–97), founder of the pan-Islamic movement to resist expansion of European power around the world, and his student Muhammad Abduh (1849–1905). Al-Afghani was a firebrand and tireless political activist who traveled widely urging Muslims to regain their identity and revivify their God-given purpose. As a supporter of pan-Islam, al-Afghani blamed Western imperialism for Muslim ills, but he also chided the *ulama* for their narrow, medieval interpretation of Islamic law. In a sense, al-Afghani called for an Islamic Reformation that would free it from its ancient chains and release the creative and intellectual potential of Muslims. He cited scripture to argue that reason was not *haram* in Islam, but that intellectual pursuits such as science and technology were acceptable and desirable. He also argued that Islam accorded well with constitu-

Introduction

tional government and Muslims' direct participation in electoral politics. Al-Afghani insisted that if Muslims were united in a pan-Islamic entity, they could realize true progress (in the Western sense) while retaining a modern yet religiously correct Islam.

Muhammad Abduh, an Egyptian religious scholar, was more of a reformist than his activist teacher. Abduh furthered his mentor's argument that Islam was compatible with the modern world and Westernization. He argued that reason was a God-given faculty that each Muslim was obliged to use not only to improve and modernize society, but also to adapt sharia to the modern world and its challenges. In other words, he recommended *ijtihad* (independent legal judgment) over traditional *taqlid* (narrow legal interpretation). Abduh organized a modernist branch of the Salafis, a group that sought to purify Islam by both reconnecting it with its roots and revitalizing it with intellectual vigor. In true Reformation style, Abduh urged all Muslims to exercise *ijtihad*. He agreed that *shura* should be extended to apply to voting for a representative government. *Ijtihad* became one of the fundamental doctrines of Salafism. Abduh taught that the uniquely religious injunctions of sharia should remain inviolate, but the parts of scripture that deal with living in the world could and should be changed by an empowered and educated *umma*. Education reform was a cornerstone of Abduh's philosophy.

Some 20th-century Islamic nations, notably Egypt, Turkey, and Iran, took up the challenge of the West. Their leaders built schools on the Western model to teach Western subjects. For the most part, this training was available only to the wealthy and political elites, who correctly viewed a Western education as a means of attaining a lucrative and powerful position in government or commerce. Confining these opportunities to more privileged classes created internal tensions over belief and policy. The vast majority of the populace was taught in underfunded, traditionally Islamic schools. The societal fissure this system produced eventually served only to fan the flames of resentment and religious revival among the majority poor.

THE IMPERFECTIONS OF SECULAR NATIONS

Westernization was embraced to some degree by some nations whose populace was fairly homogeneous in terms of language, culture, or ethnicity. Thus Turkey became a fiercely secular nation under Mustafa Kemal Atatürk (r. 1923–38); Egypt was united and ruled by the secularist Gamal Abdel Nasser (r. 1952–70); Iran, a culturally and linguistically unique nation, was led by Reza Shah Pahlavi (r. 1925–44), who was almost as vehemently secular as his Turkish counterpart. Arabic-speaking regions that had even a brief history of statehood—Morocco, Oman, Tunisia, and to a lesser extent Algeria, Kuwait, Lebanon, Sudan, and Yemen—also adopted some degree of Westernized government.

RELIGION AND THE STATE

Many of these nations adopted Western-style constitutions and, per the ideas of Abduh, citizens were given the right to vote. Thus the populace became far more politically engaged than it had been in a long time. Applying reason and judgment to their greater political activism soon made it clear to many Muslims that their vaunted Western-style, representative governments were not all they should be. In many cases, and to this day, so-called democracies maintained their power with secret police, the military, and intelligence agencies that spied on citizens and dealt harshly with dissenters who tried to rid the state of corruption.

It did not take long for widespread discontent to begin to undermine Muslim nations. Governments were repressive and undemocratic; they had not delivered on the promises of progress made during the heyday of nationalism. Many national leaders, once viewed as heroes who had led the fight for independence, lost their luster and were now reviled as tyrants. It was important that in nearly all Westernized nations, sharia courts and the *ulama* had been marginalized and played little or no role in government. Muslims began to question whether the faults found in government resulted from disparagement of these important Islamic institutions.

Many experts have cited countless reasons to explain why establishment acceptance of Western governance was so violently challenged by antiestablishment, often extremist, groups. Most cite the Six-Day War with Israel (1967) as a major factor. In this war, the major Arab powers (Egypt, Syria, and Jordan) were defeated by Israel after trying to regain control of Israeli-occupied lands in the Sinai Peninsula, the Golan Heights, and Palestine. Losing the war was a profound humiliation for Muslims, and it left deep scars. By 1967, Muslims were already restive and dissatisfied with their governments. The poor felt the government ignored them or treated them almost as badly as the imperialists. Privileged youth remained unemployed in chronically undeveloped domestic economies despite the advancement promised by their Western education. Add to this the greater popular involvement in national politics and the emphasis on the secular at the expense of religion, and one had a volatile mix that could explode with earthshaking violence.

Before discussing the development of Islamic extremism, it must be said that the overwhelming majority of the world's approximately 1.52 billion Muslims do not support or condone extremist principles or tactics.[44] Most Muslims are moderates who do the best they can to improve conditions within their nations via existing political institutions. However, it is also true that corruption often renders legitimate reform activities futile. Even in ostensibly democratic countries, leaders of parties that oppose the current regime are jailed, often along with their supporters; some opposition candidates are murdered; opposition party candidates are removed from official ballots; elections won by the opposition are declared invalid and new, "fixed" elections are held to reinstate the ruling regime. In nondemocratic states, there is little citizens can do legitimately to have an impact on government or policy.

Muslim Extremism

What follows is an overview of some major groups and thinkers who have had an important influence on the evolution of Muslim extremism. It is by no means comprehensive but highlights a few of the most influential antecedents to today's jihadists.

THE KHARIJITES

The roots of Muslim extremism can be traced back to the era of the Rightly Guided Caliphs. The Shia were not the only people to support the election of Ali as caliph and to subsequently disassociate themselves from mainstream Sunni Islam when Ali was overlooked. A small, radical sect called the Kharijites (seceders) also supported Ali, but not because he was a blood relative of the Prophet. Instead, they supported him because they felt he was the most pious man in the *umma*. For them, only perfect piety qualified one to be elected caliph. The Kharijites practiced a rigid, puritanical piety and held a literal, fundamentalist view of the Quran. After Ali entered into negotiations with the Umayyads, the Kharijites assassinated him for this impious act.

The Kharijites took literally the Quranic statement to "command the good and prohibit evil."[45] For them, actions and the people who committed them were either good (in strict accordance with sharia) or evil. Evil acts meant one was an enemy of Allah, which made one a non-Muslim subject to punishment or death. Anyone who did not agree with and live according to Kharijite principles was considered an enemy of Islam who must be destroyed. For Kharijites, maintaining a true Islamic community required rigorous oversight of all citizens' actions to ensure that they strictly followed the letter of sharia.

After seceding from the *umma*, the Kharijites formed their own fundamentalist community from where they launched attacks against non-Kharijite Muslims (evildoers). Jihad against nonfundamentalist Muslims was for them not only legitimate, it was obligatory because these apostates desecrated God's law with their "impiety." The Kharijites did not see themselves as extremists. Some scholars say they are important to Islam because "they represent the first self-conscious attempts at defining a distinctive Muslim identity. . . . [They were] obsessed with establishing who could and could not be considered a Muslim."[46] As the *umma* is the divine community of Allah, determining criteria for membership was a critical issue. Still, their extremist views and murderous violence placed the Kharijites beyond the pale for most Muslims.

IBN TAYMIYYA

The Islamic scholar and jurist Taqi al-Din Ahmad Ibn Taymiyya (d. 1328) was a chief exponent of the right wing of the orthodox and extremely conservative Hanbali School of Sunni Muslim thought. He had many scholarly forebears, but he is one thinker often cited by modern Islamic extremists. Ibn Taymiyya lived in Damascus after the Mongol invasions. Mongol culture and Greek philosophy were gaining ground at the time, and Ibn Taymiyya vociferously opposed both as un-Islamic. Ibn Taymiyya did not view himself as a radical; instead, his teachings were intended to restore orthodox Islam based on a literal interpretation of scripture and the idealization of the *umma* at the time the prophet Muhammad ruled in Medina.

Like other orthodox reformers, Ibn Taymiyya wrote and preached that Islam must be purified through strict adherence to sharia; his teachings drew on the Kharijites in sharply dividing the Islamic world into Muslims and non-Muslims based on individual and community piety and adherence to the letter of the law. He viewed religion as an inseparable, even foundational, part of the state. He was jailed, tortured, and ultimately executed for his views.

Ibn Taymiyya's greatest wrath was directed at the Mongols, not specifically for their invasion and brutality but for their conversion to Islam. The Mongols called themselves Muslims while largely adhering to a code of law promulgated by Genghis Khan. By ignoring sharia, the Mongols were, for Ibn Taymiyya, impious unbelievers who contaminated the true religion simply because they identified themselves with it. Ibn Taymiyya issued a fatwa against the Mongols, declared them unbelievers, and pronounced them excommunicated from the *umma*. Ibn Taymiyya's fatwa established a precedent that is cited by Muslim extremists to this day: For extreme Islamic fundamentalists, any person or group that identifies itself as Muslim but does not strictly follow sharia is apostate and lawfully subject to jihad. For Ibn Taymiyya and his followers, jihad against such apostasy is obligatory to maintain the purity of true Islam.

In some ways, Ibn Taymiyya's ideas may be seen as contradicting traditional Islamic teaching. For example, Islam teaches that how faithfully a Muslim follows Islamic law is a personal matter between the individual and God. One Muslim has no right to judge, condemn, or excommunicate another Muslim for lack of sufficient orthodoxy; no Muslim is authorized to target other Muslims for jihad because of their ignorance *(jahiliyyah)* or lassitude in observing God's law. Ibn Taymiyya's teachings radicalized Islamic thought and were politically explosive. However, he is a revered Islamic thinker

Introduction

whose ideas continue to have tremendous influence on Muslims, particularly Islamic extremists.

THE EARLY MUSLIM BROTHERHOOD

For Islamists, the turmoil and transformations rocking the Muslim world in the 1920s demanded a radical, activist response. Something had to be done to restore true Islam. Ataturk had created a radically secular state in Turkey, and secularism was eroding Islamic law in many newly formed Muslim nations. In 1928, Hassan al-Banna (1906–49), an Egyptian schoolteacher, founded the Muslim Brotherhood to restore the rightful place of both sharia and jihad in opposing non-Muslims (i.e., anyone who did not follow strict sharia). Like many extremist leaders, al-Banna came from a middle-class family and received a Western-style secondary education. Initially, the group used violence against the imperialist British in the name of reinstating the caliphate. By the 1940s, they had abandoned that goal and adopted "the Quran is our constitution" as their operating principle, indicating their aim to create an Islamic state built on Quranic law.[47] This motto is still used by modern Islamists.

The ideology of the Muslim Brotherhood is embraced by most extremist groups to this day. That ideology states that (1) Islam is an all-embracing guide for individuals, communities, and the state; (2) the Quran is the foundation of Muslim life; (3) sharia is the blueprint for life all true Muslims must strictly follow; (4) faithfulness to Islam brings the *umma* worldly and eternal reward; (5) faithlessness, or deviation from sharia, brings weakness and subservience; (6) only a return to Islam and sharia will restore Islamic pride and glory; and (7) reason and science can be pursued but must be guided by Islam to prevent secularization.[48] Here again there is the clear distinction between good and evil; between the good, true Muslim who follows sharia and the evil non-Muslim, or apostate, who is less orthodox.

By the 1940s, the Brotherhood had slightly altered its goal from a strict sharia state to one that was based on an ambiguous "Islamic modernity," as distinct from the Western variety. By carefully distinguishing between modernization (development that could be made compatible with Islam) and un-Islamic Westernization/secularization, the Brotherhood gained widespread popularity. The mainstream membership of the Brotherhood focused on community service, such as schools and welfare programs for the poor. However, the organization quickly became associated with its paramilitary wing, or "Secret Apparatus." This arm of the Brotherhood carried out numerous assassinations, of British colonizers in the 1930s and of officials in the Egyptian monarchy under King Farouk in the 1940s. In late 1948, a concerted effort was made to overthrow the monarchy. Many public officials

RELIGION AND THE STATE

were assassinated before the state police rounded up Brotherhood members. No evidence linked al-Banna to the assassinations, but in early 1949, he was murdered, supposedly by agents of the state secret police.

The Muslim Brotherhood went into a brief period of decline. In the early 1950s, it was revived by one of the leaders of 20th-century Islamic thought and an enormously influential writer, Sayyid Qutb (1906–66). In his youth, Qutb had loved English literature, and from 1949 to 1950 he studied educational administration in the United States. His American sojourn radicalized him. Qutb wrote letters and articles about American anti-Arab prejudice and its decadent society. His denunciations of American pastimes, such as dancing and listening to sexually nuanced pop songs, might at first seem prudish, but for Qutb these customs underlined U.S. shallowness, materialism, and sexual permissiveness. These characteristics defined the "other" against whom true Muslims must struggle. To these faults Qutb added America's ostentatious wealth, which he saw as an unforgivable insult to the millions of destitute Muslims in the Arab world. Qutb quoted liberally from the Prophet, who made redistribution of wealth and caring for the poor a cornerstone of his teaching.

After joining the Muslim Brotherhood in 1951, Qutb used his writing to promulgate a program for Muslims to realize God's plan for humans and the world. In his numerous articles and several books, Qutb explained his maturing ideology, which rested on the concept of *jahiliyya* (ignorance). In Qutb's usage, *jahiliyya* refers to anyone, even Muslims, who do not live according to the letter of God's law. God alone has sovereignty and so must be obeyed. Anyone who disobeys is an unbeliever against whom jihad is obligatory. For Qutb, there is no such thing as nationality; Muslims should identify only with the *umma*. Some of Qutb's ideas might well be viewed as a departure from the Prophet's teaching. For example, the Prophet tolerated those of other faiths, the *dhimmi,* especially People of the Book (Jews and Christians). In contrast, Qutb's writings encouraged the Brotherhood and its heirs to persecute or kill Egypt's Coptic Christians. In another departure, Qutb insisted that only leaders who obey Allah's law should themselves be obeyed. If they stray from sharia, they too should be resisted with jihad. Since all law, including state law, comes from God, it is a Muslim's obligation to overthrow non-Islamic governments. Qutb supported this view by citing a sura from the Quran that states, "Those who do not rule in accordance with what God has revealed are unbelievers."[49] Qutb was also heavily influenced by and sometimes quoted Ibn Taymiyya, whose ideas are easily recognizable in Qutb's work.

Nasser became Egypt's leader in a 1952 coup. Nasser was more of a socialist than a Muslim, and the Brotherhood soon ran afoul of his regime. The Brotherhood began a program of violence, murdering state officials and twice trying to assassinate Nasser. In 1954, along with many Brethren, Qutb

Introduction

was arrested and tortured for the attempted assassination of Nasser. Qutb was released in 1964 due to ill health. After another attempted assassination of Nasser in 1966, Qutb was rearrested, tortured, and jailed. He was hanged for attempted murder on August 29, 1966. To the end, Qutb insisted that the creation of an Islamic state based on sharia was a sacred trust worth any amount of bloodshed.

Qutb's work is an inspiration to and a blueprint for the Islamic extremist groups that came after him. He and the Brotherhood are believed to have been the "inspiration" for the assassination of Egyptian president Anwar Sadat in 1981. The ideology expressed in some of Qutb's writing is chilling in its uncompromising view of fundamentalist, literalist Islam; its Manichean good versus evil view of humans and the world; and its justification of jihad and violence. Qutb's influence on al-Qaeda and similar Islamist groups cannot be overestimated.

AL-QAEDA

Al-Qaeda's political goal is to create a righteous caliphate to rule over the world *umma*, which would be a single Islamic entity. If the group espouses Qutb's principal aims, the caliphate should ultimately become a global government ruling over humankind converted to Islam. Though its religiopolitical aims are unlikely to be realized, al-Qaeda is discussed because of its high profile and its success in carrying out the most horrific attack ever on U.S. soil—an accomplishment that has radicalized and inspired anti-Western jihadi groups around the world. Al-Qaeda's leadership, especially Osama bin Laden, was prompted to engage in jihad against the West primarily because of the military bases the United States maintained in the holy land of the Prophet, Saudi Arabia, and because of its support of Israel.

Two men who were to become crucial in developing al-Qaeda's doctrines met while attending medical school in Cairo. They were Ayman al-Zawahiri (b. 1951) and Sayyid Imam al-Sharif (n.d.). Both were Salafists insofar as they believed in a return to pure Islam. While al-Zawahiri became a public face of al-Qaeda, al-Sharif, who took the name Dr. Fadl, was the acknowledged philosophical and spiritual guide for the group. In 1988, Fadl wrote a widely read and influential book that identified jihad as the natural state of Islam and called on all true Muslims to fight the Soviets in Afghanistan. Fadl gained renown (or notoriety) as an inflexible jihadist. He became a wanted man, so he moved to Yemen where he quietly practiced medicine and continued to write books exhorting violent jihad. He cut off all contact with al-Qaeda but, in 2001, he was arrested and imprisoned.

A few years later, Fadl was transferred to an Egyptian prison, where he wrote *Rationalizing Jihad in Egypt and the World* (2007), a revolutionary work that denounces as un-Islamic most forms of external jihad, particularly the killing of Muslims and innocent civilians. The book was a bombshell that stunned Islamic extremist groups around the world, mainly because of Fadl's unparalleled reputation as a thinker, philosopher, and Islamic expert. The book's pronouncements were shattering for most jihadists, who now had to wonder if the violence they had committed was in fact justified, even glorified, by God, or if it was *haram* and they had sinned. Fadl wrote, "There is nothing in sharia about killing Jews and the Nazarenes [Christians] . . . They are the neighbors of Muslims . . . and being kind to one's neighbors is a religious duty. . . . There is no legal reason for harming people in any way."[50]

Some extremists attribute Fadl's change of heart to his mistreatment in prison. Others take him more seriously and are reevaluating their jihadist tactics. It remains to be seen if Fadl's erudite reinterpretation of the Quran and the Prophet's teachings will have any long-lasting effect in reducing extremist violence.

Islam and Democracy

The problem reconciling Islam and democracy is that democracy gives sovereignty to the people, whereas in Islam sovereignty belongs only to God. It is possible, as some experts have suggested, that the Muslim electorate be limited to voting only for leaders and laws that have been preapproved by Islamic law experts. But is that really democracy? Perhaps leaders and laws that contradict sharia can be overturned upon review by religious experts. But that is not democracy either. However, if the *umma* is the source of spiritual truth via *shura*, then as an electorate the *umma* can be seen as putting spiritual Islam into practice by voting for it. In this view, democracy is in accord with Islamic doctrine.

The Prophet denounced the rule of the pharaohs and enjoined his followers to shun tyrants. He preached equality and social justice for all. These sound like prescriptions for democracy, though they do not rule out theocracy, or the tyranny of religious zealots. Yet in the 21st century, the trend seems to be moving more toward democracy than in the opposite direction. Despite violent jihadist movements in several Muslim nations, there is a growing demand for some form of democratic government—with more rights, liberties, and economic opportunity—among the vast majority of the world's Muslims.

However, Western pressure for democratization might be doing more harm than good. Some experts think it advisable to allow Muslim nations to work out on their own what an Islamic democracy should look like and how it should function. It is clear that the Christian church in the West is an insti-

Introduction

tution that is easily separable from government. There is no such separation between Islam and the state. Therefore, it is probably more counterproductive than helpful for Western nations to expect Muslim countries to adopt the separation of church and state as it exists in the West. In Islam, such a clean break may not be possible. Yet modern, democratic states that accord with Islam may be possible if Muslims accept the challenge and create them.

---

[1] Mark Lilla. *The Stillborn God.* New York: Vintage Books, 2007, p. 21.

[2] Lilla, p. 22.

[3] Todd Lewis. "Buddhism: the Politics of Compassionate Rule." In Jacob Neusner, ed. *God's Rule: The Politics of World Religions.* Washington, D.C.: Georgetown University Press, 2003, p. 242.

[4] Lewis. In Neusner, p. 251.

[5] Lilla, p. 31.

[6] John A. Hutchison. *Paths of Faith.* New York: McGraw-Hill, 1969, p. 337.

[7] Jacob Neusner. "Judaism." In Neusner, p. 11.

[8] Justo L. Gonzalez. Vol. I. *The Story of Christianity: The Early Church to the Dawn of the Reformation.* San Francisco: HarperCollins, 1984, p. 165. Also: The Nicene Creed. Available online. URL: http://www.newadvent.org/cathen/11049a.htm. Accessed December 15, 2008.

[9] Lilla, p. 39.

[10] Bruce D. Chilton. "Primitive and Early Christianity." In Neusner, p. 53.

[11] Maurice Keen. *The Pelican History of Medieval Europe.* New York: Penguin Books, 1968, p. 67.

[12] Keen, p. 32.

[13] J. M. Roberts. *A History of Europe.* New York: Allen Lane/Penguin, 1996, p. 226.

[14] J. M. Roberts, p. 168.

[15] Gonzalez, Vol. II. *The Story of Christianity: The Reformation to the Present Day,* p. 36.

[16] Martin E. Marty. "Reformation Christianity." In Neusner, p. 122.

[17] Lilla, p. 58.

[18] Norman Davies. *Europe: A History.* New York: HarperPerennial, 1996, p. 563. The quote is from Veronica C. Wedgwood. *The Thirty Years' War.* London: Jonathan Cape, 1957, p. 460. This is considered one of the best resources about this conflict.

[19] Davies, p. 568.

[20] Charles Carlton. *The Experience of the British Civil Wars.* London: Routledge, 1992, pp. 213–214.

[21] Hobbes, *Leviathan.* Quoted in Lilla, p. 83.

[22] Thomas Hobbes. *Leviathan.* Quoted in Lilla, p. 86.

RELIGION AND THE STATE

[23] Lilla, p. 88.

[24] Two excellent books on the French Revolution are Christopher Hibbert. *The Days of the French Revolution.* New York: HarperPerennial, 1999 and Simon Schama. *Citizens: A Chronicle of the French Revolution.* New York: Vintage, 1990.

[25] Quoted in "The French Revolution." Catholic Encyclopedia. Available online. URL: http://www.newadvent.org/cathen/13009a.htm. Accessed February 5, 2009.

[26] "The French Revolution." Catholic Encyclopedia.

[27] Lilla, pp. 230, 232.

[28] Excellent resources for World War I include Barbara Tuchman. *The Guns of August.* New York: Ballantine, 1994 and Hew Strachan. *The First World War.* New York: Viking, 2004.

[29] Quoted in Lilla, pp. 245–246.

[30] Karl Barth. *The Epistle to the Romans,* 2nd ed. Quoted in Lilla, p. 263.

[31] H. Richard Niebuhr. *The Kingdom of God in America.* Quoted in Lilla, p. 248.

[32] Friedrich Gogarten. *Religion and Volkstum.* Quoted in Lilla, pp. 280, 283.

[33] Of the thousands of books written about World War II, among the best general works are James L. Stokesbury. *A Short History of World War II.* New York: HarperPerennial, 1980 and John Keegan. *The Second World War.* New York: Penguin, 2005.

[34] René Rémond. *Religion and Society in Modern Europe.* Malden, Mass.: Blackwell, 1999, p. 199.

[35] John L. Esposito. *Islam: The Straight Path.* New York: Oxford University Press, 2005, pp. 6–7.

[36] Esposito, p. 18.

[37] Esposito, p. 19.

[38] Esposito, p. 29.

[39] John L. Esposito. "Classical Islam." In Neusner, p. 131.

[40] L. Carl Brown. *Religion and State: The Muslim Approach to Politics.* New York: Columbia University Press, 2000, p. 67. Quoted from Hadith "Kitab al-Imara." *Sahih Muslim* 3:1,033.

[41] Esposito, p. 55.

[42] Peter G. Riddell and Peter Cotterell. *Islam in Context: Past, Present, and Future.* Grand Rapids, Mich.: Baker Academic, 2003, p. 97.

[43] John L. Esposito. *The Islamic Threat: Myth or Reality?* 3rd ed. New York: Oxford University Press, 1999, p. 49.

[44] Population figure from Adherents. Available online. URL: http://www.adherents.com/Religions_by_Adherents.htm. Accessed February 23, 2009.

[45] Quoted in Esposito, *The Islamic Threat,* p. 42.

[46] Reza Aslan. *No God but God.* New York: Random House, 2005, p. 132.

[47] Quoted in Gilles Kepel. *Jihad: The Trail of Political Islam.* Translated by Anthony F. Roberts. Cambridge, Mass.: Harvard University Press, 2002, p. 27.

Introduction

[48] Esposito, *The Islamic Threat*, pp. 131–132.

[49] Qur'an 5:47. Quoted in Brown, p. 156.

[50] Lawrence Wright. "The Rebellion Within: An Al-Qaeda Mastermind Questions Terrorism." *New Yorker*. Available online. URL: http://www.newyorker.com/reporting/2008/06/02/080602fa_fact_wright/. Accessed September 15, 2009.

2

Focus on the United States

THE BIRTH OF RELIGIOUS TOLERANCE
Roger Williams and the Separation of Church and State

The Massachusetts Bay Puritans vilified the "pernicious, God-provoking, truth-defacing, church-ruinating, and state-shaking toleration" espoused by the Calvinist preacher who is regarded as one of the first and greatest proponents of the separation of church and state.[1] Roger Williams (ca. 1603–83) was a godly, pious man, but he was appalled by the intolerance of the Massachusetts Bay Colony, which, in the 1600s, was a thoroughgoing theocracy. The situation in Massachusetts Bay was, for Williams, as bad as if not worse than the religious intolerance he had fled from in Europe. Massachusetts Bay Puritans believed that a state, or government, could not function and maintain civil and moral order unless it enforced strict adherence to a common religion. Any dissenters found in the colony, including Quakers and Baptists, were punished by having their ears cropped, their tongues bored or burned, or their bodies flogged. Some were even hanged (as were women during the Salem witch trials of the 1690s).

Williams's persistent arguments for the separation of church and state grated on these Puritans. Williams insisted that the "setting up of civil power and officers to judge the conviction of men's souls" was absurd.[2] To him, religious belief was a matter between the individual and God; it was an inner, spiritual relationship that no state could enforce or coerce. Williams's "blasphemy" went even further. He pointed out that a civil servant needed skills that differed from those required by a preacher. History proved that one need not be a good Christian to be a good and wise ruler: "A pagan or anti-Christian pilot may be as skillful to carry a ship to its desired port as any Christian mariner or pilot in the world."[3] Williams's notion that non-Christians and even nonbelievers might have the skills necessary to govern a Christian state was another sign of his "blasphemy." He believed that governing was a worldly skill, being a Christian was not. Thus, no "religious test" should be required for officeholders. Williams went so far as to contradict the assertion of Massachusetts Bay governor John Winthrop (1588–1649) that the American colonies were ordained by God to be a "city on a hill," or example of a perfect Christian state. Williams pointed out that nowhere in the Bible did God anoint the colonies as being especially blessed or favored. America was not a Christian nation chosen by God to carry out his divine purpose: "Government existed because God did *not* rule the world."[4]

For the devout Williams, church and state should be separate not because the church would unduly influence the state, but because the state would corrupt the spiritual nature of religion. Government was the province of people, and people are fallible; religion is the province of the infallible God. Therefore civil authorities undermine religion when they meddle in it. Since no one church or sect is possessed of all God's truth, the establishment of a state religion hinders religion's progress toward realizing God's will.

The Puritans of Massachusetts Bay feared that if they relaxed their control of religion, God would punish them and the colony would fail. No one could be permitted to undermine the purity of the colony: "In the name of our Colony . . . all Familists, Antinomians, Anabaptists, and other Enthusiasts, shall have free Liberty to keep away from us, and such as will come to be gone as fast as they can, the sooner the better."[5] By 1636, Williams could no longer be tolerated; he was banished from the colony. Roger Williams walked through the January snows to a new land where he established the colony of Rhode Island—a true island of toleration in a land of religious intolerance.

John Locke

Roger Williams had enormous influence on John Locke (1632–1704), the British philosopher and celebrated champion of religious freedom and the separation of church and state. Though the American founding fathers knew of Williams's writings (especially *The Bloudy Tenent of Persecution* [1644]), many of the ideas contained in the Declaration of Independence (1776) and the Constitution (1789) were adapted from Locke, especially his famous *Letter Concerning Toleration* (1689). The impact of Locke's ideas on the development of liberal government is beyond question. Locke reiterated and expanded Williams's differentiation between the inner realm of spiritual belief and the outer realm of civil society and government. Thus Locke wrote, "The care of souls cannot belong to the civil magistrate because his power consists only in outward force; but true and saving religion consists in the inward persuasion of the mind . . . [which] cannot be compelled to the belief of anything by outward force." For Locke, as for Williams, "liberty of conscience is everyman's natural right, equally belonging to dissenters as to [Christians] themselves."[6]

RELIGION AND THE STATE

Locke's liberal ideas (emphasizing individual freedoms) grew out of the Enlightenment, which itself was a reaction to the narrow-minded political and religious tyranny that had prevailed in Europe prior to the 18th century. "[A]ccording to Locke, men have contracted to obey civil authority not in order for that authority to tell them what to believe or how to pray, but simply for it to keep the peace," which is necessary for advancing one's self-interest in worldly affairs.[7] A church was just one type of "voluntary association" a citizen could join and, as such, it did not warrant a central role in secular society. By relegating religion to the private sphere beyond the reach of the state, Locke overturned thousands of years of state history and opened the door to a new type of government, which was born in the United States.

Before the Revolution: Virginia, Pennsylvania, and Connecticut

Virginia's 1606 charter established the Anglican Church as the official church of the colony. After 1619, the Church of England in Virginia was supported by taxes imposed by the colonial government on all residents. By the 1770s, however, Anglicanism and its clergy were detested as representatives of British oppression. The church became suspect and lost many of its followers. One fearful cleric complained to his superiors in England that "I have been obliged to shut my churches to avoid the fury of the populace who would not allow the liturgy to be used unless the . . . prayers for the King and Royal Family were omitted."[8] The growing popularity of other Christian sects, particularly Baptists and Methodists, further eroded the authority of this official church. These non-Anglican Christians vehemently protested Anglican monopolies; for example, only Anglican ministers could perform "legitimate" marriages.

One did not have to be a Baptist to pray for the demise of the Anglican Church. Rich and educated Virginians on both sides of the issue argued about the establishment of religion. Some, such as Governor Patrick Henry (1736–99), sincerely believed that an official, government-supported church was necessary for a moral and well-ordered state. Others, especially deists (who believe the deity does not interfere in human affairs) such as Thomas Jefferson (1743–1826), insisted that church and state be separate. In his *Memorial and Remonstrance* (1785), the Virginia lawmaker and future president James Madison (1743–1826) warned that Virginia would betray the American Revolution if its citizens fail "to take alarm at the first experiment on our liberties . . . [and establish Christianity] to the exclusion of all other Religions . . . [What is to prevent our being asked to establish] any particular sect of Christianity in exclusion of all other Sects?"[9] Madison's was one of the most eloquent voices in opposition to Henry's proposal of a "general assessment bill," or state tax, on all Virginians to support "the Christian Religion [which] shall be in all times . . . the established Religion of this Commonwealth."[10]

The Virginia assembly received hundreds of letters and petitions about the assessment; about 90 percent opposed it. When in 1776, Jefferson wrote the Bill for Establishing Religious Freedom, it was passed overwhelmingly by the Virginia assembly. Jefferson's bill would be the template for the debate on religious freedom at the Constitutional Convention.

In contrast to Virginia, Pennsylvania was a highly diverse and religiously tolerant colony. Though the colony's founder, William Penn (1644–1718), had originally been scathing in his opposition to the Quakers, by 1776 Quakers dominated colonial Pennsylvania. Their tolerance of dissent attracted settlers from all over Europe who were practicing Presbyterians, Baptists, Mennonites, Lutherans, Methodists, and even Jews and Roman Catholics. Anglicans both in and outside the colony were scandalized and foretold the downfall of the colony because of its "raving notions & ridiculous freaks that are every day spread & acted upon among us under the name of Religion [and are] beyond the power of description."[11] Yet this haven for dissenters of all stripes thrived, to the intense irritation of its critics. Pennsylvania embraced religious pluralism in its politics, and its society was all the better for it.

Alas, the same cannot be said of the New England colonies, where strict religious conformity, dubbed the "New England Way," was harshly enforced. Connecticut, a majority Congregationalist (Puritan) colony, had a particularly hard time adapting to the religious tolerance that was sweeping the colonies. Even after the Revolution (1775–83), Connecticut's Act of Toleration (1784) only reduced the penalties meted out to dissenters. Baptists, Methodists, and Episcopalians were required by law to obtain an official certificate as proof that they belonged to a recognized religious body. Anyone lacking a certificate, including nonbelievers, had to pay a tax to support the established Congregationalist church. Even those who had certificates found that they were stigmatized and denied rights. Schools, including Yale University, were strictly Congregationalist, and only established clergy could perform "legitimate" marriages. It was only after the election of Thomas Jefferson as U.S. president in 1801 that his party gained enough power and votes in the state to overturn Connecticut's backward practices by insisting that the state write a constitution to officially disestablish its church and guarantee complete religious freedom. In August 1818, Connecticut's constitution squeaked through in a statewide referendum by about 1,500 votes.

The Constitution

The American founders who attended the Constitutional Convention in Philadelphia during the summer of 1787 were in general agreement that

RELIGION AND THE STATE

state laws, such as the act Jefferson had written for Virginia, were sufficient to cover the issue of religion. (Jefferson, then ambassador to France, was not at the Convention.) Considering how hotly debated religious issues were in the colonies, there was remarkably little attention paid to religion at the Convention. There is no mention of God and only one mention of religion in the Constitution, at the end of the Sixth Amendment, which reads: "No religious test shall ever be required as a qualification to any office or public trust under the United States."[12]

Some delegates argued for adding a statement of rights to the Constitution, but the motion was soundly defeated. Alexander Hamilton (1757–1804), delegate from New York, explained this omission: "[W]hy declare that things shall not be done which there is no power to do! Why . . . should it be said that the liberty of the press shall not be restrained, when no power is given by which restrictions may be imposed?"[13] In other words, since the Constitution gave the federal government no authority over religion or the press, why bother to enact laws prohibiting government interference in them?

The Constitution had to be ratified by two-thirds of the states before it became the law of the land. As state legislatures debated the document, it quickly became clear that a statement of rights had to be added. Six of the 13 original states ratified the Constitution only after getting assurances from James Madison and other founders that a Bill of Rights would be appended. Some historians have marveled at the nebulous and unfocused nature of the debates and correspondence that ensued about what these rights were and how they should be protected. Neither the founders nor state leaders seemed to be overly concerned with defining precisely what they meant when they spoke of "religious liberty" or other rights.

The Bill of Rights' First Amendment

James Madison took the lead in getting the first Congress to pass a Bill of Rights. In a letter from France to Madison about a religion clause, Jefferson suggested a simple statement that "religious faith shall go unpunished."[14] The framers later suggested a version stating that no one could be "compelled to frequent or support any religious worship, place, or ministry whatever." The debate soon focused on the issue of government establishment of religion. The House of Representatives passed and sent to the Senate a bill that read: "Congress shall make no law establishing religion, or prohibiting the free exercise thereof, nor shall the rights of conscience be infringed." After proposing and voting down several variations of the bill, the Senate came up with "Congress shall make no law establishing articles of faith or a mode of worship, or prohibiting the free exercise of religion." When the two bills went to conference committee, which had to reconcile them, the House members flatly refused to consider an amendment that merely banned state preference for a specific religion. After some negotiations, on September 25, 1789, the bill agreed upon in committee was passed by two-thirds of the Senate. The final bill, in the First Amendment of the Bill of Rights, states that "Congress shall make no law respecting the establishment of religion, or prohibiting the free exercise thereof."[15]

The religion clause, like many amendments in the Bill of Rights, follows Locke's "negative" view of government: It states what government cannot do to ensure that government does not meddle in areas beyond its purview, such as religion. However, what the amendment does not do is define terms such as "establishment of religion." Does it mean government shall have no interaction with religion at all? Or does it mean that government shall not prefer one religion over another? Those who interpret the establishment clause narrowly argue that it permits federal government aid to churches as long as it does not discriminate among them. Those who view the clause more broadly cite the historical record to point out that the narrow interpretation actually adds to Congress's power. Madison explicitly described the purpose of the amendment to "limit and qualify the powers of Government," not to expand them. As the historian Leonard W. Levy remarks, "The First Amendment, like the others, was intended to restrict Congress to its enumerated powers. Since . . . Congress [had] no power to legislate on . . . religion, Congress had no such power even in the absence of the First Amendment. It is therefore unreasonable to believe that an express prohibition of power—'Congress shall make no law respecting an establishment of religion'—creates the power, previously nonexistent, of supporting religion by aid to one or all religious groups. The Bill of Rights . . . was not framed 'to imply powers not meant to be included in the enumeration.'"[16]

In an 1802 letter to the Danbury (Conn.) Baptist Association, Thomas Jefferson wrote, "I contemplate with solemn reverence that act of the whole American people which declared that their legislature should 'make no law respecting an establishment of religion, or prohibiting the free exercise thereof,' thus building a wall of separation between church and state."[17] Jefferson's "wall of separation" has been part of the American lexicon ever since. It has informed the decisions of the U.S. Supreme Court in its interpretations of the religion clause, whose precise meaning is unclear, as is Jefferson's wall itself. Throughout U.S. history, but especially in the latter 20th century, the Court has been asked repeatedly to determine just how high and solid that wall is. Does it have windows, slots, or chinks? How does it affect the religion clause and religion in American life?

RELIGION AND THE STATE

RELIGION AND THE COURTS

What follows is a brief overview of significant religion cases brought before the Supreme Court. It is by no means comprehensive, and many important cases had to be omitted due to lack of space. However, this discussion gives a flavor of the types of issues that arose around the interpretation of the First Amendment's religion clause. It also gives some idea of how contentious a single phrase in a legal document can be.

Early Cases: Sunday Mail and Bigamy

In 1810, a movement arose to repeal a federal law allowing mail delivery on Sundays. The Sabbatarians, as they were called, viewed the Sunday mail as a desecration of the Sabbath, the day set aside for God and church. From every state, petitions signed by thousands were sent to the Capitol demanding the law's repeal. Most petitions argued that Sunday delivery "made it necessary to violate the command of God . . . in which case His justice will demand that . . . punishment be initiated on our common country." Many petitioners argued that "our Government is a Christian Government . . . bound by the word of God . . . [and] . . . the obligations we owe to Him."[18] The postmaster general was willing to abandon Sunday mail delivery, but he wanted to keep mail transport throughout the week. At that time, any hiatus in moving mail would wreak havoc with schedules, raise postal rates, and compromise both business and national security. He cited the wall of separation, as well as necessity, as reasons to keep the mail moving. This contentious issue was fought over into the 1830s. Though mail continued to move on Sunday, post offices were closed and no mail was delivered. The issue had aroused state legislatures, which passed "blue laws" that prohibited a whole host of Sunday activities. Though the Sunday mail matter died quietly and in the postmaster's favor, the issue opened the door to all sorts of conflict and litigation. Most cases were eventually adjudicated by the Supreme Court, which became the final arbiter for issues regarding church and state.

One of the earliest religion clause cases heard by the Court involved Mormon polygamy, in this case bigamy. George Reynolds, a high-ranking Mormon official, had been convicted of bigamy in state court in 1875. Reynolds appealed his case to the Supreme Court (*Reynolds v. United States*, 1879), which found in favor of the state. The unanimous decision cited Jefferson's wall of separation to explain that although the Constitution gave Congress no "legislative power over mere opinion," it did have power to regulate "actions which were in violation of social duties or subversive of good order." Bigamy, the Court decided, was one of these actions. Further, "To permit [bigamy] would be to make professed doctrines of religious belief superior to the law of the land and in effect to permit every citizen to become a law unto himself."[19] In this first case dealing with the free exercise clause, the Court upheld the lower court's ruling that religious belief could not override civil law.

The Court after the Mid-Twentieth Century

The Supreme Court heard relatively few religion cases prior to the mid-20th century, after which it was inundated with them. According to the noted church historian Edwin S. Gaustad, there are several reasons for this marked increase. First, after the Civil War (1861–65) Congress passed the Fourteenth Amendment in 1868, which ensures all citizens equal rights under the law and guarantees every citizen due process of law. The passage of the Fourteenth Amendment had an enormous impact on the number and type of religion cases brought before the Court. Before the Civil War, the U.S. Constitution detailed only what Congress and the federal government could or could not do. For the most part, it did not allow the federal government to dictate or pass judgment on state law. However, with the passage of the Fourteenth Amendment, state laws touching on religion could be challenged as violations of one's civil rights under the Fourteenth Amendment. Once state law could be challenged in federal courts, a deluge of religion cases found their way to the Supreme Court. Second, organizations, such as the American Civil Liberties Union (ACLU) and Americans United for the Separation of Church and State, were formed, which challenged laws that they thought infringed on the religion clause. Third, immigration made the United States far more religiously pluralistic. New religious practices proliferated and Protestant customs could no longer be defended as traditions; religious practice had to be constitutional. Fourth, both state and federal governments were forced by changing times and technologies to legislate on issues, such as reproductive health, that had formerly been wholly personal matters. Finally, American citizens had become the most litigious in the world, ready to initiate lawsuits at the drop of a hat.[20]

ESTABLISHMENT CLAUSE CASES

Education

The case that opened the floodgates to challenges over religion and the schools was *Everson v. Board of Education* (1947). This famous, oft-cited case arose because a town in New Jersey did not have its own fleet of school buses; therefore it compensated students attending both public and private schools for their school transportation costs. The case heard by the Supreme Court challenged the use of state funds (taxpayers' money) to aid students attending church-run, parochial schools. In a "slippery" (narrow and therefore sure to be re-contested) 5-4 decision, the Court determined that paying students'

RELIGION AND THE STATE

transportation costs to and from a religious school was not an excessive degree of state support for religion and so did not violate the establishment clause. Justice Hugo Black likened this state remuneration to other forms of public services (firefighters, police) equally available to all. Black specifically cited the "wall of separation" to state that it was not breached in this case. In his opinion for the majority, Justice Black wrote what has become the most famous articulation of the meaning of the establishment clause:

> The "establishment of religion" clause of the First Amendment means at least this: Neither a state nor the Federal Government can set up a church. Neither can pass laws which aid one religion, aid all religions, or prefer one religion over another. Neither can force nor influence a person to go to or remain away from church against his will or force him to profess a belief or disbelief in any religion. No person can be punished for entertaining or professing religious beliefs or disbeliefs, for church attendance or nonattendance. No tax in any amount, large or small, can be levied to support any religious activities or institutions, whatever they may be called, or whatever form they may adopt to teach or practice religion. Neither a state nor the Federal Government can, openly or secretly, participate in the affairs of any religious organizations or groups and vice versa. In the words of Jefferson, the clause against establishment of religion by law was intended to erect "a wall of separation between church and State."[21]

The advocates of more religious involvement in schools were emboldened by the *Everson* decision to increase the role of religion in schools. Some public schools taught religion (Protestant Christianity) as part of their curriculum. In *McCollum v. Board of Education* (1948), the Court found (in an 8-1 decision) that it was unconstitutional for Champaign, Illinois, public schools to set aside 45 minutes a day for sectarian religious instruction, even though nonaffiliated students were not compelled to participate but could spend the time in study hall. In a 1952 case from New York *(Zorach v. Clausen)*, the Court ruled that it was constitutional to permit students who requested religious instruction to leave school early one day a week to attend religious classes. The 6-3 decision found in favor of the state because the religious classes were held away from school premises.

One of the most significant cases that followed involved school prayer or religious recitation in schools. New York State, for example, had required each school day to start with a prayer asking for God's blessing. In an 8-1 decision *(Engel v. Vitale,* 1962), the Court ruled that state-mandated school prayer was unconstitutional and violated the establishment clause. The justices recognized that their decision might be interpreted as "hostility toward

Focus on the United States

religion or toward prayer," but insisted that "nothing could be more wrong ... [Their decision just] put an end to governmental control of religion and prayer ... [because] a union of government and religion tends to destroy government and degrade religion."[22]

The justices were prescient about public reaction to this decision. The Court was viciously attacked from many quarters for its "godlessness." The Court's reputation among the religiously minded did not improve when, a year later, two decisions found against laws in Pennsylvania *(Abingdon v. Schempp)* and Maryland *(Murray v. Curlett)* that had required morning prayer in schools. The states had argued that reciting the Lord's Prayer was voluntary; students who did not want to pray were not forced to. Still, the Court found the states' actions in violation of the First Amendment; the Lord's Prayer is not nondenominational, as the states argued. The issue was clarified further in *Wallace v. Jaffree* (1985), when the Court ruled that setting aside time for a "moment of silence" was in violation of the Constitution. Justice Sandra Day O'Connor concurred with the 6-3 decision, explaining that the voluntary nature of prayer or contemplation was not the issue: The issue was that the government mandated it, and through this mandate "endorse[d] prayer in the public school."[23]

Another set of establishment clause cases revolved around school curriculums, particularly evolution. The issue was first litigated in Tennessee during the world-famous 1925 Scopes trial. John Scopes was tried for teaching his high school biology class evolution, a subject prohibited by state law. The trial's fame arose not only because of the issue, but because Scopes was defended by renowned attorney Clarence Darrow and prosecuted by the equally famous former presidential candidate William Jennings Bryan. The case went against Scopes, who was convicted and fined $100. After the Scopes trial, several states passed laws prohibiting the teaching of evolution. Arkansas's law was challenged in 1968 *(Epperson v. Arkansas)* and Louisiana's in 1987 *(Edwards v. Aguillard)*. In *Epperson*, the Court unanimously found that the state could not adjust its curriculum "to the principles or prohibitions of any religious sect or dogma" and that there was no doubt that Arkansas prohibited teaching evolution "because it is contrary to the belief of some that the Book of Genesis must be the exclusive source of doctrine as to the origin of man." In *Edwards,* Louisiana had mandated that creationism be taught alongside evolution. Here, again, in a 7-2 decision the Court found that the creationism law was a violation of the establishment clause because it "advanced a particular religious belief ... [that was] identical to the literal interpretation of Genesis."[24] The battle over teaching evolution rages on.

State issuance of vouchers to help parents pay for their children's education also became (and still is) a contentious constitutional issue. A 1972 New

RELIGION AND THE STATE

York law that provided educational vouchers for very poor families ($50–$100 per student for families earning less than $5,000/yr) was challenged, as most parents used the vouchers to pay tuition at parochial schools. The lawsuit contended that the use of state monies to support religiously run schools violated the establishment clause. In writing the majority opinion (*PEARL v. Nyquist*, 1973), Justice Lewis Powell acknowledged that the voucher program was well intentioned: It gave low-income families the same educational options as better-off families, it supported the diversity of private educational institutions in the state, and it helped alleviate overcrowding and fiscal strains on the public school system. Yet when weighed against the overriding importance of keeping church and state separate, these advantages could not be supported. Justice Powell found that the voucher program was essentially a state program that advanced religion and, as such, was unconstitutional. Three of the nine judges dissented, asserting that the public welfare benefit of the program was more important than its inadvertent public support for religious schools.

Ten years later, the Court reversed itself. In *Mueller v. Allen* (1983), it ruled that state income tax deductions for children attending nonpublic schools, even religious schools, did not violate the Constitution. Writing for the 5-4 majority, Chief Justice Rehnquist argued that the Minnesota law had a "secular purpose" that did not advance "sectarian aims of the nonpublic school" because the tax-based voucher went to the family, not directly to the school.[25] Justice Thurgood Marshall wrote for the four dissenting judges. He argued that the law was unconstitutional because not all parents and children benefited; only those parents sending their children to private, almost always religious, schools got the benefit. This was a disadvantage for those parents who sent their children to public schools, even though it was their tax money that was used to fund the program. Because this was a "slippery" 5-4 decision, the issue will no doubt be revisited and readjudicated.

Public Displays

For decades, if not centuries, many American towns have been decked out for Christmas in holiday lights and decorated Christmas trees, and no one cared. But in our litigious age, public displays with a whiff of religion have been challenged as violations of the establishment clause.

Pawtucket, Rhode Island, had been setting up a Christmas nativity scene, or crèche, in a public area downtown for more than 40 years. In addition to the crèche there were displays of Santa Claus, replete with sleigh and reindeer, and candy-striped poles and strings of colored lights. Some Pawtucket citizens brought suit against the town because it was using taxpayer money to pay for a religious display. In 1984, the case reached the Supreme Court.

Focus on the United States

The Court was bitterly divided, and the decision in *Lynch v. Donnelly* was 5-4 in favor of the town. Chief Justice Warren Burger ruled for the town because the crèche, an unambiguously religious image, was only one part of the entire display, which was mostly nonreligious. Taken as a whole, the justice wrote, the scene did not represent government advocacy of a religion and, if there was any advocacy implied, it was only incidental. The four dissenting justices argued that just because Santa Claus et al. were so familiar to Americans that did not mean that they were not representing a particular religious event. Thus, Pawtucket's display was an unconstitutional endorsement of a religion.

In a similar case from Pennsylvania (*Allegheny County v. ACLU*, 1989), the Court split 6-3 in supporting the display of a Christmas tree and a Jewish menorah outside the county courthouse. This dual display, they ruled, was a recognition of cultural diversity. However, the nativity scene inside the courthouse represented an endorsement of the Christian religion and was therefore unconstitutional. The justices split 5-4 on the decision about the crèche, which was draped with a banner reading "Glory to God in the Highest" in Latin. Four justices dissented, stating that the entire display was constitutionally acceptable. They argued that "Passersby who disagree with the message conveyed by these displays are free to ignore them."[26]

The most recent case (2001) involving public display of religious material played out in Alabama. Judge Roy Moore, chief justice of the Alabama Supreme Court, had installed in the courthouse rotunda a two-ton granite monument inscribed with the Ten Commandments. Moore had not gotten permission for the display, and he had it installed in the middle of the night when no one was around. Citizens complained, but Moore refused to remove it. Soon the matter was brought before the U.S. district court, which ordered Moore to remove the display. Again, Moore refused, but he was overruled by eight of his colleagues. The U.S. Supreme Court refused to hear the case or rule on Moore's appeal. Finally, the Alabama judicial ethics panel had the display taken away.

The Supreme Court later ruled on a similar, though less "weighty" case from Kentucky, which had displayed posters containing the Ten Commandments in courthouses. Kentucky insisted that the display represented the "foundations of American law and Government." In another 5-4 decision, the majority in *McCreary County v. ACLU* (2005) ruled that the display had no "secular purpose . . . [which] must be genuine, not a sham, and not merely secondary to a religious objective." Several majority opinions emphasized America's religious plurality, which must be respected in public places and by governments. In an eloquent opinion, Justice Sandra Day O'Connor concurred: "many Americans find the Commandments in accord with their personal beliefs. But we do not count heads before enforcing the First Amendment... Nor can we accept the theory that Americans who do not accept the Commandments' validity are outside the First Amendment's protection."[27]

By the 1980s, the Supreme Court had come up with a set of criteria to determine if a given action violated the establishment clause. The *Lemon* test, based on an earlier case, states that a law is constitutional under the clause if it has (1) a secular purpose; (2) secular consequences; and (3) no excessive entanglements between church and state. Although these general guidelines continue to be applied, they are obviously very vague, and new standards continue to be found to interpret the establishment clause.

FREE EXERCISE CLAUSE

The second part of the religion clause in the First Amendment is a six-word phrase that prohibits the government from infringing on citizens' free exercise of religion. Like the establishment clause, the free exercise clause has generated numerous challenges and Supreme Court cases.

The Pledge of Allegiance

In the early 1950s, a Presbyterian minister in New York gave a sermon in which he railed against the U.S. Pledge of Allegiance because it contained no references to God. According to the reverend, the American pledge could serve just as well in the atheistic Soviet Union; there was nothing in the U.S. pledge to distinguish it from an oath to the godless communist state. So in 1954, Congress passed a law that inserted the phrase "under God" into the Pledge of Allegiance. This action resulted in some of the first serious court cases regarding the free exercise clause.

A decade later, Joseph Lewis, "an avowed and flamboyant atheist," brought suit against New York for requiring citizens to utter these words in the pledge.[28] Thirty other states filed amicus (friend of the court) briefs in support of New York. The state argued that the pledge was intended to promote patriotism, not religion. Attorneys for Lewis cited Madison's *Memorial and Remonstrance* and Jefferson's "wall of separation" to argue that the state was using its authority to insinuate religion into civil policy. In the end, *Lewis v. Allen* was decided in the state's favor.

One of the first and most famous free exercise cases was brought by a Jehovah's Witnesses family whose two children were expelled from public school for refusing to salute the flag and say the pledge. Jehovah's Witnesses, a Christian sect, believe that swearing an oath to anything other than God is idolatry and therefore sacrilegious. The case was heard by the Supreme Court, which had to balance the claims of nation and religion. In the majority opinion (*Minersville School District v. Gobitis*, 1940), Justice Felix Frankfurter

Focus on the United States

wrote "because in safeguarding conscience we are dealing with interests so subtle and so dear, every possible leeway should be given to the claims of religion." Yet he and seven other justices found against Gobitis because "the flag is the symbol of our national unity, transcending all internal differences, however large, within the framework of the Constitution."[29]

Only three years later, in *West Virginia State Board of Education v. Barnett*, the Court reversed its previous ruling. This, too, was a case in which Jehovah's Witnesses refused on religious grounds to salute the flag. In this case, though, the Court ruled 8-1 in favor of the Witnesses. Writing for the majority, Justice Robert Jackson explained that

> the refusal of these persons to participate in the ceremony does not interfere with or deny rights of others to do so ... The sole conflict is between authority and rights of the individual.... [V]alidity of the asserted power to force an American citizen publicly to profess any statement of belief ... presents questions of power that must be considered independently of any idea we may have as to the utility of the ceremony in question.... If there is any fixed star in our constitutional constellation, it is that no official, high or petty, can prescribe what shall be orthodox in politics, nationalism, religion, or any other matters of opinion or force citizens to confess by word or act their faith therein."[30]

Weekends

In 1961, the Supreme Court heard cases brought by orthodox Jews who were forced by "blue laws" to shutter their stores on Sunday, even though they also closed on Saturday for the Jewish Sabbath. If the Jewish establishments opened on Sunday, they were fined by the state. Chief Justice Earl Warren wrote the majority 6-3 decision in both cases (*Braunfeld v. Brown* [Pennsylvania] and *Gallagher v. Crown Kosher Supermarket* [Massachusetts]). In finding for the state, Justice Warren argued that Sunday had become a traditional, and therefore primarily secular, day of rest for Americans of all religions. Any financial burden borne by the Jewish storeowners was "indirect." Justice William O. Douglas dissented, writing that the underlying issue was "whether a State can impose criminal sanctions on those who, unlike the Christian majority ... worship on a different day or do not share the religious scruples of the majority.... A law which compels an Orthodox Jew to choose between his religious faith and his economic survival ... is a cruel choice ... [that] no State can constitutionally demand."[31]

Orthodox Jews were not the only Americans affected by this ruling. Seventh-Day Adventists (a Protestant sect) also observe Saturday as their religious day of rest. In the early 1960s, Adell Sherbert, a Seventh-Day Adventist, was fired from her job in South Carolina because she refused to work on Saturday. The state denied her unemployment insurance benefits because, they stated, she refused "suitable employment" if it entailed working Saturdays. Sherbert's case reached the Supreme Court in 1963 *(Sherbert v. Verner).* The Court's 7-2 decision found in favor of Sherbert and used her case as a standard in adjudicating other free exercise cases. The Court stated that in denying Sherbert unemployment benefits, the state had infringed on her free exercise of religious beliefs: "To condition the availability of benefits upon this appellant's unwillingness to violate a cardinal principle of her religious faith effectively penalizes the free exercise of her constitutional liberties."[32] The majority argued that the state must be neutral in terms of religious differences.

Free Exercise of Religion versus the Law
In *Wisconsin v. Yoder* (1972), the Court was asked yet again to balance the state's duty to ensure that children are educated against a contrary religious belief. Frieda Yoder was a 15-year-old Amish girl who had graduated from the eighth grade, at which time her parents withdrew her from school. The state of Wisconsin, like all other states, has compulsory education laws and, based on these, the state sought to force her to attend school until she was 16. However, Old Order Amish religious and cultural beliefs demand that Amish children not be subjected to modern education beyond grade eight, as higher education will instill in them non-Amish values and prevent them from learning Amish ways within the community. In refusing to comply with the state education law, Frieda's and other Amish parents were fined and even jailed by the state, which claimed that enforcing education to age 16 ensures that children will be "self-reliant . . . participants in society." The Amish argued that their religion and way of life does not involve their children in modern society. In writing the majority opinion in support of the Amish, Chief Justice Burger acknowledged that a "way of life" "rooted in religious belief" cannot excuse one from following the law. However, the Court decided that religious conduct based on religious belief is also protected under the free exercise clause. Thus, religious conduct is "beyond the power of the State to control . . . A regulation neutral on its face may, in its application, nonetheless offend the constitutional requirement for governmental neutrality if it unduly burdens the free exercise of religion."[33] The Court found that the state law created such a burden for the Amish.

Supreme Court decisions rest largely on the social and political tenor of the times and on who is sitting on the Court when a particular case is heard. After the *Yoder* decision, one might think that long-practiced conduct based on religious belief would be forever deemed constitutional. *Employment*

Division v. Smith (1990) proved otherwise. In this case, the state of Oregon fired two Native American employees because they had used peyote, an illegal hallucinogenic drug, during a centuries-old religious ritual. To find for the state, all the Court had to do was establish a compelling secular purpose for the state law, but it could not find such a purpose. So rather than hearken back to *Yoder*, the Court abandoned this line of reasoning and replaced it with a standard that stated that the state had only to show a rationale for its law. In other words, if the state could explain the reasoning behind the law, this was sufficient to override the Native Americans' free exercise of religion. "*Smith* left it up to governments to choose whether or not to exempt religious behavior from laws of general application.... Virtually all religious traditions and secular civil libertarians condemned the decision and worked to restore the pre-*Smith* standard."[34]

It took the passage by Congress of the Religious Freedom and Restoration Act (RFRA, 1993) to restore "the *Sherbert* standard by stating that government actions that impose a burden on religious believers were permissible only when they serve a compelling public purpose and are the least restrictive means of accomplishing that purpose." Predictably, in a 1997 decision *(Boerne v. Flores)*, the Court struck down RFRA as unconstitutional because "interpreting the Constitution" is up to the courts, so the legislative branch of government could not pass a law that contravened a Supreme Court decision. The only way to override the Court would be to pass another amendment to the Constitution. This is a lengthy and laborious process, which requires ratification by three-fourths of the states. "*Smith* put at risk virtually every exemption that the Court had previously granted on religious grounds and made it much more difficult to sustain free exercise claims at all."[35] Perhaps at another time and with a new set of justices, the Court will hear a similar case and override *Smith*. Until then, *Smith* remains the law of the land and a severe restriction of religious freedom.

IS THE UNITED STATES A CHRISTIAN OR SECULAR NATION?

This is one of the thorniest and most divisive questions facing Americans today, and it is contested passionately by those on both sides of the issue. The most truthful answer to this question is "yes and no."

Christian Influences on Forming a Secular State

It was the Puritans' nonconformist ideas about religion that had a deep and definitive impact on the new nation. The Puritans were, after all, Dissenters who lived out their pious view of pure Christianity. This view was based on the Bible and the individual's relationship with God through the Holy Spirit. It did not depend on any state intervention or support. According to Hugh Heclo, a political scientist at George Mason University, "American politics was liberated to be religiously moralistic precisely because the government was prohibited from involving itself in the higher matters of theological doctrine and sectarian differences.... Insofar as separation of church and state in America was based on principle, it was more a product of Christian thinking than of any secular or deist or Enlightenment philosophy."[36] The United States may thus be identified as Christian because its founding principles came from deeply religious Puritan Christians; but the principles that guided these devout Christians demanded the separation of church and state, or a secular non-Christian government.

Those who have wanted to "take back America for Christ" cite the 1892 Supreme Court decision in *Church of the Holy Trinity v. United States*, in which Justice David Brewer's majority decision contained the words "this is a Christian nation." The case arose from an 1865 law passed by Congress that made it illegal for employers to pay the cost of transporting cheap labor from China to work in the mines and on the railroads of the West. The law was intended to retain these jobs for native-born American citizens. Sometime later, Holy Trinity Church hired an English reverend and paid his transoceanic travel expenses. This remuneration was challenged under the 1865 law. In his written opinion, Justice Brewer found for the church, stating that the original law applied only to "cheap and unskilled labor." The justice approved the church's action by observing that paying the reverend's expenses was a laudable thing to do in our "Christian nation." However, the justice's comment has been continually taken out of context, which made clear that he was describing the demographic and cultural nature of the country. He was not saying "that America as a nation was created or exists for the sake of advancing the cause of the Christian religion." Rather, Justice Brewer's comment can be likened to describing a parochial school by saying "It is a Catholic school." The statement is descriptive, not prescriptive. Brewer made his point clear in a 1905 book in which he "emphasized that America is not a Christian nation in the sense that anyone should be compelled by the government to support Christian doctrines ... or that Christianity should be established through state power."[37] Despite these clarifications, many on today's Christian Right continue to cite Brewer as "proof" that America is and always has been a Christian nation.

On the opposite side, secularists like to quote a 1792 treaty between the United States and the Muslim leaders of Tripoli (Libya). The treaty ratified by the U.S. Congress reads, "As the government of the United States of America is not in any sense founded on the Christian religion—as it has in itself no character of enmity against the laws, religion or tranquility of Moslems . . . it is declared by the parties that no pretext arising from religious opinions shall ever produce an interruption of the harmony existing between the two countries."[38] This official document, preceding the *Holy Trinity* case by a century, reveals the view of the founders' generation that the United States was not a Christian nation.

Religious Evolution in the United States

There is no question that Christianity was the foundation of all colonial sects. So in that sense, the United States was founded by and might be considered a Christian nation. The principal denominations dominant during the early colonial period were Anglicanism (established in charters obtained from the Mother Country) and Puritanism (Congregationalism), as well as Quakerism. Yet the colonies' reputation as a frontier where unorthodox religion could flourish attracted those who followed other forms of Christianity. By the time of the Constitutional Convention, the new republic was already religiously pluralistic. It therefore became necessary to enshrine religious freedom in the Constitution, as there were numerous sects that feared losing their freedom of worship to majority, "established" religion. This intense focus on religion, from its founding onward, makes the United States one of the most religious countries on Earth.

THE EIGHTEENTH CENTURY

Americans have always been a restless, antiauthoritarian, and nonconformist people. In the 1730s and '40s, a Great Awakening, the first of several (some would say continuous) religious revival movements, swept the new nation. The First Great Awakening was a Calvinist evangelical movement that sought to attract converts with fiery preaching and congregational ecstasy, such as loud singing, shouting, shaking, barking, speaking in tongues, and other signs of possession by the Holy Spirit. Thousands showed up at open-air or tent revivals to be converted, and many were. A large proportion of these converted Christians were poor and illiterate; folks shunned by the establishment churches.

The First Great Awakening heralded the decline of the mainline Anglican, Congregationalist, and Quaker churches, while membership in the newer Baptist and Methodist evangelical churches soared. There were several reasons for this. First, straight-laced mainline churchgoers turned their noses up at the scandalous carryings-on at revivals and at the poor folk who attended them. Second, the mainline churches had lost touch with the growing country. As settlers pushed westward, they demanded a religion they could identify with. Mainline churches were led by seminary-educated reverends. Out on the frontier, all sorts of Protestant sects arose, whose uneducated, itinerant preachers were circuit-riders who brought their sermons to the most remote towns and dusty outposts where the faithful could leave their sod huts or log cabins and gather to hear the word of God preached by one of their own in a language they could understand. America became multidenominational as preachers and their flocks reinterpreted scripture for themselves: "U.S. Protestantism uniquely abounds with . . . 'populist innovations,' or forms of worship developed by lay people."[39]

The religious landscape was shaped both by the fierce independence of the frontier and by democracy itself. Popular sovereignty combined with evangelical fervor allowed ordinary people to create new types of Christianity in their own image: ". . . common people wanted their leaders unpretentious [and] their doctrines self-evident and down-to-earth. . . . [They] denied the age-old distinction that set the clergy apart as a separate order of men [and] instinctively associated virtue with ordinary people rather than with elites."[40] Many saw their freedom of religious association as embodying the meaning of America, where their fervor might truly create God's kingdom in the new nation. Nathan O. Hatch quotes the memoir of a man who attended a religious meeting in a poor man's home: "I met the whole church of Christ in a little log house . . . we began to talk about the kingdom of God as if we had the world at our command; we talked with great confidence, and talked of big things . . . we began to talk like men in authority and power—we looked upon men of earth . . . [and] we saw by vision the church of God, a thousand times larger . . . we talked about the people coming like doves to the windows, that all nations should flock unto it . . . and of whole nations being born in one day; we talked such big things that men could not bear them."[41]

THE NINETEENTH CENTURY

By the time of the Second Great Awakening in the early 1800s, the most popular Protestant denominations were the Southern Baptists and Methodists, with Pentecostals coming in a distant third.[42] While the more politically connected mainline churches faded, these and other new denominations, including charismatics, restorationists (primitivists), Assemblies of God, holiness churches, and even their tiny but fervent offshoots, gained adherents. Sectarianism and the invention of radical new churches were the hallmark of American Protestantism. One thing all members of these myriad denominations had in common was their adamant and unwavering conviction that they wanted nothing to do with government and government had better steer clear of them. The French historian Alexis de Tocqueville (1805–59), a longtime and frequent visitor to these shores at this time and one of the most acute observers of American life, attested to the fact that "The [religious] sects that exist in the United States are innumerable . . . all [differing] in respect to [their] worship." He also noted that "Religion in America takes no direct part in the government of society, but it must be regarded as the first of their political institutions, for if it does not impart a taste for freedom, it facilitates the use of it. . . . [T]he American clergy in general . . . are all in favor of civil freedom, but they do not support any particular political system. They keep aloof from parties and from public affairs."[43]

By midcentury, Seventh-Day Adventists, millennarian Jehovah's Witnesses, and Mormons were also gaining ground on mainline churches. The Mormons, whose beliefs were truly radical (polygamy, Christ visiting America), were perhaps the only group that believed in the indispensable unity of church and state—though not the one whose seat of power was in Washington, D.C. Their Utah settlement of Deseret was, in fact, established as a theocracy ruled by the Mormon leader Brigham Young (1801–77).

Revivalism waxed and waned, but dissatisfaction with "established" churches never faded. Through the Civil War and beyond, evangelism was rampant and once-unorthodox sects often grew too complacent and "official" for frontier Christians seeking a purer religion. Newer, more radical denominations formed from dissident splinter groups. In 1850, Methodists were the largest denomination in the country, with 2.7 million members.[44] But by the 1870s, Methodism had succumbed to the allure of respectability and had become far too staid for many of its adherents who yearned for a religious rebirth. Many abandoned Methodism for holiness churches (Churches of Christ), the Baptists, or to form their own "primitive" sects that freed them from church authority to find salvation through personal experience. By World War I, restorationist and holiness churches were closing the membership gap with the Baptists. Even after the Scopes trial, when both the public and the press derided the antievolution evangelicals, membership in these and other marginal denominations continued to grow.

The democracy of revivalism had unexpected consequences. The adherence to equality and the right of individuals to pursue their own spiritual well-being melded with the right to pursue one's own temporal well-being. Instead of uniting people in a single, harmonious Christian society, the multifarious nature of homegrown religion had the opposite effect—it tended to splinter society. The religious fissures in the social fabric encouraged the growth of competition, entrepreneurship, and the every-man-for-himself form of free enterprise and capitalism that came to define American society. The longing for purity in Christian life also evolved among some Protestant denominations into a strict, moralistic "new discipline," which, like its Victorian counterpart, condemned and punished "vices" such as any hints of sexuality or imbibing alcoholic beverages. This rigid morality would later lead to Prohibition, though it also inflamed the passionate antislavery activities of the abolitionists.

Rejection of "the establishment" was made official by the election of Andrew Jackson (1767–1845) as president. This Democratic no-nonsense man-of-the-people was elected because, like most ordinary Americans, he believed in the "freedom from" government meddling, not the "freedom to" rights espoused by the Whig Party. Under Jackson, the wall of separation was tall, solid, and unbreachable. Though the Democratic Party stood for political secularism, it was supported by a large majority of evangelicals whose principal aim was to be "born again" in Christ—on their own and in their own way. The Democrats "were social levelers who believed in a limited, populist government and a society rooted in self-interest and individual autonomy. They sought a secular state that did not try to legislate social behavior and was free of church control."[45]

By the 1840s, the Democrats had the support of what are called the "liturgicals": Catholics, Episcopalians, Lutherans, and other ritual-based "established" Protestant denominations. The liturgicals were generally libertarian and egalitarian; they believed in individual autonomy and limited government. As nonmillennarians, they believed that God's kingdom was otherworldly, and they were therefore generally not social reformers. The other religious group, termed "pietists," was made up of Baptists, Methodists, Quakers, and splinter groups that generally did not see religious and civil life as separate. They were committed to purging the world of sin, and they therefore engaged in social reform as well as Christian conversion in order to usher in the millennium and the reign of Christ on Earth. Pietists opposed the Jacksonian Democrats for their perceived tacit support for slavery, alcohol, and other ills. For a time, the pietists tended to support the Whigs, even though the party was in decline. Pietists approved of the Whig goal of building a "righteous moral empire" in America. Pietists and Whigs were an odd couple. Whereas pietists were revivalist and innovative in their religion, the Whigs were essentially the party of the elite, the educated, and "established" religion. Yet the moralistic, reformist, and antislavery aims of both groups united them for a time.

Before its demise, the Whig Party was boosted by anti-immigration sentiment. The 1840s saw a large influx of Roman Catholic immigrants, mainly Irish fleeing the potato famine. Whigs found new life in enacting nativist laws to contain the Catholic "threat" to Protestant American society. These attempts to purge the "sin" of Catholicism from the nation also appealed to the evangelical pietist impulse to cleanse the world for Jesus. Yet many historians ascribe the disintegration of the Whig Party to the mismatch between it and its pietist supporters. Increasingly, the pietists demanded that the Whigs stress ethical above political goals. When the Whigs placed party above ethics, the pietists, who were in no sense party loyalists, abandoned it.

With the Whig Party defunct by the 1850s, it was for a time replaced by the infamous Know-Nothings, whose platform rested on the single anti-immigration, anti-Catholic issue. Thankfully, the party of prejudice quickly gave way to the Republican Party, which gained a broad base of support from antislavery pietists, while the Democrats gained the Catholic vote. After Abraham Lincoln (r. 1861–65) and the Civil War, and after the impeachment of the hapless Andrew Johnson (r. 1865–69), the Republican Party saw its star fading. In the 1870s and '80s, its pietist base tried to revive it with "'the politics of righteousness'—Sabbatarian and temperance laws, anti-Catholic propaganda, and defense of Protestant public schools . . . Despite these efforts, the Democrats, bolstered by the 'solid South,' surged after 1876, winning three of four presidential elections by close margins."[46]

By the 1890s, the parties further consolidated their platforms. William Jennings Bryan reshaped the Democrats into a party of reform; William McKinley turned the Republicans into the party of business that "fought against silver coinage rather than alcoholic beverages."[47] While McKinley was elected in 1896 by both Protestant and Catholic voters in the Northeast and Midwest, Bryan's support came from the South and West. The Democrats' proclivity for an activist government that supported social reform alienated a significant sector of evangelical liturgical voters who feared interference from a strong central government.

AFRICAN-AMERICAN CHURCHES

African Americans were denied universal suffrage until 1965. In the North, free black men had the franchise by the early 1800s, and most voted for the Whigs and then the Republicans because of their antislavery platform. In the South, white evangelical Protestants first began converting enslaved Africans in the 1830s. Of course, these converted Christians lacked political power, yet they generally did not use the congregation to foment rebellion. According to the historian David W. Wills, "The predominant pattern was one of accepting the power realities of the slavery system as a matter of fact but refusing to assent to them as a matter of right." Thus, the black church fostered a "culture of resistance," which persisted into the 1960s and beyond.[48]

After Reconstruction, African-American Protestant churches experienced a splintering into new denominations akin to that in the white churches, though black Baptist and Methodist denominations predominated then as now. If political power is defined as "the capacity to participate in making social decisions," the postwar African-American churches became

RELIGION AND THE STATE

and continue to be "the major vehicle for the development of black power in America. More than any other institution, the churches have provided a place where black Americans could collectively order their own lives."[49] It was primarily through the African-American churches that civil rights leaders, such as Dr. Martin Luther King, Jr. (1929–68), organized and applied the necessary political pressure to gain the vote and equal rights and opportunities for black Americans.

THE PROGRESSIVE ERA

The Progressive Era, which spanned the first two decades of the 20th century, was noted for the social reforms it enacted, supported by widespread populist sentiment. Labor laws, direct election of senators, women's suffrage, antitrust legislation and industrial regulation, and important conservation measures were all enacted during this period. At the same time, tensions within and among Protestant denominations caused deeper religious divisions. Essentially, Protestants split along fundamentalist-modernist, or conservative-liberal, lines. The split was to a great extent urban-rural, with greater sectarianism in rural areas, where the holiness and Pentecostal movements broke away from more traditional sects. Yet nearly all Protestant groups became engaged in the reform movements of the time, though the liturgicals tended more toward issues like labor reform, while the pietists focused on Prohibition.

One thing that united almost all Protestants was anti-Catholic sentiment, which was responsible for the defeat of Alfred E. Smith (1873–1944), the first Roman Catholic to run for president in 1928. Anti-Catholic feeling was most vehement in the debate about public schools. Protestants of every stripe supported free public education, and they were militantly against the rapidly expanding network of Catholic schools. For their part, Catholics insisted that public schools instilled Protestant values they did not want their children to learn. This conflict would be carried to the Supreme Court, in somewhat different form, by the middle of the century. However in the face of war (the Spanish-American War of 1898 and World War I [1914–18]), both Catholics and Protestants were united by a powerful sense of patriotism.

When the military threat ended, so did the unity. Not only did prejudice against Catholics persist, the divide between liturgical and pietist Protestants widened. Conservatism grew among pietists, among whom "there was a dramatic disappearance of interest [in social reform]—or at least a severe curtailment—by the 1920s." As the Jazz Age drew to a close, the conflict between liturgicals and pietists hardened, and there was a sense that ". . . the progressivist component of modernism [and of] the immanence of God in culture had become deeply problematic. . . . [Many] feared the demise of

Christian civilization itself [which] led many conservatives to accentuate their premillennialist views emphatically as a key to understanding God's will for the nation."[50] While the social reformers began supporting more liberal politics, the pietists rejected social reform and political involvement as incompatible with their increasingly conservative views. In a letter to the editor of *Newsweek,* one evangelical aptly summed up the conservative Christian view: "Any attempt to reduce the Son of God to [a] social reformer should be labeled for what it is—blasphemy."[51]

CHRISTIAN FUNDAMENTALISM

Religious conservatism was most pronounced in rural areas and the South. To some degree, it was primed by and arose as a backlash against newfangled technologies that threatened the rural way of life. Radio revealed formerly unknown and unwelcome, even blasphemous, ideas that preyed on the minds of the young and led them astray. It brought the city, and its "evil" ways, right into rural living rooms. Movies immersed the young in images of exciting, independent, even glamorous lives that made it increasingly difficult to "keep them down on the farm." The advent of the automobile was the last straw. New roads were cut through formerly isolated areas to allow "corrupt and godless" city dwellers to take weekend drives to the country. They inevitably brought their fancy clothes and heretical ideas to the countryside. Just the sight of them filled youngsters' heads with forbidden possibilities. After intense initial resistance, country folk began to take to motorized vehicles; for one thing, pickup trucks enabled farmers to get their produce to market more quickly and profitably. Yet cars were also places where teenagers could get up to all sorts of unthinkable and sinful shenanigans. Rural life faced a real threat to its continued existence, let alone its values, as city people began to buy up land and build first or second homes in once inaccessible, outlying areas that were now only a drive away from the city. Conservative rural residents felt like they were under siege.

Between 1910 and 1915, a set of 90 religious essays in 12 booklets was published that emphasized evangelism, conversion via the Holy Spirit, belief in the imminent end-times, and the inerrancy of the Bible. These tracts were titled *The Fundamentals.* Antimodernist religious groups and wealthy individuals paid for the publication and distribution of millions of copies of the booklets. They became so popular in the United States that those who adopted their tenets became known as fundamentalists, and a millennialist view and literal belief in the Bible became known as fundamentalism. Historically, fundamentalism first referred to 20th-century Protestant Americans who rejected science and all interpretations of the Bible that were not strictly literal. Some scholars, among them Judith Nagata, have defined fundamentalism as "a disposition characterized by a quest for certainty, exclusiveness, and unambiguous boundaries ... driven by an uncompromising mentality [that attempts] to chart a morally black and white path through the gray zones of intimidating cultural and religious complexity."[52] The boundaries delineate the true believer from the "other," anyone not a true believer, who is considered a threat and "the enemy."

Martin Marty, a noted historian of American religion, asserts that *"Fundamentalisms arise in times of crisis, real or perceived.* The sense of change may be keyed to oppressive and threatening social, economic, or political conditions, but the ensuing crisis is perceived as a *crisis of identity* by those who fear extinction as a people." This fear leads fundamentalists to "impose God's will on others, an intolerance of dissent, and a central reliance on inerrant scripture for ideology and authority."[53] The belief in the literal word of the Bible arises out of the fear that if one biblical statement is conceded to be wrong, then the entire edifice crumbles, opening up the possibility that the whole Christian faith, upon which fundamentalists base their lives, is a sham. Without the inerrant authority of the literal word of the Bible, chaos engulfs the world. It is this fearful rigidity that separates fundamentalists, whose faith rests on the absolute divine truth of every word in the Bible, from nonfundamentalist Christians, who accept that some parts of the Bible are mythic while others are truly divine.

Two crises launched the explosive growth of fundamentalism in the United States. The first crisis encompassed the Civil War and Reconstruction and lasted until the 1920s. The South was devastated and traumatized by its defeat in the Civil War and humiliated by Reconstruction. Many southerners responded to their postwar situation by adopting what some refer to as a "lost cause" theology, which teaches that the defeated (white southerners) are really the chosen people of God who have been "baptized in the blood of suffering and thus been chastened and purified," and who became "a self-identified chosen people ... who simply wouldn't let themselves be beaten, religiously or politically."[54] They believed that having survived their tribulation, God had kept faith with and redeemed them. In a social context, it became a matter of God's chosen and purified people against the heretical Yankees.

The theology of redemption and southerners' sense of separateness from, and religious superiority to, the rest of the country first came to be embodied in the Southern Baptist Convention (SBC), which was formed in 1845 as a breakaway denomination after the northern Baptists repudiated slavery. The SBC became the evangelical home of fundamentalism, as well as keeper of the flame of southern culture, a role it maintains to this day.

Focus on the United States

The second crisis that solidified fundamentalism was urbanization and the juggernaut of modernization that accompanied it. From the 1920s to the 1960s, the SBC, Pentecostals, and other splinter sects evangelized large swaths of the country, particularly in the West and in border states. Like their frontier predecessors, Christian fundamentalists avoided national political engagement to retain the purity of their beliefs and to shun to the greatest extent possible the threatening, life-altering changes that were occurring in an increasingly urban society. City life brought unacceptable innovations, such as women in the workforce, greater sexual permissiveness, hedonism, and materialism—all of which were seen as threats to conservative Christian values. Waves of non-Protestant immigrants, such as Roman Catholics and Jews, were viewed as undermining the Protestant bedrock of the "Christian nation." Science, especially, was feared and damned as heretical. From the Scopes trial onward, fundamentalists fought fiercely to keep evolution and other scientific disciplines (e.g., geology) from contaminating their schools and their worldview. Textbooks were scoured of all references that contradicted a literal reading of the Bible. Books were banned from libraries, popular music was forbidden.

Meanwhile, the northern Protestant denominations engaged in social reform activities, and they accepted modernity and science as agents of temporal progress that did not undermine their spiritual faith. The less religious or atheistic enthusiastically embraced modernization, whose innovations swelled the number of nonreligious Americans because "inevitable forces of modernization produced a secular freedom in matters of the spirit and ... skepticism toward a faith based in divine revelation ... [Yet] this tendency evoked a reactionary movement in which religious conservatism was preserved."[55] As the nation became aware of conservative Christian views and prohibitions, fundamentalists came to be viewed as narrow-minded, bigoted, and backward. To fundamentalists, their values were a badge of the purity of their Christian faith, which contrasted harshly with the "heretical and blasphemous" notions of the "enemy," their misguided critics. The religious-secular, or modernist-fundamentalist, polarization of the nation was underway.

The South had voted solidly Democratic since the Civil War as a reaction against the detested Republicans who instigated the war and destroyed the southern way of life. At the 1948 Democratic National Convention, the party adopted a platform supporting the emerging Civil Rights movements. In a "states' rights" revolt, the southern delegates stormed out of the convention, and soon most southerners abandoned the Democrats altogether. When the Catholic John F. Kennedy (1917–63) ran for president in 1960, fundamentalists voted en masse for Richard Nixon (1913–94). Under the influence of fundamentalists, the Republican Party began its inexorable slide to the right, and its candidates increasingly described themselves and their platforms in conservative Christian terms. With the exception of Democratic president Jimmy Carter (1924–   ), Christian fundamentalists consistently voted Republican. When Democratic president Lyndon B. Johnson got Congress to pass the Civil Rights Act (1964), which desegregated schools, public places, and employment, and the Voting Rights Act a year later, the president correctly predicted that the Democratic Party would lose the South for a generation or more.

THE CULTURE WARS

The rift between conservative Christians and more secular Americans came to a head during the "freewheeling" sixties. The strength of the fundamentalist reaction against the sixties was bolstered by widespread, powerful church organizations. The increasingly politically engaged evangelical churches put them center stage in the reaction against this era's liberalization.

Robert Wuthnow provides an interesting explanation of the mindset that presaged the cultural divide to come. He posits that in the 1940s and '50s, politicians and most religious leaders and their flocks subscribed to the concept that a person's values were intimately related to his behavior. If you knew someone's values, you could predict her behavior. This idea was expanded to include the nation as a whole: "Culture essentially consisted of values ... arranged in a hierarchy of priority ... [which] held the society together. It generated consensus and caused people to behave in similar ways."[56] It seemed to follow that if you wanted to shape people's behavior all you had to do was instill in them certain values, which shaped their conscience, which determined their actions. In this view, deep religious faith led to moral convictions that would ensure right action. But by the 1960s, this notion was viewed with growing skepticism.

The Civil Rights movement and the antiwar movement demonstrated that people often behaved contrary to their professed values. People who identified with egalitarian values were denying African Americans equal rights and furiously, sometimes violently, supporting segregation. People who cherished democratic values were supporting a war in which a foreign people were being denied the democratic right to choose their own government. People who valued life and the commandment not to kill were slaughtering millions to prop up a nondemocratic government. The upshot of this conundrum opened even wider the cultural gap between conservatives and liberals.

Religious conservatives retreated from the complexities of the issue and continued to insist on the primacy of values, instilled by preachers and a devout Christian community and family, in forming the all-important foundation for what one believed in one's heart; behavior took a back seat to faith. Liberals, in contrast, insisted that it was a person's behavior, the effect one had while acting in the world, that was paramount. For them, what one believed was far less important than what one did. Actions, not beliefs, made the world a better place.

This critical shift in emphasis played out before a backdrop of other great social upheavals. As modernization accelerated, people welcomed opportunities for greater mobility. Once cohesive and homogeneous communities were torn apart. New people with different, and therefore often threatening, religious and cultural ideas moved into the neighborhood. "Denominational ghettos . . . were gradually replaced by religiously and ethnically plural communities."[57] Pluralism led to religious intermarriage, something anathema to most conservative Christians (and others). The very culture of fundamentalism was compromised by children who had friends belonging to other denominations (or no denomination at all). Exposure to nonfundamentalist culture and values, spread through religiously pluralistic schools and the media, did in fact threaten the purity preserved by the isolationism of the conservative Christians.

The 1960s was also a period in which many American families sent a child to college for the first time. The college experience often radically altered the values and views of these children. Kids brought new, often unwelcome and shocking, ideas into the conservative home. Setting aside the sexually liberated ideas students carried home with them, there were ideas that challenged Christians' understanding of American history and the nation's place in the world. There were arguments for direct action against social ills, for a greater role for women in society and the workplace, and, worst of all, a questioning of Christian (and sometimes regional) values.

The Christian Right was horrified and quickly acted to retrench and mount a counterattack against what it viewed as a potentially lethal assault on its beliefs and way of life. The response, which arose mainly from the grassroots, was swift and powerful and drew the battle lines for the conflicts to come. The first salvo was fired in West Virginia in the mid-1970s, when a county board led by fundamentalists denounced its public schools' English textbooks as "disrespectful of authority and religion, destructive of social and cultural values, obscene, pornographic, unpatriotic, or in violation of individual and familial rights of privacy."[58] The issue inspired massive parent and student boycotts of the schools, wildcat strikes among miners, a teachers' strike, and a temporary shutdown of the school system to prevent the assaults and violence some protesters used to get their point across. Although eventually the textbooks were reinstated, not long after, new, more conservative texts replaced them.

RELIGION AND THE STATE

In 1977, Anita Bryant led Dade County, Florida's fundamentalists in an effort to repeal an ordinance that prohibited discrimination against homosexuals in employment, housing, and public accommodations. Conservative Christians formed organizations to fight the legislation and filed petitions against it containing tens of thousands of signatures. In a referendum on the ordinance, Floridians voted the legislation down by a 2-1 margin. At around the same time, Phyllis Schlafly, who was to become a national Christian conservative leader and spokesperson, organized massive support to defeat the Equal Rights Amendment (ERA) proposed by Congress, which would have ensured equal pay and opportunities to American women. Using a host of scare tactics, such as claiming that it would destroy the American family and that women and men would be forced to use the same public restrooms, Schlafly's "Stop-ERA" movement killed the amendment.

These initial successes laid out the issues that would delineate the battle lines in the so-called culture wars between the Christian Right and the group that has come to be called the "secular humanists," defined as those who believe more in the supremacy of humanity than of God. Bitter divisions arose over issues such as gay rights, "liberal bias" in schools and the media, the "truth" of science, sexual permissiveness, reproductive rights (especially abortion and stem cell research), and a whole host of issues that could be fought along biblical lines. Fundamentalists "rejected the division of human affairs into the 'secular' and 'sacred' . . . instead [they] insist that there is no arena of human activity, including law and politics, which is outside of God's lordship."[59]

As this worldview encompassed secular humanists, it was bound to polarize the citizenry, if not rend the fabric of society altogether. There arose a deep hostility between the divergent camps. As a National Council of Churches official described the predicament: "Liberals abhor the smugness, the self-righteousness, the absolute certainty, the judgmentalism, the lovelessness of a narrow, dogmatic faith. [Conservative Christians] scorn the fuzziness, the marshmallow convictions, the inclusiveness that makes membership meaningless—the 'anything goes' attitude that views even Scripture as relative. Both often caricature the worst in one another and fail to perceive the best."[60] The Christian Right most abhors the liberals' "moral relativism," the contention that all value systems are equally valid and have equal merit. It rejects the attendant notion that there is no such thing as absolute good, and accuses secularists of moral cowardice and hypocrisy.

The Christian Right as a Political Force

Conservative Christians continued to make inroads in local government in many parts of the country. Even in areas where they were not in the majority, their supporters voted them in to powerful positions on school boards and in municipal or county government. The Christian Right took advantage of popular indifference and low voter turnout to come to wield enormous power at the local level. Only when fundamentalist views were forced on the general population did less conservative Christians and secularists notice what was happening, as when school boards prohibited the teaching of evolution or books were banned from school and public libraries.

The power being accrued by the Christian Right did not go unnoticed nationally. Right-wing Christians who emerged as local political leaders were wooed by newly formed conservative and Christian organizations, including the Religious Roundtable, the Conservative Caucus, the National Federation for Decency, the National Conservative Political Action Committee, Dr. James Dobson's Focus on the Family, and Paul Weyrich's National Committee for the Survival of a Free Congress. Richard Viguerie became a leading fund-raiser for Christian conservative causes. Howard Phillips of the Conservative Caucus was a major player in boosting local Christian leaders onto the national stage. He forged a coalition whose main objectives were attacking "big government," gun control measures, unionization, and cuts in defense spending. Intense opposition to the 1973 Supreme Court decision in *Roe v. Wade*, which ruled that it was unconstitutional to restrict a woman's right to choose abortion to terminate a pregnancy, would become and would remain the most powerful tool in rallying and unifying the Christian Right.

The Moral Majority was a prominent Christian Right organization formed in 1979 by the televangelist Jerry Falwell (1933–2007). Falwell was also the minister in the country's largest independent Baptist church in Lynchburg, Virginia. The Christian Voice advocacy group was created in 1979 by Californians after they had failed to kill gay rights legislation. The group focused on elections: getting their candidates into office, getting evangelicals to the polls, and raising money for Christian Right candidates. Electioneering efforts were helped enormously by Richard Viguerie's innovative direct-mail appeals to evangelicals around the country. The National Christian Action Coalition, formed in 1977, lobbied to defend Christian schools from government interference (such as mandated standards and curriculum), and it created the first scorecard for grading politicians on how closely their positions aligned with the goals of the Christian Right.

By 1980, these and smaller organizations were sufficiently integrated to present a united front in pushing their issues, which were generally subsumed under the rubric "pro-family." In his "Christian Bill of Rights" published during this period, Falwell set out the evangelicals' goals of opposing abortion, supporting voluntary prayer and Bible study in public schools, lobbying for pro-family and "traditional family unit" legislation at the federal level, and government noninterference in Christian schools. Later, Christian Voice added opposition to teaching evolution, to pornography, to the "immorality" of the media, and to the use of alcohol and drugs to Falwell's manifesto. Christian leaders also lobbied for increases in defense spending as a means of defending the Gospel and their "Christian nation."

After spending years in the wilderness during the Kennedy, Johnson, and Carter administrations (and having lost many supporters after Watergate and Nixon's resignation), the Republican Party began to woo the Christian Right and adopt its views on issues. The Republican-evangelical union fulfilled mutual needs: The Republicans needed an injection of new blood, a new and large base of supporters, and a new direction; the Religious Right needed champions of its values to occupy positions of power in Washington, D.C. At the 1984 Republican National Convention, Falwell referred to the party's candidates as "God's instruments in rebuilding America."[61]

The Religious Right's support for Ronald Reagan may seem perplexing. Evangelicals hated Hollywood as a hotbed of immorality and vice, yet they gladly supported a longtime Hollywood actor. Their rigid insistence on family values was uncompromising, yet they voted overwhelmingly for a divorced man. Reagan hardly ever went to church and did not disguise his indifference to religion. Yet he was the conservative Christian's candidate for several reasons. He was amiable. He said the right things, such as his comment about the nine most dreaded words in the English language: "I'm from the government and I'm here to help." He was a true conservative who embraced the evangelical agenda. The crowds loved it. By this time, the largely southern and conservative Christian Right had been totally alienated from the Democratic Party, which just did not speak its language and did not espouse conservative values. From 1964 to 2008, the only Democratic candidates elected to the presidency were southerners. When they, too, were rejected for their northern, liberal views and legislation, the Democrats simply had to write off evangelicals. As one Christian leader explained, "They [the Democrats] attacked the integrity of the family and parental rights. They ignored traditional morality. And they still do."[62]

Some historians suggest that during this period and through the presidency of George W. Bush, the Republican Party was, in essence, becoming a religious party, something that had never before existed in the United States. The election of Bill Clinton in 1992 and 1996 was, to some extent, a protest against the capture of the Republican Party by the Religious Right. Undeterred, the Religious Right regrouped and revived. Using direct mail and what was by then the national reach of Christian and conservative talk radio, as well as nationally broadcast religious TV shows, the Christian Right galvanized a huge following. This was accomplished, in part, by a semantic change targeted to less radical Christians. Appeals were made to "religious conservatives" and then to "people of faith"; defending "Christian values" morphed into "traditional values" and the even more popular "pro-family agenda."[63]

The new language emerged from new organizations, such as the Family Research Council and Concerned Women for America. Pat Robertson's (b. 1930) Christian Coalition was the most popular and dominant of these organizations, even though Robertson was a Pentecostal (which cost him his bid for the Republican presidential nomination in 1988). Under the leadership of Ralph Reed (b. 1961), the Christian Coalition became a national political force, distributing tens of millions of letters and phoning millions of potential voters.

The Religious Right became one of the most powerful lobbying groups in Washington, D.C. As its members became more affluent (some spectacularly wealthy), they funded lobbyists who pushed the Christian Right's agenda: do away with Medicare because it undermines family unity, abolish welfare because it promotes promiscuity, reduce taxes so women could return to their rightful role in the home, and, most crucially, appoint justices to the Supreme Court who would undo "antifamily" decisions such as *Roe v. Wade*, but also decisions that maintained the separation of church and state, especially in schools. They lobbied fiercely for the Federal Communications Commission to revise its guidelines limiting the number of media outlets a single entity could own in one locality in order to permit greater expansion of the inescapable blanket of 1,600 Christian radio stations and 250 Christian TV channels.[64] These included Robertson's hugely popular Christian Broadcasting Network.

The nation was saturated by the voices of the Religious Right, and their numbers grew accordingly. The influx of new members led to the creation of megachurches the size of shopping malls where services are attended by thousands of worshippers. This enormous demographic of self-identified conservative or fundamentalist Christians helped the self-proclaimed "born again" George W. Bush gain the presidency in 2000, and again in 2004. Bush evinced the disdain for opposing viewpoints so common among right-wing Christians. He also embodied other aspects of Christian Right politics that appealed to evangelicals, who were "confident of their ability to discern the will of God, . . . quick to claim divine approval for their efforts and to treat any opposition as rebellion against God's will." Bush also mirrored their "triumphalism, the belief that they should rule by virtue of [their] moral superiority" and echoed the fundamentalist dictum to "break the back of Satan."[65] George W. Bush gave the Religious Right some of what it wanted, his faith-based initiative, for example, and he spoke the language of fundamentalism. At one 2004 gathering he declared, "I trust God speaks through me. Without that, I couldn't do my job."[66] Yet Bush was unable or unwilling to support laws, let alone constitutional amendments, that prohibited abortion and gay marriage (though he did his best to undermine science). Abortion remains legal, the nation's values overall have not shifted dramatically to the right. Many on the Christian Right feel betrayed by the current political system, and some seek to overthrow it.

AMERICAN THEOCRACY?

There is a small but significant coalition of far-right Christians who have had enough of waiting for their country to be reborn as the moral, pious nation God intended it to be. Those on the extreme Christian Right make no bones about their desire to transform the United States into a theocracy. "I hope to live to see the day when . . . we won't have any public schools. The churches will have taken them over again, and Christians will be running them" (Jerry Falwell, founder Liberty University); "the so-called 'wall of separation' between church and state is a liberal fabrication to try to put churches out of a place of influence in political life" (Bob Jones III, president Bob Jones University); "there is no way that government can operate successfully unless led by godly men and women under the laws of the God of Jacob" (Pat Robertson, founder Regent University).[67] The colleges founded and run by these evangelicals are preparing what they hope is the next generation of leaders who will create a Christian America.

In spite of their overwhelming control of government (both in the White House and in Congress) during the Bush II administration, the Religious Right whipped up a frenzy of concern about a so-called "war on Christianity" sweeping the country and threatening to annihilate its pious Christians. Robertson warned of a "spiritual battle [against] Satanic forces." The Christian conservative and judge Janice Rogers Brown warned that "these are perilous times for people of faith," or that Christians were "at a point of crisis. Our culture is in chaos. The moral foundations . . . are quickly crumbling around us, with no sign of a cure."[68] One way to overcome this chaos and win the battle for Christians is to attain enough power to gain dominion over the nation. Thus was the dominionist movement born, which took its name from the Bible (Genesis 1:26–31, where God gives humans dominion over all creation).

Both Jerry Falwell and Pat Robertson agreed that the United States suffered the attacks of September 11, 2001, because God was punishing the nation for its secular immorality. The attacks fed into the fundamentalist obsession with eschatology, or the end-times. Many fundamentalist preachers (and the best-selling Left Behind series of books coauthored by Tim LaHaye) speak of the Rapture, when the saved (fundamentalist Christians) will be raptured (alive) up to heaven at the Second Coming, when Jesus will battle the Antichrist, and the Earth and the unsaved will suffer unspeakable destruction and torment. To prepare America for this inevitability, and to save as many Americans as possible, dominionists (a term coined by the sociologist Sara Diamond) must try to save their society via direct political action, which is a mandate from God. In this view, Christian fundamentalists alone are "biblically mandated to occupy all secular institutions until Christ returns."[69] In a nutshell, they must have dominion, or power, over both the secular and religious sectors of society. The law of the land must be biblical law.

There are two flavors of dominionism. Soft dominionists are Christian nationalists who believe America to be God's chosen land and who have the same social and moral beliefs as other fundamentalists, but they stop short of advocating the overthrow of the Constitution and the government. Hard dominionists seek to make the United States a theocracy based on biblical law. The late reverend D. James Kennedy, pastor of the huge Coral Ridge Ministries, described dominionism this way in a 2005 speech: "Our job is to reclaim America for Christ, whatever the cost ... we are to exercise godly dominion and influence over our neighborhoods, our schools, our government, our literature and arts, our sports arenas, our entertainment media, our news media, our scientific endeavors—in short, over every aspect and institution of human society."[70]

Dominionism arose out of Reconstructionist Christian theology, whose goal is to politicize faith and to turn the state into a theocracy. The primary proponents of Christian Reconstructionism were Gary North (b. 1942) and R. J. Rushdoony (1916–2001). Rushdoony came to prominence as an advocate of Christian homeschooling, which would teach a Christian revisionist version of American history. Rushdoony's books, one of which drew heavily on the theocratic writings of John Calvin, were so radical (e.g., the death penalty for blasphemy and premarital sex), his ideas were rejected by even the most hard-line right-wing Christians. However, they drew on his ideas to formulate their dominionist principles and ambitions.

Though most fundamentalist Christians share the same values as the more radical dominionists—antihomosexuality, intolerance of nonbelievers, anti-intellectualism, and rejection of science—they do not subscribe to the fearsome Calvinist rigidity dominionists have adopted from Rushdoony. In this passage from *Institutes of Biblical Law* (1973), Rushdoony's ideas are uncomfortably akin to those expressed by Qutb. "Freedom must be under law or it is not freedom ... Only a law-order which holds to the primacy of God's law can bring forth true freedom.... Freedom as an absolute is simply an assertion of man's 'right' to be his own god; this means a radical denial of God's law-order. 'Freedom' thus is another name for the claim by man to divinity and autonomy."[71]

RELIGION AND THE STATE

The consequences of dominionism are not limited to the United States but have important implications for foreign and global policy. Both are forms of millennialism. Premillennialists believe that God's plan for the Earth and for humans is unfolding today. They fervently support the state of Israel because it is central to their theory of the end-times, when Jesus will return to Earth and they will be raptured into heaven. By supporting Israel and fighting secular humanism, premillennialists are helping to fulfill God's prophecy. According to Theocracy Watch, postmillennialists are Reconstructionists who are "the most extreme constituency of the Religious Right."[72] They do not believe in the Rapture, but they are the most militant group calling for the creation of a Christian theocracy in the United States. George Grant, a leading postmillennialist writer, stated: "[I]t is dominion we are after. Not just a voice. It is dominion we are after. Not just influence. It is dominion we are after. Not just equal time. It is dominion we are after. World conquest. That's what Christ has commissioned us to accomplish."[73]

Millennialism has implications for U.S. foreign policy. In 2003, General William Boykin, a fundamentalist Christian and possibly a dominionist, declared that his American troops would be triumphant over any Islamic foe because "I knew my God was bigger than his. I knew that my God was a real God and his God was an idol."[74] Such an attitude does not bode well for diplomacy or war. Neither does millennialism hold out any hope for solving environmental or social problems. Why feed people when the end of the world is nigh? Why save the Earth and its creatures when all will soon be consumed in battle with the Antichrist?

The author and former Christian seminarist Chris Hedges points out the fruitlessness of trying to reason with dominionists: "Debate with the radical Christian Right is useless. We cannot reach this movement. It does not want dialogue. It is a movement based on emotion and cares nothing for rational thought and discussion. It is not mollified because ... Jimmy Carter teaches Sunday school. Naïve attempts to reach out to the movement, to assure them that we, too, are Christian or we, too, care about moral values, are doomed. This movement is bent on our destruction. The attempts by many liberals to make peace would be humorous if the stakes were not so deadly. These dominionists hate the liberal, enlightened world formed by the Constitution, a world they blame for the debacle of their lives."[75]

Back from the Brink?

Many experts continue to debate how great a threat the dominionists really pose to the nation. Because these groups operate by stealth, it can be difficult to accurately assess their numbers and their strength. However, there is growing evidence that of the 70 million evangelical Christians in the United States, only a small percentage can be identified as part of the hard-core Religious Right, and likely even fewer would call themselves dominionists. In many ways, Christian fundamentalism is a continuum that runs from the most extreme theocrats to those who simply believe in the literal word of the Bible. In between are the millions of believers in the Rapture, in angels, and in miracles.

On the other hand, there are millions of devout evangelicals who do not identify themselves as fundamentalists and who actively oppose fundamentalist doctrine. Rev. Jim Wallis (b. 1948) is just one of an increasing number of liberal evangelicals who reject the narrowness and religious oppression espoused by fundamentalists and who actively promote social reform and environmental stewardship. Fault lines are forming even within the SBC and other traditionally right-wing Christian organizations as the membership splits between extremists and moderates. There are also millions of Christians from many denominations who are out-and-out liberals. Still, small, militant groups of radicals have often had a disproportionate effect on their societies.

The influence of the Religious Right on the nation seemed to decline in the early 21st century in response to two incidents. The first was the Terri Schiavo case, which involved the fate of a woman in a persistent vegetative state. Her husband wanted to carry out her wishes and "pull the plug," allowing her to die with dignity. Her parents argued that as a devout Roman Catholic Terri would have opposed euthanasia. In 2005, the government rallied in defense of her parents, with Congress attempting to pass special legislation to keep her on life support. President Bush even flew back to Washington, D.C., from his Texas ranch to sign the legislation. The law, intended as a gesture to pro-life Christian conservatives, was never enacted. Polls show that about 70 percent of the public was disgusted by the government's interference in such a personal family matter. Their collective revulsion is thought to have given them pause about the direction in which the Religious Right was taking the country.

The other incident was the federal response to Hurricane Katrina (2005). Many Christians expressed outrage at the casual insensitivity of the Bush administration's response to this disaster. As Americans watched the poor of New Orleans die of neglect, they were reminded of what true Christianity was all about. The disconnect between Christ's teachings and the breezy indifference of Bush's supposedly faith-based administration brought people up short and made them reevaluate the Christian Right's influence on government.

RELIGION AND THE STATE

ATHEISTS STRIKE BACK

The resurgence of the U.S. Religious Right and the 9/11 terrorist attacks perpetrated by Islamic al-Qaeda fundamentalists catapulted religious fundamentalism in general to the forefront among hot-topic public issues. The prominence of fundamentalism as a topic of public discourse, and Christian fundamentalists' inordinate influence during the Bush II administration, has in recent years led to an atheistic backlash. After decades of being referred to by fundamentalists as satanic sinners and condemned to eternal hellfire, atheists found a voice and are declaring their views openly. Yet some among them, including the author Christopher Hitchens, are in many ways as rigid and intolerant as the religions they attack.

The New Atheists' withering contempt for all believers as ignorant and misguided and their inability to accept that religion may address spiritual needs that are beyond the scope of science tend to undermine their point of view. Richard Dawkins, a Darwinian evolutionary biologist viewed by the Christian Right as the Antichrist, is quoted by the author Daniel Lazare as mocking the rise of Judaic monotheism as "dumb." Yet according to Lazare, Dawkins and New Atheists like him fail to recognize that "the idea of an all-powerful, all-knowing creator might cause worshippers to see the world as a single integrated whole and then launch them on a long intellectual journey to figure out how the various parts fit together"—by inventing the scientific method.[76]

No one can prove or disprove God's existence. Yet the New Atheists confuse science, which predicates belief on evidence, with religion, which predicates belief on faith. Religious belief cannot be belittled because it is not scientifically rational. The New Atheists' dismissive attitude toward religion and people of faith serves only to aggravate antagonisms and further polarize the country. While New Atheists deny a belief in God they offer nothing else to sustain people in their need to understand the world fully, including those realms that are beyond the reach of science. Until the rhetoric is toned down and a modicum of tolerance is embraced, the important atheistic viewpoint will likely have difficulty influencing mainstream American discourse about religion and its role in American politics and society.

IN CONCLUSION

Is the United States a Christian nation? Yes and no. Its founding Christians established it on the principles of secularism. It has since become one of the—if not the—most religiously diverse nations on Earth. Christianity was formative and is certainly culturally significant, but "the two most rapidly growing religions in our nation are Hinduism and Buddhism, the former through immigration from India, the latter through a combination of immigration and conversion."[77] A major 2008 poll conducted by the American Religious

Identification Survey found that Americans claiming "no religion" were the only demographic group that grew in all 50 states in the last 18 years.[78] Such a society cannot survive without a serious commitment to tolerance of religious pluralism. Neither the New Atheists nor the Christian Right has empirical or historical dibs on defining what this nation is or should be. If the Religious Right "is wrong for America, it must be because its message is wrong on the issues, not because its message is religious."[79] If the New Atheists are narrow-minded, the truth of scientific discovery must still be accepted. As it is likely that Americans will continue to be innovative in religion, as in nearly all other aspects of culture, the nation will progress only if it honors the wisdom of its Constitution and lets religion and the state function separately but harmoniously.

---

[1] Isaac Kramnick and R. Laurence Moore. *The Godless Constitution: The Case against Religious Correctness.* New York: W. W. Norton, 1996, p. 63.

[2] Edwin S. Gaustad. *Church and State in America.* New York: Oxford University Press, 1999, p. 20.

[3] Kramnick, p. 24.

[4] Kramnick, p. 24.

[5] Michael Corbett and Julia Mitchell Corbett. *Politics and Religion in the United States.* New York: Garland Publishing, 1999, p. 35.

[6] David Little. "Roger Williams and the Separation of Church and State." In James E. Woods, Jr. (ed.). *Religion and the State: Essays in Honor of Leo Pfeffer.* Waco, Texas: Baylor University Press, 1985, pp. 9–10.

[7] Kramnick, p. 75.

[8] Gaustad, p. 34.

[9] Edwin Scott Gaustad. "The Emergence of Religious Freedom in the Early Republic." In Woods, p. 31.

[10] Gaustad. In Woods, p. 29.

[11] Gaustad. In Woods, p. 33.

[12] Leonard W. Levy. "The Original Meaning of the Establishment Clause of the First Amendment." In Woods, p. 45.

[13] Alexander, Hamilton. *The Federalist Papers,* no. 84, pp. 575–581. Available online. URL: http://press-pubs.uchicago.edu/founders/documents/bill_of_rightss7.html. Accessed September 3, 2009.

[14] Levy. In Woods, p. 53.

[15] Levy. In Woods, pp. 59–60.

[16] Levy. In Woods, p. 61.

[17] A. E. Dick Howard. "The Wall of Separation: The Supreme Court as Uncertain Stonemason." In Woods, p. 85.

RELIGION AND THE STATE

[18] Kramnick, p. 133.

[19] Gaustad, p. 61. (Citing *Reynolds v. United States*, 1879).

[20] Gaustad, pp. 65–66.

[21] John F. Wilson. "Religion, Government, and Power in the New American Nation." In Mark A. Noll (ed.). *Religion and American Politics: From the Colonial Period to the 1980s.* New York: Oxford University Press, 1990, pp. 78–79.

[22] Gaustad, p. 89. (Citing *Engel v. Vitale*, 1962).

[23] Gaustad, pp. 91–93.

[24] Gaustad, pp. 97–98.

[25] Gaustad, p. 116.

[26] Gaustad, p. 77.

[27] Martha C. Nussbaum. *Liberty of Conscience: In Defense of America's Tradition of Religious Equality.* New York: Perseus Books, 2008, pp. 260–262.

[28] Leo Pfeffer. "The Diety in American Constitutional History." In Woods, p. 140.

[29] Gaustad, pp. 124–125.

[30] William H. Marnell. *The First Amendment: Religious Freedom in America from Colonial Days to the School Prayer Controversy.* New York: Doubleday, 1964, pp. 179–182.

[31] Gaustad, pp. 126–127.

[32] Ronald B. Flowers. *That Godless Court? Supreme Court Decisions on Church-State Relationships.* Louisville, Ky.: Westminster John Knox Press, 1994, p. 32.

[33] Nussbaum, pp. 143–144.

[34] Kenneth D. Wald. *Religion and Politics in the United States.* 4th ed. Lanham, Md.: Rowman & Littlefield Publishers, 2003, pp. 108–109.

[35] Wald, p. 109.

[36] Hugh Heclo. "Is America a Christian Nation?" *Political Science Quarterly* 122, no. 1 (2007): 77–78.

[37] Heclo, "Is America a Christian Nation?" pp. 62–63.

[38] Quoted in Heclo, p. 77.

[39] Kevin Phillips. *American Theocracy.* New York: Penguin Books, 2007, p. 103.

[40] Nathan O. Hatch. "The Democratization of Christianity and the Character of American Politics." In Noll, pp. 95–96.

[41] Hatch. In Noll, p. 104.

[42] The color and corruption of the American revivalist movement was scathingly revealed in Sinclair Lewis's 1927 novel, *Elmer Gantry*, which was also made into a brilliant, classic film (1960) of the same name starring Burt Lancaster and Jean Simmons.

[43] Alexis de Tocqueville. *Democracy in America.* Book I, chapter 17: "Indirect Influence of Religious Opinions upon Political Society in the United States." Available online. URL: http://xroads.virginia.edu/~HYPER/DETOC/religion/ch1_17.htm. Accessed April 13, 2009.

Focus on the United States

[44] Phillips, p. 109.

[45] Robert P. Swierenga. "Ethnoreligious Political Behavior in the Mid-Nineteenth Century: Voting, Values, Cultures." In Noll, p. 152.

[46] Swierenga. In Noll, pp. 160–161.

[47] Swierenga. In Noll, p. 161.

[48] David W. Willis. "Beyond Commonality and Plurality: Persistent Racial Polarity in American Religion and Politics." In Noll, p. 204.

[49] Wills, p. 208.

[50] Robert T. Handy. "Protestant Theological Tensions and Political Styles in the Progressive Period." In Noll, pp. 297–298.

[51] Wald, p. 162.

[52] Wald, p. 297.

[53] Martin Marty and Bruce Lawrence, quoted in Phillips, p. 205 (italics in original).

[54] Phillips, pp. 138, 142.

[55] Robert Wuthnow. "*Quid Obscurum:* The Changing Terrain of Church-State Relations." In Noll, p. 344.

[56] Wuthnow. In Noll, p. 347.

[57] Wuthnow. In Noll, p. 349.

[58] Wald, p. 206.

[59] Wald, p. 208.

[60] Wuthnow. In Noll, p. 340.

[61] Wald, p. 211.

[62] Wald, p. 211.

[63] Wald, p. 213.

[64] Wald, p. 221.

[65] Wald, p. 234.

[66] Phillips, p. 208.

[67] Phillips, p. 215.

[68] Quoted in Theocracy Watch. Available online. URL: http://www.theocracywatch.org/introduction2.htm. Accessed April 27, 2009.

[69] Quoted in Theocracy Watch. Available online. URL: http://www.theocracywatch.org. Accessed April 27, 2009.

[70] Quoted in Theocracy Watch. Available online. URL: http://www.theocracywatch.org. Accessed April 27, 2009.

[71] Chris Hedges. *American Fascists: The Christian Right and the War on America.* New York: Free Press, 2006, p. 14.

[72] Quoted in Theocracy Watch. Available online. URL: http://www.theocracywatch.org/christian_zionism.htm. Accessed April 27, 2009.

[73] Quoted in Theocracy Watch. Available online. URL: http://www.theocracywatch.org/christian_zionism.htm. Accessed April 27, 2009.

[74] Hedges, p. 29.

[75] Hedges, p. 202.

[76] Daniel Lazare. "Among the Disbelievers." *Nation* (5/10/07). Available online. URL: http://www.thenation.com/doc/20070528/lazare/. Accessed January 12, 2009.

[77] Nussbaum, p. 5.

[78] Laurie Goodstein. "More Atheists Shout It from the Rooftops." *New York Times* (4/27/09). Available online. URL: http://www.nytimes.com2009/04/27/us/27atheist.html. Accessed April 28, 2009.

[79] Stephen Carter. *The Culture of Disbelief: How American Law and Politics Trivialize Religious Devotion.* New York: Basic Books, 1995, p. 266.

3

Global Perspectives

ISLAMIC REVOLUTION IN IRAN

The regularly scheduled Air France flight that left Paris on February 1, 1979, was perfectly ordinary—except for one of its passengers. As the plane dipped toward the Tehran airport and taxied along the runway, the 3 million people who had come to meet the plane cheered ecstatically. When the black-robed, bearded old man emerged from the plane, the euphoric crowd chanted "Khomeini, O Emam" (Khomeini is the Perfect Imam).[1] Their revolutionary leader the Ayatollah Ruhollah Khomeini (ca. 1900–89) had come home to create and lead their Islamic state. Iran's 1979 Islamic Revolution is considered by most historians to be among the most significant historical events of the 20th century. The Iranian Revolution signaled new possibilities in the relationship between religion and the state in Muslim countries and became an inspiration for many discontented Muslims around the world.

The Persian and Safavid Empires

Persia (modern Iran) has an illustrious history dating back 2,500 years. Persians are not Arabs (Semitic people); they are Indo-Europeans who speak Farsi, not Arabic. Persians have created vast empires known for their efficient governance, exquisite art and architecture, and sublime poetry. Cyrus the Great organized the first Persian Empire in 559 B.C.E., and it stretched from Egypt to Pakistan. After Alexander the Great swept through, the Parthian Empire arose and lasted 400 years. Following its decline, it was quickly replaced by the great Sassanid Empire, which stretched from Armenia to India. The first Sassanid emperor, Ardashir I (r. 224–240), assumed the title *shahansha,* or king of kings, and the word *shah* would be used by all subsequent Persian monarchs.

The Sassanids were overrun by Muslim Arabs in the seventh century. The Umayyad conquest was a pivotal event in Iranian history. Though not overtly coerced, many Persians converted to Sunni Islam during the next few centuries. Still, a fierce resentment grew in the proud and once-powerful Persians who were now relegated to a second-rate backwater. Resentment erupted in 750, when a rebellion defeated the Umayyads, marking the beginning of the Abbasid Empire.

The Muslim Abbasids were ruled by a caliph who claimed descent from the Prophet. For the next 500 years, the Abbasids ruled a vast swath of Mesopotamia. In the ninth century, the Turks invaded, fragmenting the empire. Then the Shiite Buyids seized control of Abbasid-held Baghdad. They were followed by the Mongols in the 13th century and Tamerlane less than 100 years later. Persia languished until 1472, when the empire regained its territory around Tabriz.

Iran's golden age dates to the 16th-century Safavid Empire under Ismail, the head of a prominent Sufi order. Upon taking the throne, Ismail declared that henceforth Persia would be a Shiite nation. All Persians were required to convert to Shia Islam, a move that proved to be crucial in establishing Persia's unique religious and political identity.

Religion and the State in Premodern Iran

Zoroaster was a prophet born in a corner of Iran sometime between the 10th and seventh centuries B.C.E. His teachings became Zoroastrianism, a religion whose theology was based on duality, or the tension between good and evil in the world. Zoroastrianism teaches that there is one benevolent and just God, and it is humans who must uphold the good and practice justice to bring the highest spirituality to the world and to achieve immortality of the soul at the last judgment. A cornerstone of Zoroastrianism is the responsibility of a king or other strong political leader to embody and promote God's moral order in society.

Zoroastrianism became the major religion of Persia during the time of Cyrus the Great, who was the first of many powerful kings to whom the Persian people looked for both spiritual and political leadership. His subjects regarded the king as God's instrument on Earth, and it was he who was obligated to defend and support the good (and oppose evil) for the betterment of his people. This concept of sacred kingship persists in Iran in some form to this day.

Under the Sassanids, Persian culture flourished, but eventually the empire threw up kings more interested in power than in goodness. A powerful religious and political bureaucracy led to rigid social stratification, with priests and princes at the top, the military in the middle, and most everyone else on far lower rungs of the social ladder. Like the Indian caste system, this inflexible social structure shaped Iran's religious, social, and political life for centuries.

Global Perspectives

The introduction of Islam into Persia in 638, after Arab forces overwhelmed the empire, was experienced as an alien and cruel conquest. One of the first projects undertaken by the victorious orthodox Sunni Arabs was the destruction of magnificent Persian works of art and architecture because they were representational and thus banned by Islam. Countless books were burned and libraries destroyed. Although the Persians were horrified by these depredations, and deeply resented the Arabs, they were attracted to Islam because of its emphasis on the equality of all in the *umma*. The lure of a just social system and the abolition of the detested castelike system brought many Persians into the Islamic fold.

Though for a time Sunni Islam did away with the rule of a sacred king, that tradition reemerged after the unimaginable horrors of the Mongol invasion, which nearly exterminated the Persian people. Descendants of Tamerlane, who founded the Persian Timurid Empire, embraced Sufism, the mystical, devotional, and most tolerant branch of Islam. The Safavids arose as just one of many Sufi sects in Persia during the 13th century, but they emerged as leaders who reinvigorated the tradition of the sacred king. As so often happens, the more power the Safavid kings got, the more they wanted and the less interest they had in being moral exemplars to their people. Power struggles within the ruling family forced some into exile among the Shiite Turkoman peoples of Turkey and Syria. Eventually, one of these exiles, Ismail, reconquered his homeland and established Shia Islam as the official religion.

Shia Islam turned out to be a good fit with Persian tradition. The Shiite preoccupation with martyrdom resonated with the sufferings the Persians had endured from the Mongols and Tamerlane. The Shiite idolization of Ali meshed with the Persian political ideal of the just ruler or sacred king. The Shia teachings about the Last Days when the Mahdi will redeem them echoed the Zoroastrian teachings about immortality and the last judgment. Finally, the Shiite acceptance of *ijtihad,* or interpretation of the Sunna, dovetailed well with an intellectual and sophisticated Persian society. Under Abbas the Great (1571–1629), who ruled Safavid Persia at its height, the shah became the religiously sanctioned sacred king. Ever since, the Iranians have looked to their head of state for both spiritual guidance and powerful political leadership.

Modern Iranian History

The 18th-century Qajar dynasty attempted to modernize Persia. However, inept rule made most of the Qajari period one of imperial retraction and decline. The Qajari ruler Nasir al-Din Shah (r. 1848–96) lured Western investors

RELIGION AND THE STATE

to Persia. In what Patrick Clawson and Michael Rubin have described as "the most complete and extraordinary surrender of the entire industrial resources of a kingdom into foreign hands that had probably ever been dreamed of," in 1872, the shah handed monopoly control of Persia's railways and mineral, forest, and water resources to an English investor.[2] Persians were furious. His 1891 attempt to give foreigners total control over Persia's tobacco industry caused a two-year-long nationwide Tobacco Protest. The *ulama*, which had always been quiescent in public matters, issued a fatwa sanctioning the tobacco boycott. The shah withdrew his offer.

A reengaged *ulama* emboldened Persians to more vocal protests against European interference. By the early 20th century, the British held powerful interests in the south, as did the Russians in northern Persia. Persians organized mass protests against the imperialists. When the troops of Muzaffar al-Din Shah (r. 1896–1907) stormed a mosque where protesters had taken sanctuary, the nation erupted, demanding a more representative government. The 1905 Constitutional Revolution forced the shah to institute Persia's first representative assembly, or *majlis*, which henceforth would be a part of government.

In 1907, Britain and Russia signed a treaty they had negotiated without Persia's knowledge to divide Persia between them. For decades afterward, Persia was carved into spheres of influence, with Britain controlling the south and Russia the north; central Persia was a neutral zone. Humiliation at being used so shabbily intensified Persian nationalism. The Persians grew to loathe and distrust both the West and the East.

It was in this poisonous and chaotic atmosphere that Ruhollah Khomeini grew up. In 1921, he was a mullah (local religious leader) teaching Islam in Qom and preaching against foreign interference and for Persian independence. Khomeini drew on the Shiite principle of a juristic clergy and its history of protest and opposition to argue for the establishment of an Islamic state with an Islamic leader. The British, too, were engaged in finding a Persian ruler. The British installed as shah a former army commander and minister of war. Reza Khan was to mold Persia into a pro-Western, secular state that would do Britain's bidding. Upon assuming the Peacock Throne, Reza Khan (r. 1925–41) took the name Pahlavi, meaning "heroic" in ancient Farsi.

Reza Shah's rule was tyrannical, brutal, and corrupt. In his attempts to modernize Persia, he weakened the *ulama* by attempting to wrest from it control of schools and the legal system and establishing Western-style secular versions of both. He filled the *majlis* with his supporters and got them to rubber-stamp laws—such as requiring men to wear Western suits and banning the veil for women—that infuriated large sectors of the populace. His opponents were jailed, tortured, and frequently executed. His admiration for the Nazis finally alienated the British, and they forced him to abdicate and go into exile in 1941. He did leave his mark on his nation, however; in 1935, he changed the country's name from Persia to Iran.

Mohammad Reza Pahlavi (r. 1941–79) succeeded his father as shah. Though at first he was less dictatorial than his father, the man who came to be known as the shah of Iran was still a British puppet. He was undone by the outrageously one-sided contracts he signed with the Anglo-Iranian Oil Company (AIOC) (today's British Petroleum). The contracts gave AIOC total control over and nearly all the profits from Iranian oil. The unfairness of the deal, the appalling conditions of Iranian oil workers, and the grinding poverty of most Iranians galvanized nearly all sectors of society to form a nationalist coalition called the National Front. The coalition was led by Mohammad Mossadeq (1882–1967), a charismatic leader who had served in the *majlis* since 1924.

MOSSADEQ AND THE ROAD TO REVOLUTION

As leader of the National Front, Mossadeq built vast public support for renegotiating AIOC's contract. The British adamantly refused to negotiate. In the face of British obstinacy, in 1951 the *majlis* unanimously voted to nationalize the oil company. The outraged British sent warships to blockade Iran and deprive it of oil revenues. Still, Iranians overwhelmingly supported nationalization. As the situation deteriorated, the shah asked Mossadeq to be prime minister and de facto head of government.

For the next two years, the British tried, in vain, to persuade U.S. president Harry S. Truman (1945–53) to join an invasion of Iran to take the oil fields by force. It was the height of the cold war, and the British raised the specter of the Soviet Union invading Iran and taking the oil. Yet Truman was sympathetic to Mossadeq. Said one unnamed U.S. diplomat, "Since nationalization is an accomplished fact, it would be wise for Britain to adopt a conciliatory attitude. Mossadeq's National Front party is the closest thing to a moderate and stable political element in the national parliament."[3]

Mossadeq visited Washington, D.C., and the United Nations in late 1951. At the United Nations, Mossadeq stated that "The oil resources of Iran, like its soil, its rivers and mountains, are the property of the people of Iran. They alone have the authority to decide what should be done with it, by whom, and how."[4] The British were humiliated when the United Nations refused to issue a condemnation of Iran.

The tenor of the conflict changed with the election of U.S. president Dwight D. Eisenhower in 1952. With the support of the State Department, the stage was set for the CIA to plan a covert operation to overthrow Mossadeq.

RELIGION AND THE STATE

The operation would entail creating an underground network of anti-Mossadeq activists in Iran and providing them with funds to hire thousands of poor Iranians as anti-Mossadeq demonstrators. July 1953 saw the first organized anti-Mossadeq demonstrations. A first coup attempt failed, but the next one achieved the desired result. CIA agents scoured Tehran, paying off mullahs, thugs, ex-soldiers, and anyone else who, for money, could muster a crowd to demonstrate against the prime minister. On August 19, 1953, thousands of protesters surged onto the streets and toward Mossadeq's home. Mossadeq surrendered the next day. The deposed Mossadeq was sentenced to life under house arrest.

While CIA-backed Iranians were rioting in Tehran, the shah had escaped to Rome where he assumed he would spend the rest of his life in exile. But days after the coup, a CIA-chartered plane flew the shah back to Iran. He disembarked with a CIA agent at his side. For the next 26 years, the increasingly megalomaniacal and brutal shah would rule Iran in the interest of the United States, whose government and corporations remunerated him handsomely. Since it was the CIA that had carried out the coup, Iran's oil was shared between British and U.S. oil companies. While the shah stashed his billions in kickbacks in Swiss banks, repression by SAVAK, his secret police, became intolerable to Iran's citizens, who were both oppressed and impoverished.

As the facts emerged about U.S. involvement in the coup against Mossadeq, Iranians' attitudes toward representative government changed. As Ebrahim Yazdi, head of the Iranian Freedom Movement, put it, "The Mossadeq affair was the big turning point in modern Iranian history. It killed our experiment with popular government. It also blackened the image of America, which . . . had been our ideal of freedom and democracy. I think there was a good chance for our democracy had Mossadeq survived. Instead the Shah came back and, in the eyes of all Iranians, he was an American agent. The Shah never overcame that, and neither did the Americans."[5] Those who engineered the coup did not anticipate the world-changing forces their rash actions had unleashed. Intelligence agencies call this "blowback," the unforeseen consequences arising from an operation based on expediency but without consideration of its potential repercussions.

THE IRANIAN REVOLUTION

The shah's despotic rule lasted until 1979. His modernization efforts benefited urban elites but left most Iranians behind. Under his orders, SAVAK arrested, tortured, executed, or "disappeared" anyone who opposed him. One of his most outspoken critics was Khomeini, who had become an ayatollah ("mirror of god"; highest-ranking cleric) in 1961. SAVAK arrested the ayatollah, provoking violent protests in Tehran. He was released, but Khomeini

Global Perspectives

would not be silenced. He was rearrested, then rereleased. In 1964, the government exiled him to Turkey; he later settled in Najaf, a Shiite city in Iraq.

From exile, the ayatollah preached and wrote prolifically against the shah and for the formation of an Islamic state in Iran. His writings and recorded speeches were smuggled into Iran and widely distributed. He was in constant contact with rebellious clerics in Iran and guided their revolutionary actions. Khomeini began to argue for an Islamic theocracy, or governance by a supreme religious jurist *(velayat i-faqih)*, who would have supreme political and religious power and who would act with the infallible authority of the Hidden Imam (the Mahdi).

In his book *Islamic Government: Regency of the Jurist* (1970), Khomeini explained his concept of an Islamic state. For Khomeini, in Shia Islam religious and political authority should be one; that is, the *ulama*, or a *mujtahid* (Shiite legal scholar), should rule directly. In contrast to Sunni fundamentalism (e.g., Wahhabism), which considers *bidaa* (innovation) sinful, Shia Islam embraces *ijtihad*, interpretation of the Sunna by the *mujtahid*, as an acceptable way of adapting Islam to changing conditions. Khomeini greatly expanded this principle in his concept of the *velayat i-faqih*, or rule (mandate) of the jurist. Khomeini asserted that the *velayat i-faqih* is the heir to the Hidden Imam, or Mahdi, and thus he alone has the ability to correctly interpret Islamic law *(fiqh)* and to mandate that his interpretations become the law of the land. As the infallible *velayat i-faqih*, Khomeini would embody the religious authority of the *ulama* and the political authority of the state. According to Khomeini, "The mandate of the jurist is to govern ... and implement the provisions of the sacred law.... [Only] those acquainted with the law or, more precisely, religion must supervise its functioning ... The jurist's regency will be the same as [that] enjoyed by the Prophet ... and it is incumbent on all Muslims to obey him."[6]

Khomeini's ideas were revolutionary, but turmoil in Iran and fear of fracturing the united front against the shah made it impossible for the *ulama* to debate the notion of a single ruling *mujtahid*. By 1977, the shah's vicious repression of dissent and the savagery of SAVAK had alienated the entire population. In 1978, with little left to lose, Iranians engaged in mass protests against the shah, and several people were shot. The shah declared martial law but, on September 8, thousands of demonstrators took to the streets in cities across Iran. The shah sent tanks and helicopter gunships to fire on the protesters. "Black Friday" was the Iranian people's Rubicon; their bitterness and revulsion at the shah's rule could not be stifled. By December, millions of Iranians thronged the streets demanding that the "Yazid government" (Yazid refers to the hated son of Muawiya) give way to Khomeini.[7] When troops defected to support the protesters, the game was up. On January 16, 1979, the shah fled Iran. Ayatollah Khomeini returned to establish the Islamic Republic of Iran.

RELIGION AND THE STATE IN THE ISLAMIC REPUBLIC OF IRAN

Khomeini understood that his revolution would endure only if it were legitimized by the population. A month after Khomeini's return, 98 percent of voters in a national referendum approved his formation of an Islamic state.[8] Officials in Khomeini's government set about writing a constitution that, when finalized, was a radical departure from traditional Shiite skepticism about temporal, corruptible government. The constitution institutionalizes the rule for life of the infallible *velayat i-faqih*, who has the power to appoint government officials and approve all candidates running for president. The Council of Guardians (clerics appointed by the ayatollah) oversees the suitability of candidates (who do not have to be clerics) running for election to the single-chamber parliament *(majlis)*. All laws and regulations have to be "based on Islamic criteria," and the legal system is run by clerics who enforce the "limited personal freedom" approved by Shia Islam.[9] As a consequence, all things Western and un-Islamic are banned. Every neighborhood has its *komiteh*, or local guardians of Islam, who patrol their area and attack anyone guilty of anything impermissible.

The United States was stunned by the revolution and refused to extradite the shah, who was in New York for cancer treatment. This galvanized a group of Iranian students to storm the U.S. Embassy in Tehran in November 1979 and take 52 American staff hostage. The ayatollah supported the action as a deserving humiliation of the Great Satan (America). Those in Khomeini's government who opposed the hostage-taking were dismissed. Iranians crowed at the helplessness of the United States. (The hostages were kept for 444 days and then released.)

With his power growing, Khomeini filled his government with orthodox clerics and maneuvered *mujtahid* into important political positions in towns and cities across Iran. He openly supported Islamic extremists, such as Hezbollah in Lebanon, who fought against their "un-Islamic" governments and Western powers. According to Robin Wright, "Iran redefined the nature of warfare by weaker Third World nations against the superpowers ... Under Iranian tutelage, political violence and terrorism crossed a threshold in the 1980s."[10] In 1981, Ayatollah Ali Khamenei, a rigid hard-liner, became president.

Khomeini was dismantling the Iranian military when, in September 1980, Iraqi troops invaded. No one knows exactly why the Iraqi dictator Saddam Hussein attacked Iran, but the United States supplied him with vast numbers of weapons to help him defeat the dreaded Iranians. The eight-year-long war cost more than a million lives on both sides. Khomeini hoped to use the war to promote his idea for "exporting the revolution," with highly secular Iraq as the first conquest in a worldwide Islamic revolution.[11] It was not to be. With their cities bombed to rubble, the combatants signed a UN ceasefire agreement in July 1988.

Khomeini did manage to galvanize the world's Muslims in 1989 when he issued a fatwa against the author Salman Rushdie for his novel *The Satanic Verses*. Khomeini raged that it was every Muslim's duty to assassinate Rushdie for "insulting" Islam and the Prophet. It is doubtful that Khomeini or most other Muslims had read the book (Muslim countries banned it), but the fatwa unified the Muslim world in indignation. (The fatwa was later rescinded.)

POST-KHOMEINI IRAN

Ayatollah Khomeini died on July 3, 1989, and he was universally mourned in Iran. Yet Khomeini's Islamic state was not as it seemed. Many Iranians are grateful to the ayatollah for freeing them from U.S. interference and for restoring their self-respect and identity. They are more ambivalent about the religious strictures imposed on them by their Islamic constitution.

Khomeini did not consider himself a fundamentalist; in fact, he had issued fatwas approving women TV news anchors and the sale of musical instruments. More orthodox Shia Muslims denounced the rulings, but the ayatollah reminded them that Shia Islam does not demand that "civilization should be destroyed ... or the people should live in shackles."[12] Still, Khomeini had kept Iran in isolation to maintain its religious and political purity. Many Iranians who remembered modernization under the shah chafed at the restrictions Khomeini imposed.

Khamenei succeeded Khomeini as ayatollah. Khamenei is a true hardliner and has imposed the most burdensome Islamic laws, prohibiting music, applause, foreign news, and a host of restrictions on women's behavior and dress. With Khamenei elevated to ayatollah, Iranians elected a new president. In 1989, Iranians elected the wealthy and urbane Akbar Hashemi Rafsanjani president. Rafsanjani promised reform and an opening of Iran to international trade. His ambitions were hampered by U.S. economic sanctions and the country's lack of up-to-date facilities for oil refining. Charges of corruption and lack of real economic progress made Rafsanjani's presidency, which lasted until 1997, seem a failure.

Mohammad Khatami was Iran's president from 1997 to 2005. He was a reformer who had been allowed to run because the Guardian Council thought he had no chance of winning. Iranians were hopeful that he would stand up to religious leaders and implement the reforms they so desperately wanted. In his speeches, Khatami quoted John Locke, but as president he proved to be too weak to overcome a council that opposed reforms and modernization. In the end, the electorate abandoned him.

RELIGION AND THE STATE

In 2004, the mayor of Tehran, a slightly built man who lived in a poor, working-class neighborhood, decided to run for president. A former Revolutionary Guard, Mahmoud Ahmadinejad (b. 1956) ran a grassroots campaign, traveling the country in his 1977 jalopy. He was a populist, an "Iranian Robin Hood," who promised the poor a better life.[13] When Ahmadinejad was elected president in 2005, he turned back the clock on reform. As the hardest of hard-liners, he has banned satellite dishes and foreign news and programming; prohibited Western music (including classical music); and shut down blogs, chat rooms, and Web sites. Severe restrictions and oversight have been imposed on citizens, and their behavior is closely monitored. Fundamentalists have formed thuggish vigilante groups, called *basijees*, made up mostly of former Revolutionary Guardsmen, who prowl the streets and confront or attack anyone who appears or acts "Western" or "un-Islamic." Ahmadinejad's politics is encapsulated in his statement, "We did not have a revolution in order to have democracy.... Today we should define our ... policies based on the [Twelfth] Imam Mahdi's return."[14]

There arose a yearning for greater social liberalization and reform among Iranians, especially the young. After the failure of Khatami's presidency, Abdulkarim Soroush, a respected Iranian thinker, predicted that if a more flexible, secular government were not established "the hypocrisies of politics and government would discredit religion in Iran and alienate the young. That is precisely what happened."[15]

Many young, Western-oriented Iranians have abandoned politics because clerical control makes reform unachievable; their favored candidates are consistently disqualified by the ayatollah or the Council of Guardians. There is increasing evidence that a significant proportion of Iranians is skeptical of the religious leadership and clearly would prefer a more secular state. Yet the poor and those who fear a reversal of the Islamic Revolution seem, for the time being, to have their way.

THE 2009 PRESIDENTIAL ELECTION

A few weeks before the June 12, 2009, presidential elections, Mir-Hussein Mousavi, a "reformed" former minister in Khomeini's government, began garnering widespread popularity among voters. Mousavi's campaign rallies attracted thousands of supporters, and he soon acquired the aura of a true reformist candidate. A large percentage of the electorate turned out on June 12, and polls indicated that Mousavi was destined for victory.

Yet only two days after the election, reportedly before all of the millions of votes could be counted, the ayatollah pronounced Ahmadinejad the winner. On June 15, a crowd of an estimated million or more Iranians, both young and old, swarmed onto the streets of Tehran to protest what they viewed as a fixed election. For days, massive protests choked the streets of

Iran's cities. Investigations soon revealed disturbing inconsistencies in the vote count: In Mousavi's home district, his opponent supposedly trounced him. In other known anti-Ahmadinejad districts, the incumbent allegedly defeated his opponent by wide and often identical margins. Electoral irregularities like these convinced Iranians, and international observers, that election fraud was widespread and the election was therefore illegitimate.

Unrest on the streets was mirrored by disunity among the ruling elite. It was reported that Khatami and Rafsanjani were furious and were working behind the scenes to garner support for a recount or a new vote. They tried to convince Ayatollah Khamenei to call for new elections, but though Khamenei was no fan of Ahmadinejad he feared that the reforms that Mousavi might enact would undermine clerical authority. Khamenei threw his support behind Ahmadinejad, using his authority as *velayat-i-faqih* to proclaim Ahmadinejad's election a "divine assessment."[16]

Meanwhile, huge public demonstrations continued. As the situation became critical and the clerics feared for their rule, the *basijees* were called out to put down the protests. Several people were killed, many were beaten, and hundreds were arrested. (The hard-liners wanted 100 of those arrested [and tortured] to be tried for treason and executed, but the charge was reduced. As of this writing, their trial is ongoing.) In fear for their lives, the protesters abandoned the streets but not their protests. Although all outside media were banned from Iran, Iranians used their cell phones to videotape and record their dissent. In stirring scenes reminiscent of the 1979 revolution, Iranians flocked to their rooftops at night, holding candles and chanting *"Allahu Akbar"* and "Death to tyrants." The same actions had heralded the end of the shah's rule 30 years before.

Ayatollah Khamenei swore in Ahmadinejad as president, and he warned Iranians and the world not to criticize or undermine the legitimacy of the two-term leader. The West has demonized the outspoken and confrontational Ahmadinejad, and he has played his role as the West's nemesis to the hilt. Yet those who know Iran know that it is not Ahmadinejad who wields power; it is the less visible clerics who run the country. Still, as political discontent swells in Iran, the day may come, sooner or later, when the people reclaim their republican government. As Fareed Zakaria wrote, "We are watching the fall of Islamic theocracy in Iran . . . the failure of the ideology that lay at the basis of the Iranian government."[17]

SAUDI ARABIA: THEOCRATIC MONARCHY

The uniformly white-draped devotees were filled with religious fervor as the imam of the Grand Mosque, the holiest shrine in Islam, ended the first prayer of the day shortly after 5:00 A.M. on November 20, 1979, just as the sun was rising over Mecca. The many thousands of hajj pilgrims at the Grand Mosque that morning were looking forward to days dedicated to prayer and spiritual renewal. As the imam's prayer ended, a ripple of anxiety flowed through the crowd. There was a disturbance; something strange was happening. Those up front saw an armed man shove the imam aside. Everyone heard the shots ring out. Then 250 armed men swarmed into the mosque and took it over. A voice boomed over the microphone, announcing that the Grand Mosque had been seized and would remain under the control of the rebels until the infidel Saudi government was deposed and replaced by a truly pious Islamic leadership that followed the strictest form of sharia.

The Saudi king and his ministers were initially too stunned to act. At first, the royal leaders assumed the rebels were Shia demanding equal rights or a Shiite state in Saudi Arabia. It was, after all, only months since the Islamic Revolution in Iran, where a Shiite government had taken over the country. But the rebels in the Grand Mosque were not Shia. It seemed unbelievable to the rulers, but the mosque rebels were ultraconservative Sunnis, mostly Saudi Arabian, who had committed this blasphemous act to "purify" Saudi Arabia—a country that prided itself on being the embodiment of the purest Sunni Islam.

Days went by and the siege continued, with thousands trapped inside the mosque. The Saudi leadership was frightened and humiliated, but Islamic law constrained its options in regaining control of the mosque. Attempts at negotiation had failed. Shedding blood in the Grand Mosque is a terrible sin, but force seemed necessary. Five days after the siege began, the king got the *ulama* to assert that, under these grave circumstances, Islamic law permitted sending in troops to retake the mosque. It took 2,000 Saudi troops more than nine days to overcome the rebels and retake the mosque. At least 255 people were killed in the operation; hundreds more were injured. More than 60 surviving Sunni fundamentalists were tried (secretly) and beheaded publicly in cities throughout the country.

A Brief History of Saudi Arabia

The seeds of Islamic extremism that inspired the rebels had been sown in the sands of Arabia during the 18th century. They grew into a fundamentalist Islam that would challenge Arabia and other Muslim nations around the world.

A thousand years after the death of Muhammad and the disintegration of his ideal state, Muhammad ibn Abd al-Wahhab (ca. 1703–92) wandered the deserts of Arabia, Syria, and Iran preaching a revitalized, pure Islam as it had existed at the time of the Prophet. Everywhere he traveled, Abd al-Wahhab had seen a distressing laxity (even debauchery) in Muslim adherence to Islamic law. After studying Islamic philosophy, Abd al-Wahhab aligned himself with the highly orthodox and rigid Hanbali school of Islam and the teachings of one of its most extreme exponents, Ibn Taymiyya. One of Ibn Taymiyya's most influential teachings was his denunciation of *bidaa* ("innovation"), beliefs, activities, and institutions that are not mentioned by either the Quran or the Sunna. *Bidaa* was prohibited even as a response to changing worldly conditions. For Abd al-Wahhab, a Muslim who engaged in *bidaa* was an infidel for committing this most grievous sin.

Abd al-Wahhab sought to rid Islam of its moral degradation by stressing its core monotheism. Backsliding was universal among the nomadic Bedouin in Arabia, who, soon after the Prophet's death, had reverted to their traditional polytheistic worship of local saints, idols, ancestors, and natural objects, such as trees and stones. Their identification with the *umma* had given way to traditional tribal loyalty. For Abd al-Wahhab, polytheists were guilty of *bidaa* because they endowed objects with a divine power that belonged only to Allah. Abd al-Wahhab considered Muslim sects that diverged from Hanbali orthodoxy guilty of *bidaa*, and he condemned them as infidels. The absolute conformity with strict sharia embodied in Hanbali Islam made numerous everyday behaviors taboo: using tobacco or prayer beads; listening to music; singing and dancing; and all forms of public immodesty. Abd al-Wahhab demonstrated his no-nonsense dedication to a literal interpretation of sharia when, while preaching at an oasis, he helped carry out the public stoning to death of a woman accused of fornication.

THE AL SAUD–WAHHABI ALLIANCE

What Abd al-Wahhab needed was a fighting force to help him impose Hanbali Islam via jihad. In 1744, Abd al-Wahhab settled in the oasis town of al-Diriya, whose local emir was Muhammad ibn Saud (d. 1765). Ibn Saud was an ambitious man who wanted to expand his region of control. The ambitions of the two men were a perfect fit. Ibn Saud would lead his forces (called the Ikhwan, or Brothers) in the service of Abd al-Wahhab. Abd al-Wahhab granted Saud religious legitimacy and political authority by giving him the title of imam (leader of the Muslim community, not to be confused with the Shiite Imams). The alliance they formed, cemented by marriage, created an inseparable link between the destinies of Wahhabism and the family of Al Saud.

What followed is a long story of conquest and intrigue, whose upshot was the formation of a nascent Saudi state. As one by one tribes were overcome by Ibn Saud's forces and oases fell under Ibn Saud's control, Arabia began to experience the first inklings of a type of political unity. The wars for control over ever-larger areas of Arabia were carried on by the male descendants of the original allies. The Ikhwan eventually defeated the Ottomans

RELIGION AND THE STATE

(who ruled 18th-century Arabia) and the Egyptians who the Ottomans sent to defeat them.

By 1915, the Ikhwan was a formidable fighting force of more than 100,000 (described by one witness as "utterly fearless of death . . . determined to annihilate the enemy . . . veritable messengers of death from whose grasp no one escapes"[18]). The new emir, Abd al-Aziz, used this fearsome army in his conquest of Mecca and Medina. By the 1930s, the Wahhabi-Saudi conquest of Arabia was complete. Abd al-Aziz (r. 1890–1953) took the title of king. The formation of an Islamic state was accomplished; militancy was abandoned and maintaining social order became the paramount goal. The king reigned from his capital, Riyadh, and strove to make his nation a model Islamic state. The fundamentalist revolution having achieved its purpose, the king's primary concern was preventing *fitna* (disorder) by maintaining the status quo via the imposition of strict sharia. At that time, no state was more Islamic than the Kingdom of Saudi Arabia, a nation created on September 23, 1932, and the only state named after its ruling (Al Saud) family.

As emir of the holy cities of Mecca and Medina, King al-Aziz had the religious and political authority to unite the peoples of the Arabian Peninsula (except for ethnically distinct Yemen). His crowning as king was blessed by the highest *ulama* in Arabia; his religious authority was now inseparable from his political power.

One of the first problems the king faced was the seemingly uncontrollable zealotry and violence of the fanatical Ikhwan, who continued to rampage through the country slaughtering non-Wahhabi Muslims and even Wahhabis who were, in their view, insufficiently orthodox. The Ikhwan could not be talked down, and in 1929 the king decided that force was necessary. Before taking action, he obtained approval for the campaign from the *ulama*. Religious sanction gave him the authority he needed to raise a large army. After years of intense fighting, by the late 1930s most of the Ikhwan were destroyed or disbanded.

MODERN SAUDI ARABIA

By the mid-1930s, geologists who had been poking around in the sand in the Eastern Province made a discovery that would transform the kingdom's fortunes. Though most Saudi kings were reformers who used some of the nation's immense oil wealth to improve the lives of its citizens, the royal family itself was awash in a sea of money. Many were educated in the West and privately engaged in decidedly un-Islamic behavior. That their *bidaa* was paid for by Western money derived from the oceans of oil beneath their feet made it all the more offensive. The luxurious, un-Islamic life led by the royals engendered real resentment among the people. Worse was the presence on

Global Perspectives

Arabian soil of Western oil company workers and families, as well as the U.S. troops who protected them. Although they lived segregated from the general population, the mere presence of Westerners sullied the sacred land of the Prophet. When in the mid-1950s, King Saud (r. 1953–64) granted the United States permission to maintain the Dhahran air base near the oil fields, many Muslims, in Arabia and elsewhere, were outraged at an infidel presence in the holy land.

In 1965, King Faisal (1904–75) called a summit of Arab leaders in an attempt to revivify the orthodox practice of Islam as a counterweight to the increasing secularization of many Muslim nations. Although his argument that religion must be a part of politics and governance was not adopted by most attendees, Faisal was honored for his integrity and dignity. His exemplary management of the hajj (to Mecca) and his virulent opposition to Zionism also earned him widespread respect among the Arabs.

As a descendant of Abd al-Wahhab, Faisal's religious credentials enabled him to take small, incremental steps toward modernization. Arabian schools and universities taught some modern subjects. Radio and television were introduced (though not without vehement protest), though they were state controlled and broadcast exclusively Islamic programming (radio broadcasts consisted only of Quran reading). For the first time, girls were permitted to attend girls' elementary schools. Because of these nods toward Westernization, King Faisal was assassinated by his nephew, who had protested the coming of television to Saudi Arabia.

The seizure of the Grand Mosque occurred during the reign of King Khalid (r. 1975–82). The king had helped organize the Arab League (1976) and had also expanded Saudi Arabia's industrial base, improved its agricultural output, and made other domestic reforms. Both before and after the mosque siege, the king faced massive protests among the minority Shia in the Eastern Province. Most Shia, were employed in the oil fields and earned decent salaries, but the government neglected them. Sunni Arabs looked down on and despised the Shia who were treated as second-class citizens. The violent Shiite protests that occurred just after the Grand Mosque incident were certainly inspired by the events in Iran. Shaken by the growing *fitna* in his country, King Khalid acceded to Shiite demands and provided them with more hospitals and schools and greater equality and justice within the kingdom.

Khalid died in 1982 and was succeeded by Fahd, who ruled until 2005. During the first Gulf War in 1991, King Fahd allowed U.S. troops to use Saudi Arabia as a base of operations (American forces left in 2003). This foreign contamination of Saudi soil ignited new and more violent protests by Islamic fundamentalists. Saudi Arabia suffered several major terrorist attacks, and the king began a strong campaign against domestic terrorism. The current ruler of Saudi Arabia is King Abdullah, who has continued along his predecessors' path of cautious reform. However, he too is caught between the divergent forces of fundamentalist Islam and modernization that are threatening to tear Saudi Arabia apart.

Religion and Politics in Saudi Arabia

The Al Saud kings are absolute monarchs, but their power has always been circumscribed by Islamic law. It is only by publicly upholding strict Wahhabi sharia that the family maintains its legitimacy to rule. The *ulama* play a key role in legitimizing royal proclamations. Without the approval of the *ulama*, it is doubtful that a royal decree would be implemented. There has in recent decades existed a tension between the *ulama*, which guards Islamic orthodoxy, and the reformist inclinations of the monarchy. However, the Quran continues to be the only constitution recognized by the Saudi government. Issues not covered in the Quran are regulated by the 1992 Basic Law, created by royal decree, which deals with the running of the bureaucracy, commerce, business, and similar worldly affairs.

The Saudi king has ultimate authority in virtually every aspect of government, and most laws and regulations are enacted by royal decree. In the 1960s, a large segment of the Saudi population pushed for the creation of a popularly elected representative legislature. The king resisted and bolstered his position by getting the *ulama* to declare such an assembly un-Islamic on the grounds that man-made laws are *bidaa* and cannot supersede or impinge on divine law. In 2003, the king relented somewhat and announced that local officials and one-third of the 150-member Consultative Council *(Majlis al-Shura)* could be popularly elected. It was not stated how candidates would run for office, as no political parties are allowed. To date, no elections have taken place.

Saudi Arabia is one of the only countries in which the *ulama* plays a direct role in government. The Council of Senior Ulama generally works hand-in-glove with the king to give his decrees the sharia stamp of approval. For his part, the king treads carefully to craft legislation that does not overtly conflict with sharia. When there is a disagreement, however, it is often the king who prevails. In 1992, for example, a few members of the *ulama* supported some ultraconservatives who criticized the king for lack of subservience to the *ulama*. The king responded by rebuking the *ulama* and actually dismissing some from their posts.

Discontent

The Al Saud view themselves as the protectors of pure Sunni Islam. They are therefore truly shaken by antigovernment protests by Wahhabi funda-

Global Perspectives

mentalists. As one expert noted regarding the siege of the Grand Mosque, "In the final analysis, what stunned the royal family was the audacity of the dissidents' Islamic claims. The Sauds have always taken pride in their piety. They never describe their foes as fundamentalists because they reserve the term to describe themselves.... They denounce dissidents as fanatics who are degrading Islam to promote impious ends. But they could not conceal their pain, since what the dissidents were doing was challenging them at their own Islamic game."[19]

Some well-placed Arabian officials see the ongoing protests and terrorist attacks as a latter-day resurgence of the fanatically orthodox Ikhwan. There have been car bombings near Riyadh (1995) and the Dhahran air base (1996). The perpetrators were caught and publicly beheaded. In August 2009, a member of the royal family who is also the deputy interior minister in charge of antiterrorism was injured when an extremist blew himself up at a gathering at the minister's home. Since then, hundreds, if not thousands, of Saudis who have dared to openly criticize the royal family have been jailed. Press criticism of the royal family, Islam, or the state is censored in Saudi Arabia (it may cause *fitna*), but antigovernment pamphlets circulate clandestinely. Political organizing, too, is unlawful, so there is little or nothing reformers can do within the establishment to effect change.

Some radicals have left the country to militate for change from abroad. Some of them are religious fundamentalists who seek to rid Saudi Arabia of all *bidaa*; to, in effect, immunize it against all things modern, including democracy, and return it to a type of medieval Islamic purity. Other expats are just trying to establish some form of accountability among the untouchable royals; they want some oversight of the royal family to ensure that they live according to sharia and that they are working toward instituting a representative *Majlis al-Shura,* at least some of whose members are elected by the people.

Another cause of general discontent within Saudi Arabia arises from Western support for the country's authoritarian regime. Many Saudis wish that Western leaders were less hypocritical about their support for democracy when it comes to their oil-rich allies. The desire for representative government has considerable support in Saudi Arabia, although there is a significant segment of the population that opposes these reforms as un-Islamic. The tension between greater liberalization and democratization and strict adherence to Hanbali sharia will probably continue to plague Saudi Arabia for the foreseeable future. In the meantime, the *ulama* continue to struggle with the often awkward task of applying sharia to the modern world. In 2008, the *ulama* issued a decree pronouncing the use of biofuels un-Islamic. Why? Because ethanol is a form of alcohol, and alcohol is *haram.*

RELIGION AND THE STATE

TIBET: THEOCRACY, IDENTITY, AND AUTONOMY
A Brief History of Tibet

The ancient history of Tibet is lost in the snows of the Himalayan peaks, but folklore tells that Tibet came into being when the "land rose above the waters."[20] This myth reflects the geological uplifting of the Tibetan Plateau, the highest on Earth, and the surrounding Himalaya Mountains. Stories of the original inhabitants of Tibet recount how their first king came to them from India. The early dynastic kings who followed were believed to have descended from Heaven and thus were divine rulers who exercised supreme power. These kings of the Yarlung dynasty were adherents of the indigenous religion called Bön. Bön was an animistic religion in which shamans performed rituals to honor and appease its many gods and demons. Life on the harsh, cold, and largely barren Tibetan Plateau was and is extremely hard. Little wonder, then, that in this magnificent but overwhelming environment, the mountains, rivers, and weather were viewed as being governed by capricious gods or demons. Ritual appeasement of the gods gave Tibetans a feeling of greater control over their lives in their frequently hazardous habitat; religious rites kept demons at bay and encouraged the gods to bestow good harvests, healthy livestock, and life and safety to worshippers.

In the sixth century, Tibet was a conquering power whose armies invaded the minuscule country of Nepal, where Tibetans first encountered Buddhism, and even parts of western China. For a short time in the early ninth century, the Chinese emperor was required to pay tribute to the Yarlung kings who ruled the Tibetan Empire. During this period China and Tibet were viewed as equal, major powers in Central Asia.

Legend has it that Buddhism first came to Tibet around 233 C.E. when a Buddhist religious text and holy relics of the bodhisattva Avalokiteśvara fell from the sky and crashed through the palace roof of the 23rd Yarlung king. Unfortunately, the king could not decipher the text, which was written in Sanskrit. The first religious king, Songtsen Gampo (ca. 618–650), moved the royal palace to Lhasa (the capital and religious center of Tibet) and took as a wife a devout Chinese Buddhist princess. She is viewed as an incarnation of the bodhisattva Tara and is credited with converting the king to Buddhism. Gampo and later kings faced fierce opposition to the new religion from government ministers who remained adherents of Bön. Therefore, the second religious king, Trisong Detsen (ca. 740–798), sent to India for a Buddhist holy man to defeat the Bön deities once and for all. The great Buddhist adept Padmasambhava is said to have read Detsen's thoughts and left for Tibet before he was actually summoned. Stopped en route by a howling snowstorm (caused by the enraged Bön gods), Padmasambhava took refuge in a cave. There he meditated on the destruction of the Bön deities. So great was Padmasambhava's power, he overcame them single-handedly (or single-mindedly). Padmasambhava helped the Tibetan king to establish Buddhism throughout the country, to found monasteries, and to translate the "heaven sent" and other sacred Buddhist texts into Tibetan.

The third religious king, Relbachen (r. 815–836), firmly established Buddhism throughout Tibet. Relbachen was a truly pious, some say fanatical, Buddhist. Alas, he was not a very good governor. The official opposition to him that swelled during his reign was inspired more by his ineptitude as a politician and financial manager than by his devout Buddhism. However, Buddhists credit Relbachen with the translation into Tibetan of many important Buddhist texts.

The Buddhism that was established in Tibet incorporated elements of the indigenous Bön religion to create a uniquely Tibetan form of Buddhism. Tibetan Buddhism has transformed some indigenous gods into incarnations of bodhisattvas. The famous images of fierce demonlike gods that appear on many Tibetan ritual objects and in temples are likenesses of Bön gods reincarnated, so to speak, in their new roles as bodhisattvas. The melding of the indigenous religion with Buddhism smoothed the way for the popular acceptance of the new teachings and gave the world a truly unique form of Buddhism.

THE MONGOL HORDE AND THE DALAI LAMA

Tibet continued to be a major power in Central Asia until the reign of the last Yarlung king, Lang Darma. More attracted to Bön than Buddhism, Lang Darma was a divisive force in Tibet and an incompetent leader. The Yarlung dynasty died with him, leaving Tibet weak and vulnerable to outside forces. In a short time, China regained the territory it had lost to Tibet. After a period of internal instability and persecution of Buddhism, Buddhism experienced its second wave of transmission to Tibet. A key figure in this revival was a Bengali nobleman and Buddhist monk named Atisa (fl. 11th century). After arriving in Tibet from India, the elderly monk translated important Buddhist scriptures, reinvigorated the monasteries, and trained disciples.

Buddhism continued to gain adherents during the following, generally peaceful centuries. Then in 1240, led by Godan (Köten) Khan, the grandson of Genghis (Chinggis), the Mongols invaded Tibet. After years of looting, in 1249 Godan summoned the Sa-skya Pandit, Tibet's highest religious leader, to ask him to surrender the nation. However, when the Mongol leader met the sage, he was so impressed that he converted to Buddhism. Godan made a deal with Sa-skya Pandit: Godan would be protector of Tibet if the holy man would convert the Mongol khans to Buddhism. It was an offer Sa-skya

Pandit could not refuse. Thereafter, the Mongols used their military power to safeguard Tibet, and Sa-skya Pandit devoted himself to the spiritual training of the khans. This "patron-priest" relationship lasted through the rule of Kublai (Khubilai) Khan and to the end of Mongol hegemony in Tibet in the early 1600s.[21]

In 1578, Sönam Gyatso (1543–88), a major religious leader, visited Altan Khan (1508–82), then a Mongol chieftain. Though it was the waning days of Mongol power (they had abandoned China), at this meeting Altan conferred the title of *ta le* ("ocean"), on Lama (monk) Gyatso, indicating that he was an "ocean of wisdom." With this title, Gyatso assumed both the religious and political leadership of Tibet, which thus became a theocracy. Lama Gyatso's title—*ta le lama*—became Dalai Lama, the title used by all religious and secular leaders of Tibet. Over time, the Dalai Lama was viewed as an incarnation of Avalokiteśvara and thus as an incarnation of the Buddha. From the time of Lama Gyatso, when the Dalai Lama died his Buddha-soul reincarnated in a new Dalai Lama. It was the job of high religious officials to seek out the new incarnation of the Dalai Lama via a system of signs and tests.[22]

Religion and the State in Pre-1949 Tibet

Lama Gyatso was one of the most powerful rulers in Tibetan history. With the strong backing of the departed but neighboring Mongols, Gyatso's rule created a Buddhist theocracy in Tibet, led by the Dalai Lama. The fifth Dalai Lama, Ngawang Losan Gyatso (1617–82), called the "Great Fifth," was an absolute theocrat who exercised his power to unify Tibet.

In 1706, a small Manchu army marched into Tibet, after the Manchus had conquered most of China. The Manchus maintained a presence in Tibet until 1722, when they largely lost interest in it, keeping a low profile and exercising little power. In 1747, a new series of Dalai Lamas once again regained both spiritual and religious power in Tibet. The theocratic reign of the Dalai Lamas lasted 130 years, after which time Tibet began to be governed by a succession of monk regents. At this time, as previously, a period of stable government led foreign nations, particularly China, to abandon their interests in the region.

The Tibetan people greatly resented foreign rule, even though it usually brought a modicum of political stability to the country. Whenever the Mongols, and later the Manchus, quit Tibet, and when the process of choosing a new Dalai Lama was challenged, the instability that resulted often led to strife. Monks from rival monasteries, housing rival Tibetan Buddhist sects, often used extreme violence in contending for power over greater regions of the country. At times, extreme intolerance led to murder and assassination among rival sects.

Global Perspectives

For most of its Buddhist history, the various areas of Tibet were governed by the regional monastery and its head lama. Although a powerful Dalai Lama might govern overall, local governance rested primarily with the regional monastery, which usually owned most of the land in the area. Ordinary Tibetans were essentially serfs who worked the land for the benefit of the monastic landlord. Though there was a tiny "middle class" of merchants and still fewer "free peasants," most Tibetans lived as virtual slaves of the landowner, who could, and often did, mistreat them horribly. To a great extent, Buddhist teachings were used to maintain this unjust and inhumane social system. Theocratic leaders at nearly every level of society instilled in the Tibetan people the idea that their predicament arose from bad karma they had accumulated in previous incarnations. Acceptance of their lifelong misery would rid them of some of this bad karma.

Although Tibet's theocracy was based on the compassionate teachings of the Buddha, it did not always practice these teachings. The mythic image of an ideal "Shangri-La" in the Himalayas is to a great extent a fantasy. Some Dalai Lamas, especially those of the modern age, have been true practitioners of compassionate Buddhism. Yet the theocracy of Tibet has a checkered history in terms of human rights. However, the claim by the Chinese that their "liberation" of Tibet in 1949 arose from an altruistic desire to destroy Tibetan feudalism and that for this reason they were welcomed as saviors by the Tibetan people is equally false.

CHINESE INVASION AND "LIBERATION"

In 1911, Chinese nationalists, led by Sun Yat-sen, overthrew China's Manchu rulers and took over the country. They also cast covetous eyes on Tibet, which they wanted to control primarily for its strategic location, as it shares borders with India, Nepal, Mongolia, and Russia. The new Chinese regime also wanted access to the vast natural resources of Tibet, which in Chinese is called "Xizang," meaning "western treasure house." The nationalists began to claim that Tibet had been a Chinese "vassal" and thus a part of China since the 12th century. The Chinese date this claim from the time that Satya Pandit and Godan Khan entered into their long-lasting "patron-priest" relationship. The fact that this arrangement involved a Mongol chieftain and not a Chinese ruler has always been conveniently overlooked. It was only a few decades after Godan Khan that the Mongols took control of China, thus making China and Tibet part of the same, Mongol-controlled political entity. As one scholar of Tibetan history wrote:

> There is no substance to the [Chinese] claim that Tibet was in unbroken subordination to China from the time of the Mongol dynasty. The link between [Beijing] and Tibet came into being only through the conquest of

RELIGION AND THE STATE

> *China by [the Mongols, who] had already been accepted by the Tibetans as their overlord.... Although the Chinese recovered their own territory from the erstwhile foreign conqueror, they did not take possession of ... nor did they exercise or attempt to exercise any authority in Tibet. China and Tibet had each recovered its independence of the Mongols in its own way and at different times.*[23]

The Chinese claim on Tibet only intensified after the communist revolution of Mao Zedong in 1949. The 13th Dalai Lama, Tupden Gyatso (1876–1933), recognized the threat China posed to Tibetan autonomy and cultural and political independence. He sought to modernize and safeguard Tibet by attempting to create its first standing army, set up a Western-style educational system, and send emissaries to the West both to learn from Westerners and to inform them about conditions in Tibet. Unfortunately, these efforts were defeated by powerful monks, who saw them as a threat to their power and traditional Tibetan culture. On his deathbed in 1933, the Dalai Lama warned that Tibet might perish if his reforms were not implemented.

While the current 14th Dalai Lama, Hlamo Döndrup, was being educated and trained in Lhasa, the Chinese communist leadership announced that China would immediately begin to "liberate" Tibet. In October 1950, 20,000 Chinese soldiers from the People's Liberation Army soon appeared on Tibet's border and quickly crushed the ill-equipped and outnumbered Tibetan forces. The Chinese army began its march toward Lhasa.

The newly installed Dalai Lama immediately appealed to the United Nations to help Tibet repel Chinese aggression, but no nation was willing to provoke a conflict with a country as large and powerful as China to help a tiny and obscure Himalayan nation. It did not help that Tibet was not a member of the United Nations, so its appeal was turned down. The Dalai Lama sought repeatedly to negotiate with the Chinese to find a peaceful arrangement both parties could live with. But the Chinese were intransigent. In September 1951, the Red Army marched into Lhasa. Within months, Tibetans were in the streets protesting the occupation, but all acts of defiance were harshly suppressed. The Chinese tried to convince the Tibetans that they were bringing them progress and real happiness. But it quickly became clear that the ideology of the atheistic and materialistic Chinese was antithetical to Tibetan belief and culture. The more the Chinese expected Tibetans to "see the light" and embrace "progress," the more disillusioned and resentful the Tibetans became. As historian David Patt explains:

Global Perspectives

> *[The Chinese] must have believed their own propaganda, that the Tibetan serfs would rise up and join their Chinese brothers ... to throw off the chains of feudalism. But events proved that the vast chasm that separated Communist China from Buddhist Tibet—in terms of religion, culture, language, history, and political ethos—was so vast, so utterly unbridgeable, that in the end the Chinese must have come to the conclusion that the only way they could liberate Tibet was to destroy it.[24]*

The Dalai Lama accepted an invitation to visit Beijing in 1954, and the talks were reportedly cordial though fruitless. He returned to a Tibet in which communist collectivization was well underway. Chinese troops were confiscating all Tibetan property, temples were being ransacked, monks were being publicly humiliated, and protesters were arrested, beaten, and sometimes killed. Tibetan monks and nuns were publicly tortured and "reactionary elements" were arrested and executed. Thousands of people died. Tibet and its unique culture were being annihilated.

By 1959, the situation had grown so dire, the monks feared for the Dalai Lama. The Chinese leaders feared him because he was a symbol of Tibetan culture and religion around whom Tibetans rallied and from whom they drew the strength to resist. After receiving thinly veiled threats from the Chinese, the Dalai Lama was persuaded to flee the country. Though highly reluctant to leave his people, the Dalai Lama was persuaded that he could do more to save Tibet and its culture from a safe haven outside the country than he could if he remained (and was assassinated). On March 10, 1959, tens of thousands of Tibetans massed outside the Dalai Lama's residence to prevent his capture by the Chinese. The crowds remained for several days, shouting anti-Chinese slogans. On March 14, the Chinese began shelling the area with mortar rounds, to "free" the Dalai Lama from the "reactionary citizens" who "held him captive."[25] That night, disguised as a soldier, the Dalai Lama left his residence and headed out of Tibet toward India. When the Chinese found out about the escape, they immediately dissolved the Tibetan government and took direct and total control of Tibet.

With the Dalai Lama gone, the Chinese embarked on an orgy of destruction aimed at eradicating Tibetan identity and subsuming it under Chinese communist control. Monasteries, temples, and sacred sites were bombed into rubble, and monks and nuns were slaughtered, as were thousands of ordinary Tibetans. The practice of Tibetan Buddhism was forbidden and harshly punished. To end Tibetan resistance, the Chinese government's policy of "population transfer" encouraged hundreds of thousands of ethnic Chinese to settle in Tibet, where their cultural and economic dominance overwhelmed the native population.

RELIGION AND THE STATE

Experts estimate that about 1.2 million Tibetans died or were killed during the first decade of Chinese rule. Of the 6,254 original monasteries, only 13 remained.[26] During the Cultural Revolution of the 1960s, Red Guards invaded Tibet and carried out some of the most harrowing persecutions of traditional Tibetans, with mass executions, widespread torture, and near-total destruction of religious sites and symbols.

Though in the 1970s the Chinese president Deng Xiaoping promised to ease the intense oppression, Chinese policies continued to undermine all things Tibetan. Most expressions of Tibetan Buddhism were severely punished and monks were prohibited from studying or practicing their religion.

EXILE AND UNCERTAINTY

The Dalai Lama settled in the northern Indian town of Dharamsala, where he remains to this day. From this sanctuary, he has tried tirelessly to gain the world's support for Tibetan autonomy. Though millions of ordinary citizens throughout the world support the Tibetan cause, few, if any, national leaders have been willing to confront China in any meaningful way. China is just too economically powerful for anyone to risk a severing of trade over the issue of Tibet.

As conditions in Tibet worsened, more Tibetans fled. Today there are about 100,000 Tibetan refugees living in India, with another 25,000 or so in Nepal, Bhutan, and other nations.[27] Many refugee monks and nuns have attempted, with some success, to establish Tibetan Buddhist monasteries in exile. The exile communities, wherever they are, are trying to keep their culture and religion alive. The guidance of the Dalai Lama is crucial to this effort because he is the center of religious and cultural life.

The Dalai Lama may be a globally respected religious leader, but he is also a pragmatist. Throughout his exile he has tried to compromise with the Chinese government. He has supported a "middle way," in which Tibet would remain part of China and accept Beijing's political control. In exchange, China would grant Tibet enough autonomy to maintain its ethnic, cultural, and religious identity. For example, in 1987, the Dalai Lama proposed a "five point plan" for peace in Tibet, which was lauded by world leaders and won the Dalai Lama the Nobel Peace Prize in 1989, but it was spurned by China. Beginning in the 1980s, Chinese leaders began easing restrictions on Tibetan Buddhist practices and publications. Some monasteries were reopened. Yet anti-Chinese protests and political dissidence continue to be severely punished. To this day, the Chinese fear the power the Dalai Lama has over Tibetans and continually seek to undermine him, both in Tibet and internationally.

For years, the Chinese authorities had refused even to meet with the Dalai Lama, calling him an evil "dog" and a "wolf" who seeks to "split the motherland."[28] The global attention the 2008 Beijing Olympics drew to the plight of Tibet turned out to be an acute embarrassment and source of indignation among Chinese officials. Wherever the Olympic torch touched down, it was met by mass protests against China's treatment of Tibet. The issue could not be ignored by the host nation, which wanted to show the world how enlightened it had become. So in early autumn 2008, Chinese officials agreed to host a delegation sent by the Dalai Lama. The negotiations in Beijing yielded no compromises from the Chinese. Later that year, the Dalai Lama called a mass meeting of Tibetans in exile to have them decide how to proceed. There had been serious protests in Tibet prior to and during the Beijing Olympic games, with violent acts committed by both Tibetans and Chinese police. The Dalai Lama, who condemns all violence, vowed to resign if the violence continued. However, he recognized that his "middle path" of reasonable negotiation to achieve autonomy for Tibet was just not working. He would accede to the wishes expressed by the convening exiles, and he offered to step down as Dalai Lama. After much debate about whether Tibetans should fight for their independence, the exiles decided that they would continue to pursue negotiations. They also refused to accept the resignation of the Dalai Lama.

The Dalai Lama has said that he will likely choose not to reincarnate because the Chinese occupation of Tibet makes the system of discovering the new Dalai Lama impossible. The current Dalai Lama has suggested that it might be preferable to have elections to choose future Dalai Lamas. He has also supported a transformation of Tibet's political system from a theocracy to a democracy. Many Tibetans also support this vision. It would alter some important aspects of Tibetan culture, which is so imbued with religion. It would also limit the hugely important influence of religion on the state. Yet it would guarantee a clean break with a feudal past and align Tibet politically with the world's advanced democracies. Unfortunately, there is little likelihood that communist China would tolerate any political—let alone democratic—transformation in Tibet.

HINDU NATIONALISM IN INDIA

On January 30, 1948, Mohandas K. Gandhi (1869–1948), the revered spiritual and independence leader of India, was walking to a prayer meeting at his compound in New Delhi when a man emerged from the crowd that had come to see and honor the Mahatma ("great soul"). The man calmly pulled out a gun and fired four shots point-blank into the Mahatma's body. Gandhi died instantly. Millions of Indians were in shock at the cold-blooded murder of the man who had shown the world that ahimsa, nonviolence, could overthrow an empire and free a nation. Added to their shock was the dread that the assassin would be a Muslim. Had this been the case, the horrific ethnic violence that was torturing the newly partitioned nation (Pakistan had been created for Indian Muslims) would get immeasurably worse. So, in some ways, it was a relief when the assassin, who gave himself up at the scene of the crime, turned out to be a Hindu. Relief turned to anxiety and confusion as Hindus tried to understand why one of their own had murdered the most beloved Hindu leader of all time.

Gandhi's assassin, Nathuram Godse, was a member of the RSS (Rashitriya Swayamsevak Sangh/National Volunteers Association), a militant anti-Muslim, Hindu nationalist organization. Formed in 1925, the RSS was just one of a number of groups that believed India should be a strictly Hindu nation. At his trial in early 1948, just three months after independence, Godse proudly proclaimed that the murder was motivated by Gandhi's "consistent pandering to the Muslims . . . [and the] vivisection of our motherland." Godse said he hoped that with Gandhi dead "the nation would be saved from the inroads of Pakistan . . . [and become the] land of the Hindus."[29] Godse, a martyr for Hindu nationalism, sang songs to the Hindu Motherland as he cheerfully marched to his death on the gallows.

A Brief History of Hindu Nationalism

The drive toward Hindu nationalism arose as part of the Indian independence movement. Hindu nationalists, who seek to regain a true, or "pure," Indian identity, argue that throughout its history, India has been a single civilization that has absorbed the invading "other." *Hindutva*, a term coined in 1915 by V. D. Savarkar (1883–1966), defines the identity of the true Indian as encompassing not just Hinduism as a religion but the complete history and culture of Hindu civilization. All who lived within this civilization, from the Indus River to the Bay of Bengal, since ancient times, such as Sikhs, Jains, and Buddhists, are part of the Hindutva if they identify with this civilization and with the birthplace of Hinduism, the holy land of India. All differences in geography, religion, ethnicity, or language (there are 16 official languages in India) are subsumed within the essential oneness of Hindu culture. Savarkar defined the Hindus as a race united by "common blood" from which Muslims and Christians are excluded. These foreign invaders are the "other" who must be dominated.

For some nationalist groups, the Hindu religion, not its culture, takes precedence above all else; for them Hinduism is the foundation of identity, maintains the fabric of society, and should inform governance while unifying the nation under one religion. Through Hindutva, the nationalists seek "not simply to conserve Hinduism but to develop the latent power of the Hindu community" whose goal is "promoting the unity *(sangathan)* of Hindus as a political entity."[30]

In a philosophy redolent of modern Islamic fundamentalism, some Hindu nationalist groups reject modern Hinduism as contaminated by imperial and Western influences and look back to Hinduism's ancient roots as an "ideal" period when the religion was "pure." It is this idealized religious state (or *dharma-raja,* dharmic kingdom) that the nationalists seek to re-create via a unified Hindu community. Hindu nationalism even gained the support of respected spiritual teachers who were caught up in the independence movements of their time, though their expressions of nationalism in no way compromised their spiritual teachings. The ideology was expounded in the late 1890s by Swami Vivekananda (1863–1902) through his concept of the "religion of patriotism," which identifies Mother India with the Supreme God, reinstates the active role of Kshatriyas (the warrior caste) in fighting to re-create the ideal Hindu state, and sees Indian Hinduism's destiny as teaching the world about the one true spiritual reality. Empires may come and go, the swami explained, but the ideal Indian civilization based on pure Hinduism remains "indestructible and eternal." Later, Aurobindo Ghose (1872–1950) would cite the Bhagavad Gita (a holy Hindu text) as the only legitimate basis for both religion and politics. He believed that "the nation [India] was a divine expression of God . . . [so that] nationalism is a religion that has come from God."[31]

HINDUISM AND THE STATE IN INDIA

The diversity of Hindu worship has generally made Hindus highly tolerant of other religions and able to absorb or ignore the religions of the many different peoples who came to conquer or settle India. The primary unifying aspect of Hinduism was, and to some extent still is, that it gives structure to Hindu society. From its earliest days, Hinduism established one of the most rigid caste systems in the world. Kings were regarded as divine, but they maintained their legitimacy only via the consent of the highest social caste, the Brahmins, or priests. The king earned legitimacy by ruling in accordance with Hindu scripture and the dharma as prescribed by the Brahmins.

This method of governance prevailed for centuries in India. It also was a good fit with the manner of kingship of the Muslim Mughal emperors who conquered and ruled India (1526–1857). Only after the fall of the Mughal Empire and the ascendancy of the British Raj did the religiously based rule of Brahmins and princes begin to unravel. Yet the British bureaucracy in India paved the way for the democratic government that followed independence. Hindutva arose in reaction to the weakening of traditional Indian society under the British. Indian Hindus had for so long lived under foreign, non-Hindu rule that some independence groups insisted that only a Hindu-based government was suitable or acceptable in India. That India had by then become a very religiously diverse society made achieving the goals of Hindutva, especially within a democracy, highly problematic. The constitution approved after independence ensured that the Indian state would be secular and religiously inclusive, a state the supporters of Hindutva found hard to accept.

MODERN HINDU NATIONALISM

Over the millennia, India has absorbed peoples with different cultures and religions. Although 80 percent of its 1.15 billion people are Hindu, India is home to more than 130 million Muslims, and small but significant populations of Sikhs, Jains, and Christians.[32] Because of its diversity, India's first independent government determined that a secular state, separate from all religions, would best serve the multicultural, multiethnic population. The constitution approved under India's first president, Jawaharlal Nehru of the Congress Party, codified the separation of religion and the state and established a clearly secular government—a polity that has been challenged by Hindu nationalists ever since. They have also fought for changing the constitution to eliminate its affirmative-action provisions intended to help low-caste Hindus and ethnic minorities, including Muslims and Dalits (Untouchables), achieve parity with more privileged sectors of society.

Gandhi was assassinated by a Hindu extremist who rejected ahimsa and instead promoted *himsa,* violence, carried out by militant Kshatriyas to rid the nation of the "other" so that an ideal Hindutva state might be created. Since 1948, a number of more or less militant Hindu nationalist organizations have arisen. Some have faded away, others have evolved into major players in modern Indian politics. The Jana Sangh, Indian People's Party, was formed in the 1950s. It viewed as Hindus all Indians who identified with an ancient, Sanskrit-based cultural heritage. The 1960s saw the rise of the Shiv Sena (Hindu Nationalist Party), a virulently anti-Muslim organization. In 1977, the Jana Sangh disintegrated and some of its members regrouped to form the Bharatiya Janata Party (BJP, Hindu People's Party), which has become a powerful force in modern Indian politics.

The BJP aligns itself strongly with the worship of Rama as the supreme incarnation of Vishnu. Rama worship has been a major form of Hinduism in northern India since the 11th century and throughout India since the 13th. The story of Rama is told in the Hindu scriptural epic the Ramayana. In the epic, Rama is the ideal dharmic king who rules over the perfect Hindu kingdom, or Rama-Raj. As the highest avatar of Vishnu, Rama had been worshipped as the embodiment of the ideal Hindu man and hero-king, an avatar filled with love and compassion. However, the nationalist form of Rama worship reflects significant changes. Prior to the 20th century, Rama worship involved a deep, spiritual love of this benevolent god, a form of bhakti yoga. Since being adopted by Hindu nationalists, Rama no longer represents devotion and compassion; instead, Rama has been transformed into an aggressive Kshatriya "holy warrior" who fights for Hindutva. Whereas in the epic Rama battles and overcomes the demon Ravana, modern nationalists depict Rama as annihilating Muslims.

The modern cult of Rama is germane because of the symbolic importance nationalists have given to the god's supposed birthplace in the town of Ayodhya in Uttar Pradesh in northern India. A temple to Rama once stood on this most sacred spot in India where the avatar was born. Nationalists contend that when Babur and the Mughals conquered India, they deliberately destroyed this temple and built a mosque on the site to insult Hindus. Ayodhya has become a flashpoint and rallying cry for Hindu nationalists who use it to stir up anti-Muslim sentiment. The Congress Party preserved the Ayodhya mosque as a national symbol of India's multicultural secularism and tolerance. But in December 1992 a mob of about 300,000 fanatical Hindu nationalists attacked the mosque and destroyed it completely. They built a small shrine to Rama on the rubble-strewn site. The attack, instigated by the BJP, was followed by days of rioting that left more than 1,500 people, mostly Muslims, dead.[33]

Building on growing Hindu militancy, the BJP began to broaden its electoral appeal. After years of only modest gains in the Indian parliament, in 1998 the BJP gained control of the government, and the BJP candidate A. B. Vajpayee became prime minister. For the first time in decades, the Congress Party lost control of government. One BJP supporter explained the victory: "The Congress policy of appeasement has merely widened national resistance and has gravely jeopardized the legitimate rights of Hindus."[34] Yet once in power, Vajpayee toned down his BJP nationalist rhetoric and policies; he did not want a religious civil war occurring on his watch.

Violence engendered violence, especially in the BJP stronghold of Gujarat State. On February 27, 2002, a small mob attacked a train full of Hindus returning from a pilgrimage to Ayodhya. Though the exact circumstances remain unclear, when the train was in the tiny station of Godhra, several cars were set alight. At least 58 people, mostly women and children, were trapped in the train cars and burned to death. The BJP immediately accused Muslims of planning and carrying out this horrific carnage, though this has never been proven.[35]

Revenge for the atrocity was meticulously planned and carried out by members and supporters of the BJP. Between February 28 and March 2, militia-like Hindu mobs descended on the city of Ahmedabad, in Gujarat, with the sole aim of killing Muslims. That the attacks were planned in advance was proved by the computer printouts each attacker carried listing the name and address of every Muslim home, shop, and business in the city. Chanting anti-Muslim and Hindu nationalist slogans, the attackers, armed with swords, spears, firearms, gas cylinders, and explosives, hunted down and slaughtered more than 2,000 Muslim men, women, and children. Human Rights Watch detailed the brutality and according to its report, "Women were gang-raped before being killed. Children were burned alive . . . most bodies were burned and butchered beyond recognition. Many were missing body parts."[36] The police not only ignored calls for help, they provided cover for the bloodthirsty mob. National security forces, too, failed to respond to the days of bloodshed until long after the event ended.[37]

Ashok Singal, president of the nationalist World Hindu Council, called the massacre "a victory for Hindu society." An RSS official explained, "Let Muslims understand that their safety lies in the goodwill of the majority."[38] Most BJP leaders felt that it was wiser not to comment on the attacks, which in time became a source of some national shame and international scandal.

The public seemed to reject militant Hindu nationalism in the 2004 elections, when the BJP lost to the Congress Party and Manmohan Singh became India's first non-Hindu prime minister. Even the BJP's Ayodhya candidate lost the election, and the party no longer dominates government in its stronghold of Gujarat. However, some Hindu extremists claim they did not vote BJP because Vajpayee had been too "soft" on Muslims and insufficiently supportive of Hindu nationalist aims. Some analysts see the Congress victory as the expression of an electorate fearful of possible reprisals by Muslims or their turning to violent Islamic extremism. Others view it as an affirmation of the Indian people's dedication to pluralism and democracy. Whatever the case, ethnic tensions in India remain high. It is possible that as India's economy grows and modernization accelerates, ethnic conflict may abate. The tug of war between 21st-century secularism and the dream of re-creating the Rama-Raj may be resolved if India finds a way to meld its glorious cultural heritage with educational and economic opportunities for all its citizens.

Public repudiation of the BJP was evident after the May 2009 national elections, which were won handily by the Congress Party. In fact, Congress gained twice as many votes as it had in 2004, while the BJP lost 22 percent of its support.[39] The monthlong elections, in which at least 700 million people voted, were viewed as a repudiation of the BJP's polarizing nationalism.

Global Perspectives

WESTERN EUROPE: SECULARISM AND THE PARADOX OF TOLERANCE

The Muslim populations of Europe immigrated to their respective countries mainly from former colonies. Thus, the majority of French Muslims came from Algeria and other parts of North Africa; British Muslims hail mainly from India and Pakistan. The first wave of migration occurred in the 1950s and '60s, as Europe was rebuilding its bombed-out industries and needed to import a large, unskilled labor force. The original immigrant population was mainly adult males who worked in factories. It eventually became clear that these "temporary" workers were needed long term and would not be returning to their native countries. Humanitarian policies were instituted that permitted the wives and families of these workers to immigrate as well. In a short time, a large population of European-born offspring swelled the number of immigrants.

It is the changing demographics of Europe that has many white, Christian Europeans worried. A society must maintain a birthrate of at least 2.0 (two children per woman) to keep it from dying out. On average, the birthrate for white Europeans is 1.4. In contrast, each Muslim woman in Europe produces 3.5 children. If current trends continue, by 2050, 30 percent of Europe's population will be Muslim.[40] This burgeoning population, which could one day surpass that of white Europeans, has profound and, to some, troubling implications—especially regarding the nature of the state and the continuation of long-held Enlightenment values.

European Commissioner Fritz Bolkestein commented in 2004, "[E]ither Islam gets Europeanized or Europe gets Islamized.... The problem is not whether the majority of Europeans is Islamic but rather which Islam—*shari'a* Islam or Euro-Islam—is to dominate in Europe."[41] What frightens some white Europeans is not only the possible imposition of a sharia Islam in Europe (creating "Eurabia") but also that they might become a minority in their own country. This anxiety is exacerbated by the perceived chasm between European and Islamic values. Today, Europe is viewed by many as the most secular, nonreligious place on Earth. Religious observance and identification has plummeted among white Europeans, and many churches fear the total disappearance of Christianity in Europe. Plummeting church attendance supports this view. In the 1950s, church attendance among European Protestants hovered around 60 to 70 percent, on average, with similar or greater numbers for those attending weekly Catholic mass. In most of Europe by 2000 or so, less than 20 percent of Protestants and Catholics were believed to attend church weekly. In Ireland, half of Catholics (down from about 90 percent in the 1970s) and in Italy only about one-third of Catholics attend Sunday mass.[42] In a sense, secularism is the new European religion, though Christianity has strong historical and cultural traditions. Secularism is based on core Enlightenment values of individual liberty, freedom of speech and belief, tolerance, and gender equality. To the extent that the European Muslim population accepts these core values, they smoothly and peacefully assimilate into European culture. However, many of these secular values are antithetical to Muslim teachings that, thus, pose a direct challenge to European society. Though the majority of Europe's Muslims seek to harmonize their religion and way of life with Western mores, there is a sector of the Muslim population that confronts or rejects traditional Western values; in an estimated 3 percent of western European mosques, militant anti-Western extremism is openly preached.[43]

European v. Muslim Customs

The most obvious difference is perhaps the least immediately threatening: the Muslim belief that religion must be an integral part of the state and inform its policies. There are some radical extremists who do denounce democracy as un-Islamic because the rule of the majority undermines religious law. Most European Muslims, however, are content to be allowed to freely practice their religion and live a good Muslim life within their community. Actual conflict has come from what might be considered more mundane differences: the family, for instance. In the West, where religion and the state are strictly separate, civil law determines acceptable behavior within families. Islamic laws regarding family are sometimes in direct conflict with related secular laws and values. Polygamy, domestic violence (particularly wife-beating), and honor killings (the murder by relatives of a woman who is seen to have compromised her chastity by, for example, being alone with a male nonrelative) are all believed by some to be sanctioned by Islamic scripture, yet all are anathema to Western customs and laws. In many parts of Europe, governments maintain a respect for multiculturalism (another linchpin of secularism) to the extent that they discourage law enforcement from intervening in cases of polygamy or domestic violence, as such interference is considered an infringement of both cultural and (male) individual rights, as well as an erosion of tolerance for other cultures. Yet to the extent that governments tolerate certain of other cultures' customs they undermine some of their own core values.

The same holds true for freedom of speech. Several famous incidents illustrate the divergence of views on this principle. The first is the well-known Muslim condemnation of Salman Rushdie's *The Satanic Verses* in response to the Ayatollah Khomeini's death sentence against the author. When the fatwa was issued, thousands of Muslims took to the streets of European cities to protest the book's alleged insult to Islam. Virtually all Western writers, journalists, and libertarians were vehement in their defense of freedom of expression, even if that expression might be viewed by some as offensive. A similar but opposite unanimity was found among Europe's (and the world's) Muslims, only some of whom supported the fatwa but many of whom wanted the book banned for blasphemy. European blasphemy laws had not been invoked for decades, if not longer. The Egyptian Nobel Prize–winning writer Naguib Mahfouz supported the Muslim majority, saying "different cultures have different attitudes towards freedom of speech. What might be endured in Western cultures might not be acceptable in Muslim countries."[44] Yet, the question must be asked: To what extent must Muslims resident in the West accede to Western standards of freedom?

The second infamous incident occurred in 2005, when the Danish newspaper *Jyllands-Posten* published 12 cartoons lampooning Islam and Muslims. The most insulting cartoon showed the prophet Muhammad with a bomb in his turban. Muslims throughout Europe rioted; Christian churches were burned and people were killed during violent protests in Pakistan, Libya, and Nigeria. In Britain, some protests were peaceful, though many younger and more militant demonstrators carried placards declaring "Behead those who insult Islam," "Europe you will pay—your 9/11 is on its way," and similarly threatening messages. Many Western observers dubbed the protests the "cartoon jihad" to belittle what they viewed as a petty overreaction to a silly cartoon in a second-rate rag.[45] In the aftermath of the incident, law enforcement officials in Britain and other European nations uncovered domestic terrorist plots to retaliate against this unforgivable insult to Islam. While many in the chattering classes lectured or wrote about the impossibility of assimilating anti–free speech Muslims into Western society, European Muslim leaders pointed out hypocrisies that go unnoticed by most Westerners. For example, cartoons or other published materials that are clearly anti-Semitic, racist, or offensive to homosexuals elicit righteous outrage from the champions of secularism. If hate speech is now illegal in much of the West, why should Muslims be condemned for finding certain speech offensive? It was, they declared, a clear double standard. Citing anti-Semitic cartoons in German newspapers of the 1930s, the German writer Günter Grass wrote, "Where does the West come by all this arrogance in dictating what is right and wrong?"[46]

The ultimate threat to free speech occurred with the murder of the Dutch filmmaker Theo van Gogh after he made *Submission* (2004), a searing attack against Muslim treatment of women. Van Gogh's assassin, Mohammed Bouyeri, pinned a note to the dead man's body warning that others faced the same fate if they used a religious and scriptural context to condemn Islamic customs. To say that this murder had a chilling effect on free speech is an understatement. Individuals and governments worried openly about the effects death threats would have on self-censorship and the freedom of expression that is central to public discourse in a democracy. One European Union justice minister was so shaken by the murder, he suggested that the media accept a voluntary "code of conduct" when referring to Muslims or Islam, so that "the press will give the Muslim world the message: We are aware of the consequences of exercising the right of free expression, we can and we are ready to self-regulate that right."[47] Needless to say, his remarks were greeted with outrage and horror by those who legitimately feared losing one of the West's most cherished rights. Most nations dissociated themselves from the minister's remarks. Yet the situation remains unresolved. Is it possible to practice free speech when members of your society may kill you for doing so? Should the state rein in freedom of expression to "protect" the sensibilities of some citizens (as it has done with hate speech), or must all citizens come to accept that they may find some speech personally or communally offensive?

Britain: Taking Tolerance Too Far?

In recent decades, many Muslims entering Britain (and other European countries) have been asylum seekers, those who flee their native country to avoid persecution, prison, and torture because of their religious or political beliefs. Britain is viewed as one of the most tolerant and generous nations in admitting asylum seekers. However, its famed hospitality has been offered to some of the world's most extreme Islamist radicals, known terrorists who faced prison in their home countries because of their violent actions or extremist views. These extremists soon learn that Britain is free speech heaven. Whereas the threat of jail or torture forced them to voice their views clandestinely in their home countries, Britain's absolute commitment to freedom of speech and religion allows them to advocate for their extreme Islamist views openly. There are several mosques in Britain where many of the world's most ardent promoters (if not proven actors) of terrorism have preached their message of violent jihad against targeted Muslim nations and for the establishment of sharia law in Europe.

The British government's seeming unwillingness to impinge on freedom of religion or speech has riled many moderate British Muslims. Muhammed Sifaoui, a British Muslim writer, noted that "[T]he most sought-after terrorists in the world have found shelter in the UK [where] they propagate their ideology ... The majority of young guys ... who left to go to training camps in Afghanistan ... went through London to Pakistan ... to Afghanistan."[48] The despairing parents of disaffected Muslim youths complain that the preaching of these radical Islamists may turn their impressionable, surly teenagers into Islamic extremists, or even global or domestic terrorists. While Islam obliges Muslim immigrants not to harm a host "infidel" nation that welcomes them, second- and third-generation Muslim youth are under no such obligation. As described by the author Aatish Sateer, "Most of our [radicalized] . . . youth are British citizens. They owe nothing to the Government. They did not ask to be born here; neither did they ask to be protected by Britain."[49] High unemployment and racism make these young Muslims easy targets for radical recruiters.

Britain's super-tolerance drives other nations to distraction. It is not only the radicals' home nations (Egypt, Saudi Arabia) that want these supposed extremists extradited and tried. It is also other Western nations that fear that Britain's policies make it a breeding ground for the export of terrorism. A French intelligence agent believes that Britain's openness and the subsequent establishment of extremist groups and networks there poses "an immediate, grave, and specific risk to the survival of our democracy and constitutional order."[50]

Yet there may be method in this perceived madness. British intelligence officials claim that by allowing Islamic extremist groups to operate openly, they are much easier to monitor and infiltrate. British intelligence has uncovered and foiled a number of planned attacks through careful surveillance of mosques known to harbor radicals. When extremist preaching gets too violent, the offender(s) may be arrested or deported. Yet extremists are given asylum mainly because the British are so committed to human rights and due process of law, two cornerstones of Western secularism rarely found in Muslim nations. The fact is, some so-called extremists were actually political dissidents who opposed authoritarian regimes at home. Some were arrested, jailed, and tortured on trumped-up charges and without due process. The British have chosen to give asylum seekers the benefit of the doubt. If they occasionally err by admitting a true extremist, they feel that is preferable to compromising their secular humanitarian principles.

France's "Homogenized" Citizens

Most French Muslims come from North Africa, especially France's former colonies in Morocco and Algeria. The first wave of immigrants had supported the French military against the Algerian independence movement and emigrated for political asylum. Today, many come from the same region and from former colonies in West Africa for economic reasons. France has the largest Muslim population in Europe: about 5 million, or one-tenth of the population (and growing). The nature of the French state, and its constitution, make peaceful assimilation of its Muslim population highly problematic.

RELIGION AND THE STATE

France's Muslims obviously have a different cultural and religious background from native French people. However, there are also distinct differences among Muslims hailing from North and West Africa. Though all are part of the *umma*, their cultural and religious differences serve to separate rather than unite them. Since the French Revolution, France's constitution has mandated a policy of total *egalité* (equality) that essentially views all French people as being the same—everyone is fully French, no one gets special treatment because differences are papered over or ignored. The goal is to mold everyone into a French person and meld all together into a "homogenized" French society. This attitude refuses to acknowledge that some groups have special disadvantages that the government needs to address. Thus, as industries shuttered and unemployment skyrocketed in France's *banlieues* (poor suburban immigrant enclaves), no action was taken to ameliorate the situation.

To complicate matters, the French Religious Affairs Bureau deals with the nation's religious groups via the national association each group forms to interact with the government. It was only after 1981 that Muslims began forming religious associations, but these have been mostly local. The French Muslim community has been too fragmented to set aside their differences and create a national association. Lack of formal input with the government prevents the community from getting needed assistance and further alienates Muslims from mainstream French society.

The principle of a secular society in France *(laïcité)* protects religious freedom but refuses to countenance religious activity that flouts French law. This has led to conflict between Muslims who want to follow Islamic law and what is written in the French legal code. Polygamy among West African immigrants is one example. Charles Pasqua, a former French minister of the interior, has said that "There must be a French Islam," but one that does not "challenge the integrity of French society."[51]

The French "affair of the headscarf" has drawn international attention. Ongoing since 1989, the affair began when three Muslim girls wore traditional headscarves *(hijab)* to school. Religious symbols are strictly prohibited in French schools, and the girls were told to either take off the *hijab* or face expulsion. The prohibition on religious symbols dates from Voltaire (1694–1778), a leading philosopher of the Enlightenment, and was originally intended to curb the power of the Catholic Church. *Laïcité* mandates that all religions be treated equally and prohibits the state from supporting religious schools; the *hijab* purportedly tinged schools with religion. Muslims responded that the *hijab* is not a religious but a cultural symbol, so *laïcité* does not apply. They argued that prohibiting wearing of the *hijab* was an infringement of their freedom of expression. The French counterargument emphasized the role of schools to "imbue students with a common dedication to French culture" and that the role of French education is "incompatible with the preservation of immigrant cultures."[52]

The *hijab* became a symbol of Muslim identity and independence. It became a cause célèbre as more and more girls began wearing it to school. Outraged teachers and some sectors of the public began viewing the *hijab* as a symbol of Islamic extremism. As the conflict escalated, the appeal of Jean-Marie Le Pen and his right-wing, anti-immigration National Front Party spread widely among growing numbers of "nativist" French. Then in 1994, the French government issued a decree stating that religious symbols would be allowed in schools unless they were "outrageous, ostentatious, or meant to proselytize."[53] School principals were left to interpret this vague pronouncement on their own. No one was satisfied, and wearing the *hijab* continues to be a hot-button issue in France.

The French insistence on *laïcité*, as well as increasing racism and xenophobia, has left France with the least assimilated immigrant population in Europe. Neglected by the state, the large population of young, unemployed Muslims in the nation's impoverished *banlieues* has led to smoldering unrest and outbreaks of violence. Many Muslims claim that racism is rampant; as one anonymous unemployed youth said, "... with a name like mine, I couldn't even get an interview; they take one look at my name and I have no chance [at getting a job]."[54] As in many other urban ghettos in the West, some kids turn to gangs, crime, or drug dealing to earn money. Even if they do not, there is ample evidence that nonwhite French youths are disproportionately targeted and abused by the police. "Muslims are at the bottom of the social heap," Areski Dahmani of the Muslim France Plus organization said, "because France has no policy to end racial discrimination and massive unemployment."[55] Despite adoption of a Charter of Muslim Faith that affords Muslims greater participation and voice in government, the social and economic situation in the *banlieues* has worsened.

In November 2005, the world watched as angry youths from France's *banlieues* rioted. Night after night, cars were set aflame around France. The riots were sparked when two young boys were electrocuted while climbing a metal fence to escape the police; the boys had done nothing wrong. The *banlieues* erupted. Protesters threw Molotov cocktails, setting alight non-Muslim stores. Police were bombarded with rocks, and arsonists burned parts of more than 30 French suburbs. Then minister of the interior (now president) Nicolas Sarkozy denounced the rioters as scum *(racaille),* which only made matters worse. Newspaper headlines screamed that the intifada (uprising) had come to France or that jihadists were on the verge of conquering the country. Yet the riots were instigated by economic deprivation and racial discrimination; they were not a call for jihad.

After things settled down, analyses showed that the riots were not wholly Muslim. As described by Philip Jenkins, experts reported that "The chief causes were found in issues of class and race, flaws in education and housing, perceptions of official racism and police brutality."[56] To address these issues, the government should acknowledge that racism exists, revise its view of a homogenized French citizenry, and act to redress the grievances of distinct sectors of society. Philip Jenkins argues that the secular *laïcité* should be eased to assimilate cultural differences into French society. Issues of racism, unemployment, and police brutality must be dealt with in France, as in other Western nations, to foster peaceful coexistence between Islamic belief and the core values of the secular state.

---

[1] Michael Axworthy. *Empire of the Mind: A History of Iran.* New York: Perseus Books, 2008, p. 260.

[2] Patrick Clawson and Michael Rubin. *Eternal Iran: Continuity and Chaos.* New York: Palgrave Macmillan, 2005, p. 40.

[3] Stephen Kinzer. *All the Shah's Men: An American Coup and the Roots of Middle East Terror.* New York: John Wiley & Sons, 2003, p. 93.

[4] Kinzer, p. 125.

[5] Milton Viorst. *In the Shadow of the Prophet: The Struggle for the Soul of Islam.* New York: Anchor Books, 1998, p. 187.

[6] Viorst, pp. 189–190.

[7] Axworthy, p. 256.

[8] Viorst, p. 192.

[9] Viorst, p. 193.

[10] Robin Wright. *In the Name of God: The Khomeini Decade.* New York: Touchstone, 1989, pp. 26–27.

[11] Viorst, p. 195.

[12] Viorst, p. 201.

[13] Robin Wright. *Dreams and Shadows: The Future of the Middle East.* New York: Penguin, 2008, p. 318.

[14] Wright. *Dreams and Shadows,* pp. 316, 330.

[15] Axworthy, pp. 271–272.

[16] Fareed Zakaria. "Theocracy and Its Discontents." *Newsweek* 153 (6/29/09), no. 26, p. 30.

[17] Zakaria, p. 30.

Global Perspectives

[18] Robin Wright. *Sacred Rage: The Wrath of Militant Islam.* New York: Simon & Schuster, 1985, p. 162.

[19] Viorst, p. 214.

[20] John Powers. *Introduction to Tibetan Buddhism.* Ithaca, N.Y.: Snow Lion Publications, 1995, p. 122.

[21] Powers, pp. 139–140, 146.

[22] Powers, pp. 162–164.

[23] Powers, p. 140.

[24] Powers, p. 172.

[25] Powers, p. 175.

[26] Powers, p. 181.

[27] Powers, p. 177.

[28] Powers, p. 185.

[29] Pankaj Mishra. "The Other Face of Fanaticism." *New York Times* (2/2/03). Available online. URL: http://www.nytimes.com/2003/02/02/magazine/the-other-face-of-fanaticism.html. Accessed March 13, 2009.

[30] Arun K. Swamy. "Hindu Nationalism: What's Religion Got to Do with It?" Asia-Pacific Center for Security Studies (March 2003). Available online. URL: http://www.apcss.org/Publications/Ocasional%20Papers/OPHinduNationalism.pdf. Accessed March 12, 2009.

[31] Tapio Tamminen. "Hindu Revivalism and the Hindutva Movement." *Temenos* 32 (1996). Available online. URL: http://web.abo.fi/comprel/temenos/temeno32/tamminen.htm. Accessed March 9, 2009.

[32] India. CIA Factbook. Available online. URL: http://www.cia.gov/library/publications/the-world-factbook/in.html. Accessed March 13, 2009.

[33] Sharif Shuja. "Indian Secularism: Image and Reality." *Contemporary Review* 287 (July 2005), no. 1674, p. 39.

[34] Swamy. "Hindu Nationalism."

[35] Celia W. Dugger. "The World: Gandhi's Dream and India's Latest Nightmare." *New York Times* (3/10/02). Available online. URL: http://nytimes.com/gst/fullpage.html?res=9500EFDC1F30F933A25750C0A9649C8B63. Accessed March 16, 2009.

[36] Mishra, "The Other Face of Fanaticism."

[37] Shuja, "Indian Secularism."

[38] Mishra, "The Other Face of Fanaticism."

[39] Indian Election Results. News bulletin on the home page of Bloomberg News. Available online: URL: http://www.bloomberg.com. Accessed May 18, 2009. See also BBC News. Available online. URL: http://news.bbc.co.uk/2/hi/south_asia/8055055.stm. Accessed May 18, 2009.

[40] Philip Jenkins. *God's Continent: Christianity, Islam, and Europe's Religious Crisis.* New York: Oxford University Press, 2007, p. 8.

[41] Jenkins, p. 4.

[42] Jenkins, pp. 27–32.

[43] Jenkins, p. 220.

[44] John L. Esposito. *The Islamic Threat: Myth or Reality?* New York: Oxford University Press, 1999, p. 250.

[45] Jenkins, p. 238.

[46] Jenkins, p. 240.

[47] Jenkins, p. 241.

[48] Jenkins, p. 223.

[49] Jenkins, p. 219.

[50] Jenkins, p. 221.

[51] Viorst, p. 282.

[52] Viorst, p. 286.

[53] Viorst, p. 287.

[54] Viorst, p. 153.

[55] Viorst, p. 294.

[56] Jenkins, p. 177.

PART II

Primary Sources

4

United States Documents

The documents contained in this section relate to issues of religion and the state in the United States, from its inception to current issues. As indicated, some documents are excerpts taken from the longer originals.

"The Virginia Act for Establishing Religious Freedom" by Thomas Jefferson, 1786

This act was written by Jefferson three years after he wrote the Declaration of Independence. Though fiercely opposed by some who thought the state should help support all religious institutions, the act passed the Virginia legislature in 1786, when Jefferson was in Paris as the U.S. ambassador to France.

> Well aware that Almighty God hath created the mind free; that all attempts to influence it by temporal punishments or burdens, or by civil incapacitations, tend only to beget habits of hypocrisy and meanness, and are a departure from the plan of the Holy Author of our religion, who being Lord both of body and mind, yet chose not to propagate it by coercions on either, as was in his Almighty power to do; that the impious presumption of legislators and rulers, civil as well as ecclesiastical, who, being themselves but fallible and uninspired men, have assumed dominion over the faith of others, setting up their own opinions and modes of thinking as the only true and infallible, and as such endeavoring to impose them on others, hath established and maintained false religions over the greatest part of the world, and through all time; that to compel a man to furnish contributions of money for the propagation of opinions which he disbelieves, is sinful and tyrannical; that even the forcing him to support this or that teacher of his own religious persuasion, is depriving him of the comfortable liberty of giving his contributions to the particular pastor whose morals he would make his pattern, and whose powers he feels most persuasive to righteousness, and is withdrawing from the ministry those

RELIGION AND THE STATE

temporal rewards, which proceeding from an approbation of their personal conduct, are an additional incitement to earnest and unremitting labors for the instruction of mankind; that our civil rights have no dependence on our religious opinions, more than our opinions in physics or geometry; that, therefore, the proscribing any citizen as unworthy the public confidence by laying upon him an incapacity of being called to the offices of trust and emolument, unless he profess or renounce this or that religious opinion, is depriving him injuriously of those privileges and advantages to which in common with his fellow citizens he has a natural right; that it tends also to corrupt the principles of that very religion it is meant to encourage, by bribing, with a monopoly of worldly honors and emoluments, those who will externally profess and conform to it; that though indeed these are criminal who do not withstand such temptation, yet neither are those innocent who lay the bait in their way; that to suffer the civil magistrate to intrude his powers into the field of opinion and to restrain the profession or propagation of principles, on the supposition of their ill tendency, is a dangerous fallacy, which at once destroys all religious liberty, because he being of course judge of that tendency, will make his opinions the rule of judgment, and approve or condemn the sentiments of others only as they shall square with or differ from his own; that it is time enough for the rightful purposes of civil government, for its officers to interfere when principles break out into overt acts against peace and good order; and finally, that truth is great and will prevail if left to herself, that she is the proper and sufficient antagonist to error, and has nothing to fear from the conflict, unless by human interposition disarmed of her natural weapons, free argument and debate, errors ceasing to be dangerous when it is permitted freely to contradict them.

Be it therefore enacted by the General Assembly, That no man shall be compelled to frequent or support any religious worship, place, or ministry whatsoever, nor shall be enforced, restrained, molested, or burdened in his body or goods, nor shall otherwise suffer on account of his religious opinions or belief; but that all men shall be free to profess, and by argument to maintain, their opinions in matters of religion, and that the same shall in nowise diminish, enlarge, or affect their civil capacities.

And though we well know this Assembly, elected by the people for the ordinary purposes of legislation only, have no powers equal to our own and that therefore to declare this act irrevocable would be of no effect in law, yet we are free to declare, and do declare, that the rights hereby asserted are of the natural rights of mankind, and that if any act shall be hereafter passed to repeal the present or to narrow its operation, such act will be an infringement of natural right.

Source: Available online. URL: http://www.religiousfreedom.lib.virginia.edu/sacred/vaact.html. Accessed November 26, 2008.

The "Wall of Separation Letter" of Thomas Jefferson, 1802

In 1802, the Danbury Baptist Association wrote Jefferson to request that a day of fasting and thanksgiving be set aside as an official Christian national holiday. Such a holiday had been granted by presidents Washington and Adams. In this letter, Jefferson explains why he opposes such a holiday and, for the first time, uses the phrase "wall of separation" to describe the relationship between the state and religion in the United States. [Note that the bracketed, italicized section in the letter had been blocked off in the original for deletion, though it was never deleted.]

Jefferson's Wall of Separation Letter

Gentlemen

The affectionate sentiments of esteem & approbation which you are so good as to express towards me, on behalf of the Danbury Baptist association, give me the highest satisfaction. My duties dictate a faithful & zealous pursuit of the interests of my constituents, and in proportion as they are persuaded of my fidelity to those duties, the discharge of them becomes more & more pleasing.

Believing with you that religion is a matter which lies solely between man & his god, that he owes account to none other for his faith or his worship, that the legitimate powers of government reach actions only, and not opinions, I contemplate with sovereign reverence that act of the whole American people which declared that their legislature should make no law respecting an establishment of religion, or prohibiting the free exercise thereof, thus building a wall of separation between church and state. *[Congress thus inhibited from acts respecting religion, and the Executive authorised only to execute their acts, I have refrained from presenting even occasional performances of devotion presented indeed legally where an Executive is the legal head of a national church, but subject here, as religious exercises only to the voluntary regulations and discipline of each respective sect.]* Adhering to this expression of the supreme will of the nation in behalf of the rights of conscience, I shall see with sincere satisfaction the progress of those sentiments which tend to restore to man all his natural rights, convinced he has no natural right in opposition to his social duties.

I reciprocate your kind prayers for the protection and blessing of the common Father and creator of man, and tender you for yourselves and your religious association, assurances of my high respect & esteem.

(signed)
Th Jefferson
Jan.1.1802.

Source: Available online. URL: http://www.constitution.org/tj/sep_church_state.htm. Accessed October 30, 2008.

From *Democracy in America* by Alexis de Tocqueville, 1835/1840 (excerpt)

In the early 19th century, the Frenchman Alexis de Tocqueville spent some years touring the newly formed United States of America. He recorded his experiences in the two-volume Democracy in America. *De Tocqueville is renowned as one of the keenest and most insightful observers and analysts of the American psyche and way of life. Some of his insights about life two centuries ago still seem pertinent. The passage below is excerpted from that part of the book in which de Tocqueville describes Americans' attitudes toward religion and the state.*

There is an innumerable multitude of sects in the United States. They are all different in the worship they offer to the Creator, but all agree concerning the duties of men to one another. Each sect worships God in its own fashion, but all preach the same morality in the name of God. Though it is very important for man as an individual that his religion should be true, that is not the case for society. Society has nothing to fear or hope from another life, what is most important for it is not that all citizens should profess the true religion but that they should profess religion. Moreover, all the sects in the United States belong to the great unity of Christendom, and Christian morality is everywhere the same.

One may suppose that a certain number of Americans, in the worship they offer to God, are following their habits rather than their convictions. Besides, in the United States the sovereign authority is religious, and consequently hypocrisy should be common. Nonetheless, American is still the place where the Christian religion has kept the greatest real power over men's souls; and nothing better demonstrates how useful and natural it is to man, since the country where it now has widest sway is both the most enlightened and the freest.

I have said that American priests proclaim themselves in general terms in favor of civil liberties without excepting even those who do not admit religious freedom; but none of them lend their support to any particular political system. They are at pains to keep out of affairs and not mix in the combinations of parties. One cannot therefore say that in the United States religion influences the laws or political opinions in detail, but it does direct mores, and by regulating domestic life it helps to regulate the state.

I do not doubt for an instant that the great severity of mores which one notices in the United States has its primary origin in beliefs. There religion is often powerless to restrain men in the midst of innumerable temptations which fortune offers. It cannot moderate their eagerness to enrich themselves, which everything contributes to arouse, but it reigns supreme in the souls of the women, and it is women who shape mores. Certainly of all countries in the World America is the one in which the marriage tie is most respected and where the highest and truest conception of conjugal happiness has been conceived.

In Europe almost all the disorders of society are born around the domestic hearth and not far from the nuptial bed. It is there that men come to feel scorn for natural ties and legitimate pleasures and develop a taste for disorder, restlessness of spirit, and instability of desires. Shaken by the tumultuous passions which have often troubled his own house, the European finds it hard to submit to the authority of the state's legislators. When the American returns from the turmoil of politics to the bosom of the family, he immediately finds a perfect picture of order and peace. There all his pleasures are simple and natural and his joys innocent and quiet, and as the regularity of life brings him happiness, he easily forms the habit of regulating his opinions as well as his tastes.

Whereas the European tries to escape his sorrows at home by troubling society, the American derives from his home that love of order which he carries over affairs of state.

In the United States it is not only mores that are controlled by religion, but its sway extends even over reason. . . .

RELIGION AND THE STATE

Religion, which never intervenes directly in the government of American society, should therefore be considered as the first of their political institutions, for although it did not give them the taste for liberty, it singularly facilitates their use thereof.

The inhabitants of the United States themselves consider religious beliefs from this angle. I do not know if all Americans have faith in their religion—for who can read the secrets of the heart?—but I am sure that they think it necessary to the maintenance of republican institutions. That it is not the view of one class or party among the citizens, but of the whole nation; it is found in all ranks. . . .

For the Americans the ideas of Christianity and liberty are so completely mingled that it is almost impossible to get them to conceive of the one without the other; it is not a question with them of sterile beliefs bequeathed by the past and vegetating rather than living in the depths of the soul. . . .

Eighteenth-century philosophers had a very simple explanation for the gradual weakening of beliefs. Religious zeal, they said, was bound to die down as enlightenment and freedom spread. It is tiresome that the facts do not fit this theory at all.

There are sections of the population in Europe where unbelief goes hand in hand with brutishness and ignorance, whereas in America the most free and enlightened people in the world zealously perform all the external duties of religion.

The religious atmosphere of the country was the first thing that struck me on arrival in the United States. The longer I stayed in the country, the more conscious I became of the important political consequences resulting from this novel situation.

In France I had seen the spirits of religion and of freedom almost always marching in opposite directions. In America I found them intimately linked together in joint reign over the same land.

My longing to understand the reason for this phenomenon increased daily.

To find this out, I questioned the faithful of all communions; I particularly sought the society of clergymen, who are the depositaries of the various creeds and have a personal interest in their survival. As a practicing Catholic

United States Documents

I was particularly close to the Catholic priests, with some of whom I soon established a certain intimacy. I expressed my astonishment and revealed my doubts to each of them; I found that they all agreed with each other except about details; all thought that the main reason for the quiet sway of religion over their country was the complete separation of church and state. I have no hesitation in stating that throughout my stay in America I met nobody, lay or cleric, who did not agree about that. . . .

I then wished to trace the facts down to their causes. I wondered how it could come about that by diminishing the apparent power of religion one increased its real strength . . .

I know that, apart from influence proper to itself, religion can at times rely on the artificial strength of laws and the support of the material powers that direct society. There have been religions intimately linked to earthly governments, dominating men's souls both by terror and by faith; but when a religion makes such an alliance, I am not afraid to say that it makes the same mistake as any man might; it sacrifices the future for the present, and by graining a power to which it has no claim, it risks its legitimate authority.

When a religion seeks to found its sway only on the longing for immortality equally tormenting every human heart, it can aspire to universality; but when it comes to uniting itself with a government, it must adopt maxims which apply only to certain nations. Therefore, by allying itself with any political power, religion increases its strength over some but forfeits the hope of reigning over all. . . .

So long as a religion derives its strength from sentiments, instincts, and passions, which are reborn in like fashion in all periods of history, it can brave the assaults of time, or at least it can only be destroyed by another religion. But when a religion chooses to rely on the interests of this world, it becomes almost as fragile as all earthly powers. Alone, it may hope for immortality; linked to ephemeral powers, it follows their fortunes and often falls together with the passions of a day but sustaining them.

Hence any alliance with any political power whatsoever is bound to be burdensome for religion. It does not need their support in order to live, and in serving them it may die. . . .

When a nation adopts a democratic social state and communities show republican inclinations, it becomes increasingly dangerous for religion to ally itself with authority. For the time is coming when power will pass from hand to hand, political theories follow one another, and men, laws, and even constitutions vanish or alter daily, and that not for a limited time but continually. Agitation and instability are natural elements in democratic republics, just as immobility and somnolence are the rule in absolute monarchies.

If the Americans, who change the head of state every four years, elect new legislators every two years and replace provincial administrators every year, and if the Americans, who have handed over the world of politics to the experiments of innovators, had not placed religion beyond their reach, what could it hold on to in the ebb and flow of human opinions? Amid the struggle of parties, where would the respect due to it be? What would become of its immortality when everything around it was perishing?

The American clergy were the first to perceive this truth and to act in conformity with it. They saw that they would have to give up religious influence if they wanted to acquire political power, and they preferred to lose the support of authority rather than to share its vicissitudes.

In America religion is perhaps less powerful than it has been at certain times and among certain peoples, but its influence is more lasting. It restricts itself to its own resources, of which no one can deprive it; it functions in one sphere only, but it pervades it and dominates there without effort.

Source: Available online. URL: http://www.churchstatelaw.com/historicalmaterials/8_2_5.asp. Accessed October 25, 2008.

Wisconsin v. Yoder Supreme Court decision, 1972 (excerpt)

This excerpt is from a famous U.S. Supreme Court decision regarding the separation of church and state. The decision, written by Chief Justice Warren Burger, supports the right of Amish children not to be forced to attend a secular high school.

Respondents, members of the Old Order Amish religion and the Conservative Amish Mennonite Church, were convicted of violating Wisconsin's compulsory school-attendance law (which requires a child's school attendance until age 16) by declining to send their children to public or private school after they had graduated from the eighth grade. The evidence showed that the Amish provide continuing informal vocational education to their children designed to prepare them for life in the rural Amish community. The evidence also showed that respondents sincerely believed that high school attendance was contrary to the Amish religion and way of life and that they would endanger their own salvation and that of their children by complying with the law. The State Supreme Court sustained respondents' claim that application of the compulsory school-attendance law to them violated their rights under the Free Exercise Clause of the First Amendment, made applicable to the States by the Fourteenth Amendment.

Held:

    1. The State's interest in universal education is not totally free from a balancing process when it impinges on other fundamental rights, such as those specifically protected by the Free Exercise Clause of the First Amendment and the traditional interest of parents with respect to the religious upbringing of their children.

    2. Respondents have amply supported their claim that enforcement of the compulsory formal education requirement after the eighth grade would gravely endanger if not destroy the free exercise of their religious beliefs.

    3. Aided by a history of three centuries as an identifiable religious sect and a long history as a successful and self-sufficient segment of American society, the Amish have demonstrated the sincerity of their religious beliefs, the interrelationship of belief with their mode of life, the vital role that belief and daily conduct play in the continuing survival of Old Order Amish communities, and the hazards presented by the State's enforcement of a statute generally valid as to others. Beyond this, they have carried the difficult burden of demonstrating the adequacy of their alternative mode of continuing informal vocational education in terms of the overall interests that the State relies on in support of its program of compulsory high school education. In light of this showing, and weighing the minimal difference between what the State would require and what the Amish already accept, it was incumbent on the State to show with more particularity how its admittedly strong interest in compulsory education would be adversely affected by granting an exemption to the Amish.

    4. The State's claim that it is empowered, as parens patriae, to extend the benefit of secondary education to children regardless of the wishes of their parents cannot be sustained against a free exercise claim of the nature revealed by this record, for the Amish have introduced convincing evidence that accommodating their religious objections by forgoing one or two additional years of compulsory education will not impair the

physical or mental health of the child, or result in an inability to be self-supporting or to discharge the duties and responsibilities of citizenship, or in any other way materially detract from the welfare of society. . . .

Amish objection to formal education beyond the eighth grade is firmly grounded in these central religious concepts. They object to the high school, and higher education generally, because the values they teach are in marked variance with Amish values and the Amish way of life; they view secondary school education as an impermissible exposure of their children to a "worldly" influence in conflict with their beliefs. The high school tends to emphasize intellectual and scientific accomplishments, self-distinction, competitiveness, worldly success, and social life with other students. Amish society emphasizes informal learning-through-doing; a life of "goodness," rather than a life of intellect; wisdom, rather than technical knowledge; community welfare, rather than competition; and separation from, rather than integration with, contemporary worldly society. . . .

The Amish do not object to elementary education through the first eight grades as a general proposition because they agree that their children must have basic skills in the "three R's" in order to read the Bible, to be good farmers and citizens, and to be able to deal with non-Amish people when necessary in the course of daily affairs. They view such a basic education as acceptable because it does not significantly expose their children to worldly values or interfere with their development in the Amish community during the crucial adolescent period. While Amish accept compulsory elementary education generally, wherever possible they have established their own elementary schools in many respects like the small local schools of the past. In the Amish belief higher learning tends to develop values they reject as influences that alienate man from God. . . .

There is no doubt as to the power of a State, having a high responsibility for education of its citizens, to impose reasonable regulations for the control and duration of basic education. Providing public schools ranks at the very apex of the function of a State. Yet even this paramount responsibility was, in *Pierce*, made to yield to the right of parents to provide an equivalent education in a privately operated system. There the Court held that Oregon's statute compelling attendance in a public school from age eight to age 16 unreasonably interfered with the interest of parents in directing the rearing of their offspring, including their education in church-operated schools. As that case suggests, the values of parental direction of the religious upbringing and education of their children in their early and formative years have a high place in our society. Thus, a State's interest in universal education, however highly we rank it, is not totally free from a balancing process when it impinges on fundamental rights and interests, such as those specifically protected by the Free Exercise Clause of the First Amendment, and the traditional interest of parents with respect to the religious upbringing of their children so long as they, in the words of Pierce, "prepare [them] for additional obligations."

It follows that in order for Wisconsin to compel school attendance beyond the eighth grade against a claim that such attendance interferes with the practice of a legitimate religious belief, it must appear either that the State does not deny the free exercise of religious belief by its requirement, or that there is a state interest of sufficient magnitude to override the interest claiming protection under the Free Exercise Clause. Long before there was general acknowledgment of the need for universal formal education, the religion clauses had specifically and firmly fixed the right to free exercise of religious beliefs, and buttressing this fundamental right was an equally firm, even if less explicit, prohibition against the establishment of any religion by government. The values underlying these two provisions relating to religion have been zealously protected, sometimes even at the expense of other interests of admittedly high social importance.

The essence of all that has been said and written on the subject is that only those interests of the highest order and those not otherwise served can overbalance legitimate claims to the free exercise of religion. We can accept it as settled, therefore, that, however strong the State's interest in universal compulsory education, it is by no means absolute to the exclusion or subordination of all other interests.

Although a determination of what is a "religious" belief or practice entitled to constitutional protection may present a most delicate question, the very concept of ordered liberty precludes allowing every person to make his own standards on matters of conduct in which society as a whole has important interests. Thus, if the Amish asserted their claims because of their subjective evaluation and rejection of the contemporary secular values accepted by the majority, much as Thoreau rejected the social values of his time and isolated himself at Walden Pond, their claims would not rest on a religious basis. Thoreau's choice was philosophical and personal rather than religious, and such belief does not rise to the demands of the religion clauses.

Giving no weight to such secular considerations, however, we see that the record in this case abundantly supports the claim that the traditional way of life of the Amish is not merely a matter of personal preference, but one of deep religious conviction, shared by an organized group, and intimately related to daily living. That the Old Order Amish daily life and religious practice stem from their faith is shown by the fact that it is in response to their literal interpretation of the biblical injunction from the Epistle of Paul to the Romans, "be not conformed to this world. . . ." This command is fundamental to the Amish faith. Moreover, for the Old Order Amish, religion is not simply a matter of theocratic belief. As the expert witnesses explained, the Old Order Amish religion pervades and determines virtually their entire way of life, regulating it with the detail of the Talmudic diet through the strictly enforced rules of the church community. . . .

As the society around the Amish has become more populous, urban, industrialized, and complex, particularly in this century, government regulation of human affairs has correspondingly become more detailed and pervasive. The Amish mode of life has thus come into conflict increasingly with requirements of contemporary society exerting a hydraulic insistence on conformity to majoritarian standards. So long as compulsory education laws were confined to eight grades of elementary basic education imparted in a nearby rural schoolhouse, with a large proportion of students of the Amish faith, the Old Order Amish had little basis to fear that school attendance would expose their children to the worldly influence they reject. But modern compulsory secondary education in rural areas is now largely carried on in a consolidated school, often remote from the student's home and alien to his daily home life. As the record so strongly shows, the values and programs of the modern secondary school are in sharp conflict with the fundamental mode of life mandated by the Amish religion; modern laws requiring compulsory secondary education have accordingly engendered great concern and conflict. The conclusion is inescapable that secondary schooling, by exposing Amish children to worldly influences in terms of attitudes, goals, and values contrary to beliefs, and by substantially interfering with the religious development of the Amish child and his integration into the way of life of the Amish faith community at the crucial adolescent stage of development, contravenes the basic religious tenets and practice of the Amish faith, both as to the parent and the child.

The impact of the compulsory-attendance law on respondents' practice of the Amish religion is not only severe, but inescapable, for the Wisconsin law affirmatively compels them, under threat of criminal sanction, to perform acts undeniably at odds with fundamental tenets of their religious beliefs. See *Braunfeld v. Brown*. Nor is the impact of the compulsory-attendance law confined to grave interference with important Amish religious tenets from a subjective point of view. It carries with it precisely the kind of objective danger to the free exercise of religion that the First Amendment was designed to prevent.

Wisconsin concedes that under the religion clauses religious beliefs are absolutely free from the State's control, but it argues that "actions," even though religiously grounded, are outside the protection of the First Amendment. But our decisions have rejected the idea that religiously grounded conduct is always outside the protection of the Free Exercise Clause. It is true that activities of individuals, even when religiously based, are often subject to regulation by the States in the exercise of their undoubted power to promote the health, safety, and general welfare, or the Federal Government in the exercise of its delegated powers. But to agree that religiously grounded conduct must often be subject to the broad police power of the State is not to deny that there are areas of conduct protected by the Free Exercise Clause of the First Amendment and thus beyond the power of the State to control, even under regulations of general applicability. This case, therefore, does not become easier because respondents were convicted for their "actions" in refusing to send their children to the public high school; in this context belief and action cannot be neatly confined in logic-tight compartments.

Nor can this case be disposed of on the grounds that Wisconsin's requirement for school attendance to age 16 applies uniformly to all citizens of the State and does not, on its face, discriminate against religions or a particular religion, or that it is motivated by legitimate secular concerns. A regulation neutral on its face may, in its application, nonetheless offend the constitutional requirement for governmental neutrality if it unduly burdens the free exercise of religion.

We turn, then, to the State's broader contention that its interest in its system of compulsory education is so compelling that even the established religious practices of the Amish must give way. Where fundamental claims of religious freedom are at stake, however, we cannot accept such a sweeping claim; despite its admitted validity in the generality of cases, we must searchingly examine the interests that the State seeks to promote by its requirement for compulsory education to age 16, and the impediment to those objectives that would flow from recognizing the claimed Amish exemption.

The State advances two primary arguments in support of its system of compulsory education. It notes, as Thomas Jefferson pointed out early in our history, that some degree of education is necessary to prepare citizens to participate effectively and intelligently in our open political system if we are to preserve freedom and independence. Further, education prepares individuals to be self-reliant and self-sufficient participants in society. We accept these propositions.

However, the evidence adduced by the Amish in this case is persuasively to the effect that an additional one or two years of formal high school for Amish children in place of their long-established program of informal vocational education would do little to serve those interests. Respondents' experts testified at trial, without challenge, that the value of all education must be assessed in terms of its capacity to prepare the child for life. It is one thing to say that compulsory education for a year or two beyond the eighth grade may be necessary when its goal is the preparation of the child for life in modern society as the majority live, but it is quite another if the goal of education be viewed as the preparation of the child for life in the separated agrarian community that is the keystone of the Amish faith.

The State attacks respondents' position as one fostering "ignorance" from which the child must be protected by the State. No one can question the State's duty to protect children from ignorance but this argument does not square with the facts disclosed in the record. Whatever their idiosyncrasies as seen by the majority, this record strongly shows that the Amish community has been a highly successful social unit within our society, even if apart from the conventional "mainstream."

The State, however, supports its interest in providing an additional one or two years of compulsory high school education to Amish children because of the possibility that some such children will choose to leave the Amish community, and that if this occurs they will be ill-equipped for life. The State argues that if Amish children leave their church they should not be in the position of making their way in the world without the education available in the one or two additional years the State requires. However, on this record, that argument is highly speculative. There is no specific evidence of the loss of Amish adherents by attrition, nor is there any showing that upon leaving the Amish community Amish children, with their practical agricultural training and habits of industry and self-reliance, would become burdens on society because of educational shortcomings. Indeed, this argument of the State appears to rest primarily on the State's mistaken assumption, already noted, that the Amish do not provide any education for their children beyond the eighth grade, but allow them to grow in "ignorance." To the contrary, not only do the Amish accept the necessity for formal schooling through the eighth grade level, but continue to provide what has been characterized by the undisputed testimony of expert educators as an "ideal" vocational education for their children in the adolescent years. There is nothing in this record to suggest that the Amish qualities of reliability, self-reliance, and dedication to work would fail to find ready markets in today's society. Absent some contrary evidence supporting the State's position, we are unwilling to assume that persons possessing such valuable vocational skills and habits are doomed to become burdens on society should they determine to leave the Amish faith, nor is there any basis in the record to warrant a finding that an additional one or two years of formal school education beyond the eighth grade would serve to eliminate any such problem that might exist.

Insofar as the State's claim rests on the view that a brief additional period of formal education is imperative to enable the Amish to participate effectively and intelligently in our democratic process, it must fall. The Amish alternative to formal secondary school education has enabled them to function effectively in their day-to-day life under self-imposed limitations on relations with the world, and to survive and prosper in contemporary society as a separate, sharply identifiable and highly self-sufficient community for more than 200 years in this country. For the reasons stated we hold, with the Supreme Court of Wisconsin, that the First and Fourteenth Amendments prevent the State from compelling respondents to cause their children to attend formal high school to age 16. Our disposition of this case, however, in no way alters our recognition of the obvious fact that courts are not school boards or legislatures, and are ill-equipped to determine the "necessity" of discrete aspects of a State's program of compulsory education. This should suggest that courts must move with great circumspection in performing the sensitive and delicate task of weighing a State's legitimate social concern when faced with religious claims for exemption from generally applicable educational requirements. It cannot be overemphasized that we are not dealing with a way of life and mode of education by a group claiming to have recently discovered some "progressive" or more enlightened process for rearing children for modern life.

Aided by a history of three centuries as an identifiable religious sect and a long history as a successful and self-sufficient segment of American society, the Amish in this case have convincingly demonstrated the sincerity of their religious beliefs, the interrelationship of belief with their mode of life, the vital role that belief and daily conduct play in the continued survival of Old Order Amish communities and their religious organization, and the hazards presented by the State's enforcement of a statute generally valid as to others. Beyond this, they have carried the even more difficult burden of demonstrating the adequacy of their alternative mode of continuing informal vocational education in terms of precisely those overall interests that the State advances in support of its program of compulsory high school education. In light of this convincing showing, one that probably few other religious groups or sects could make, and weighing the minimal difference between what the State would require and what the Amish already accept, it was incumbent on the State to show with more particularity how its admittedly strong interest in compulsory education would be adversely affected by granting an exemption to the Amish.

RELIGION AND THE STATE

Nothing we hold is intended to undermine the general applicability of the State's compulsory school-attendance statutes or to limit the power of the State to promulgate reasonable standards that, while not impairing the free exercise of religion, provide for continuing agricultural vocational education under parental and church guidance by the Old Order Amish or others similarly situated. The States have had a long history of amicable and effective relationships with church-sponsored schools, and there is no basis for assuming that, in this related context, reasonable standards cannot be established concerning the content of the continuing vocational education of Amish children under parental guidance, provided always that state regulations are not inconsistent with what we have said in this opinion.

Affirmed.

Source: Available online. URL: http://caselaw.lp.findlaw.com/scripts/getcae.pl?court=us&vol=406&invol=205. Accessed November 20, 2008.

"Remarks by the President in Announcement of the Faith-Based Initiative," President George W. Bush, 2001 (excerpt)

In this announcement, President George W. Bush presented his faith-based initiative program, which would use federal funds to support churches and other religious organizations that provide assistance to their community. The president presents his reasons for establishing the program, which was challenged by some as being in violation of the separation of church and state.

THE PRESIDENT: I take great joy in making this announcement. It's going to be one of the most important initiatives that my administration not only discusses, but implements.

First, it's good to have so many groups represented here—religious and non-religious; Catholic, Jewish, Protestant, and Muslim; foundations and other nonprofits. I want to thank you all for coming. . . .

This is a diverse group, but we share things in common. They provide more than practical help to people in need. They touch and change hearts. And for this, America is deeply appreciative. . . .

United States Documents

It is one of the great goals of my administration to invigorate the spirit of involvement and citizenship. We will encourage faith-based and community programs without changing their mission. We will help all in their work to change hearts while keeping a commitment to pluralism.

I approach this goal with some basic principles: Government has important responsibilities for public health or public order and civil rights.... Yet when we see social needs in America, my administration will look first to faith-based programs and community groups, which have proven their power to save and change lives. We will not fund the religious activities of any group, but when people of faith provide social services, we will not discriminate against them.

As long as there are secular alternatives, faith-based charities should be able to compete for funding on an equal basis, and in a manner that does not cause them to sacrifice their mission. And we will make sure that help goes to large organizations and to small ones as well....

In a few moments, I will sign two executive orders. The first executive order will create a new office, called the White House Office of Faith-based and Community Initiatives. The head of this office will report directly to me and be charged with important responsibilities. He will oversee our initiatives on this issue. He will make sure our government, where it works with private groups, is fair and supportive. And he will highlight groups as national models so others can learn from them.

The second executive order will clear away the bureaucratic barriers in several important agencies that make private groups hesitate to work with government. It will establish centers in five agencies to ensure greater cooperation between the government and the independent sector....

I look forward to working with the people in this room and the social entrepreneurs all across America who have heard the universal call to love a neighbor like they'd like to be loved themselves; to exist and work hard, not out of the love of money, but out of the love of their fellow human beings. I'm absolutely convinced the great fabric of the nation exists in neighborhoods, amongst unsung heroes who do heroic acts on a daily and hourly basis. It's the fabric of the country that makes America unique....

RELIGION AND THE STATE

I am confident that this initiative, when fully implemented, will help us realize the dream that America, its hopes, its promise, its greatness, will extend its reach throughout every single neighborhood, all across the land.

And now it is my honor to sign the two executive orders.

Source: Available online. URL: http://www.whitehouse.gov/news/releases/print/20010129-5.html. Accessed November 9, 2008.

"Judicial Tyranny" by Dr. James Dobson, 2003 (excerpt)

This is the text of a speech the Christian fundamentalist leader James Dobson gave in Montgomery, Alabama, in support of keeping a stone tablet with the Ten Commandments in the state courthouse. The Alabama attorney general had installed the large tablet, but its location in a public building was challenged in court as a violation of the separation of church and state. Dobson viewed court decisions that the Ten Commandments must be removed from a public building as a form of "judicial tyranny" over the rights of Americans.

I came here to remind us of what you already know—that it is very ironic that this event and this confrontation is occurring in Montgomery, where a little black lady, by the name of Rosa Parks, led a movement that began in 1955. She had no power. She had no influence. She had no money. She was not a political leader, yet she saw something that she felt was evil. Yeah, it was imposed on her and all black people by "the rule of law" that we've been hearing about this last week, but it was wrong. It was wrong. She determined not to obey the order, because her people were oppressed and being sent to the back of the bus.

She is a Christian woman, as you know. She has a deep faith in God, but in 1955 the governor didn't help her. And the Attorney General was not there for her, and the legislators ran for the tall grass, and the power structure of the day did not offer its help. Nevertheless, Rosa prevailed, because she believed in the rightness of her cause.

Therefore, we honor her and invoke her name here today, because in a very real sense, we're in a great moral struggle of our own. We as people of faith are also being sent to the back of the bus. And we're not going to go there.

This great monument has now been put in the back of the bus, and it ought to be out on display where people can see it. But in a larger context, this struggle that we're involved in is not really about the Ten Commandments.

United States Documents

It's not about the monument. It is not even about that wonderful man, Judge Moore, who has had the courage of his convictions to put it on the line. It will cost him professionally, but he has been willing to suffer the loss. But there is something even more significant at play here. This struggle is primarily a battle against judicial tyranny.

The liberal elite and the federal court judges and some members of the media, are determined to remove every evidence of faith in God from this entire culture. They are determined to control more and more of our private lives, and it is time that we said, "Enough is enough."

They want to redefine us as a nation and deny the spiritual heritage that brought us to this point. On the United States Supreme Court building are three depictions to the same Ten Commandments and to Moses. The sergeant of arms has opened every workday since 1777 by shouting, "God bless the United States and this Court."

The National Archives building displays the Constitution, the Bill of Rights and the Declaration of Independence. In order to see them, you have to walk past the Ten Commandments. There are evidences [sic] of early faith in God throughout the Capitol building in Washington, where I was yesterday, in the inscriptions, in the statutes, in the art displayed on the walls and in the chamber of the House of Representatives. Written behind the speaker are the words "In God We Trust."

Surrounding that chamber are depictions of the great lawgivers down through history. They are all facing away from the speaker. They're all looking at the person in the center. Moses is depicted there. He is the only one that is shown full-face, looking down on the Speaker and the representatives. The rest are looking to him, because our law is based on the Judeo-Christian system of values.

Throughout Washington, you see evidences of faith. In Philadelphia, the Liberty Bell has a Scripture inscribed from the book of Leviticus. The other examples are evident throughout the historic monuments and governmental buildings. If the ACLU and if the People for the American Way and if Americans United for the Separation of Church and State and all the other liberal organizations are going to accomplish their goal, they're going to have to sandblast half the buildings in Washington. And we're not going to let them do that.

So, we are here today to defend the things we believe. Now why has this confrontation occurred in Montgomery? Why didn't the leftist organizations

RELIGION AND THE STATE

start by removing references to God in Washington? Why did they come down here to beat up on the people of Alabama? The reason is because they were afraid to do it elsewhere. That will be done later when the nation has been "softened up"! Thus, they have come to Alabama, and they think they can intimidate you. But we must not allow that to happen.

The question is, what is the legal basis for these attacks on religious faith? It is the liberal interpretation of the Constitution. Everything that represents God or things that are holy are considered to be unconstitutional. The Ten Commandments represent our historic spiritual heritage on which all other law is based.

It's been a 41-year struggle that started in 1962 with prayer in public schools. And in 1963, they removed Bible reading from the public schools, and most of us sat in silence. Christians are a people that reverence the law and abide by the rule of law. So we said nothing. And the liberals were on a roll then. They removed voluntary prayer from the schools, and then banned prayer at graduations and even silent prayer. In the 1980s, they required the state of Kentucky to take down the Ten Commandments from high school bulletin boards.

And it's gone from one thing to the other until it reached a low point last year when Judge Goodwin of the 9th Circuit in California ruled that schoolchildren could not say the Pledge of Allegiance because it contained those "offensive" words "under God." Everybody was shocked by the audacity of that decision. It was terrible, and in fact, it frightened members of Congress. They came stumbling out of the Capitol building, trying to get to the microphones to say they were opposed to Judge Goodwin's order.

Senator Daschle was one of the first ones to get to the microphones. This is "just nuts," he said. But ever since then he has been working tirelessly to preserve that kind of leftist judiciary and prevent conservative men and women from being confirmed to the U.S. Senate who have been nominated by President Bush. It is time for us to let the Democrats know that their filibustering is unacceptable to us.

Did you know that Thomas Jefferson was worried about the development of an oligarchy (which is defined as "government by a few") that would gain judicial power and be beyond the reach of the other two branches of government? When I was in the fourth grade, back in the days when school taught history—I was sitting in class one day, and my teacher went to the board and talked about the principle of checks and balances between the three branches of government. They put within the Constitution the responsibility in the Congress to check the courts. But the Congress has totally abdicated that responsibility, and what we have now is the kind of oligarchy that Thomas Jefferson was worried about.

Both Jefferson and Franklin submitted designs for the seal of the United States, and they each suggested depictions of Moses.

For the past few weeks, I've been watching the developing story in Alabama on CNN and FOX News. I've heard the various news media as they've described this event in Montgomery. They've totally missed the point. They've described it as the work of an out-of-control judge *[Moore]* who has a personal motive or ambition in defending the monument. I don't know how losing his job can be interpreted as an expression of ambition. The media have not understood the issue at all, and that's why I came here, to say to you, it's not about the Ten Commandments. It's about everything else.

It is mostly about an unelected, unaccountable, arrogant, imperious judiciary that is appointed for life and is determined to make all of us dance to their music. That is not the way a democracy is supposed to function. We need to go to the Congress and demand—absolutely demand—that they rein in this runaway court.

It's not just about removing God from the public square. Look at what they've done to us. In 1973, the *Roe v. Wade* decision was an outrage. We followed the rule of law, despite our agitation about the ruling. So we worked within the system. Now, 30 years have gone by, and over 40 million babies are dead, and they're still being murdered.

Most recently, the Justices have ruled that homosexuals have the constitutional right to practice sodomy. Writing for the majority was Justice Anthony Kennedy, whom I consider to be one of the most dangerous men in this country. Somebody ought to tell him he could be impeached.

The Court appears to be headed straight as an arrow for the sanction and supposed constitutionality of same-sex marriage. That is what will happen if we don't act to stop this out-of-control Court. What they are doing is wrong, and we must oppose it. It will destroy the family and bring down this nation if a family can consist of gay marriage or "group marriage." If marriage means everything, it ceases to mean anything. We must stop this movement in its tracks.

RELIGION AND THE STATE

The best way to protect the family is with the passage of the Federal Marriage Amendment. Congress needs to give that message to the Court. Time is very short. I'm absolutely convinced of that. This country could very easily be like Canada is today, where pending legislation could one day make it illegal to ever preach the first chapter of Romans.

There was a time, when I was younger that it stung me to be called a "right winger." There was a time when I didn't want to take that heat. There was a time when I wanted to say what I needed to say, but then I tried to keep my head down. I've got to tell you. Those days are over.

Do you think it's time to limit the power of the oligarchy? Do you believe the redefinition of marriage will undermine and threaten its legal underpinnings? Are you fed up with the courts tampering with the schools and warping the minds of kids? Do you want kids to say the Pledge of Allegiance every day? Are you going to make these convictions known in the wider public square? Are you going to oppose any legal action taken against Judge Moore?

You may have to do it, because the judiciary believes they have him by the neck. I believe that God has another plan.

One of my great heroes is Winston Churchill. I have his memorabilia displayed all around my office in Colorado Springs. I have a big portrait of him in my office. I love what he said during Britain's very darkest hour, when it looked like there was no hope against the Nazis. He said, "We will never, never, never, never, never give up." And never will we! God bless you all.

Source: Available online. URL: http://www2.focusonthefamily.com/docstudy/newsletters/a000000770.cfm. Accessed November 9, 2008.

"Call to Renewal" Keynote Address by Barack Obama, 2006 (excerpt)

In this speech, then Senator Barack Obama discusses the interaction among faith and religion and government. He cogently argues that faith has its place in American public life and that it can play a significant role in the lives of individuals and communities while not violating constitutional principles.

Today I'd like to talk about the connection between religion and politics and perhaps offer some thoughts about how we can sort through some of the often bitter arguments that we've been seeing over the last several years.

United States Documents

I do so because, as you all know, we can affirm the importance of poverty in the Bible ... and we can discuss the religious call to address poverty and environmental stewardship all we want, but it won't have an impact unless we tackle head-on the mutual suspicion that sometimes exists between religious America and secular America.

I want to give you an example that I think illustrates this fact. As some of you know, during the 2004 U.S. Senate general election I ran against a gentleman named Alan Keyes. Mr. Keyes is well-versed in the Jerry Falwell-Pat Robertson style of rhetoric that often labels progressives as both immoral and godless.

Indeed, Mr. Keyes announced towards the end of the campaign that, "Jesus Christ would not vote for Barack Obama. Christ would not vote for Barack Obama because Barack Obama has behaved in a way that it is inconceivable for Christ to have behaved."

Jesus Christ would not vote for Barack Obama.

Now, I was urged by some of my liberal supporters not to take this statement seriously, to essentially ignore it. To them, Mr. Keyes was an extremist, and his arguments not worth entertaining. And since at the time, I was up 40 points in the polls, it probably wasn't a bad piece of strategic advice.

But what they didn't understand, however, was that I had to take Mr. Keyes seriously, for he claimed to speak for my religion, and my God. He claimed knowledge of certain truths.

Mr. Obama says he's a Christian, he was saying, and yet he supports a lifestyle that the Bible calls an abomination.

Mr. Obama says he's a Christian, but supports the destruction of innocent and sacred life.

And so what would my supporters have me say? How should I respond? Should I say that a literalist reading of the Bible was folly? Should I say that Mr. Keyes, who is a Roman Catholic, should ignore the teachings of the Pope?

Unwilling to go there, I answered with what has come to be the typically liberal response in such debates—namely, I said that we live in a pluralistic society, that I can't impose my own religious views on another, that I was running to be the U.S. Senator of Illinois and not the Minister of Illinois.

But Mr. Keyes's implicit accusation that I was not a true Christian nagged at me, and I was also aware that my answer did not adequately address the role my faith has in guiding my own values and my own beliefs.

Now, my dilemma was by no means unique. In a way, it reflected the broader debate we've been having in this country for the last thirty years over the role of religion in politics.

RELIGION AND THE STATE

For some time now, there has been plenty of talk among pundits and pollsters that the political divide in this country has fallen sharply along religious lines. Indeed, the single biggest "gap" in party affiliation among white Americans today is not between men and women, or those who reside in so-called Red States and those who reside in Blue, but between those who attend church regularly and those who don't.

Conservative leaders have been all too happy to exploit this gap, consistently reminding evangelical Christians that Democrats disrespect their values and dislike their Church, while suggesting to the rest of the country that religious Americans care only about issues like abortion and gay marriage; school prayer and intelligent design.

Democrats, for the most part, have taken the bait. At best, we may try to avoid the conversation about religious values altogether, fearful of offending anyone and claiming that—regardless of our personal beliefs—constitutional principles tie our hands. At worst, there are some liberals who dismiss religion in the public square as inherently irrational or intolerant, insisting on a caricature of religious Americans that paints them as fanatical, or thinking that the very word "Christian" describes one's political opponents, not people of faith.

Now, such strategies of avoidance may work for progressives when our opponent is Alan Keyes. But over the long haul, I think we make a mistake when we fail to acknowledge the power of faith in people's lives—in the lives of the American people—and I think it's time that we join a serious debate about how to reconcile faith with our modern, pluralistic democracy.

And if we're going to do that then we first need to understand that Americans are a religious people. 90 percent of us believe in God, 70 percent affiliate themselves with an organized religion, 38 percent call themselves committed Christians, and substantially more people in America believe in angels than they do in evolution.

This religious tendency is . . . a hunger that goes beyond any particular issue or cause.

Each day, it seems, thousands of Americans are going about their daily rounds—dropping off the kids at school, driving to the office, flying to a business meeting, shopping at the mall, trying to stay on their diets—and they're coming to the realization that something is missing. They are deciding that their work, their possessions, their diversions, their sheer busyness, is not enough.

They want a sense of purpose, a narrative arc to their lives. They're looking to relieve a chronic loneliness, a feeling supported by a recent study that shows Americans have fewer close friends and confidants than ever before. And so they need an assurance that somebody out there cares about them, is listening to them—that they are not just destined to travel down that long highway towards nothingness . . .

. . . When we ignore the debate about what it means to be a good Christian or Muslim or Jew; when we discuss religion only in the negative sense of where or how it should not be practiced, rather than in the positive sense of what it tells us about our obligations towards one another; when we shy away from religious venues and religious broadcasts because we assume that we will be unwelcome—others will fill the vacuum, those with the most insular views of faith, or those who cynically use religion to justify partisan ends.

More fundamentally, the discomfort of some progressives with any hint of religion has often prevented us from effectively addressing issues in moral terms. Some of the problem here is rhetorical—if we scrub language of all religious content, we forfeit the imagery and terminology through which millions of Americans understand both their personal morality and social justice.

Imagine Lincoln's Second Inaugural Address without reference to "the judgments of the Lord." Or King's I Have a Dream speech without references to "all of God's children." Their summoning of a higher truth helped inspire what had seemed impossible, and move the nation to embrace a common destiny.

Our failure as progressives to tap into the moral underpinnings of the nation is not just rhetorical, though. Our fear of getting "preachy" may also lead us to discount the role that values and culture play in some of our most urgent social problems. . . .

I am not suggesting that every progressive suddenly latch on to religious terminology—that can be dangerous. Nothing is more transparent than inauthentic expressions of faith.

But what I am suggesting is this—secularists are wrong when they ask believers to leave their religion at the door before entering into the public square. Frederick Douglass, Abraham Lincoln, Williams Jennings Bryan, Dorothy Day, Martin Luther King—indeed, the majority of great reformers in American history—were not only motivated by faith, but repeatedly used religious language to argue for their cause. So to say that men and women should not inject their "personal morality" into public policy debates is a practical absurdity. Our law is by definition a codification of morality, much of it grounded in the Judeo-Christian tradition.

Moreover, if we progressives shed some of these biases, we might recognize some overlapping values that both religious and secular people share when it comes to the moral and material direction of our country. We might recognize that the call to sacrifice on behalf of the next generation, the need

RELIGION AND THE STATE

to think in terms of "thou" and not just "I," resonates in religious congregations all across the country. And we might realize that we have the ability to reach out to the evangelical community and engage millions of religious Americans in the larger project of American renewal . . .

So the question is, how do we build on these still-tentative partnerships between religious and secular people of good will? It's going to take more work, a lot more work than we've done so far. The tensions and the suspicions on each side of the religious divide will have to be squarely addressed. And each side will need to accept some ground rules for collaboration.

While I've already laid out some of the work that progressive leaders need to do, I want to talk a little bit about what conservative leaders need to do—some truths they need to acknowledge.

For one, they need to understand the critical role that the separation of church and state has played in preserving not only our democracy, but the robustness of our religious practice. Folks tend to forget that during our founding, it wasn't the atheists or the civil libertarians who were the most effective champions of the First Amendment. It was the persecuted minorities, it was Baptists like John Leland who didn't want the established churches to impose their views on folks who were getting happy out in the fields and teaching the scripture to slaves. It was the forebearers of the evangelicals who were the most adamant about not mingling government with religious, because they did not want state-sponsored religion hindering their ability to practice their faith as they understood it.

Moreover, given the increasing diversity of America's population, the dangers of sectarianism have never been greater. Whatever we once were, we are no longer just a Christian nation; we are also a Jewish nation, a Muslim nation, a Buddhist nation, a Hindu nation, and a nation of nonbelievers.

And even if we did have only Christians in our midst, if we expelled every non-Christian from the United States of America, whose Christianity would we teach in the schools? Would we go with James Dobson's, or Al Sharpton's? Which passages of Scripture should guide our public policy? Should we go with Leviticus, which suggests slavery is ok and that eating shellfish is abomination? How about Deuteronomy, which suggests stoning your child if he strays from the faith? Or should we just stick to the Sermon on the Mount—a passage that is so radical that it's doubtful that our own Defense Department would survive its application? So before we get carried away, let's read our Bibles. Folks haven't been reading their Bibles.

This brings me to my second point. Democracy demands that the religiously motivated translate their concerns into universal, rather than religion-specific, values. It requires that their proposals be subject to argument, and amenable to reason. I may be opposed to abortion for religious reasons, but if I seek to pass a law banning the practice, I cannot simply point to the teachings of my church or evoke God's will. I have to explain why abortion violates some principle that is accessible to people of all faiths, including those with no faith at all.

Now this is going to be difficult for some who believe in the inerrancy of the Bible, as many evangelicals do. But in a pluralistic democracy, we have no choice. Politics depends on our ability to persuade each other of common aims based on a common reality. It involves the compromise, the art of what's possible. At some fundamental level, religion does not allow for compromise. It's the art of the impossible. If God has spoken, then followers are expected to live up to God's edicts, regardless of the consequences. To base one's life on such uncompromising commitments may be sublime, but to base our policy making on such commitments would be a dangerous thing.

Finally, any reconciliation between faith and democratic pluralism requires some sense of proportion.

This goes for both sides.

Even those who claim the Bible's inerrancy make distinctions between Scriptural edicts, sensing that some passages—the Ten Commandments, say, or a belief in Christ's divinity—are central to Christian faith, while others are more culturally specific and may be modified to accommodate modern life.

The American people intuitively understand this, which is why the majority of Catholics practice birth control and some of those opposed to gay marriage nevertheless are opposed to a Constitutional amendment to ban it. Religious leadership need not accept such wisdom in counseling their flocks, but they should recognize this wisdom in their politics.

But a sense of proportion should also guide those who police the boundaries between church and state. Not every mention of God in public is a breach to the wall of separation—context matters. It is doubtful that children reciting the Pledge of Allegiance feel oppressed or brainwashed as a consequence of muttering the phrase "under God." I didn't. Having voluntary student prayer groups use school property to meet should not be a threat, any more than its use by the High School Republicans should threaten Democrats. And one can envision certain faith-based programs—targeting ex-offenders or substance abusers—that offer a uniquely powerful way of solving problems.

So we all have some work to do here. But I am hopeful that we can bridge the gaps that exist and overcome the prejudices each of us bring to this debate. And I have faith that millions of believing Americans want that to happen. No matter how religious they may or may not be, people are tired of seeing faith used as a tool of attack. They don't want faith used to belittle or to divide. They're tired of hearing folks deliver more screed than sermon. Because in the end, that's not how they think about faith in their own lives.

Source: Available online. URL: http://www.barackobama.com/2006/06/28/call_to_renewal_keynote_address.php. Accessed July 28, 2009.

Debate on His Book *God Is Not Great* between the Author Christopher Hitchens and the Reverend Al Sharpton, 2007 (excerpt)

Christopher Hitchens has become one of the most outspoken proponents of agnosticism and atheism in the United States. He argues against the belief in God in his controversial book God Is Not Great. *In this debate with the Reverend Al Sharpton, held at the New York Public Library, Hitchens argues his case. This excerpt provides Hitchens's viewpoint to show the nature of the current "atheistic" backlash against surging religiosity in the United States.*

JACOB WEISBERG: Christopher, I would like to start with you. What have you got against God?

CHRISTOPHER HITCHENS: Good grief, sir, it hadn't really sunk in on me, that as you were being ordained, when I was nine, I was just getting out of there completely. I was nine when I thought I saw through it, when my biology teacher told me that God was so good as to have made vegetation green because it was the color most restful to our eyes. And I thought, "Mrs. Watts, this is nonsense." I knew nothing about chlorophyll or photosynthesis, nothing about the theory of evolution, nothing about adaptation, nothing of the sort, I just knew she'd got everything all wrong.

And of course the argument against faith, against religion, falls into two essential halves, not necessarily congruent, but I *believe* congruent. The first is it's not true. Religion comes from the infancy of our species—I won't say race, because I don't think our species is subdivided by races—infancy of our species, when we didn't know that the Earth went round the sun, we didn't know that germs caused disease, we didn't know when we were told in Genesis, "you're given dominion over all creatures," that this did not include microorganisms, because we didn't know they were there, so you didn't know they had dominion over *us*. When diseases broke out, it was blamed on wickedness, or sometimes on the Jews, or if it was by Jews, on the Amalekites, or as you will. We didn't know *anything* about the nature of the earth's crust, how it was cooling, earthquakes, storms, all of this were a mystery. Well, we are at least to that extent, a reasoning species. Even a conspiracy theory is often better than no theory at all. The mind searches for form. We are now stuck with the forms that we found in our infancy, in our primitive, barbaric past.

Well, that could be fine, still, no nation can be without mythology, or myth, or legend. And there are people who say, "Well, it's not exactly true, virgins don't conceive, okay, bushes don't burn forever," though why that would be so impressive, I've never understood, "dead men don't walk, and so on. Okay, all right, it's not really true, it does come from a rather fearful period of the Dark Ages, but at least it's nice to believe it. It teaches good precepts." This, I think, is very radically untrue.

I give in my book the example, which I'll give you now, of a person very much influential on my youth . . . Dr. Martin Luther King . . . And everybody literate here knows the story of Exodus and understands what Dr. King meant when he demanded that his people be free of bondage, but if you think about it for a second, it's a very good thing that the good doctor was only using this metaphorically. If he'd really been invoking the lessons of Genesis and Exodus, he would have been saying that his people had the right to kill anyone who stood in their way, to exterminate all other tribes . . . to make slaves of those they captured, to take the land and property of others . . .

In other words, in these books there are the warrants for genocide, for slavery, for the torture of children for disobedience, for genital mutilation, for annexation, for rape, and all the rest of it. That it's a very *good* thing that this is man-made. There are those who say that they wish they could believe. I suppose a decent atheist could say that if only for lack of evidence, he wishes he or she could. I can't be among their number. I'm very glad it is not true that there is a permanent, unshakeable, unchallengeable celestial supervision, a divine North Korea in which no privacy, no liberty, is possible from the moment of conception not just until the moment of death but until well after. I've been to North Korea, and now I know what a prayerful state would look like. I know what it would be like to praise God from dawn till dusk. I've seen it happen, and it's the most disgusting and depressing and pointless and soulless thing you can picture, but at least with North Korea you can die and you can leave.

Christianity won't let you do that. Because I mentioned another thing about the Old Testament. The Old Testament may have . . . genocide, rape, racism, all the rest of the things I've mentioned, but it never mentions punishment of the dead. When you're done, when you're in the mass grave into which you've been thrown as an Amalikite, it's over. Not until gentle Jesus meek and mild is the concept of Hell introduced. Eternal torture, eternal punishment, for you and all your family for the smallest transgression. I have no hesitation in saying this is a *wicked* belief. I also have no hesitation in saying . . . that we don't need it in two senses. One is it's wicked. Two, we

RELIGION AND THE STATE

have and always have had a much superior tradition. We know that Democritus and Epicurus worked out in ancient Athens, the world was made of atoms, that the gods did not exist, and certainly took no interest in human affairs and would be foolish to do so and would be wicked if they did. We have a tradition that brings us through Galileo and Spinoza and Thomas Paine and Voltaire and Thomas Jefferson and Bertrand Russell and Albert Einstein. Men of great wisdom and insight, by all means struck by the awe-inspiring character of our universe, by all means open to devotional music and architecture and poetry, by all means aware of the transcendent, but look through the Hubble Telescope if you want to see something that is awe-inspiring, and don't look to bloodstained old myths.

Now, why now? Why am I doing this now, people ask. Well, I'll tell you why now, because in the last few years it's become impossible to turn a page of a newspaper without being, as the religious would say, offended. In other words, I don't think I sound self-pitying if I say that I'm offended that a cartoonist in a tiny democratic country in Scandinavia, Denmark, can't do his job without a death threat, and that no American magazine or newspaper would reprint those cartoons, either to elucidate the question or in solidarity. I'm offended that civil society in Iraq is being destroyed, leveled, by the parties of God. I'm offended that people in this country believe that they have the right to advocate the teaching of garbage to children under the fatuous name of "intelligent design." . . . Just as I believe that where religion ends, philosophy begins; where alchemy ends, chemistry begins; where astrology ends, astronomy begins and now would the people say, well let's give equal time to astrology in the schools? It's nonsense, dangerous and sinister and nonsense. The pope says, "AIDS may be bad, but condoms are much worse." What kind of moral teaching is this, and how many people are going to die for such dogma? You see what I mean. . . . There's an end to this, an end particularly to the cultural fringe that says that if someone can claim to be a religious spokesman, they are entitled to respect. . . .

AL SHARPTON: You make a very interesting analysis of how people use or misuse God, but you made no argument about God Himself . . . [C]learly, people have misused God as they've misused other things that are possibly positive, but its existence is not in any way proven or disproven by you giving a long diatribe on those that have mishandled and misused God, because there are many that you can cite that have acted in a way that shows the goodness of God . . .

CHRISTOPHER HITCHENS: Now, I didn't say that God was misused. I hope I wasn't so poorly understood by everybody. I said that the idea of God is a dictatorial one to begin with, the belief in a supreme, eternal, invigilating Creator who knows what you think, and what you do, and cares about it, and will reward or punish you and watches you while you sleep, is I think a horrific belief, and a man-made one fortunately, I'm very glad there's no evidence for it. Let me . . . let me assert again. I think it's *innately* an awful belief. However, the cleverest theologian, and there have been some, has never been able to demonstrate that such a person exists. It's impossible to do so. It's not possible, either, for me to demonstrate conclusively that *no* such person exists. That cannot be done, either.

But one thing *can* be done. A person who claims not to know only that this person exists—a task beyond our brain—but who claim to know his or her mind, to say, I know, because I'm in holy orders, what this entity wants you to do, what he wants you to eat, who he wants you to go to bed with, and *how* he wants you to go to bed with them, what you may read, and what associations in private you may form, what thoughts you may have. That person is out of the argument now, it seems to me. We know that no one knows that. So the claim made by the religious that they know God and they know his mind and they can tell us what to do in his name is, I think, exploded.

Further, it is not argued by my side, at any rate, and by no one I know on it, that our presence here on the planet is something that is susceptible of the smooth, logical, reasonable explanation. To the contrary. We are still very much in doubt about precisely how we came to be human and to separate ourselves from some of our common ancestors. We also know that of the species that have been on this small planet in this tiny solar system, since the beginning of measurable time, of the number that were ever in existence, more than 98.9 percent have become extinct. A certain solipsism, I think, is required to believe that we, as a result, as a species are somehow the center of the creative cosmos. This is not modesty, as the Christians call it, it's not humility, it's an *unbelievably* arrogant claim to make. But at least it makes up for the other claim we're supposed to put with, which is well, yes, but we're also miserable sinners conceived in filth and doomed to abject our selves. Both of these positions are too extreme, too strenuous, too fanatical. Both of them reinforce each other in unpleasant ways and both should be outgrown by us.

...

AL SHARPTON: I pose the question: When you raise the issue of morality, if there is no supervisory being, then what do we base morality on? Is it based on who has the might at any given time? Who's in power? What is morality based on if there is no order to the universe and therefore some being, some force that ordered it, then who determines what is right or wrong, what is moral or immoral?

CHRISTOPHER HITCHENS: If there was no one in charge how would we know how to act morally? This is indeed a very profound observation . . . It's argued by Smerdyakov in *The Brothers Karamazov,* he said, "Without God, anything is permissible." Some people believe that. Some people believe that without the fear of divine total surveillance and supervision, everyone would do exactly as they wished, and we would all be wolves to each other. I think there's an enormous amount of evidence that that's not the case, that morality is innate in us and solidarity is part of our self-interest in society as well as our own interests. And very much to argue the contrary, when you see something otherwise surprising to you, such as a good person acting in a wicked manner, it's very often because they believe they are under divine orders to do so. Steven Weinberg puts it very well. He says, "Left to themselves, evil people will do evil things and good people will try and do good things. If you want a good person to do a wicked thing, that takes religion.

For example, I don't believe that my Palestinian friends I've known for years think that to blow yourself up outside an orphanage is a moral act, or inside one, is a moral act, or in an old people's home in Netanya is a moral action, that anything in their nature makes them think this but their mullahs tell them that it is. And that the person doing this is a hero. I do not think that any person looking at a newborn baby would think, "How wonderful. What a gift. But now just let's start sawing away at his genitalia with a sharp stone." Who would give them that idea if not the godly? And what kind of argument from design is this? "Babies are not born beautiful. They're born ugly, they need to be sawn a bit, because the handiwork of God is such garbage." Well, honestly, this is what I mean when I saw that those who think there's any connection between ethics and religion have their all work still ahead of them and after thousands of years still have it all ahead of them more and more . . .

Source: Available online. URL: http://www.nypl.org/research/calendar/imagesprog/hitchens5707.pdf. Accessed November 7, 2008.

"Christian Reconstruction: A Call for Reformation and Revival" by Robert Parsons, 2008

This article, first published in the Christian journal The Forerunner, *argues that the United States was and should always be a Christian nation governed by the laws of the Bible. The author claims that the nation has lost its way and must adopt strict biblical law in order to reestablish its true identity. This reconstructionist argument represents the views of one wing of extreme Christian fundamentalists in the United States.*

Christian Reconstruction is a call to the Church to awaken to its biblical responsibility to revival and the reformation of society. While holding to the priority of individual salvation, Christian Reconstruction also holds that cultural renewal is to be the necessary and expected outworking of the gospel as it progressively finds success in the lives and hearts of men. Christian Reconstruction therefore looks for and works for the rebuilding of the institutions of society according to a biblical blueprint.

Christian Reconstruction is also an attempt to answer the unprecedented threat facing the Church of Jesus Christ in the 20th century resurgence of secular humanism and parallel rise of statism. The state threatens to swallow the Church by such actions such as property taxation, zoning laws, and direct court action, all directly contrary to the Word of God.

There are two fatal errors facing the Church as it is being called upon to respond to this threat.

Fatal Error #1: Retreat

Retreat is failing to apply the Word of God to society and culture. It seems as though many Christians are guided more by Plato in some aspects of their thinking than by Christ. They tend to deny the application of scripture to the secular. They fail to recognize that every sphere is spiritual and subject to the Word of God.

This shows up in a studied indifference to biblical teaching on civil law, economics, government and other cultural applications. It is pietism as opposed to true piety. There was, for example, little response to the abortion holocaust from the evangelical Church for over 10 years after the 1973 Supreme Court ruling.

Fatal Error #2: Accommodation

Accommodation is misapplying the Word of God in society and culture. This is by far the more subtle error. One glaring example would be "Christian socialism" like that espoused by Ron Sider in Rich Christians in an Age of Hunger. This perspective down plays biblical charity and poor laws (such as gleaning) in favor of the anti-biblical "solution" of government taxation and redistribution of wealth.

RELIGION AND THE STATE

By way of contrast, the truly biblical welfare is local, personal, voluntary and usually requires the poor to work (2 Thes. 3:10).

The Christian Reconstruction movement has been raised up by God to awaken the Church to the reality of these two fatal errors.

Christian Reconstruction is a call to return to the vision of the Reformation, where men sought to restructure every sphere of life according to the Word of God. This is true biblical revival. Every example of revival in Scripture extended beyond individual repentance to impact every facet of culture. For example, rediscovery of the Law by King Josiah (2 Kings 22,23) produced a reformation (but not a revival) leading to reconstruction of the entire Hebrew culture. In the New Testament, proclamation of the crown rights of King Jesus resulted in changes to all life, it being said that the world had been turned upside down (Acts 17).

The Foundation: Sovereignty of God

Christian Reconstruction rests on one solid foundation stone: the sovereignty of God. Sovereignty refers to God's supreme power and rule. His reign and control extends into every sphere of life, here and now, not just in eternity. To defer His Kingship is to deny His Kingship. The Bible contains the directives of the King of kings for every area of human activity, including civil government, economics, art, science, family, church, and more. Activity in each sphere is to be governed by the Law of God, with minimal interference from civil government. There are no neutral zones.

God exercises His sovereignty through many secondary agencies. For example, civil government is responsible to God to bear the sword, executing God's wrath against violators of His Law. The Church, as the depository of the Law of God, is to provide Biblical instruction for every sphere, including civil government. She is not to control civil government, but rather to provide expert legal counsel (Deut.17:8-13). Many of her sons are expected to assume the mantle of civil leadership.

Resting on the foundation of God's sovereignty, four vital pillars support the Christian Reconstruction movement:

Pillar #1: Redemption

This is the sovereignty of God in salvation. All men are disobedient and worthy of eternal separation from God in Hell. But Jesus Christ, the perfect man, died as a substitute for sinners. Because Christ shed His blood in their stead, God justly pardons everyone who believes the Gospel, granting them eternal life. This is called justification (Rom. 6:23).

Justification is accomplished entirely by the grace and mercy of God. Sinful man, being totally depraved, is utterly dependent on the provision of God for salvation, including the ears to hear and even the faith to believe the Gospel. Salvation does not rest primarily on the "decision" of a particular man for God, but rather on God's decision to save that particular man. Jesus said: "Ye have not chosen Me, but I have chosen you . . ." (John 15:16).

Pillar #2: Law of God

Christian Reconstruction upholds the authority of the Law of God in every sphere of society. This is the sovereignty of God in ethics. 1 Tim. 1:8 implies a lawful and an unlawful use of the Law of God. It is unlawful to seek acceptance with God by trying to obey the Law of God, the ceremonial law, or any manmade additions to the Law. We are justified by faith alone (Ephesians 2:8). On the other hand, man must look to the Law of God as his guide for holy living and civil statutes. The perfect standard of the Law shows us how we are to live, how far short we fall and how much we need a Savior.

"We know that the law is good if anyone uses it lawfully" (1 Tim. 1:8).

Unlawful Uses of the Law

1. Salvation by Works

2. Sacrificial Observances (Gal. 3:24)

3. Man made Traditions Added to the Law (Mk. 7:7ff.)

Lawful Uses of the Law

1. Guide for Life

2. Convict of Sin (Rom. 3:20)

3. Civil Use (1 Timothy 1:8,9)

Therefore, "not under the law" means that we are no longer condemned by the Law of God since we are justified by faith. It does NOT mean we are no longer ethically and morally bound to obey Old Testament law. Legalism results from a misapplication of God's moral Law or from traditions added to the Law. Simple childlike obedience to the Law of God does NOT equal legalism.

RELIGION AND THE STATE

The faulty interpretive principle of Old Testament law is to assume the Old Testament is invalid unless confirmed by the New Testament.

The faithful interpretive principle is to assume that the Old Testament is valid and still in effect unless specifically changed by the New Testament.

Covenantal shifts have occurred in areas such as sacrificial laws, ceremonial laws, Sabbath laws, dietary laws and agricultural laws. 1 Timothy 1:9 goes on to list a category of civil crimes that the Law of God is to restrain under the New Covenant: murder, kidnapping, adultery, perjury, etc. Therefore, one useful use of the Law of God is to restrain evil doers in society.

The theological name for this approach is "theonomy," from the Greek words "theos" meaning God and "nomos" meaning law. When men reject the Law of God as a standard, they are left with autonomy (self-law). This takes many forms, including common sense, pluralism, natural law, democracy (law of the people), and statutory law. The result of rejecting God's absolutes is always chaos.

When the Church rejects God's Law, it usually adopts what it calls the "law of love" in its place as the guide to action. Often this is a love devoid of content, that exalts unity over truth to avoid confrontation. But true biblical love goes hand in hand with the Law. Jesus said, "If you love me, you will keep my commandments" (John 14:15,21). By rejecting the standard of God's Law, the Church has nothing of substance to offer the world and becomes irrelevant.

Pillar #3: Presuppositionalism

Presuppositionalism is the self-sufficiency of an authoritative Bible. This is the sovereignty of God in revelation. Presuppositionalism defines our approach to the sovereign Word of God. Too often Christians try to "prove" the Bible to the natural man by presenting evidences from creation or logic. They assume the problem is merely intellectual and that belief will flow naturally from an airtight presentation of the facts.

But the Bible says that natural man willfully suppresses the truth (Rom. 2:15). The problem is not, therefore, a lack of evidence, but the basic tendency to set oneself up as the ultimate judge of truth. The heart of Eve's sin lay in exalting herself as the judge of what God had said. (Gen. 3:5,6).

These presuppositions radically alter our approach to the non-believer. If our defense of the faith consists solely of presenting evidences to his supposed independent reason, we are simply encouraging his independence, Instead of a focus on persuasion with facts and logic, Christian Reconstruction challenges the natural man, who presumes himself to be the ultimate judge of truth. The sword of the Spirit does not need to be proved, it needs to be used. We presuppose that the sword of the Spirit will penetrate the hearts of natural men knowing that the Law of God in their hearts confirms its truth.

Pillar #4: Assurance of Earthly Victory

This is the sovereignty of God in history. The Bible insists that God's Law is to hold full sway in every sphere of earthly activity, in history as well as eternity (Mat. 6:10). God's sovereignty ensures it will hold sway. He has commanded His Church to carry His gospel ("teaching them to observe all things"—Matt. 28:20 includes God's Law) to the nations. He has given us power for this task. The only hindrance is a faithless Church that can only see giants in the promised land of earthly victory.

Some Christians say God has turned world rulership over to Satan until the second coming of Christ. But this denies God's explicit claim to ownership (Ps. 24:1) and the decisive work of Christ in destroying the power of the devil (Col. 2:15, 1 Jn. 3:8).

This view overlooks the various meanings of the word "world" (Compare John 3:16 with 1 John 2:15). Satan may be the god of the world system that opposes God, but to grant him a sovereignty that belongs to God alone borders on blasphemy.

In The *American Covenant,* Marshall Foster observes that the implications of which view you hold are profound.

If you see God as ruling the earth

1. Your commission is to subdue the earth and build Christian nations through evangelizing and discipleship.

2. You see Christian culture to be the only acceptable culture and you see all others as aberrations.

3. All of God's world is holy and every activity in life is a religious activity to be seen as a spiritual work for God.

4. Reformation is expected.

RELIGION AND THE STATE

If you see Satan as ruling the earth

1. You must just concentrate on saving souls from this evil world.

2. You see Christian culture as a counter-culture, a persecuted minority in an evil world.

3. Church activity is primary and spiritual, while worldly pursuits are secular and to be dealt with only as a necessity.

4. Reformation is impossible and suspect, since things must get worse before Christ returns.

The above dichotomy illustrates the importance of ideas in determining consequences, because to the degree Christians have abdicated their leadership role and denied the "crown rights of Jesus Christ," to that degree the humanists have filled the void.

In summation, Christian Reconstruction is the only view that biblically answers the question of how Christians should relate to their culture.

Not RETREAT, that fails to apply the Bible to the problems of society (Fatal Error #1).

Not ACCOMMODATION, that misapplies the Bible to endorse various forms of humanism (Fatal Error #2). But RECONSTRUCTION according to the Law of God.

Individual salvation is the necessary priority, but Christian Reconstruction teaches that cultural renewal is an expected outworking of the Gospel. When Jesus said "make disciples of all nations," He meant it literally. The very cultural/governmental fabric of the nations is to be transformed by the preservative effect of their Christian citizens. This is the vision of the Reformers, the Puritans and the Pilgrims. This is the vision that we must rekindle anew today.

Source: Available online. URL: http://www.forerunner.com/forerunner/X0505_Parsons_-_What_is_Re.html. Accessed November 9, 2008.

5

International Documents

The material presented in this section include a cross section of historical documents regarding the world religions discussed in the text. As indicated, some documents are excerpts taken from longer originals.

HINDUISM

The "Quit India" Speech of Mahatma Gandhi (1942) (excerpts)

Gandhi made this speech on August 8, 1942, when the Quit India movement against British occupation was gaining strength. Given to a large gathering of independence leaders in Bombay (Mumbai), it became famous for its passionate call for ahimsa, or nonviolent resistance.

. . .

Let me explain my position clearly. God has vouchsafed to me a priceless gift in the weapon of Ahimsa.... If in this present crisis, when the earth is being scorched by the flames of Himsa [violence] and crying for deliverance, I failed to make use of [my] God-given talent, God will not forgive me and I shall be judged....

Ours is not a drive for power, but a purely non-violent fight for India's independence.... The Congress [party] is unconcerned as to who will rule when freedom is attained. The power, when it comes, will belong to the people of India, and it will be for them to decide [to whom they should give their trust]. Maybe the reins will be placed in the hands of the Parsis, for instance—as I would love to see happen—or they may be handed to some others whose names are not heard in the Congress today. It will not be for you then to object, saying "This community is microscopic. That party did not play its due part in the freedom's struggle, why should it have all the power?" Ever since its inception, the Congress has kept itself meticulously free of the communal taint. It has thought always in terms of the whole nation and has acted accordingly.

. . .

I believe that in the history of the world there has not been a more genuinely democratic struggle for freedom than ours . . . In the democracy which I have envisaged, a democracy established by nonviolence, there will be equal freedom for all. Everybody will be his own master. It is to join a struggle for such a democracy that I invite you today. Once you realize this, you will forget the differences between Hindus and Muslims, and think of yourselves as Indians only, engaged in the common struggle for independence.

Then there is the question of your attitude towards the British. I have noticed that there is hatred towards the British among the people. The people say they are disgusted with their behavior. The people make no distinction between British imperialism and the British people. To them, the two are one. . . . We must get rid of this feeling. Our quarrel is not with the British people, we fight their imperialism. The proposal for the withdrawal of British power did not come out of anger. It came to enable India to play its due part at the present critical juncture. . . . We cannot evoke the true spirit of sacrifice and valour so long as we are not free. I know the British Government will not be able to withhold freedom from us when we have made enough self-sacrifice. We must therefore purge ourselves of hatred. Speaking for myself, I can say that I have never felt any hatred. . . . At a time when I may have to launch the biggest struggle of my life, I may not harbor hatred against anybody.

Source: "The Quit India Speech by Mahatma Gandhi." Available online. URL: http://www.wordpower.ws/speeches/gandhi-quit-india.html. Accessed August 3, 2009.

BUDDHISM

The Edicts of Ashoka, ca. Third Century B.C.E. (excerpt)

The edicts are Buddhist teachings about dharma that were inscribed on stone tablets. These were erected throughout King Ashoka's realm in India and beyond. The king was a devout Buddhist who viewed the purpose of his government as showing compassion to all beings, improving people's lives, and helping them live in accordance with the dharma. The references to King Piyadasi are to Ashoka, who uses this term (from Priya-darshi, or Beloved of God) for himself.

1

Beloved-of-the-Gods, King Piyadasi, has caused this Dhamma edict to be written. Here (in my domain) no living beings are to be slaughtered or offered in sacrifice. Nor should festivals be held, for Beloved-of-the-Gods, King Piyadasi, sees much to object to in such festivals, although there are some festivals that Beloved-of-the-Gods, King Piyadasi, does approve of.

Formerly, in the kitchen of Beloved-of-the-Gods, King Piyadasi, hundreds of thousands of animals were killed every day to make curry. But now with the writing of this Dhamma edict only three creatures, two peacocks and a deer are killed, and the deer not always. And in time, not even these three creatures will be killed.

2

Everywhere within Beloved-of-the-Gods, King Piyadasi's domain, and among the people beyond the borders ... King Piyadasi made provision for two types of medical treatment: medical treatment for humans and medical treatment for animals. Wherever medical herbs suitable for humans or animals are not available, I have had them imported and grown. Wherever medical roots or fruits are not available I have had them imported and grown. Along roads I have had wells dug and trees planted for the benefit of humans and animals.

3

Beloved-of-the-Gods, King Piyadasi, speaks thus: Twelve years after my coronation this has been ordered—Everywhere in my domain the Yuktas, the Rajjukas and the Pradesikas shall go on inspection tours every five years for the purpose of Dhamma instruction and also to conduct other business. Respect for mother and father is good, generosity to friends, acquaintances, relatives, ...

In the past, for many hundreds of years, killing or harming living beings and improper behavior towards relatives, and improper behavior towards Brahmans and ascetics has increased. But now due to Beloved-of-the-Gods, King

RELIGION AND THE STATE

Piyadasi's Dhamma practice, the sound of the drum has been replaced by the sound of the Dhamma. And the sons, grandsons and great-grandsons of Beloved-of-the-Gods, King Piyadasi, too will continue to promote Dhamma practice until the end of time; living by Dhamma and virtue, they will instruct in Dhamma. Truly, this is the highest work, to instruct in Dhamma. But practicing the Dhamma cannot be done by one who is devoid of virtue and therefore its promotion and growth is commendable.

6

Beloved-of-the-Gods, King Piyadasi, speaks thus: In the past, state business was not transacted nor were reports delivered to the king at all hours. But now I have given this order that … reporters are to be posted with instructions to report to me the affairs of the people so that I might attend to these affairs wherever I am. And whatever I orally order in connection with donations or proclamations, or when urgent business presses itself on the Mahamatras, if disagreement or debate arises in the Council, then it must be reported to me immediately. This is what I have ordered. I am never content with exerting myself or with despatching business. Truly, I consider the welfare of all to be my duty, and the root of this is exertion and the prompt despatch of business. There is no better work than promoting the welfare of all the people and whatever efforts I am making is to repay the debt I owe to all beings to assure their happiness in this life, and attain heaven in the next.

7

Beloved-of-the-Gods, King Piyadasi, desires that all religions should reside everywhere, for all of them desire self-control and purity of heart. But people have various desires and various passions, and they may practice all of what they should or only a part of it. But one who receives great gifts yet is lacking in self-control, purity of heart, gratitude and firm devotion, such a person is mean.

12

Beloved-of-the-Gods, King Piyadasi, honors both ascetics and the householders of all religions, and he honors them with gifts and honors of various kinds. But Beloved-of-the-Gods, King Piyadasi, does not value gifts and honors as much as he values this—that there should be growth in the essentials of all religions. Growth in essentials can be done in different ways, but all of them have as their root restraint in speech, that is, not praising one's own religion, or condemning the religion of others without good cause. And if there is cause for criticism, it should be done in a mild way. But it is better to honor other religions for this reason. By so doing, one's own religion benefits, and so do other religions, while doing otherwise harms one's own religion and the religions of others. Whoever praises his own religion, due to excessive devotion, and condemns others with the thought "Let me glorify my own religion," only harms his own religion. Therefore contact (between religions) is good. One should listen to and respect the doctrines professed by others. Beloved-of-the-Gods, King Piyadasi, desires that all should be well-learned in the good doctrines of other religions.

Source: Available online. URL: http://www.cs.colorado.edu/~malaiya/ashoka.html. Accessed January 4, 2008.

Nobel Lecture of the 14th Dalai Lama (1989) (excerpt)

This speech was given by the Dalai Lama at the Nobel awards ceremony in Oslo, Norway. The Dalai Lama was awarded the Nobel Peace Prize in 1989 for his Five Point Peace Plan, which sets out a method for achieving peace between occupied Tibet and the People's Republic of China.

Brothers and Sisters,

It is an honour and pleasure to be among you today.... I am always reminded that we are all basically alike: we are all human beings. Maybe ... our skin is of a different colour or we speak different languages.... But basically, we are the same ... [that] is what binds us to each other.

I decided to share with you some of my thoughts concerning the common problem all of us face as members of the human family. Because we all share this small planet earth, we have to learn to live in harmony and peace with each other and with nature. That is not a dream, but a necessity.

I also wish to share with you today my feelings concerning the plight and aspirations of the people of Tibet.... As a spokesman for my captive countrymen and -women, I feel it is my duty to speak out on their behalf. I speak not with a feeling of anger or hatred towards those who are responsible for the immense suffering of our people and the destruction of our land, homes, and culture. They too are human beings who struggle to find happiness and deserve our compassion. I speak to inform you of the sad situation in my country today and of the aspirations of my people, because in our struggle for freedom, truth is the only weapon we possess....

RELIGION AND THE STATE

Peace, in the sense of the absence of war, is of little value to someone who is dying of hunger or cold. It will not remove the pain of torture inflicted on a prisoner of conscience. It does not comfort those who have lost their loved ones in floods caused by senseless deforestation in a neighboring country. Peace can only last where human rights are respected, where the people are fed, and where individuals and nations are free. True peace with oneself and with the world around us can only be achieved through the development of mental peace . . .

Material progress is of course important for human advancement. In Tibet, we paid much too little attention to technological and economic development, and today we realize that this was a mistake. At the same time, material development without spiritual development can also cause serious problems. In some countries, too much attention is paid to external things and very little importance is given to inner development. I believe both are important and must be developed side by side . . . Tibetans are always described by foreign visitors as being a happy, jovial people. This is part of our national character, formed by cultural and religious values that stress the importance of mental peace through the generation of love and kindness to all other living sentient beings, both human and animal. Inner peace is the key . . . without this inner peace no matter how comfortable your life is materially, you may still be worried, disturbed, or unhappy because of circumstances. . . .

. . . There are ways in which we can consciously work to develop feelings of love and kindness. For some of us, the most effective way to do so is through religious practice. For others, it may be non-religious practices. What is important is that we each make a sincere effort to take our responsibility for each other and for the natural environment we live in seriously. . . .

As you know, Tibet has, for forty years, been under foreign occupation. Today, more than a quarter of a million Chinese troops are stationed in Tibet. . . . During this time, Tibetans have been deprived of their most basic human rights, including the right to life, movement, speech, [and] worship. . . . More than one-sixth of Tibet's population of six million died as a direct result of the Chinese invasion and occupation. Even before the Cultural Revolution started, many of Tibet's monasteries, temples, and historic buildings were destroyed. Almost everything that remained was destroyed during the Cultural Revolution. . . . [D]espite the limited freedom granted after 1979 to rebuild parts of some monasteries and other such tokens of liberalization, the fundamental human rights of the Tibetan people are still today being systematically violated. In recent months, this bad situation has become even worse.

International Documents

If it were not for our community in exile, ... our nation would today be little more than a shattered remnant of a people. Our culture, religion, and national identity would have been effectively eliminated. As it is, we have built schools and monasteries in exile and have created democratic institutions to serve our people and preserve the seeds of our civilization. With this experience, we intend to implement full democracy in a future free Tibet. ...

[My] Five-Point Peace Plan addresses the principal and interrelated issues [of] (1) Transformation of the whole of Tibet ... into a Zone of Ahimsa [nonviolence]; (2) Abandonment of China's population transfer policy; (3) Respect for the Tibetan people's fundamental rights and democratic freedoms; (4) Restoration and protection of Tibet's natural environment; and (5) Commencement of earnest negotiations on the future status of Tibet and of relations between the Tibetan and Chinese people. ...

I would like to take this opportunity to explain the Zone of Ahimsa, or peace sanctuary concept, which is the central element of the [plan]: ... It is my dream that the entire Tibetan Plateau should become a free refuge where humanity and nature can live in peace and in harmonious balance. It would be a place where people from all over the world could come to seek the true meaning of peace within themselves, away from the tensions and pressures of so much of the rest of the world.

Let me end with a personal note of thanks to all of you. ... [Your] concern and support ... continue to give us courage to struggle for freedom and justice: not through the use of arms, but with the powerful weapons of truth and determination. ... [Do] not forget Tibet at this critical time in its history. ... A future free Tibet will seek to help those in need throughout the world, to protect nature, and to promote peace. ... This is my hope and prayer. ...

Source: The Nobel Lectures. The 14th Dalai Lama: The Nobel Peace Prize 1989. December 11, 1989. Available online. URL: http://nobelprize.org/nobel-prizes/peace/laureates/1989/lama-lecture.html. Accessed August 3, 2009.

CHRISTIANITY

The Edict of Milan by Constantine, 313 (excerpt)

This edict by Constantine, a leader of the Roman Empire, set out the extent to which the state and its people and institutions were willing to tolerate new religions, particularly early Christianity. Constantine later became the first world leader to convert to Christianity and make it the official religion of the Roman Empire.

RELIGION AND THE STATE

When I, Constantine Augustus, as well as I Licinius Augustus fortunately met near Mediolanurn (Milan), and were considering everything that pertained to the public welfare and security, we thought, among other things which we saw would be for the good of many, those regulations pertaining to the reverence of the Divinity ought certainly to be made first, so that we might grant to the Christians and others full authority to observe that religion which each preferred; whence any Divinity whatsoever in the seat of the heavens may be propitious and kindly disposed to us and all who are placed under our rule And thus by this wholesome counsel and most upright provision we thought to arrange that no one whatsoever should be denied the opportunity to give his heart to the observance of the Christian religion, of that religion which he should think best for himself, so that the Supreme Deity, to whose worship we freely yield our hearts, may show in all things His usual favor and benevolence. Therefore, your Worship should know that it has pleased us to remove all conditions whatsoever, which were in the rescripts formerly given to you officially, concerning the Christians and now any one of these who wishes to observe Christian religion may do so freely and openly, without molestation. We thought it fit to commend these things most fully to your care that you may know that we have given to those Christians free and unrestricted opportunity of religious worship. When you see that this has been granted to them by us, your Worship will know that we have also conceded to other religions the right of open and free observance of their worship for the sake of the peace of our times, that each one may have the free opportunity to worship as he pleases; this regulation is made that we may not seem to detract from any dignity or any religion.

Source: Available online. URL: http://www.fordham.edu/halsall/source/edict-milan.html. Accessed November 9, 2008.

Dictatus Papae by Pope Gregory VII, 1075 (excerpt)

This dictat of the pope was issued to make absolutely clear to kings and peasants alike that the ultimate arbiter of power in this world and the world to come was the Catholic Church in the person of the pope.

1. That the Roman church was founded by God alone.

2. That the Roman pontiff alone can with right be called universal.

3. That he alone can depose or reinstate bishops.

4. That, in a council his legate, even if a lower grade, is above all bishops, and can pass sentence of deposition against them.

...

7. That of the pope alone all princes shall kiss the feet.

8. That his name alone shall be spoken in the churches.

9. That this is the only name in the world.

10. That it may be permitted to him to depose emperors.

11. That he may be permitted to transfer bishops if need be.

12. That he has power to ordain a clerk of any church he may wish.

...

14. That no synod shall be called a general one without his order.

15. That no chapter and no book shall be considered canonical without his authority.

16. That a sentence passed by him may be retracted by no one; and that he himself, alone of all, may retract it.

17. That he himself may be judged by no one.

18. That no one shall dare to condemn one who appeals to the apostolic chair.

...

20. That the Roman church has never erred; nor will it err to all eternity, the Scripture bearing witness.

21. That the Roman pontiff, if he have been canonically ordained, is undoubtedly made a saint by the merits of St. Peter; St. Ennodius, bishop of Pavia, bearing witness, and many holy fathers agreeing with him. As is contained in the decrees of St. Symmachus the pope.

22. That, by his command and consent, it may be lawful for subordinates to bring accusations.

23. That he may depose and reinstate bishops without assembling a synod.

RELIGION AND THE STATE

24. That he who is not at peace with the Roman church shall not be considered catholic.

25. That he may absolve subjects from their fealty to wicked men.

Source: Available online. URL: http://www.fordham.edu/halsall/source/g7-dictpap.html. Accessed November 9, 2008.

The Constitutions of Clarendon by King Henry II, 1164 (excerpt)

When the British king Henry II installed Thomas Becket as archbishop of Canterbury, he thought he had an ally who would support the claims to power of the king over those of the church. Henry was mistaken, and an epic battle of wills ensued. As archbishop, Becket became an extremely devout and immovable supporter of the ultimate power of the Catholic Church over that of monarchs. This document sets out Henry's claim to supremacy over the church and to royal prerogatives of all types that had existed during the reigns of previous English kings. Shortly afterward, the king had Becket assassinated in Canterbury Cathedral.

From the year of our Lord's incarnation 1164, the fourth year of the papacy of Alexander, the tenth of the most illustrious Henry, king of the English, in the presence of the same king, was made this remembrance or recognition of a certain part of the customs, liberties, and dignities of his predecessors, that is to say of King Henry his grandfather and others, which ought to be observed and held in the kingdom. And because of dissensions and discords which had arisen between the clergy and the lord king's justices and the barons of the kingdom concerning the customs and dignities, this recognition has been made before the archbishops and bishops and clergy, and the earls and barons and great men of the kingdom. And these same customs declared by the archbishops, bishops, earls, and barons, and by the nobler and older men of the kingdom, Thomas archbishop of Canterbury and Roger archbishop of York ... and many other great men and nobles of the kingdom both clergy and laymen.

A certain part of the customs and dignities which were recognized is contained in the present writing. Of which part these are the articles:

1. If a controversy arise between laymen, or between laymen and clerks, or between clerks concerning patronage and presentation of churches, it shall be treated or concluded in the court of the lord king. . . .

International Documents

3. Clerks charged and accused of any matter, summoned by the king's justice, shall come into his court to answer there to whatever it shall seem to the king's court should be answered there; and in the church court to what it seems should be answered there; however the king's justice shall send into the court of holy Church for the purpose of seeing how the matter shall be treated there. And if the clerk be convicted or confess, the church ought not to protect him further.

4. It is not permitted the archbishops, bishops, and priests of the kingdom to leave the kingdom without the lord king's permission. And if they do leave they are to give security, if the lord king please, that they will seek no evil or damage to king or kingdom in going, in making their stay, or in returning . . .

6. Laymen ought not to be accused save by dependable and lawful accusers and witnesses in the presence of the bishop, yet so that the archdeacon lose not his right or anything which he ought to have thence. And if there should be those who are deemed culpable, but whom no one wishes or dares to accuse, the sheriff, upon the bishop's request, shall cause twelve lawful men of the neighborhood or the vill to take oath before the bishop that they will show the truth of the matter according to their conscience.

7. No one who holds of the king in chief or any of the officials of his demesne is to be excommunicated or his lands placed under interdict unless the lord king, if he be in the land, or his justiciar, if he be outside the kingdom, first gives his consent, that he may do for him what is right: yet so that what pertains to the royal court be concluded there, and what looks to the church court be sent thither to be concluded there . . .

10. If any one who is of a city, castle, borough, or demesne manor of the king shall be cited by archdeacon or bishop for any offense for which he ought to be held answerable to them and despite their summonses he refuse to do what is right, it is fully permissible to place him under interdict, but he ought not to be excommunicated before the king's chief official of that vill shall agree, in order that he may authoritatively constrain him to come to his trial. But if the king's official fail in this, he himself shall be in the lord king's mercy; and then the bishop shall be able to coerce the accused man by ecclesiastical authority . . .

12. When an archbishopric or bishopric, or an abbey or priory of the king's demesne shall be vacant, it ought to be in his hands, and he shall assume its revenues and expenses as pertaining to his demesne. And when the time comes to provide for the church, the lord king should

notify the more important clergy of the church, and the election should be held in the lord king's own chapel with the assent of the lord king and on the advice of the clergy of the realm whom he has summoned for the purpose. And there, before he be consecrated, let the elect perform homage and fealty to the lord king as his liege lord for life, limbs, and earthly honor, saving his order.

13. If any of the great men of the kingdom should forcibly prevent archbishop, bishop, or archdeacon from administering justice in which he or his men were concerned, then the lord king ought to bring such an one to justice. And if it should happen that any one deforce the lord king of his right, archbishops, bishops, and archdeacons ought to constrain him to make satisfaction to the lord king.

14. Chattels which have been forfeited to the king are not to be held in churches or cemetaries against the king's justice, because they belong to the king whether they be found inside churches or outside.

15. Pleas concerning debts, which are owed on the basis of an oath or in connection with which no oath has been taken, are in the king's justice.

16. Sons of villeins should not be ordained without the consent of the lord on whose land it is ascertained they were born.

The declaration of the above-mentioned royal customs and dignities has been made by the archbishops, bishops, earls, barons, and the nobler and older men of the kingdom, at Clarendon on the fourth day before the Purification of the Blessed Virgin Mary, lord Henry being present there with the lord king his father. There are, indeed, many other great customs and dignities of holy mother church and of the lord king and barons of the kingdom, which are not included in this writing, but which are to be preserved to holy church and to the lord king and his heirs and the barons of the kingdom, and are to be kept inviolate for ever.

Source: Available online. URL: http://www.fordham.edu/halsall/source/cclarendon.html. Accessed November 24, 2008.

The Bull *Unam Sanctam* by Pope Boniface VIII, 1302 (excerpt)

This document is another in the ongoing tug-of-war between monarchs and the pope. The bull (official papal statement) states unequivocally that the pope is the head of the church, that all who seek eternal salvation must obey him, that he is infallible, and that his is the ultimate authority in Christendom. This bull

International Documents

is one of the most famous and powerful salvos in the battle between the church and the state. In this case, the pope was putting King Phillip the Fair of France in his "rightful" and subservient place in relation to the church.

UNAM SANCTAM (PROMULGATED NOVEMBER 18, 1302)

Urged by faith, we are obliged to believe and to maintain that the Church is one, holy, catholic, and also apostolic. We believe in her firmly and we confess with simplicity that outside of her there is neither salvation nor the remission of sins, as the Spouse in the Canticles [Sgs 6:8] proclaims: 'One is my dove, my perfect one. She is the only one, the chosen of her who bore her,' and she represents one sole mystical body whose Head is Christ and the head of Christ is God [1 Cor 11:3]. In her then is one Lord, one faith, one baptism [Eph 4:5]. . . . We venerate this Church as one, the Lord having said by the mouth of the prophet: 'Deliver, O God, my soul from the sword and my only one from the hand of the dog.' [Ps 21:20] He has prayed for his soul, that is for himself, heart and body; and this body, that is to say, the Church, He has called one because of the unity of the Spouse, of the faith, of the sacraments, and of the charity of the Church. This is the tunic of the Lord, the seamless tunic, which was not rent but which was cast by lot [Jn 19:23–24]. Therefore, of the one and only Church there is one body and one head, not two heads like a monster; that is, Christ and the Vicar of Christ, Peter and the successor of Peter, since the Lord speaking to Peter Himself said: 'Feed my sheep' [Jn 21:17], meaning, my sheep in general, not these, nor those in particular, whence we understand that He entrusted all to him [Peter]. Therefore, if the Greeks or others should say that they are not confided to Peter and to his successors, they must confess not being the sheep of Christ, since Our Lord says in John 'there is one sheepfold and one shepherd.' We are informed by the texts of the gospels that in this Church and in its power are two swords; namely, the spiritual and the temporal. For when the Apostles say: 'Behold, here are two swords' [Lk 22:38] that is to say, in the Church, since the Apostles were speaking, the Lord did not reply that there were too many, but sufficient. Certainly the one who denies that the temporal sword is in the power of Peter has not listened well to the word of the Lord commanding: 'Put up thy sword into thy scabbard' [Mt 26:52]. Both, therefore, are in the power of the Church, that is to say, the spiritual and the material sword, but the former is to be administered for the Church but the latter by the Church; the former in the hands of the priest; the latter by the hands of kings and soldiers, but at the will and sufferance of the priest.

However, one sword ought to be subordinated to the other and temporal authority, subjected to spiritual power. For since the Apostle said: 'There is no power except from God and the things that are, are ordained of God' [Rom

13:1–2], but they would not be ordained if one sword were not subordinated to the other and if the inferior one, as it were, were not led upwards by the other.

For, according to the Blessed Dionysius, it is a law of the divinity that the lowest things reach the highest place by intermediaries. Then, according to the order of the universe, all things are not led back to order equally and immediately, but the lowest by the intermediary, and the inferior by the superior. Hence we must recognize the more clearly that spiritual power surpasses in dignity and in nobility any temporal power whatever, as spiritual things surpass the temporal. This we see very clearly also by the payment, benediction, and consecration of the tithes, but the acceptance of power itself and by the government even of things. For with truth as our witness, it belongs to spiritual power to establish the terrestrial power and to pass judgement if it has not been good. Thus is accomplished the prophecy of Jeremias concerning the Church and the ecclesiastical power: 'Behold to-day I have placed you over nations, and over kingdoms' and the rest. Therefore, if the terrestrial power err, it will be judged by the spiritual power; but if a minor spiritual power err, it will be judged by a superior spiritual power; but if the highest power of all err, it can be judged only by God, and not by man, according to the testimony of the Apostle: 'The spiritual man judgeth of all things and he himself is judged by no man' [1 Cor 2:15]. This authority, however, (though it has been given to man and is exercised by man), is not human but rather divine, granted to Peter by a divine word and reaffirmed to him (Peter) and his successors by the One Whom Peter confessed, the Lord saying to Peter himself, 'Whatsoever you shall bind on earth, shall be bound also in Heaven' etc. [Mt 16:19]. Therefore whoever resists this power thus ordained by God, resists the ordinance of God [Rom 13:2], unless he invent like Manicheus two beginnings, which is false and judged by us heretical, since according to the testimony of Moses, it is not in the beginnings but in the beginning that God created heaven and earth [Gen 1:1]. Furthermore, we declare, we proclaim, we define that it is absolutely necessary for salvation that every human creature be subject to the Roman Pontiff.

Source: Available online. URL: http://www.fordham.edu/halsall/source/b8-unam.html. Accessed December 15, 2008.

The Ninety-five Theses by Martin Luther, 1517 (excerpts)

By the 16th century, the corruption in the Roman Catholic Church was so egregious, many people sought a purer, more Christian way to worship. The

International Documents

monk and theologian Martin Luther took it upon himself to write a treatise exposing the church's corruption, particularly the selling of indulgences, and describing the true Christian principles that should guide believers. The 95 theses that Luther wrote, most of which are included here, were famously posted on the door of a church in Wittenberg, Germany. This public protestation was one of the driving forces behind the Reformation that followed.

Out of love for the truth and the desire to bring it to light, the following propositions will be discussed at Wittenberg, under the presidency of the Reverend Father Martin Luther, Master of Arts and of Sacred Theology, and Lecturer in Ordinary on the same at that place. Wherefore he requests that those who are unable to be present and debate orally with us, may do so by letter.

In the Name our Lord Jesus Christ. Amen.

1. Our Lord and Master Jesus Christ, when He said Poenitentiam agite, willed that the whole life of believers should be repentance.

2. This word cannot be understood to mean sacramental penance, i.e., confession and satisfaction, which is administered by the priests.

3. Yet it means not inward repentance only; nay, there is no inward repentance which does not outwardly work divers mortifications of the flesh.

4. The penalty [of sin], therefore, continues so long as hatred of self continues; for this is the true inward repentance, and continues until our entrance into the kingdom of heaven.

5. The pope does not intend to remit, and cannot remit any penalties other than those which he has imposed either by his own authority or by that of the Canons.

6. The pope cannot remit any guilt, except by declaring that it has been remitted by God and by assenting to God's remission; though, to be sure, he may grant remission in cases reserved to his judgment. If his right to grant remission in such cases were despised, the guilt would remain entirely unforgiven.

7. God remits guilt to no one whom He does not, at the same time, humble in all things and bring into subjection to His vicar, the priest. . . .

10. Ignorant and wicked are the doings of those priests who, in the case of the dying, reserve canonical penances for purgatory.

11. This changing of the canonical penalty to the penalty of purgatory is quite evidently one of the tares that were sown while the bishops slept....

14. The imperfect health [of soul], that is to say, the imperfect love, of the dying brings with it, of necessity, great fear; and the smaller the love, the greater is the fear.

15. This fear and horror is sufficient of itself alone (to say nothing of other things) to constitute the penalty of purgatory, since it is very near to the horror of despair.

16. Hell, purgatory, and heaven seem to differ as do despair, almost-despair, and the assurance of safety.

17. With souls in purgatory it seems necessary that horror should grow less and love increase.

18. It seems unproved, either by reason or Scripture, that they are outside the state of merit, that is to say, of increasing love.

19. Again, it seems unproved that they, or at least that all of them, are certain or assured of their own blessedness, though we may be quite certain of it.

20. Therefore by "full remission of all penalties" the pope means not actually "of all," but only of those imposed by himself.

21. Therefore those preachers of indulgences are in error, who say that by the pope's indulgences a man is freed from every penalty, and saved;

22. Whereas he remits to souls in purgatory no penalty which, according to the canons, they would have had to pay in this life.

23. If it is at all possible to grant to any one the remission of all penalties whatsoever, it is certain that this remission can be granted only to the most perfect, that is, to the very fewest.

24. It must needs be, therefore, that the greater part of the people are deceived by that indiscriminate and highsounding promise of release from penalty.

25. The power which the pope has, in a general way, over purgatory, is just like the power which any bishop or curate has, in a special way, within his own diocese or parish.

26. The pope does well when he grants remission to souls [in purgatory], not by the power of the keys (which he does not possess), but by way of intercession.

International Documents

27. They preach . . . that so soon as the penny jingles into the money-box, the soul flies out [of purgatory].

28. It is certain that when the penny jingles into the money-box, gain and avarice can be increased, but the result of the intercession of the Church is in the power of God alone. . . .

31. Rare as is the man that is truly penitent, so rare is also the man who truly buys indulgences, i.e., such men are most rare.

32. They will be condemned eternally, together with their teachers, who believe themselves sure of their salvation because they have letters of pardon.

33. Men must be on their guard against those who say that the pope's pardons are that inestimable gift of God by which man is reconciled to Him;

34. For these "graces of pardon" concern only the penalties of sacramental satisfaction, and these are appointed by man.

35. They preach no Christian doctrine who teach that contrition is not necessary in those who intend to buy souls out of purgatory or to buy confessionalia.

36. Every truly repentant Christian has a right to full remission of penalty and guilt, even without letters of pardon.

37. Every true Christian, whether living or dead, has part in all the blessings of Christ and the Church; and this is granted him by God, even without letters of pardon. . . .

41. Apostolic pardons are to be preached with caution, lest the people may falsely think them preferable to other good works of love.

42. Christians are to be taught that the pope does not intend the buying of pardons to be compared in any way to works of mercy.

43. Christians are to be taught that he who gives to the poor or lends to the needy does a better work than buying pardons;

44. Because love grows by works of love, and man becomes better; but by pardons man does not grow better, only more free from penalty.

45. Christians are to be taught that he who sees a man in need, and passes him by, and gives [his money] for pardons, purchases not the indulgences of the pope, but the indignation of God.

RELIGION AND THE STATE

46. Christians are to be taught that unless they have more than they need, they are bound to keep back what is necessary for their own families, and by no means to squander it on pardons.

47. Christians are to be taught that the buying of pardons is a matter of free will, and not of commandment.

48. Christians are to be taught that the pope, in granting pardons, needs, and therefore desires, their devout prayer for him more than the money they bring.

49. Christians are to be taught that the pope's pardons are useful, if they do not put their trust in them; but altogether harmful, if through them they lose their fear of God.

50. Christians are to be taught that if the pope knew the exactions of the pardon-preachers, he would rather that St. Peter's church should go to ashes, than that it should be built up with the skin, flesh and bones of his sheep.

51. Christians are to be taught that it would be the pope's wish, as it is his duty, to give of his own money to very many of those from whom certain hawkers of pardons cajole money, even though the church of St. Peter might have to be sold.

52. The assurance of salvation by letters of pardon is vain, even though the commissary, nay, even though the pope himself, were to stake his soul upon it. . . .

55. It must be the intention of the pope that if pardons, which are a very small thing, are celebrated with one bell, with single processions and ceremonies, then the Gospel, which is the very greatest thing, should be preached with a hundred bells, a hundred processions, a hundred ceremonies.

56. The "treasures of the Church," out of which the pope. grants indulgences, are not sufficiently named or known among the people of Christ.

57. That they are not temporal treasures is certainly evident, for many of the vendors do not pour out such treasures so easily, but only gather them. . . .

60. Without rashness we say that the keys of the Church, given by Christ's merit, are that treasure;

61. For it is clear that for the remission of penalties and of reserved cases, the power of the pope is of itself sufficient.

62. The true treasure of the Church is the Most Holy Gospel of the glory and the grace of God.

63. But this treasure is naturally most odious, for it makes the first to be last.

64. On the other hand, the treasure of indulgences is naturally most acceptable, for it makes the last to be first.

65. Therefore the treasures of the Gospel are nets with which they formerly were wont to fish for men of riches.

66. The treasures of the indulgences are nets with which they now fish for the riches of men.

67. The indulgences which the preachers cry as the "greatest graces" are known to be truly such, in so far as they promote gain.

68. Yet they are in truth the very smallest graces compared with the grace of God and the piety of the Cross. . . .

75. To think the papal pardons so great that they could absolve a man even if he had committed an impossible sin and violated the Mother of God—this is madness.

76. We say, on the contrary, that the papal pardons are not able to remove the very least of venial sins, so far as its guilt is concerned.

77. It is said that even St. Peter, if he were now Pope, could not bestow greater graces; this is blasphemy against St. Peter and against the pope.

78. We say, on the contrary, that even the present pope, and any pope at all, has greater graces at his disposal; to wit, the Gospel, powers, gifts of healing, etc., as it is written in I. Corinthians xii.

79. To say that the cross, emblazoned with the papal arms, which is set up [by the preachers of indulgences], is of equal worth with the Cross of Christ, is blasphemy.

80. The bishops, curates and theologians who allow such talk to be spread among the people, will have an account to render. . . .

84. Again:—"What is this new piety of God and the pope, that for money they allow a man who is impious and their enemy to buy out of purgatory the pious soul of a friend of God, and do not rather, because of that pious and beloved soul's own need, free it for pure love's sake?"

85. Again:—"Why are the penitential canons long since in actual fact and through disuse abrogated and dead, now satisfied by the granting of indulgences, as though they were still alive and in force?"

86. Again:—"Why does not the pope, whose wealth is to-day greater than the riches of the richest, build just this one church of St. Peter with his own money, rather than with the money of poor believers?" . . .

90. To repress these arguments and scruples of the laity by force alone, and not to resolve them by giving reasons, is to expose the Church and the pope to the ridicule of their enemies, and to make Christians unhappy.

91. If, therefore, pardons were preached according to the spirit and mind of the pope, all these doubts would be readily resolved; nay, they would not exist.

92. Away, then, with all those prophets who say to the people of Christ, "Peace, peace," and there is no peace!

93. Blessed be all those prophets who say to the people of Christ, "Cross, cross," and there is no cross!

94. Christians are to be exhorted that they be diligent in following Christ, their Head, through penalties, deaths, and hell;

95. And thus be confident of entering into heaven rather through many tribulations, than through the assurance of peace.

Source: Available online. URL: http://www.iclnet.org/pub/resources/text/wittenberg/luther/web/ninetyfive.html. Accessed October 31, 2008.

A Letter Concerning Toleration by John Locke, 1689 (excerpt)

John Locke was one of the brightest minds of the European Enlightenment. This English philosopher wrote extensively on the superiority of reason over superstition and intolerance. This letter is considered one of the greatest arguments for religious tolerance and the separation of church and state ever written. It profoundly influenced the Founding Fathers of the United States, as well as the leaders of the French Revolution.

Honoured Sir,

Since you are pleased to inquire what are my thoughts about the mutual toleration of Christians in their different professions of religion, I must needs answer you freely that I esteem that toleration to be the chief characteristic mark of the true Church. For whatsoever some people boast of the antiquity of places and names, or of the pomp of their outward worship; others, of the reformation of their discipline; all, of the orthodoxy of their faith—for everyone is orthodox to himself—these things, and all others of this nature, are much rather marks of men striving for power and empire over one another than of the Church of Christ. Let anyone have never so true a claim to all these things, yet if he be destitute of charity, meekness, and good-will in general towards all mankind, even to those that are not Christians, he is certainly yet short of being a true Christian himself . . . Whosoever will list himself under the banner of Christ, must, in the first place and above all things, make war upon his own lusts and vices. It is in vain for any man to usurp the name of Christian, without holiness of life, purity of manners, benignity and meekness of spirit. "Let everyone that nameth the name of Christ, depart from iniquity." . . . It would, indeed, be very hard for one that appears careless about his own salvation to persuade me that he were extremely concerned for mine. For it is impossible that those should sincerely and heartily apply themselves to make other people Christians, who have not really embraced the Christian religion in their own hearts. If the Gospel and the apostles may be credited, no man can be a Christian without charity and without that faith which works, not by force, but by love. Now, I appeal to the consciences of those that persecute, torment, destroy, and kill other men upon pretence of religion, whether they do it out of friendship and kindness towards them or no? And I shall then indeed, and not until then, believe they do so, when I shall see those fiery zealots correcting, in the same manner, their friends and familiar acquaintance for the manifest sins they commit against the precepts of the Gospel . . .

The toleration of those that differ from others in matters of religion is so agreeable to the Gospel of Jesus Christ, and to the genuine reason of mankind, that it seems monstrous for men to be so blind as not to perceive the necessity and advantage of it in so clear a light . . . I esteem it above all things necessary to distinguish exactly the business of civil government from that of religion and to settle the just bounds that lie between the one and the other. If this be not done, there can be no end put to the controversies that will be always arising between those that have, or at least pretend to have, on the one side, a concernment for the interest of men's souls, and, on the other side, a care of the commonwealth.

The commonwealth seems to me to be a society of men constituted only for the procuring, preserving, and advancing their own civil interests.

Civil interests I call life, liberty, health, and indolency of body; and the possession of outward things, such as money, lands, houses, furniture, and the like.

RELIGION AND THE STATE

It is the duty of the civil magistrate, by the impartial execution of equal laws, to secure unto all the people in general and to every one of his subjects in particular the just possession of these things belonging to this life. If anyone presume to violate the laws of public justice and equity, established for the preservation of those things, his presumption is to be checked by the fear of punishment, consisting of the deprivation or diminution of those civil interests, or goods, which otherwise he might and ought to enjoy. But seeing no man does willingly suffer himself to be punished by the deprivation of any part of his goods, and much less of his liberty or life, therefore, is the magistrate armed with the force and strength of all his subjects, in order to the punishment of those that violate any other man's rights.

Now that the whole jurisdiction of the magistrate reaches only to these civil concernments, and that all civil power, right and dominion, is bounded and confined to the only care of promoting these things; and that it neither can nor ought in any manner to be extended to the salvation of souls, these following considerations seem unto me abundantly to demonstrate.

First, because the care of souls is not committed to the civil magistrate, any more than to other men. It is not committed unto him, I say, by God; because it appears not that God has ever given any such authority to one man over another as to compel anyone to his religion. Nor can any such power be vested in the magistrate by the consent of the people, because no man can so far abandon the care of his own salvation as blindly to leave to the choice of any other, whether prince or subject, to prescribe to him what faith or worship he shall embrace. For no man can, if he would, conform his faith to the dictates of another . . .

In the second place, the care of souls cannot belong to the civil magistrate, because his power consists only in outward force; but true and saving religion consists in the inward persuasion of the mind, without which nothing can be acceptable to God. And such is the nature of the understanding, that it cannot be compelled to the belief of anything by outward force. Confiscation of estate, imprisonment, torments, nothing of that nature can have any such efficacy as to make men change the inward judgement that they have framed of things . . .

In the third place, the care of the salvation of men's souls cannot belong to the magistrate; because, though the rigour of laws and the force of penalties were capable to convince and change men's minds, yet would not that help at all to the salvation of their souls. For there being but one truth, one way to heaven, what hope is there that more men would be led into it if they had no rule but the religion of the court and were put under the necessity to quit the light of their own reason, and oppose the dictates of their own consciences, and blindly to resign themselves up to the will of their governors and to the religion which either ignorance, ambition, or superstition had chanced to establish in the countries where they were born? In the variety and contradiction of opinions in religion, wherein the princes of the world are as much divided as in their secular interests, the narrow way would be much straitened; one country alone would be in the right, and all the rest of the world put under an obligation of following their princes in the ways that lead to destruction; and that which heightens the absurdity, and very ill suits the notion of a Deity, men would owe their eternal happiness or misery to the places of their nativity.

These considerations, to omit many others that might have been urged to the same purpose, seem unto me sufficient to conclude that all the power of civil government relates only to men's civil interests, is confined to the care of the things of this world, and hath nothing to do with the world to come.

Let us now consider what a church is. A church, then, I take to be a voluntary society of men, joining themselves together of their own accord in order to the public worshipping of God in such manner as they judge acceptable to Him, and effectual to the salvation of their souls.

I say it is a free and voluntary society ... No member of a religious society can be tied with any other bonds but what proceed from the certain expectation of eternal life. A church, then, is a society of members voluntarily uniting to that end.

It follows now that we consider what is the power of this church and unto what laws it is subject.

But since the joining together of several members into this church-society, as has already been demonstrated, is absolutely free and spontaneous, it necessarily follows that the right of making its laws can belong to none but the society itself; or, at least (which is the same thing), to those whom the society by common consent has authorised thereunto ...

[L]et us inquire, in the next place: How far the duty of toleration extends, and what is required from everyone by it? ...

RELIGION AND THE STATE

[N]o private person has any right in any manner to prejudice another person in his civil enjoyments because he is of another church or religion. All the rights and franchises that belong to him as a man, or as a denizen, are inviolably to be preserved to him. These are not the business of religion. No violence nor injury is to be offered him, whether he be Christian or Pagan. Nay, we must not content ourselves with the narrow measures of bare justice; charity, bounty, and liberality must be added to it. This the Gospel enjoins, this reason directs, and this that natural fellowship we are born into requires of us. If any man err from the right way, it is his own misfortune, no injury to thee; nor therefore art thou to punish him in the things of this life because thou supposest he will be miserable in that which is to come . . .

Nobody, therefore, in fine, neither single persons nor churches, nay, nor even commonwealths, have any just title to invade the civil rights and worldly goods of each other upon pretence of religion. Those that are of another opinion would do well to consider with themselves how pernicious a seed of discord and war, how powerful a provocation to endless hatreds, rapines, and slaughters they thereby furnish unto mankind. No peace and security, no, not so much as common friendship, can ever be established or preserved amongst men so long as this opinion prevails, that dominion is founded in grace and that religion is to be propagated by force of arms.

[L]et us see what the duty of toleration requires from those who are distinguished from the rest of mankind (from the laity, as they please to call us) by some ecclesiastical character and office; whether they be bishops, priests, presbyters, ministers, or however else dignified or distinguished. It is not my business to inquire here into the original of the power or dignity of the clergy. This only I say, that, whencesoever their authority be sprung, since it is ecclesiastical, it ought to be confined within the bounds of the Church, nor can it in any manner be extended to civil affairs, because the Church itself is a thing absolutely separate and distinct from the commonwealth. The boundaries on both sides are fixed and immovable.

But this is not all. It is not enough that ecclesiastical men abstain from violence and rapine and all manner of persecution. He that pretends to be a successor of the apostles, and takes upon him the office of teaching, is obliged also to admonish his hearers of the duties of peace and goodwill towards all men, as well towards the erroneous as the orthodox; towards those that differ from them in faith and worship as well as towards those that agree with them therein. And he ought industriously to exhort all men, whether private persons or magistrates (if any such there be in his church), to charity, meekness, and toleration, and diligently endeavour to ally and temper all that heat and unreasonable averseness of mind which either any man's fiery zeal for his own sect or the craft of others has kindled against dissenters.

In the last place, let us now consider what is the magistrate's duty in the business of toleration, which certainly is very considerable.

We have already proved that the care of souls does not belong to the magistrate. Not a magisterial care, I mean (if I may so call it), which consists in prescribing by laws and compelling by punishments. But a charitable care, which consists in teaching, admonishing, and persuading, cannot be denied unto any man. The care, therefore, of every man's soul belongs unto himself and is to be left unto himself. But what if he neglect the care of his soul? I answer: What if he neglect the care of his health or of his estate, which things are nearer related to the government of the magistrate than the other? Will the magistrate provide by an express law that such a one shall not become poor or sick? Laws provide, as much as is possible, that the goods and health of subjects be not injured by the fraud and violence of others; they do not guard them from the negligence or ill-husbandry of the possessors themselves. No man can be forced to be rich or healthful whether he will or no. Nay, God Himself will not save men against their wills . . .

Having thus at length freed men from all dominion over one another in matters of religion, let us now consider what they are to do. All men know and acknowledge that God ought to be publicly worshipped; why otherwise do they compel one another unto the public assemblies? Men, therefore, constituted in this liberty are to enter into some religious society, that they meet together, not only for mutual edification, but to own to the world that they worship God and offer unto His Divine Majesty such service as they themselves are not ashamed of and such as they think not unworthy of Him, nor unacceptable to Him; and, finally, that by the purity of doctrine, holiness of life, and decent form of worship, they may draw others unto the love of the true religion, and perform such other things in religion as cannot be done by each private man apart.

These religious societies I call Churches; and these, I say, the magistrate ought to tolerate, for the business of these assemblies of the people is nothing but what is lawful for every man in particular to take care of—I mean the salvation of their souls; nor in this case is there any difference between the National Church and other separated congregations . . .

RELIGION AND THE STATE

As the magistrate has no power to impose by his laws the use of any rites and ceremonies in any Church, so neither has he any power to forbid the use of such rites and ceremonies as are already received, approved, and practised by any Church; because, if he did so, he would destroy the Church itself: the end of whose institution is only to worship God with freedom after its own manner ...

[W]e see what difference there is between the Church and the Commonwealth. Whatsoever is lawful in the Commonwealth cannot be prohibited by the magistrate in the Church. Whatsoever is permitted unto any of his subjects for their ordinary use, neither can nor ought to be forbidden by him to any sect of people for their religious uses. If any man may lawfully take bread or wine, either sitting or kneeling in his own house, the law ought not to abridge him of the same liberty in his religious worship; though in the Church the use of bread and wine be very different and be there applied to the mysteries of faith and rites of Divine worship. But those things that are prejudicial to the commonweal of a people in their ordinary use and are, therefore, forbidden by laws, those things ought not to be permitted to Churches in their sacred rites. Only the magistrate ought always to be very careful that he do not misuse his authority to the oppression of any Church, under pretence of public good ...

Now whosoever maintains that idolatry is to be rooted out of any place by laws, punishments, fire, and sword, may apply this story to himself. For the reason of the thing is equal, both in America and Europe. And neither Pagans there, nor any dissenting Christians here, can, with any right, be deprived of their worldly goods by the predominating faction of a court-church; nor are any civil rights to be either changed or violated upon account of religion in one place more than another ...

Thus far concerning outward worship. Let us now consider articles of faith ...

[T]he magistrate ought not to forbid the preaching or professing of any speculative opinions in any Church because they have no manner of relation to the civil rights of the subjects. If a Roman Catholic believe that to be really the body of Christ which another man calls bread, he does no injury thereby to his neighbour. If a Jew do not believe the New Testament to be the Word of God, he does not thereby alter anything in men's civil rights. If a heathen doubt of both Testaments, he is not therefore to be punished as a pernicious citizen. The power of the magistrate and the estates of the people may be equally secure whether any man believe these things or no. But the business of laws is not to provide for the truth of opinions, but for the safety and security of the commonwealth and of every particular man's goods and person. And so it ought to be . . .

A good life, in which consist not the least part of religion and true piety, concerns also the civil government; and in it lies the safety both of men's souls and of the commonwealth. Moral actions belong, therefore, to the jurisdiction both of the outward and inward court; both of the civil and domestic governor; I mean both of the magistrate and conscience. Here, therefore, is great danger, lest one of these jurisdictions intrench upon the other, and discord arise between the keeper of the public peace and the overseers of souls. But if what has been already said concerning the limits of both these governments be rightly considered, it will easily remove all difficulty in this matter.

Every man has an immortal soul, capable of eternal happiness or misery; whose happiness depends upon his believing and doing those things in this life which are necessary to the obtaining of God's favour, and are prescribed by God to that end. It follows from thence, first, that the observance of these things is the highest obligation that lies upon mankind and that our utmost care, application, and diligence ought to be exercised in the search and performance of them; because there is nothing in this world that is of any consideration in comparison with eternity. Secondly, that seeing one man does not violate the right of another by his erroneous opinions and undue manner of worship, nor is his perdition any prejudice to another man's affairs, therefore, the care of each man's salvation belongs only to himself.

These things being thus explained, it is easy to understand to what end the legislative power ought to be directed and by what measures regulated; and that is the temporal good and outward prosperity of the society; which is the sole reason of men's entering into society, and the only thing they seek and aim at in it. And it is also evident what liberty remains to men in reference to their eternal salvation, and that is that every one should do what he in his conscience is persuaded to be acceptable to the Almighty, on whose good pleasure and acceptance depends their eternal happiness. For obedience is due, in the first place, to God and, afterwards to the laws . . .

Another more secret evil, but more dangerous to the commonwealth, is when men arrogate to themselves, and to those of their own sect, some peculiar prerogative covered over with a specious show of deceitful words, but in effect opposite to the civil right of the community . . . What else do they mean who teach that faith is not to be kept with heretics? Their meaning, forsooth, is that the privilege of breaking faith belongs unto themselves; for they declare all that are not of their communion to be heretics, or at least may declare them so whensoever they think fit. What can be the meaning of their asserting that kings excommunicated forfeit their crowns and kingdoms? It is evident that they thereby arrogate unto themselves the power of deposing kings, because they challenge the power of excommunication, as the peculiar right of their hierarchy ... These, therefore ... who attribute unto ... themselves, any peculiar privilege or power above other mortals, in civil concerns; or who upon pretence of religion do challenge any manner of authority over such as are not associated with them in their ecclesiastical communion, I say these have no right to be tolerated by the magistrate; as neither those that will not own and teach the duty of tolerating all men in matters of mere religion. For what do all these and the like doctrines signify, but that they may and are ready upon any occasion to seize the Government and possess themselves of the estates and fortunes of their fellow subjects; and that they only ask leave to be tolerated by the magistrate so long until they find themselves strong enough to effect it? ...

Lastly, those are not at all to be tolerated who deny the being of a God. Promises, covenants, and oaths, which are the bonds of human society, can have no hold upon an atheist. The taking away of God, though but even in thought, dissolves all; besides also, those that by their atheism undermine and destroy all religion, can have no pretence of religion whereupon to challenge the privilege of a toleration. As for other practical opinions, though not absolutely free from all error, if they do not tend to establish domination over others, or civil impunity to the Church in which they are taught, there can be no reason why they should not be tolerated ...

That we may draw towards a conclusion. The sum of all we drive at is that every man may enjoy the same rights that are granted to others. Is it permitted to worship God in the Roman manner? Let it be permitted to do it in the Geneva form also. Is it permitted to speak Latin in the market-place? Let those that have a mind to it be permitted to do it also in the Church. Is it lawful for any man in his own house to kneel, stand, sit, or use any other posture; and to clothe himself in white or black, in short or in long garments? Let it not be made unlawful to eat bread, drink wine, or wash with water in the church. In a word, whatsoever things are left free by law in the common occasions of life, let them remain free unto every Church in divine worship. Let no man's life, or body, or house, or estate, suffer any manner of prejudice upon these accounts. Can you allow of the Presbyterian discipline? Why should not the Episcopal also have what they like? Ecclesiastical authority, whether it be administered by the hands of a single person or many, is everywhere the same; and neither has any jurisdiction in things civil, nor any manner of power of compulsion, nor anything at all to do with riches and revenues.

. . . If anything pass in a religious meeting seditiously and contrary to the public peace, it is to be punished in the same manner and no otherwise than as if it had happened in a fair or market. . . . But those whose doctrine is peaceable and whose manners are pure and blameless ought to be upon equal terms with their fellow-subjects. Thus if solemn assemblies, observations of festivals, public worship be permitted to any one sort of professors, all these things ought to be permitted to the Presbyterians, Independents, Anabaptists, Arminians, Quakers, and others, with the same liberty. Nay, if we may openly speak the truth, and as becomes one man to another, neither Pagan nor Mahometan, nor Jew, ought to be excluded from the civil rights of the commonwealth because of his religion. The Gospel commands no such thing. The Church which "judgeth not those that are without" wants it not. And the commonwealth, which embraces indifferently all men that are honest, peaceable, and industrious, requires it not. Shall we suffer a Pagan to deal and trade with us, and shall we not suffer him to pray unto and worship God? If we allow the Jews to have private houses and dwellings amongst us, why should we not allow them to have synagogues? Is their doctrine more false, their worship more abominable, or is the civil peace more endangered by their meeting in public than in their private houses? But if these things may be granted to Jews and Pagans, surely the condition of any Christians ought not to be worse than theirs in a Christian commonwealth . . .

God Almighty grant, I beseech Him, that the gospel of peace may at length be preached, and that civil magistrates, growing more careful to conform their own consciences to the law of God and less solicitous about the binding of other men's consciences by human laws, may, like fathers of their country, direct all their counsels and endeavours to promote universally the civil welfare of all their children, except only of such as are arrogant, ungovernable, and injurious to their brethren; and that all ecclesiastical men, who boast themselves to be the successors of the Apostles, walking peaceably and modestly in the Apostles' steps, without intermeddling with State Affairs, may apply themselves wholly to promote the salvation of souls.

Source: Available online. URL: http://www.constitution.org/jl/tolerati.htm. Accessed October 31, 2008.

RELIGION AND THE STATE

Theological Declaration of Barmen by Karl Barth, 1934

The Barmen Declaration, written by theologian Karl Barth, is a statement issued and signed by most of the Protestant church leaders in Germany after the election of Adolf Hitler as chancellor. The declaration uses scripture and other arguments to explain why the distortion of Christian teachings by the National Socialists is anathema to true Christians. It urges the state to desist from corrupting the church's teachings and urges both church officials and laypeople to reject the Nazi perversion of Christianity.

II. THEOLOGICAL DECLARATION CONCERNING THE PRESENT SITUATION OF THE GERMAN EVANGELICAL CHURCH

8.05 According to the opening words of its constitution of July 11, 1933, the German Evangelical Church is a federation of Confessional Churches that grew out of the Reformation and that enjoy equal rights. The theological basis for the unification of these Churches is laid down in Article 1 and Article 2(1) of the constitution of the German Evangelical Church that was recognized by the Reich Government on July 14, 1933:

- Article 1. The inviolable foundation of the German Evangelical Church is the gospel of Jesus Christ as it is attested for us in Holy Scripture and brought to light again in the Confessions of the Reformation. The full powers that the Church needs for its mission are hereby determined and limited.
- Article 2 (1). The German Evangelical Church is divided into member Churches *Landeskirchen.*

8.06 We, the representatives of Lutheran, Reformed, and United Churches, of free synods, Church assemblies, and parish organizations united in the Confessional Synod of the German Evangelical Church, declare that we stand together on the ground of the German Evangelical Church as a federation of German Confessional Churches. We are bound together by the confession of the one Lord of the one, holy, catholic, and apostolic Church.

8.07 We publicly declare before all evangelical Churches in Germany that what they hold in common in this Confession is grievously imperiled, and with it the unity of the German Evangelical Church. It is threatened by the teaching methods and actions of the ruling Church party of the "German Christians" and of the Church administration carried on by them. These have become more and more apparent during the first year of the existence of the German

Evangelical Church. This threat consists in the fact that the theological basis, in which the German Evangelical Church is united, has been continually and systematically thwarted and rendered ineffective by alien principles, on the part of the leaders and spokesmen of the "German Christians" as well as on the part of the Church administration. When these principles are held to be valid, then, according to all the Confessions in force among us, the Church ceases to be the Church and the German Evangelical Church, as a federation of Confessional Churches, becomes intrinsically impossible.

8.09 In view of the errors of the "German Christians" of the present Reich Church government which are devastating the Church and also therefore breaking up the unity of the German Evangelical Church, we confess the following evangelical truths: . . .

8.18 We reject the false doctrine, as though the Church were permitted to abandon the form of its message and order to its own pleasure or to changes in prevailing ideological and political convictions . . .

8.20 The various offices in the Church do not establish a dominion of some over the others; on the contrary, they are for the exercise of the ministry entrusted to and enjoined upon the whole congregation.

8.21 We reject the false doctrine, as though the Church, apart from this ministry, could and were permitted to give itself, or allow to be given to it, special leaders vested with ruling powers.

8.22–5. "Fear God. Honor the emperor." (1 Peter 2:17.)

Scripture tells us that, in the as yet unredeemed world in which the Church also exists, the State has by divine appointment the task of providing for justice and peace. [It fulfills this task] by means of the threat and exercise of force, according to the measure of human judgment and human ability. The Church acknowledges the benefit of this divine appointment in gratitude and reverence before him. It calls to mind the Kingdom of God, God's commandment and righteousness, and thereby the responsibility both of rulers and of the ruled. It trusts and obeys the power of the Word by which God upholds all things.

8.23 We reject the false doctrine, as though the State, over and beyond its special commission, should and could become the single and totalitarian order of human life, thus fulfilling the Church's vocation as well.

8.24 We reject the false doctrine, as though the Church, over and beyond its special commission, should and could appropriate the characteristics, the tasks, and the dignity of the State, thus itself becoming an organ of the State.

8.26 The Church's commission, upon which its freedom is founded, consists in delivering the message of the free grace of God to all people in Christ's stead, and therefore in the ministry of his own Word and work through sermon and sacrament.

8.27 We reject the false doctrine, as though the Church in human arrogance could place the Word and work of the Lord in the service of any arbitrarily chosen desires, purposes, and plans.

8.28 The Confessional Synod of the German Evangelical Church declares that it sees in the acknowledgment of these truths and in the rejection of these errors the indispensable theological basis of the German Evangelical Church as a federation of Confessional Churches. It invites all who are able to accept its declaration to be mindful of these theological principles in their decisions in Church politics. It entreats all whom it concerns to return to the unity of faith, love, and hope.

Source: Available online. URL: http://www.sacred-texts.com/chr/barmen.htm. Accessed October 21. 2008.

United Nations Declaration on the Elimination of All Forms of Intolerance and of Discrimination Based on Religion or Belief, 1981

This is the first official document produced by the United Nations that sets out the right of individuals not to be victims of discrimination based on religious belief. The declaration's signatories supposedly ban intolerance based on religion in their nations and officially guarantee freedom of religion.

The General Assembly,

Considering that one of the basic principles of the Charter of the United Nations is that of the dignity and equality inherent in all human beings, and that all Member States have pledged themselves to take joint and separate action in co-operation with the Organization to promote and encourage universal respect for and observance of human rights and fundamental freedoms for all, without distinction as to race, sex, language or religion,

International Documents

Considering that the Universal Declaration of Human Rights and the International Covenants on Human Rights proclaims the principles of nondiscrimination and equality before the law and the right to freedom of thought, conscience, religion and belief,

Considering that the disregard and infringement of human rights and fundamental freedoms, in particular of the right to freedom of thought, conscience, religion or whatever belief, have brought, directly or indirectly, wars and great suffering to mankind, especially where they serve as a means of foreign interference in the internal affairs of other States and amount to kindling hatred between peoples and nations,

Considering that religion or belief, for anyone who professes either, is one of the fundamental elements in his conception of life and that freedom of religion or belief should be fully respected and guaranteed, . . .

Convinced that freedom of religion and belief should also contribute to the attainment of the goals of world peace, social justice and friendship among peoples and to the elimination of ideologies or practices of colonialism and racial discrimination, . . .

Concerned by manifestations of intolerance and by the existence of discrimination in matters of religion or belief still in evidence in some areas of the world,

Resolved to adopt all necessary measures for the speedy elimination of such intolerance in all its forms and manifestations and to prevent and combat discrimination on the ground of religion or belief,

Proclaims this Declaration on the Elimination of All Forms of Intolerance and of Discrimination Based on Religion or Belief:

Article 1

1. Everyone shall have the right to freedom of thought, conscience and religion. This right shall include freedom to have a religion or whatever belief of his choice, and freedom, either individually or in community with others and in public or private, to manifest his religion or belief in worship, observance, practice and teaching.

2. No one shall be subject to coercion which would impair his freedom to have a religion or belief of his choice.

RELIGION AND THE STATE

3. Freedom to manifest one's religion or belief may be subject only to such limitations as are prescribed by law and are necessary to protect public safety, order, health or morals or the fundamental rights and freedoms of others.

Article 2

1. No one shall be subject to discrimination by any State, institution, group of persons, or person on the grounds of religion or other belief.

2. For the purposes of the present Declaration, the expression "intolerance and discrimination based on religion or belief" means any distinction, exclusion, restriction or preference based on religion or belief and having as its purpose or as its effect nullification or impairment of the recognition, enjoyment or exercise of human rights and fundamental freedoms on an equal basis.

Article 3

Discrimination between human beings on the grounds of religion or belief constitutes an affront to human dignity and a disavowal of the principles of the Charter of the United Nations, and shall be condemned as a violation of the human rights and fundamental freedoms proclaimed in the Universal Declaration of Human Rights and enunciated in detail in the International Covenants on Human Rights, and as an obstacle to friendly and peaceful relations between nations.

Article 4

1. All States shall take effective measures to prevent and eliminate discrimination on the grounds of religion or belief in the recognition, exercise and enjoyment of human rights and fundamental freedoms in all fields of civil, economic, political, social and cultural life.

2. All States shall make all efforts to enact or rescind legislation where necessary to prohibit any such discrimination, and to take all appropriate measures to combat intolerance on the grounds of religion or other beliefs in this matter. . . .

Article 6

In accordance with article 1 of the present Declaration, and subject to the provisions of article 1, paragraph 3, the right to freedom of thought, conscience, religion or belief shall include, inter alia, the following freedoms:

(a) To worship or assemble in connection with a religion or belief, and to establish and maintain places for these purposes;

(b) To establish and maintain appropriate charitable or humanitarian institutions;

(c) To make, acquire and use to an adequate extent the necessary articles and materials related to the rites or customs of a religion or belief;

(d) To write, issue and disseminate relevant publications in these areas;

(e) To teach a religion or belief in places suitable for these purposes;

(f) To solicit and receive voluntary financial and other contributions from individuals and institutions;

(g) To train, appoint, elect or designate by succession appropriate leaders called for by the requirements and standards of any religion or belief;

(h) To observe days of rest and to celebrate holidays and ceremonies in accordance with the precepts of one's religion or belief;

(i) To establish and maintain communications with individuals and communities in matters of religion and belief at the national and international levels.

Article 7

The rights and freedoms set forth in the present Declaration shall be accorded in national legislation in such a manner that everyone shall be able to avail himself of such rights and freedoms in practice.

Source: Available online. URL: http://www.unhchr.ch/html/menu3/b/d_intole.htm. Accessed November 23, 2008.

ISLAM

Quran: Suras Relating to Governance
Hadith: *Sahih Muslim* by Muslim ibn al-Hajjaj, Ninth Century (excerpts)

All excerpted text in this section relates to original Islamic teachings on rulers and governance and on jihad and martyrdom. The sayings, or suras, in the first group, come from the Quran and are therefore the word of God as transmitted to the Prophet Muhammad. Note sura 2, verse 256: One point of divergence between the Quran and traditionalist Islamists is the latter's application of severe penalties to people reluctant to follow the precepts of Islam. This is against the Quran.

Also excerpted below are hadiths, short reports, stories, or traditions about what Muhammad did and did not say and do. The thousands of hadiths that circulated in the Muslim community in the first century after Muhammad's

RELIGION AND THE STATE

death were eventually collected into books during the ninth and 10th centuries. One of the most authoritative collections of hadiths recognized by Sunnis is by Muslim ibn al-Hajjaj (d. 874), called Sahih Muslim. *The collections are arranged by subject, and* The Book of Jihad and Expedition *and* The Book on Government *are two sections within the* Sahih Muslim.

Quran

[2:255] GOD: there is no other god besides Him, the Living, the Eternal. Never a moment of unawareness or slumber overtakes Him. To Him belongs everything in the heavens and everything on earth. Who could intercede with Him, except in accordance with His will? He knows their past, and their future. No one attains any knowledge, except as He wills. His dominion encompasses the heavens and the earth, and ruling them never burdens Him. He is the Most High, the Great.

[2:256] There shall be no compulsion in religion; the right way is now distinguished from the wrong way.

[3:26] Say, "Our god: possessor of all sovereignty. You grant sovereignty to whomever You choose, You remove sovereignty from whomever You choose. You grant dignity to whomever You choose, and commit to humiliation whomever You choose. In Your hand are all provisions. You are Omnipotent.

[4:58] God commands you to render back your trusts to those to whom they are due; and when you judge between man and man, that you judge with justice.

[4:59] Obey God, and obey His messenger and those charged with authority among you . . .

[5:8] O you who believe! Stand up as a witness for God in all fairness, and do not let the hatred of a people deviate you from justice. Be just.

[5:48] Then we revealed to you this scripture, truthfully, confirming previous scriptures, and superseding them. You shall rule among them in accordance with GOD's revelations, and do not follow their wishes if they differ from the truth that came to you. For each of you, we have decreed laws and different rites. Had GOD willed, He could have made you one congregation. But He thus puts you to the test through the revelations He has given each of you. You shall compete in righteousness. To GOD is your final destiny—all of you—then He will inform you of everything you had disputed.

International Documents

[5:49] You shall rule among them in accordance with GOD's revelations to you. Do not follow their wishes, and beware lest they divert you from some of GOD's revelations to you. If they turn away, then know that GOD wills to punish them for some of their sins. Indeed, many people are wicked.

[5:50] Is it the law of the days of ignorance that they seek to uphold? Whose law is better than GOD's for those who have attained certainty? . . .

[42:40] Although the just requital for an injustice is an equivalent retribution, those who pardon and maintain righteousness are rewarded by GOD. He does not love the unjust.

[42:41] Certainly, those who stand up for their rights, when injustice befalls them, are not committing any error.

[42:42] The wrong ones are those who treat the people unjustly, and resort to aggression without provocation. These have incurred a painful retribution.

[42:43] Resorting to patience and forgiveness reflects a true strength of character.

[60:8] God does not forbid you from being kind and acting justly towards those who did not fight over faith with you, nor expelled you from your homes. God indeed loves those who are just.

Sahih Muslim: The Book of Jihad and Expedition
(Kitab Al-Jihad wal-Siyar)

Book 019, Number 4313:
It has been narrated on the authority of Abu Huraira that the Messenger of Allah (may peace be upon him) said: Do not desire an encounter with the enemy; but when you encounter them, be firm.

Book 019, Number 4314:
It is narrated by Abu Nadr that he learnt from a letter sent by a man from the Aslam tribe, who was a Companion of the Holy Prophet (may peace be upon him) and whose name was 'Abdullah b. Abu Aufa, to 'Umar b. 'Ubaidullah when the latter marched upon Haruriyya (Khawarij) informing him that the Messenger of Allah (may peace be upon him) in one of those days when lie was confronting the enemy waited until the sun had declined. Then he stood up (to address the people)

and said: O ye men, do not wish for an encounter with the enemy. Pray to Allah to grant you security; (but) when you (have to) encounter them exercise patience, and you should know that Paradise is under the shadows of the swords. Then the Messenger of Allah (may peace be upon him) stood up (again) and said: O Allah Revealer of the Book, Disperser of the clouds, Defeater of the hordes, put our enemy to rout and help us against them.

Book 019, Number 4319:

It is narrated on the authority of 'Abdullah that a woman was found killed in one of the battles fought by the Messenger of Allah (may peace be upon him). He disapproved of the killing of women and children.

Book 019, Number 4320:

It is narrated by Ibn 'Umar that a woman was found filled in one of these battles; so the Messenger of Allah (may peace by upon him) forbade the killing of women and children.

Sahih Muslim: The Book on Government (Kitab Al-Imara)

Book 020, Number 4477:

It has been narrated on the authority of Jabir b. Samura who said: I joined the company of the Holy Prophet (may peace be upon him) with my father and I heard him say: This Caliphate will not end until there have been twelve Caliphs among them. All of them will be from the Quraish.

Book 020, Number 4491:

It has been narrated on the authority of Abu Dharr who said: I said to the Holy Prophet (may peace be upon him): Messenger of Allah, will you not appoint me to a public office? He stroked my shoulder with his hand and said: Abu Dharr, thou art weak and authority is a trust. and on the Day of judgment it is a cause of humiliation and repentance except for one who fulfils its obligations and (properly) discharges the duties attendant thereon.

Book 020, Number 4518:

It has been narrated on the authority of Abu Huraira that the Holy prophet (may peace be upon him) said: Whoso obeys me obeys God, and whoso disobeys me disobeys God. Whoso obeys the commander (appointed by me) obeys me, and whoso disobeys the commander disobeys me.

International Documents

Book 020, Number 4524:

It has been narrated on the authority of Abu Huraira that the Messenger of Allah (may peace be upon him) said: It is obligatory for you to listen to the ruler and obey him in adversity and prosperity, in pleasure and displeasure, and even when another person is given (rather undue) preference over you.

Book 020, Number 4533:

It has been narrated on the authority of Ibn 'Umar that the Holy Prophet (may peace be upon him) said: It is obligatory upon a Muslim that he should listen (to the ruler appointed over him) and obey him whether he likes it or not, except that he is ordered to do a sinful thing. If he is ordered to do a sinful act, a Muslim should neither listen to him nor should he obey his orders.

Book 020, Number 4542:

It has been narrated on the authority of Abu Huraira that the Prophet of Allah (may peace be upon him) said: A commander (of the Muslims) is a shield for them. They fight behind him and they are protected by (him from tyrants and aggressors). If he enjoins fear of God, the Exalted and Glorious, and dispenses justice, there will be a (great) reward for him; and if he enjoins otherwise, it redounds on him.

Book 020, Number 4543:

It has been narrated by Abu Huraira that the Holy Prophet (may peace be upon him) said: Banu Isra'il were ruled over by the Prophets. When one Prophet died, another succeeded him; but after me there is no prophet and there will be caliphs and they will be quite large in number. His Companions said: What do you order us to do (in case we come to have more than one Caliph)? He said: The one to whom allegiance is sworn first has a supremacy over the others. Concede to them their due rights (i.e. obey them). God (Himself) will question them about the subjects whom He had entrusted to them.

Book 020, Number 4545:

It has been narrated on the authority of 'Abdullah who said: The Messenger of Allah (may peace be upon him) said: After me there will be favouritism and many things that you will not like. They (his Companions) said: Messenger of Allah, what do you order that one should do if anyone from us has to live through such a time? He said: You should discharge your own responsibility (by obeying your Amir), and ask God to concede your right (by guiding the Amir to the right path or by replacing him by one more just and God-fearing).

RELIGION AND THE STATE

Book 020, Number 4560:
It has been narrated (through a different chain of transmitters) on the authority of Ibn Abbas that the Messenger of Allah (may peace be upon him) said: One who dislikes a thing done by his Amir should be patient over it, for anyone from the people who withdraws (his obedience) from the government, even to the extent of a handspan and died in that conditions, would die the death of one belonging to the days of jahilliyya.

Book 020, Number 4565:
It has been narrated on the authority of 'Arfaja who said: I have heard the Messenger of Allah (may peace be upon him) say: Different evils will make their appearance in the near future. Anyone who tries to disrupt the affairs of this Umma while they are united you should strike him with the sword whoever he be. (If remonstrance does not prevail with him and he does not desist from his disruptive activities, he is to be killed.)

Book 020, Number 4569:
It has been narrated on the authority of Umm Salama that the Messenger of Allah (may peace be upon him) said: In the near future there will be Amirs and you will like their good deeds and dislike their bad deeds. One who sees through their bad deeds (and tries to prevent their repetition by his band or through his speech), is absolved from blame, but one who hates their bad deeds (in the heart of his heart, being unable to prevent their recurrence by his hand or his tongue), is (also) safe (so far as God's wrath is concerned). But one who approves of their bad deeds and imitates them is spiritually ruined. People asked (the Holy Prophet): Shouldn't we fight against them? He replied: No, as long as they say their prayers.

Book 020, Number 4631:
It has been narrated on the authority of Abu Huraira who said: I heard the Messenger of Allah (may peace be upon him) say: I would not stay behind (when) an expedition (for Jihad was being mobilised) if it were going to be too hard upon the believers.... By the Being in Whose Hand is my life, I love that I should be killed in the way of Allah; then I should be brought back to life and be killed again in His way...."

Book 020, Number 4634:
It has been narrated on the authority of Anas b. Malik that the Messenger of Allah (may peace be upon him) said: "Nobody who dies and has something good for him with Allah will (ever like to) return to this world even though he were offered the whole world and all that is in it (as an

inducement), except the martyr who desires to return and be killed in the world for the (great) merit of martyrdom that he has seen."

Book 020, Number 4696:
It has been narrated on the authority of Abu Huraira that the Messenger of Allah (may peace be upon him) said: One who died but did not fight in the way of Allah nor did he express any desire (or determination) for Jihad died the death of a hypocrite.

Sources: Qur'an: Available online. URL: http://www.submission.org/suras/sura5.html, http://www.quranic.org/quran_article/30/the_quran_and_government.htm, http://www.submission.org/suras/sura42.html, http://www.submission.org/suras/sura3.html, and http://www.submission.org/suras/sura2.html; Hadith: Center for Muslim-Jewish Engagement. Available online. URL: http://www.usc.edu/schools/college/crcc/engagement/resources/texts/muslim/hadith/muslim/020 .smt. Accessed December 21, 2008.

The Uprising of Khurdad 15, 1979 by Ayatollah Ruhollah Khomeini

In this document, the Ayatollah Khomeini extols those who aided in the victory of the Iranian Revolution that overthrew the shah of Iran in 1979. Khomeini had just returned to Iran from exile in Paris. He would be the supreme, theocratic authority in Iran until his death in 1989. (Note that Khurdad 15 refers to a date in the Islamic calendar.)

Those who are ignorant must be guided to a correct understanding. We must say to them: "You who imagine that something can be achieved in Iran by some means other than Islam, you who suppose that something other than Islam overthrew the Shah's regime, you who believe non-Islamic elements played a role—study the matter carefully. Look at the tombstones of those who gave their lives in the movement of Khurdad 15. If you can find a single tombstone belonging to one of the non-Islamic elements, it will mean they played a role. And if, among the tombstones of the Islamic elements, you can find a single tombstone belonging to someone from the upper echelons of society, it will mean that they too played a role. But you will not find a single tombstone belonging to either of those groups. All the tombstones belong to Muslims from the lower echelons of society: peasants, workers, tradesmen, committed religious scholars. Those who imagine that some force other than Islam could shatter the great barrier of tyranny are mistaken. As for those who oppose us because of their opposition to Islam, we must cure them by means of guidance, if it is at all possible; otherwise, we will destroy these agents of foreign powers with the same fist that destroyed the Shah's regime.

RELIGION AND THE STATE

Your opponents, oppressed people, have never suffered. In the time of the *taghut*, they never suffered because either they were in agreement with the regime and loyal to it, or they kept silent. Now you have spread the banquet of freedom in front of them and they have sat down to eat. Xenomaniacs, people infatuated with the West, empty people, people with no content! Come to your senses; do not try to westernize everything you have! Look at the West, and see who the people are in the West that present themselves as champions of human rights and what their aims are. Is it human rights they really care about, or the rights of the superpowers? What they really want to secure are the rights of the superpowers. Our jurists should not follow or imitate them. You should implement human rights as the working classes of our society understand them. Yes, they are the real Society for the Defense of Human Rights. They are the ones who secure the well-being of humanity; they work while you talk; for they are Muslims and Islam cares about humanity. You who have chosen a course other than Islam—you do nothing for humanity. All you do is write and speak in an effort to divert our movement from its course.

But as for those who want to divert our movement from its course, who have in mind treachery against Islam and the nation, who consider Islam incapable of running the affairs of our country despite its record of 1,400 years—they have nothing at all to do with our people, and this must be made clear. How much you talk about the West, claiming that we must measure Islam in accordance with Western criteria! What an error! It was the mosques that created this Revolution, the mosques that brought this movement into being. The *mihrab* was a place not only for preaching, but also for war—war against both the devil within and the tyrannical powers without. So preserve your mosques, O people. Intellectuals, do not be Western-style intellectuals, imported intellectuals; do your share to preserve the mosques!

Source: Modern History Sourcebook. Available online. URL: http://www.fordham.edu/halsall/mod/1979khom1.html. Accessed December 15, 2008.

U.S. Muslims Issue Fatwa against Religious Extremism, 2008

This document was drawn up by the Fiqh Council (legal council) to express their vehement condemnation of terrorist acts committed by Islamic extremists. They cite the Quran and other religious texts in support of their argument.

The Fiqh Council of North America wishes to reaffirm Islam's condemnation of terrorism and religious extremism. Islam strictly condemns religious extremism

International Documents

and the use of violence against innocent lives. There is no justification in Islam for extremism or terrorism. Targeting civilians' life and property through suicide bombings or any other method of attack is haram—prohibited in Islam—and those who commit these barbaric acts are criminals, not "martyrs."

The Qur'an, Islam's revealed text, states: "Whoever kills a person, unless it be for murder or for spreading mischief in the land, it is as though he has killed all mankind. And whoever saves a person, it is as though he had saved all mankind." (Qur'an, 5:32)

Prophet Muhammad said there is no excuse for committing unjust acts: "Do not be people without minds of your own, saying that if others treat you well you will treat them well, and that if they do wrong you will do wrong to them. Instead, accustom yourselves to do good if people do good and not to do wrong (even) if they do evil." (Al-Tirmidhi)

God mandates moderation in faith and in all aspects of life when He states in the Qur'an: "We made you to be a community of the middle way, so that (with the example of your lives) you might bear witness to the truth before all mankind." (Qur'an, 2:143)

In another verse, God explains our duties as human beings when he says: "Let there arise from among you a band of people who invite to righteousness, and enjoin good and forbid evil." (Qur'an, 3:104)

Islam teaches us to act in a caring manner to all of God's creation. The Prophet Muhammad, who is described in the Qur'an as "a mercy to the worlds," said: "All creation is the family of God, and the person most beloved by God (is the one) who is kind and caring toward His family."

In the light of the teachings of the Qur'an and Sunnah we clearly and strongly state:

    1. All acts of terrorism targeting the civilians are Haram (forbidden) in Islam.

    2. It is Haram for a Muslim to cooperate or associate with any individual or group that is involved in any act of terrorism or violence.

    3. It is the duty of Muslims to cooperate with the law enforcement authorities to protect the lives of all civilians.

We issue this fatwa following the guidance of our scripture the Qur'an and the teachings of our Prophet Muhammad—peace be upon him. We urge all people to resolve all conflicts in just and peaceful manners. We have deep concern for the suffering and pain of millions of Muslims in different parts of the world. We deplore those who cause death and destruction to them. However, we urge Muslims to not lose their moral grounds. God's help is with those who follow the right path.

We pray for the defeat of extremism, terrorism and injustice. We pray for the safety and security of our country [the] United States and its people. We pray for the safety and security of all inhabitants of this globe. We pray that interfaith harmony and cooperation prevail both in United States and every where in the world.

Source: Fiqh Council. Available online. URL: http://www.fiqhcouncil.org/FatwaBank/tabid/176/ctl/Detail/mid/600/xmid/25/smfid/3/Default.aspx. Accessed December 21, 2008.

Muslims of Europe Charter, 2008

This charter was drawn up by the Federation of Islamic Organizations in Europe to set out the principles by which European Muslims can and should participate in society and politics. The document explains how participating as a citizen of a nation can be in accord with Muslim teachings. It also describes ways European Muslims can maintain their unique identity while acting as full citizens of European nations.

Since early 2000, the Federation of Islamic Organisations in Europe (FIOE) debated the establishment of a charter for the Muslims of Europe, setting out the general principles for better understanding of Islam, and the bases for the integration of Muslims in society, in the context of citizenship . . .

After amendments were approved, and duly incorporated, the final version of the charter was ready. It was signed by Muslim organisations from 28 European states . . .

Despite their diversity, Muslims of Europe share common values and principles. In order to portray this to European society they need to clearly express their religious convictions and the nature of their presence in Europe.

This charter aims to define a number of principles in accordance with the common understanding of Islam within the European context and to set thenceforth the foundations of greater positive interaction with society.

International Documents

The rationale for such a charter includes:

The contribution of Islam to modern Europe as well as the rooted Islamic presence as represented by Muslims in many of the Eastern European states. Likewise, the establishment of Muslim communities in several Western European countries has witnessed a shift from a transitory presence of foreign migrants to a more permanent presence.

The Muslim presence in Europe requires a framework of citizenship based on justice, equality of rights, with respect for difference, and the recognition of Muslims as a European religious community.

The need to enhance the values of mutual understanding, working for peace and the welfare of society, moderation and inter-cultural dialogue, removed from all inclinations of extremism and exclusion.

The importance of Islam in the world and its spiritual, human and civilisational potential requires a rapprochement with the West, and Europe in particular, in order to ensure justice and peace in the world. . . .

Articles of the Charter
Section one: on the understanding of Islam:

1. Our understanding of Islam is based on immutable, basic principles that are derived from the authentic sources of Islam: the Qur'an and the Prophetic traditions (Sunnah), within the framework of Muslim scholarly consensus and with consideration for the time factor as well as the specifics of the European reality.

2. The true spirit of Islam is based on moderation as extended from the Universal Objectives (Maqasid) of this religion. This moderation avoids both laxity and excessiveness and reconciles reason and divine guidance, taking into consideration the material and spiritual needs of man, with a balanced outlook on life which brings together the reality of the next life with constructive work in this world.

3. In its principles, rulings and values, Islam can be structured around the following three areas: the creed as expressed in the six pillars of faith—Belief in God, the Angels, the revealed books, the messengers, the Hereafter and Divine Decree; the Shari'ah as expressed in acts of Worship and human interaction; and the Ethical code which lays down the foundations for living a good life. These three interconnected areas

RELIGION AND THE STATE

are complementary and aim to fulfil the Interests (Maslaha) of humanity and avert harm from it.

4. The emphasis on the human dimension, legislative flexibility and respect for diversity and natural differences among human beings are general characteristics of Islam.

5. Islam honours human beings. This honour embraces all the children of Adam, both male and female, without discrimination. By virtue of this honour, human beings are to be protected from anything that is an affront to their dignity, is harmful to their mental faculties, is damaging to their health or which abuses their rights by exploiting their vulnerabilities.

6. Islam gives particular emphasis to the social dimension and calls for compassion, mutual support, co-operation and brotherhood. These values apply particularly to the rights of parents, relatives and neighbours but also to the poor, the needy, the sick, the elderly and others, regardless of their race or creed.

7. Islam calls for equality between man and woman within the framework of human dignity and mutual respect and views that a balanced life is one in which the relationship between man and woman is harmonious and complementary. It unequivocally rejects all notions or actions that undermine women or deprive them of their legitimate rights, regardless of certain customs and habits of some Muslims. Islam rather confirms women's indispensable role in society and strongly opposes the exploitation of women and their treatment as mere objects of desire.

8. Islam considers that a family based on the bonds of marriage between a man and a woman is the natural and necessary environment for the raising of future generations. The family is an indispensable condition for the happiness of the individual and stability of society. Thus, Islam emphasises the significance of taking all measures in order to reinforce the family and protect it from all things that will weaken or marginalise its role.

9. Islam respects human rights and calls for equality among all human beings; it rejects all forms of racial discrimination and calls for liberty. It condemns compulsion in religion and allows the individual freedom of conscience. However, Islam encourages that freedom should be exercised in accordance with moral values, such that it does not infringe upon the rights of others.

10. Islam calls for mutual acquaintance, dialogue and co-operation among people and nations so as to enhance stability and guarantee peace in the world. The term Jihad that occurs in Islamic texts means to exert all efforts towards good, starting from reforming oneself to spreading truth and justice between people. Jihad in its understanding as warfare is regarded as one of the means available to any sovereign state when it needs to defend itself against aggression. The teachings of Islam, in this respect, are in line with international law. Based on such an understanding of Jihad, Islam rejects violence and terrorism, supports just causes and affirms the right of all people to defend themselves by legitimate means.

11. Islam enjoins Muslims to be honest and to respect their pledges; forbidding treason and treachery. It also commands them to pursue excellence in dealings with other people, as well as with the rest of creation.

12. Given the virtues of consultation (Shura) and with consideration to human experience in the political, legislative and constitutional realms, Islam affirms the principles of democracy based on pluralism, freedom to choose one's political institutions and peaceful alternation of power.

13. Islam urges human beings to use nature in a responsible manner. This requires the preservation of the environment and its protection from all causes of pollution and harm as well as from anything that may destroy the delicate balance of nature. Likewise, it requires the protection of natural resources and forbids cruelty to animals, over consumption and wastage of wealth.

Section two: the Muslim Presence in Society:

The principles of interaction among Muslims:

14. Despite their ethnic and cultural diversity and their affiliations to various schools of Islamic law and thought, Muslims of Europe constitute one religious entity within the framework of Islamic principles, united by fraternity. They are also tied with each other, in each European country, by their belonging to the same national entity. Any discrimination arising between them based on ethnic origin is against the value of Islam which emphasises unity.

15. Considering the basic principles of their religion and their common interests, Muslims of Europe are urged to come together, co-operate

and co-ordinate the efforts of their different institutions and organisations. This should not fail to recognise the natural diversity that exists among them, within the framework of Islam as generally agreed by scholarly consensus.

16. In addition to their belonging to the country in which they reside and their commitment to the demands of citizenship, Muslims of Europe retain their links with fellow Muslims by virtue of the normal relationship which exists between members of the same community.

On Citizenship:

17. Muslims of Europe respect the laws of the land and the authorities that uphold them. This should not prevent them from individually or collectively defending their rights and expressing their opinions based on their specific concerns as a religious community or on any general matter that concerns them as citizens. Whenever there is a conflict with regard to certain laws and matters that are specific to religion, the relevant authorities should be approached in order to arrive at suitable and viable solutions.

18. Muslims of Europe adhere to the principle of neutrality of the state regarding religious affairs. This means dealing fairly with all religions and allows those who hold religious values to express their beliefs and practise the rites of their religion either as individuals or groups, in conformity with European and international human rights charters and treaties. Muslims have, therefore, the right, as religious communities, to establish mosques, religious, educational and welfare institutions, to practise their religion in day-to-day affairs such as diet, clothing and other needs.

19. As European citizens, Muslims of Europe consider it their duty to work for the common good of society. Their endeavour for the common good is as important as defending their rights. Finally, an authentic understanding of Islam requires of Muslims to be active and productive citizens who are useful to society.

20. Muslims of Europe are urged to integrate positively in their respective societies, on the basis of a harmonious balance between preservation of Muslim identity and the duties of citizenship. Any form of integration that fails to recognise the right of Muslims to preserve their Islamic personality and the right to perform their religious obligations does not serve the interests of Muslims nor the European societies to which they belong.

International Documents

21. Muslims of Europe are encouraged to participate in the political process as active citizens. Real citizenship includes political engagement, from casting one's vote to taking part in political institutions. This will be facilitated if these institutions open up to all members and sections of society, an opening up which takes into account competence and ideas.

22. Muslims of Europe emphasise their respect for pluralism and the religious and philosophical diversity of the multicultural societies they live in. They believe that Islam affirms the diversity and differences that exists between people and is not discomforted by this multicultural reality. Rather, Islam calls for members of society to appreciate and enrich one another through their differences.

Islam's Contribution to Europe:

23. Through its universal and humane principles, Islam adheres to the rapprochement of all people who respect the rights of others and their particularities, who abide by the rules of fairness among people in matters of dealings and co-operation. Starting from these principles, Muslims of Europe consider it their duty to participate in strengthening relations between Europe and the Muslim World. This requires the removal of all the prejudices and negative images which stand between Islam and the West in order to build bonds of rapprochement between people and to establish bridges of fruitful exchanges among different civilizations.

24. Given its culturally rich heritage and emphasis on humanity, Islam, through its presence in Europe, can participate in enhancing important values in contemporary society such as justice, freedom, fraternity, equality and solidarity. Islam gives primacy to moral considerations as well as to scientific, technical and economic progress. This participation can be beneficial and enriching for the whole of society.

25. The Muslim presence in Europe represents a key element in establishing better communication and co-existence between the different religions and beliefs by encouraging discussion between different faiths and ideologies. This will no doubt bolster the path towards global peace.

26. Through their religious and cultural legacy as well as their presence in many European states, Muslims of Europe represent an enhancing element to the efforts of strengthening the European Union. With its diverse religious and cultural make up, Europe can act as an important

civilisational signpost with a key role in maintaining international stability between influential world powers.

"O Mankind, indeed we created you from a male and female and have made you different nations and tribes so that you may get to know one another." (Qur'an; Chapter 49: Verse 13)

Source: Euro-Islam. Available online. URL: http://www.euro-islam.info/2008/01/10/muslims-of-europe-charter/. Accessed December 21, 2008.

"Advice to the Community to Reject the Fatwa of Sheikh Bin Baz Authorizing Parliamentary Representation" by Ayman al-Zawahiri, 2008 (excerpt)

These are excerpts from a longer essay in which the al-Qaeda leader explains why Muslims should not participate in democratic elections. Zawahiri cites the Quran and some of its radical commentators to refute the argument of a sheikh who defended Muslim participation in democratic elections.

The Legal Means of Eliminating the Corruption That Affects Our Lands

... Preserving the state of the world and eliminating corruption, dear Muslim brother, depends on carrying out God's rulings, pronounced to reform his creatures.... When the impure-unbelievers came to dominate Muslim countries at the end of the nineteenth century, the revealed law of Islam was put aside in governing our countries, and they brought in impious positive law instead. When they left, the colonizers handed the reins to a group of Muslims who had reached power through these laws, which do not give truth and error their real importance: they allow such illicit behavior, as fornication, usury, wine, and gambling but forbid that which is licit, like jihad along God's path, commanding good, and forbidding evil. These positive laws protect the corruption spreading through the land and are a threat to all those who do not want to obey them and who call for reform.

Evil, my brothers, lies in the group that defends positive law, the rulers and their assistants; these rulers are unbelieving apostates whom it is necessary to fight until the unbelief and the corruption that hover over our countries are eliminated.

The fact that they are apostates is proved by God's word: "And if any fail to judge by (the light of) what god has revealed, they are (no better than) wrong-doers." What they are doing is the very same thing that caused the revelation: they are abandoning government according to revealed law and creating a new authority imposed on all men, just as the Jews abandoned stoning according to the Torah and created another legislation. . . .

The Essence of Democracy

Democracy is a new religion. In Islam, legislation comes from God; in a democracy, this capacity is given to the people. Therefore, this is a new religion, based on making the people into gods and giving them God's rights and attributes. This is tantamount to associating idols with God and falling into unbelief, since God said: "The command is for none but God. He has commanded that you worship none but Him."

Sovereignty in Islam is God's alone; in a democracy, it belongs to the people. That is why Abul-Ala al-Mawdudi said of Western-style democracy that it gives godlike powers to the people. . . . In democracy, the people legislate through the majority of deputies in parliament.

These deputies are men and women, Christians, communists, and secularists. Their legislation becomes a law imposed on all people, according to which taxes are levied and death sentences are passed. Take the example of the Egyptian constitution: article 3 proclaims that "sovereignty is for the people alone who will practise and protect this sovereignty and safeguard national unity in the matter specified by the Constitution," . . . In this manner, they made the people equal to and similar to God. God said: "Have they partners (in godhead), who have established for them some religion without the permission of God?"

According to one definition, religion is a system of life for men, whether true or false. God said: "To you be your Way, and to me mine." He therefore called the infidels' unbelief a religion; in consequence, the human beings who legislate for the people in a democracy are idols, associated with God and worshipped in his place. . . . Is there a worse form of unbelief? . . .

Let us briefly cite what Sayyid Qutb said about God's words, "that we erect not, from among ourselves, Lords and patrons other than God." . . . There is no corruption like that which spreads when gods multiply on the earth, when men worship men, when one of God's creatures claims the right to be obeyed as such, and claims the right to legislate, and establish values and rules as such. All of this is tantamount to claiming divinity, even if the creature does not claim, as Pharaoh did: "I am your Lord, Most High." . . .

In all earthly systems, men take each other as lords instead of God . . . They worship this group instead of God, even if they do not prostrate themselves or kneel before it . . .

RELIGION AND THE STATE

As you can see, my dear Muslim brother, democracy is based on the principle of the power of creatures over other creatures, and rejects the principle of God's absolute power over all creatures; it is also based on the idea that men's desires, whatever they may be, replace God absolutely, and on the refusal to obey God's law.

In Islam, when there is a disagreement or a difference of opinion, one refers to God, his Prophet, and the commands of sharia: "If you differ in anything among yourselves, refer it to God and His Messenger, if you do believe in God and the Last Day." He also said: "Whatever it be wherein you differ, the decision thereof is with God." But in a democracy, one has recourse to human beings (the people) in case of disagreement: Can one go further in unbelief? God commands that decisions be referred to him, and democracy commands that decisions be referred to the people; can one go further in unbelief?

In addition, they call their countries republics to show that legitimacy is derived from the masses and not from God's commands. Thus, in the Egyptian constitution (article 1): "The Arab Republic of Egypt is a democratic, socialist state."

In some countries, the people are even consulted and their opinion is solicited with regard to implementation of the sharia: Do the people agree or not? This shows clearly that in a democracy, when disagreements arise, the people, rather than God and his Prophet, resolve them. This means that the ruler and the people give themselves the right to judge what God has revealed . . .

Islam has no need of all these impious principles. God said: "This day have I perfected your religion for you." So whoever thinks Islam is not perfect and may need the unbelievers' systems is himself an unbeliever and goes against the verse we have just cited. God said: "None but Unbelievers reject our signs." Islam is elevated, and has no need of elevation; it does not accept mingling with anything else. God said: "Say: O you that reject Faith! . . . To you be your Way, and to me mine." This is a total break and an utter disavowal. God said: "Verily it is We Who have revealed the Book to you in Truth: so serve God, offering Him sincere devotion. / Is it not to God that sincere devotion is due?" Sincere, here, means exempt from mixing of any sort.

This is what impious democracy is like, my brother; and the members of the People's Assembly are lords who seek to take God's place; those who elect them and take them for lords in God's place make them tyrants and worship them instead of God.

And if a member of that assembly were to tell us that he serves in it not to legislate but to advise, we would reply: What about the oath of unbelief you took when you entered? What about the fact that you recognize democracy as a regime? and the fact that the majority opinion applies to all? Remember, if he refused the majority opinion, he would not have been allowed to be a candidate, let alone to stay in the assembly. . . .

You will readily understand, dear brother, that it is impossible for anyone who rejects idolatrous democracy to enter this assembly. No one enters it who has not recognized democracy and committed to it. . . .

If you consider, my dear brother, that positive law is impious, as well you should, you must also know that democracy is more impious still, because the capacity to legislate in positive law is in the hands of legal specialists, whereas in a democracy, the capacity to legislate is entirely in the hands of the people . . .

Conditions for a Legal Opinion

You must know that legal opinions are "the knowledge of duty in reality." Therefore, someone who does not know the real circumstances to which a question relates, or does not know which legal judgment applies in a given case, can only err in his legal opinion.

Ibn Qayyim said: "The mufti or the judge cannot give a legal opinion or judge according to law if he does not possess two sorts of understanding: 1) an understanding of reality and jurisprudence, and deduction of what really happened through signs, traces, and indications; 2) an understanding of duty, meaning that one must understand God's command as delivered in his book or through the mouth of his Prophet on a given subject, since one of the two applies to the other." . . .

Does Sheikh Bin Baz know that the laws that members of parliament swear to respect fornication between consenting adults, usury, consumption of alcohol, gambling, and apostasy, which in the name of freedom of belief it does not punish (article 46)? We think Sheikh Bin Baz does not know these things.

This is why his legal opinion is not based on precise knowledge of reality. It is erroneous, and this constitutes the error of a religious scholar.

Harmful Consequences of a Religious Scholar's Error

Omar Ibn al-Khattab said: "Three things can harm Islam: a religious scholar's error; a hypocrite's contestation of the Quran; and a lying imam's ruling." . . .

Advice to Sheikh Bin Baz

God's messenger said: "Religion is sincere counsel." We would therefore advice the sheikh to investigate the situation to which his legal opinion relates. We also advise him to promulgate another fatwa, abrogating his previous one, because God's messenger said: "If someone promulgates a legal opinion without knowledge, the sin falls upon the person who requested it." ... What use was it if the sheikh spent his life preaching monotheism, rejecting idolatry, and dismissing pretexts for paganism, if he is now authorizing participation in idolatrous democracy, whether through participation in the People's Assembly or through elections?

This legal opinion emitted by Sheikh Bin Baz leads to the suspension of jihad against tyrants who rule without bothering with revealed law. By making it licit to follow the democratic path, the sheikh opened the door for Muslims to forsake this jihad, which is an individual duty; he is even combating it. That is why his legal opinion is deplorable from a religious perspective, now and in the future. We therefore request that God will inspire him to revise his legal opinion, and we ask God to give the sheikh and all of us a favorable conclusion. God's messenger said: "The (results of) deeds done depend upon the last actions" (accepted hadith) . . .

Source: Kepel, Gilles, and Jean-Pierre Milelli. *Al Qaeda in Its Own Words.* Cambridge, Mass.: Belknap Press, 2008, pp. 182–192.

PART III:

Research Tools

6

How to Research Religion and the State

Throughout human history there have been innumerable religions and countless states, which have interacted with and affected one another in a wide variety of ways. Researching such a broad topic can be a challenge. This section provides some ideas and practical advice that should help when researching this subject.

One bit of advice that must be mentioned up front is a reminder that the word *state* refers to "condition" as well as to a nation and its government. Be aware of this to save time and ensure that the research does not yield information on the "condition of religion," unless of course that is what one is after. Note, too, that the phrase "church and state" will most frequently turn up information about the United States, where this phrase has been used to refer to the relationship between religion and the government for centuries.

BOOK RESEARCH

The annotated bibliography in this volume lists many reliable books that can be used as jumping-off points to begin research on a topic related to religion and the state. The notes appended at the end of each chapter list pertinent books. Use the author's name or the book title to find a book that fits the topic of research or interest. If the exact title is unavailable at the library or bookstore, try to find titles by the same author. Sometimes these may also provide needed and useful information.

When looking for other books on a topic, whether searching in an online bookstore or the library catalogue, it is usually advisable to search by subject rather than by title. Sometimes, titles do not contain words that specifically refer to what the book is about. If you know the name of an author who is an expert on a topic, a search by author name will likely yield useful results.

RELIGION AND THE STATE

Libraries categorize their books by set subject words established by the Library of Congress (LOC). If a researcher does not use these exact topic words, it may sometimes be difficult to find books on a subject. However, library search pages or card catalogues often provide the searcher with a list of LOC subject words and phrases. Choose one of the LOC subjects that matches the research topic and use that to start another search. For example, if the research topic is the history of Islam in Iran, searching for a book using the words "Muslims Iran" might not yield any books. The library Web page or catalogue card may suggest that the searcher use the LOC words "Iran—religion." A search using this LOC subject will very likely yield a list of useful books.

When books have been found in the library that seem like they may be useful, there are several things that should be checked. After looking at the title and subtitle, read the blurb that is printed on the inside flap of the book cover. A blurb is a brief description of the subject matter the book covers. The back flap, or the back cover of the book, usually provides some information about the author. It is important to know about the author's expertise, background, or possible bias. If the author is a well-respected journalist or a college professor who is an expert on the topic, then it is likely that the book contains reliable information. Bias is less easy to discern. Even college professors have opinions about subjects they know a lot about. However, a book that makes a cogent argument for one point of view can be balanced by finding a book by an equally qualified author who expresses an opposing viewpoint. In any case, make sure the book's author is knowledgeable and has a solid background on the subject.

It is a good idea to read the book's table of contents. Look to see if the research subject is named in one of the chapter titles. Sometimes, chapter titles are rather fanciful and don't reveal what the chapter is about. In that case, flip to the index at the back of the book. Subjects and names are listed alphabetically in the index. Check the index to see if the desired subject is listed. When a relevant listing is found, notice the page numbers that indicate where in the book that subject is mentioned. Sometimes the page numbers shown are not continuous. For example, if the research topic is the Ayatollah Khomeini, the index may list it as: Khomeini, Ayatollah, 11, 34, 178, 229. This indicates that the subject is mentioned only on these four pages, which may not contain all the information sought. However, if the index listing reads: Khomeini, Ayatollah, 128–176, then this subject is covered extensively throughout these pages. It is likely that the latter type of listing will provide more detailed and useful information.

Another thing to keep in mind when choosing books for research is the date of publication. In some cases, an old book can be just as or more useful than a new book. For example, an old book that contains primary source material or eyewitness accounts or one that is a classic background source on a subject may be highly useful and informative. However, if the research topic requires up-to-date information, look for books that have been published recently. The date of publication is given on the book's copyright page, which is the flip side of the page that shows the title and author. The date is often given in very small type, but it is there and looking will determine how timely the information in the book really is.

Like this book, many nonfiction books have notes either after each chapter or at the end of the book. The notes correspond to superscript numbers in the text and tell where the author got the information included in the book. A book's notes are a good place to start looking for reliable sources for a research topic. Look at the name of the book or article cited in the notes. Try to find the cited source or other materials by the same author. Jot down the book or article title and the name of the author cited. Using this information is a good way to begin researching a topic. Once a reliable and relevant book is found on the research topic, it will almost certainly have a bibliography and/or notes that will lead to other books and articles that are also useful and relevant.

PERIODICALS RESEARCH

Periodicals are magazines, newspapers, and journals. Many libraries allow users to search a comprehensive periodicals database, or complete listing (some with complete text), of a wide variety of magazines, journals, and newspapers. In many cases, this search can be conducted on a computer from home or in the library.

As with book searches, unless one can search under a known author's name, it is a good idea to search keywords related to the topic. Some databases use LOC subject words. Many, however, search the titles or even the text of the articles in the database. In the latter case, the researcher can search using a wider range of words or phrases. However, the database search engine finds all occurrences of the words searched, so some of the results produced may not be relevant. For example, if the search is "Christian state," one may get a list that includes articles about the "state" of actor "Christian" Bale's career. This is not what the researcher wants. If most of the articles listed are relevant to the topic, one can ignore the few that are off target. If most of the articles listed are not on the topic, the search terms must be revised; for example, try "Christianity government."

The recommendations made about author expertise and date of publication in books also apply to articles. In searching articles, one also should look at the name of the magazine, journal, or newspaper. Some newspapers and magazines are known to publish mainly sensationalist articles that have little basis in fact or reality. If articles from these periodicals are retrieved and listed after a search, it is advisable to ignore them. Also, look for clues about bias in the publication name. For example, if an article was published in the *Christian Fundamentalist Monthly,* the researcher should recognize that it will probably present one point of view that may be biased. However, not all periodicals that contain the name of a religion are biased, and some that one might think are biased are not. Be sure to look at the magazine or journal name to be alert to the possibility of bias. If possible, click on the listing and read the abstract, or summary, of the article. The abstract will give some idea about the content and bias, if any, of the article. Also, look for publications that are known to have high standards regarding the objectivity of their articles, such as respected newspapers and news magazines, and that employ and publish work by knowledgeable writers who thoroughly research the articles they write.

Boolean Search Terms

A periodicals database includes a space where search terms are typed in. Many databases allow Boolean search terms, which make the search more specific. Boolean search terms include the words AND, OR, and NOT (always in capital letters).

The Boolean NOT eliminates the word or phrase that follows it from the articles returned in a search. For example, if the research topic is religion in Turkey, using Boolean terms will help weed out articles with recipes for cooking a turkey for Christmas. The researcher might type *[Turkey NOT cook]* or *[Turkey NOT recipe]* in the search space. The NOT eliminates those articles that also have the word "cook" (or cooking) and the word "recipe." So one would also want to use the NOT to eliminate the animal: *[Turkey NOT bird]* to eliminate articles about turkey hunting or turkey habitat.

The Boolean AND searches for articles that have both the word before the AND plus the word after it. Use the Boolean AND to find articles about religion: *[Turkey AND religion].* In this case, the list of results will be of articles that contain both these words. This search will likely yield results about Islam in the nation of Turkey.

What if one wants to find out not about Shia Muslims, but about Sufis or Christians in Turkey? This search might use OR, which finds articles that contain either of the words around OR: *[Turkey AND Sufis OR Christians].* This search will yield results about Sufis or Christians in Turkey.

Boolean searches can be very powerful in retrieving the most useful articles. Sometimes, a very long Boolean search may be used; for example, *[Turkey NOT cook NOT bird AND Sufi OR Christian NOT Islam].* In most instances, these long Boolean phrases can be broken down. First, one would search for *[Turkey NOT cook NOT bird]*. Then one can search within these results for *[Turkey AND Sufi OR Christian]* to see if this search yields useful articles. Try using a variety of Boolean combinations until relevant articles are retrieved.

Dates

Most periodicals databases allow the researcher to limit the search by date of publication. The database may have drop-down menus that allow one to automatically choose the dates to be searched. Other databases require that the researcher type in the dates that delimit the search. For example, if the researcher needs general background on a topic, then leaving the dates open, either indicating a wide range of dates or clicking "All" dates, may yield the best results because more articles will be retrieved. However, if the researcher needs information on a particular incident, then limiting the dates searched will provide more targeted results.

A researcher who is looking for information on the Islamic Revolution in Iran, for example, would indicate that the search should begin with articles published after September 1979. If one wants primarily eyewitness accounts of the revolution or information on the immediate reaction to the revolution, one might limit the end date of the search to 1980 or 1981.

INTERNET SEARCHES

Most Internet search engines do not use Boolean terms. When using an Internet search engine, a researcher must carefully determine the best word(s) or phrase to get relevant results. A good rule of thumb is to use the most specific word or combination of words possible. If the results retrieved from the search are too narrow or do not cover all the aspects of the research topic, try adding relevant words to the search. If search results still seem incomplete, it is often helpful to click on a listing that seems the most relevant. When that Web page opens, read its contents. The contents on a partly relevant Web page may contain words or phrases that one had not thought of before. One may be able to use these words or phrases in a new search to find more complete information. Nearly all Web pages provide links that can be clicked on to open a new Web page. Clicking on what looks like a relevant link may take the researcher to a Web page that has the relevant information or terms being sought. In all cases, one should not limit oneself to looking at only those Web pages listed on the first page of search results. Click through two, three, or more pages of result listings to find the Web site that is most relevant and useful to the topic and is likely to have the most complete information on the research subject.

Search terms should be as precise as possible. If one is doing research on Muslims in Europe, it is inadvisable to begin a Web search with the word *Europe*. That term is so broad, it will yield a gazillion Web pages, most of which will have nothing to do with the research topic. A better, more targeted search might be *European Muslims* or *Muslims in Europe*. In the latter case, some search engines require apostrophes around the phrase *Muslims in Europe* in order to find Web sites that contain the full phrase and not just Web sites that contain these words randomly. However, be aware that sometimes using apostrophes around a phrase limits the number of Web sites retrieved.

While maintaining focus on the research topic, it is often helpful to be flexible in changing one's search terms to get the best results. For example, if searching with the word *Muslim* yields too many irrelevant results, try using the word *Islam* in the search phrase. The list of search results may also suggest new search terms that can be used to revise and improve the search. Thus, a Web site listing that is titled "Islam's New Front Line: Germany" suggests that doing a search with the word "Germany" might yield a new and useful listing of informative and reliable Web sites. Being open to refining the search by using new relevant keywords and terms almost always yields positive results.

Once a list of Web pages is displayed, the researcher must determine which are likely to have reliable information and which are not. Listings displayed by most search engines will show the title of an article or similar content at the top of the listing. As with magazine articles, the article title often provides clues about its content or bias. Thus, an article entitled "Is Europe a Province of Islam?" might well be biased and unreliable and should be ignored. Look for reasonable, authoritative titles relevant to the research topic. Ignore obviously biased or irrelevant Web sites. Check Web site listings on several pages of search results to find the best sources.

Remember that the best research draws from several sources of information. One should not limit information gathering to a single Web site, even if it is a good one. Try to find different types of Web sites that confirm each other's information but that also offer different "flavors" that can be incorporated into the research report. For example, a researcher may draw on a well-written and descriptive newspaper report to give the research project a personal tone and mix in factual data taken from a Web site about history and statistics derived from an encyclopedia. Do not use too many sources, but using a variety of reliable and relevant sources should improve and enliven the research project.

Assessing Web Sites

Below the title, there will be the Web site address where the article is found. One should always look at the Web site address extension to determine who

How to Research Religion and the State

or what type of organization or publication runs the Web site. Knowing who owns or runs the Web site gives information that helps one evaluate the validity of the information found on the site. The most common Web site extensions are .com (dot com), which indicates a commercial, for-profit site; .org, which indicates a Web site run by an organization of some sort; .edu, which indicates that the Web site is run by a college or university; and .gov, which are Web sites run by government agencies. Web sites with .tv, .biz, or similar extensions are generally unreliable and should be avoided.

Some .com Web sites are reliable, even though they are commercial sites. For example, the Web site for the *New York Times* (www.nytimes.com) is a .com, but most articles found on the site of this respected newspaper are reliable, factual, and objective. Dot com newspapers and magazines can be very useful in finding timely information, but look for sites run by respected magazines and newspapers. Encyclopedias, too, are commercial sites (e.g., www.britannica.com), but most have well-researched and reliable information. Other .com Web sites may be unreliable and biased. A Web site whose address is www.christianityisforfools.com is one to avoid. If one is not sure about the reliability of a Web site, click on the Web site address and scan the site's home page. One can often tell from the home page if the site contains useful and unbiased information. Look at the text on the home page, its clickable links, any list of articles the site contains, the names of the people who write for the Web site, etc., to get a good idea about the reliability, objectivity, and relevance of the Web site. A Web site may be reliable, but it must also have the information needed for the research topic.

Web sites that have a .org extension may or may not be useful. Some very trusted and reliable organizations have Web sites. Then again, so do biased and hate-mongering organizations. Remember that religion and politics are "hot topics," and some organizations have an axe to grind on religious or political issues. If one is uncertain about a .org Web site, click on the Web address and scan the site's home page for clues to its bias and its relevance to the research topic. Just remember that anyone can put up a Web site and fill it with all kinds of nonsense. So be discriminating and take a minute or two to read what is on the site to see if it is useful and objective.

Every college and university has its own .edu Web site. Some college Web sites have pages that contain journal articles written by professors. These articles are usually well researched and reliable. However, there are things to keep in mind when reviewing these Web pages. Professors are experts in their field, but they may have a strong point of view about a topic. So one professor's article on religion may be biased one way, and another professor's article on the same topic may have a different bias. The information within the articles may be accurate, but each professor may use it to make his or her own point.

RELIGION AND THE STATE

A good way to test the reliability of the information on one particular Web site is to find the same information on a different Web site. If one finds information about Tibet and China on a .org Web site, and the information seems reliable, double-check it by looking for the same information on a government Web site (e.g., www.state.gov, the State Department Web site) or on a university or encyclopedia Web site.

A NOTE ABOUT BIAS

Bias is slanting information to argue one particular point of view. If one is looking for an objective overview of a subject, bias should be avoided. Bias may be recognized because it uses emotional terms or obviously tells only one side of an issue. However, bias is not always bad. For example, one might read accounts of Christianity in Turkey on a Christian Web site and on an Islamic or Turkish Web site. Both accounts may present viable and interesting points of view. But one then should check the accuracy of the factual information in both articles through a government or encyclopedia Web site.

Sometimes a researcher wants to understand both sides of an issue. This requires reading biased material, or material that presents a particular point of view. This type of bias can be stimulating as long as one recognizes that opinions are being expressed. Generally, one wants to avoid using biased material that expresses irrational or emotional prejudice on an issue. That is especially important in studying religion or politics. Experts may have differing points of view on the Israeli-Palestinian question, and reading these divergent points of view will be enlightening. Yet there are many Web sites intended only to promulgate religious hatred, such as anti-Semitic or anti-Islamic views. Learn to recognize the inflammatory, emotional language used by these Web sites in order to steer clear of them.

EXPANDING AND REFINING THE SEARCH

Once a researcher has found a reliable Web site with factual, relevant information, an examination of the Web site's links may lead to new and interesting sources of information. Generally, reliable Web sites link to other reliable Web sites. Click on buttons that read Links, More Information, Articles, News, Publications, or other terms that indicate that clicking on the button will open up a new page that may have more useful information.

There are literally billions of Web sites on the Internet, most of them biased or unreliable for a serious researcher. Unless one carefully chooses one's search terms and, if necessary, continues to make them more specific to all the information needed, one will quickly be overwhelmed by, or lost in, a maze of irrelevant Web site information. It might be helpful to jot down key terms to look for on a Web site that help in evaluating its relevance. Some terms from this book might help in this regard. After scanning the Web site's home page and its About Us page, Web sites or links from Web sites that do not contain the desired key terms may be eliminated as irrelevant to the research. However, Web sites and links may also provide new, more pertinent search terms, and they may discuss new aspects of the topic the researcher has not thought of before. The most important skill is to keep the research topic and its key terms in focus. Once this is accomplished, apply evaluation skills to the Web site or other source of information to ensure that it is factual, reliable, and relevant.

Blogs and Wikis

For the most part, blogs should be avoided as sources of information. Anyone can write anything on a blog and there is no one to assure its accuracy or reliability. In fact, most blogs contain nothing but people's opinions about various subjects. These may be interesting to read, and some people may present cogent arguments for their point of view, but the fact is that these entries are still opinion, or bias, and not something to include in a research report.

There are some blogs—for example, those run by college professors, experienced reporters, or other experts in a field—that may contain useful information. The problem is that it can be very hard to distinguish reliable blogs from the zillions of useless blogs. If your research leads you to a blog by a professor or other expert, carefully evaluate the information on the site. If the primary blogger (the owner of the site) cites an official report or source of information, seek out that information for the research project rather than using the blog itself. Any information the researcher finds on a respected and is tempted to use should always be double-checked against another reliable source.

Many Web search engines list Wikipedia articles in their search results. Be aware that many teachers take a dim view of the information on Wikipedia. However, Wikipedia has been taking steps to ensure that the information in its articles is reliable. Those articles that do not cite sources for their information are now flagged by a notice at the top of the Web page that tells the researcher that the article needs more source citations or that the article may be biased. Before you read a Wikipedia article, look for any warnings at the top of the page that indicate that the article may be unreliable or inaccurate. Even if no such warnings are posted assess the quality of the information as you would with any other source by double-checking information and looking for signs of bias.

If your teacher will not accept Wikipedia citations, look at the bottom of the Wikipedia article. All reliable Wiki articles list citations that tell where they got the information that is in the article. They may also list a number of books and Web sites as references. In many cases, one can click on the citation or reference and be taken to the Web site that is the source of the information. If the Web site is reliable (if it is a university, encyclopedia, or other respected source), then use that Web site (not Wiki) as the source of information for the research project.

LEGAL ISSUES

Plagiarism is copying other people's work and passing it off as one's own. Plagiarism is cheating, is a form of copyright infringement, and is illegal. When picking up text from a book, article, or Web site, always set it off in the research paper with quotation marks. At the end of the quotation, add a note number. Write a corresponding note that includes the source of the quote, text, or information. Notes, at the bottom of the page or at the end of the research paper, should include the name of the author or speaker, the source the quote came from (book, article, Web site), and in the case of books the publisher, place, and date of publication, and page number(s). When citing a Web site in notes, include the complete Web site address and the date on which the information was accessed. Look at the notes following the chapters in this book to recognize how citations should be presented.

Nearly every book one gets in the library or buys in a bookstore is protected by copyright and must be cited if it is quoted in the research project. The same applies to magazine, journal, and newspaper articles published within the last 75 years (or more). One may face fines or jail for failing to cite a source or for plagiarizing material without crediting the original author. Unattributed use of material that is in the public domain is also plagiarism and is equally unacceptable because it is cheating, even if it is not illegal. The same holds true for Web sites. Articles written by professionals on Web sites are copyrighted. Look for the copyright sign © on the Web site. It indicates that any quoted or cited material must be sourced in the research report's notes. Additionally, all data, such as statistics, must also be sourced. A reader wants to know where the researcher got the numbers included in the data so they can be checked for accuracy. Finally, any images used in research must indicate where the image came from. Any tables or charts picked up or created from another source must also be given a citation. That's the law.

7

Facts and Figures

INTRODUCTION

1.1 Percentage of World Population for Major Religions

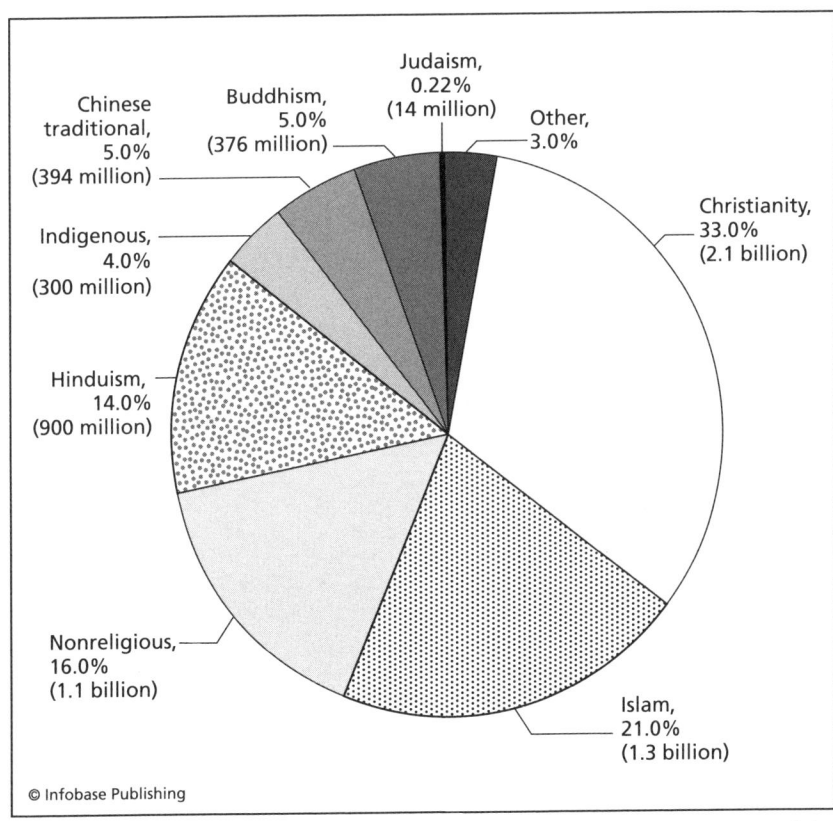

The pie chart shows the percentage of the world population who are adherents of the major world religions for the year 2005.

Source: Numbers are based on "Major Religions of the World Ranked by Number of Adherents." Available online. URL: http://www.adherents.com/Religions_By_Adherents.html. Accessed on July 28, 2009.

1.2 How Select Nationalities View Religious Influence on Government

Should religious leaders try to influence government decisions?	
Country	Yes (%)
Americans (U.S.)	37
Italians	30
Canadians	25
Australians	22
Koreans	21
Germans	20
British	20
Spanish	17
French	12

Source: Philips, Kevin. *American Theocracy.* New York: Penguin Books, 2004, p. 197.

Facts and Figures

1.3 Religion(s) and Government of Selected World Nations

Nation	Major Religion(s)* [percent]	Government
Afghanistan	Sunni Muslim 80%; Shia Muslim 19%	Islamic Republic
Algeria	Sunni Muslim 99%	Republic
Angola	Indigenous 47%; Catholic 38%; Protestant 15%	Republic
Bahrain	Muslim (Shia & Sunni) 81%; Christian 9%	Constitutional Monarchy
Bangladesh	Muslim 83%; Hindu 16%	Parliamentary Democracy
Bhutan	Buddhist (Lamaistic) 75%; Hindu 25%	Constitutional Monarchy
Bosnia/Herzegovina	Muslim 40%; Chr. Orthodox 31%; Catholic 15%; Other 14%	Emerging Federal Democratic Republic
Brunei	Muslim (official) 67%; Buddhist 13%; Christian 10%; Indigenous & Other 10%	Constitutional Sultanate
Burma (Myanmar)	Buddhist 89%; Christian 4%; Muslim 4%	Military Junta Dictatorship
Cambodia	Buddhist (Theravada) 95%	Democracy under a Constitutional Monarchy
China	(Officially Atheist) Taoist 4%; Buddhist 4%; Christian 4%; Muslim 2%; (+Tibetan Buddhism)	Communist
Cyprus	Greek Orthodox 78%; Muslim 18%	Republic (ethnic communities separated)
Egypt	Muslim (mostly Sunni) 90%; Coptic Christian 9%	Republic
France	Catholic ~ 85%; Muslim ~ 10%	Republic
Greece	Greek Orthodox 98%; Muslim 1.5%	Parliamentary Republic
India	Hindu 81%; Muslim 13%; Christian 2%; Sikh 2%	Federal Republic
Indonesia	Muslim 86%; Christian 9%; Hindu 2%	Republic
Iran	Muslim 98% (Shia 89%, Sunni 9%)	Theocratic Republic
Iraq	Muslim 97% (Shia 65%, Sunni 32%)	Emerging Parliamentary Democracy
Israel	Jewish 76%; Muslim 16%; Druze 2%; Christian 2%	Parliamentary Democracy
Laos	Buddhist 67%; Christian 2%; None or other 31%	Communist

(continues)

RELIGION AND THE STATE

1.3 Religion(s) and Government of Selected World Nations *(continued)*

Nation	Major Religion(s)* [percent]	Government
Lebanon	Muslim (six sects) 60%; Christian (14 sects) 39%	Republic
Libya	Sunni Muslim 97%	Authoritarian state
Malaysia	Muslim 60%; Buddhist 19%; Christian 9%; Hindu 6%; Confucianism/Taoism 3%	Constitutional Monarchy
Mauritius	Hindu 48%; Catholic 24%; Muslim 17%; Other Christian 9%	Parliamentary Democracy
Nepal	Hindu ~ 100% (official)	Democratic Republic
Pakistan	Muslim 95% (Sunni 75%, Shia 20%); Christian or Hindu 5%	Federal Republic
Qatar	Muslim 78%; Christian 8%; Other 14%	Emirate
Saudi Arabia	Muslim (Sunni) ~ 100%	Monarchy
Singapore	Buddhist 42%; Muslim 14%; Taoist 9%; Hindu 4%; Catholic 5%; Other Christian 10%	Parliamentary Republic
Sri Lanka	Buddhist 69%; Muslim 8%; Hindu 7%; Christian 6%	Republic
Taiwan	Buddhist/Taoist 93%; Christian 5%	Democracy
Tanzania	Christian 30%; Muslim 35%; Indigenous 35%	Republic
Thailand	Buddhist 95%; Muslim 5%	Constitutional Monarchy
Turkey	Muslim ~ 100% (mostly Sunni)	Parliamentary Democracy
United Arab Emirates	Muslim 96% (80% Sunni; 16% Shia)	Federation
United Kingdom	Christian 72%; Muslim 3%; Hindu 1%; None 23%	Constitutional Monarchy
United States	Protestant 51%; Catholic 24%; Mormon & Other 3%; Jewish 2%; Buddhist 1%; Muslim 0.6%; None or unaffiliated 16%	Constitutional Federal Republic

* Religions classified as "other" not included unless they make up a large percentage of the population.

Source: CIA World Factbook, 2008. Available online. URL: http://www.cia.gov/library/publications/the-world-factbook/fields/2122.html&/fields/2128.html. Accessed December 29, 2008.

Facts and Figures

1.4 Holy Roman Empire, 1215–1250

RELIGION AND THE STATE

1.5 Spread of Islam, 632–2000

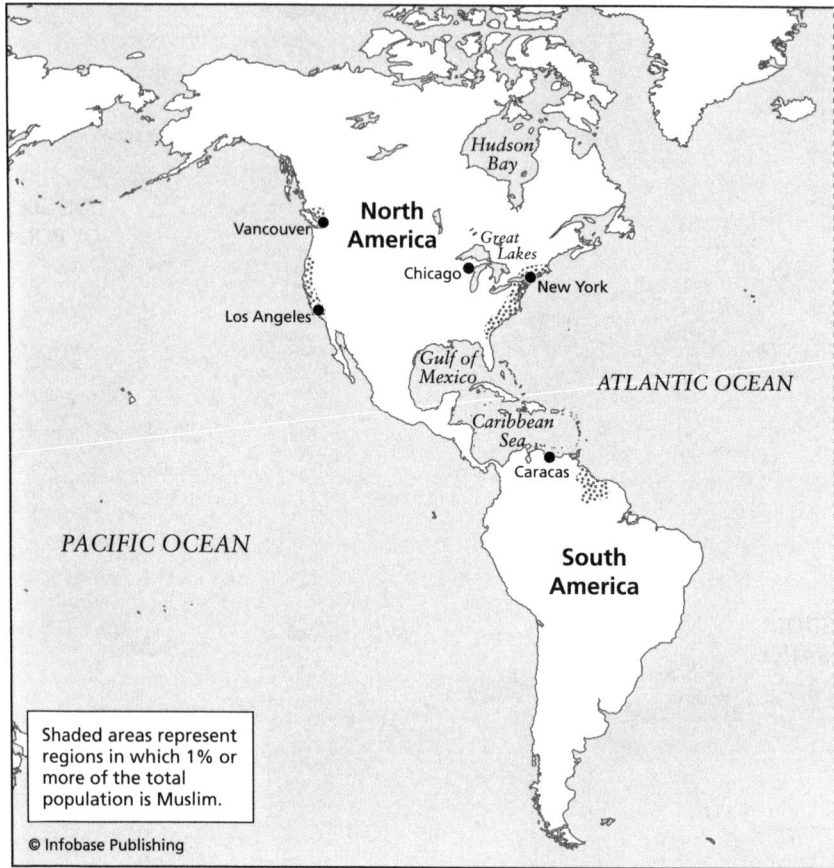

This map shows the spread of Islam throughout the world in the years since the death of Muhammad in 632 C.E. In all cases, shaded areas represent regions in which 1 percent or more of the population is Muslim.

Facts and Figures

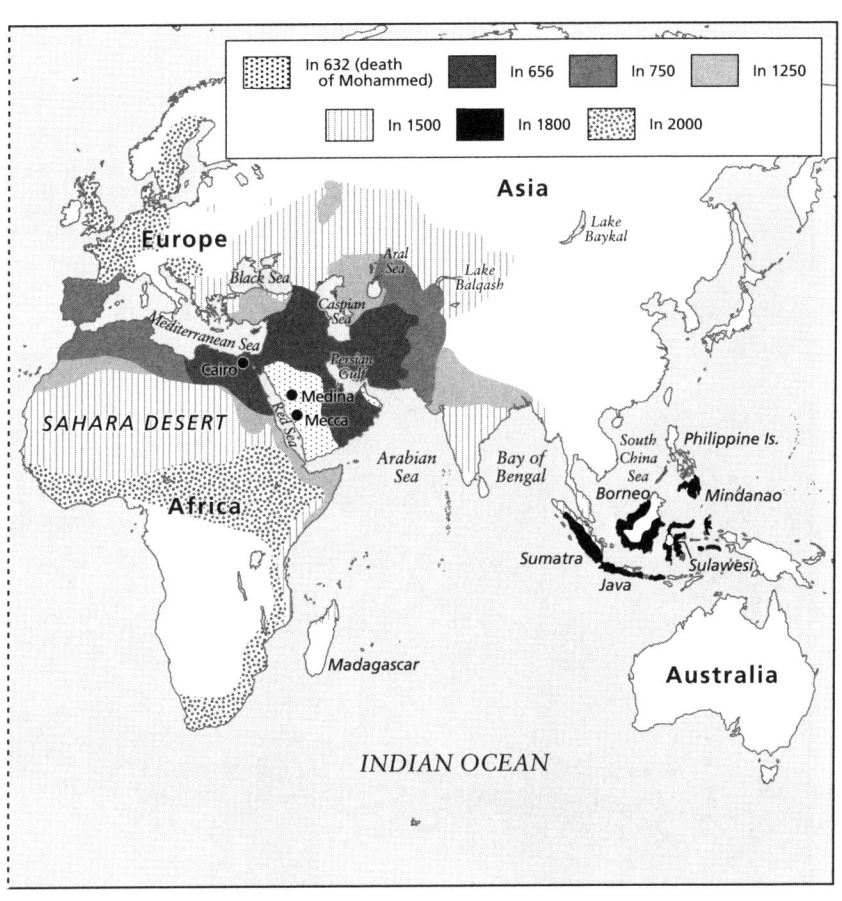

RELIGION AND THE STATE

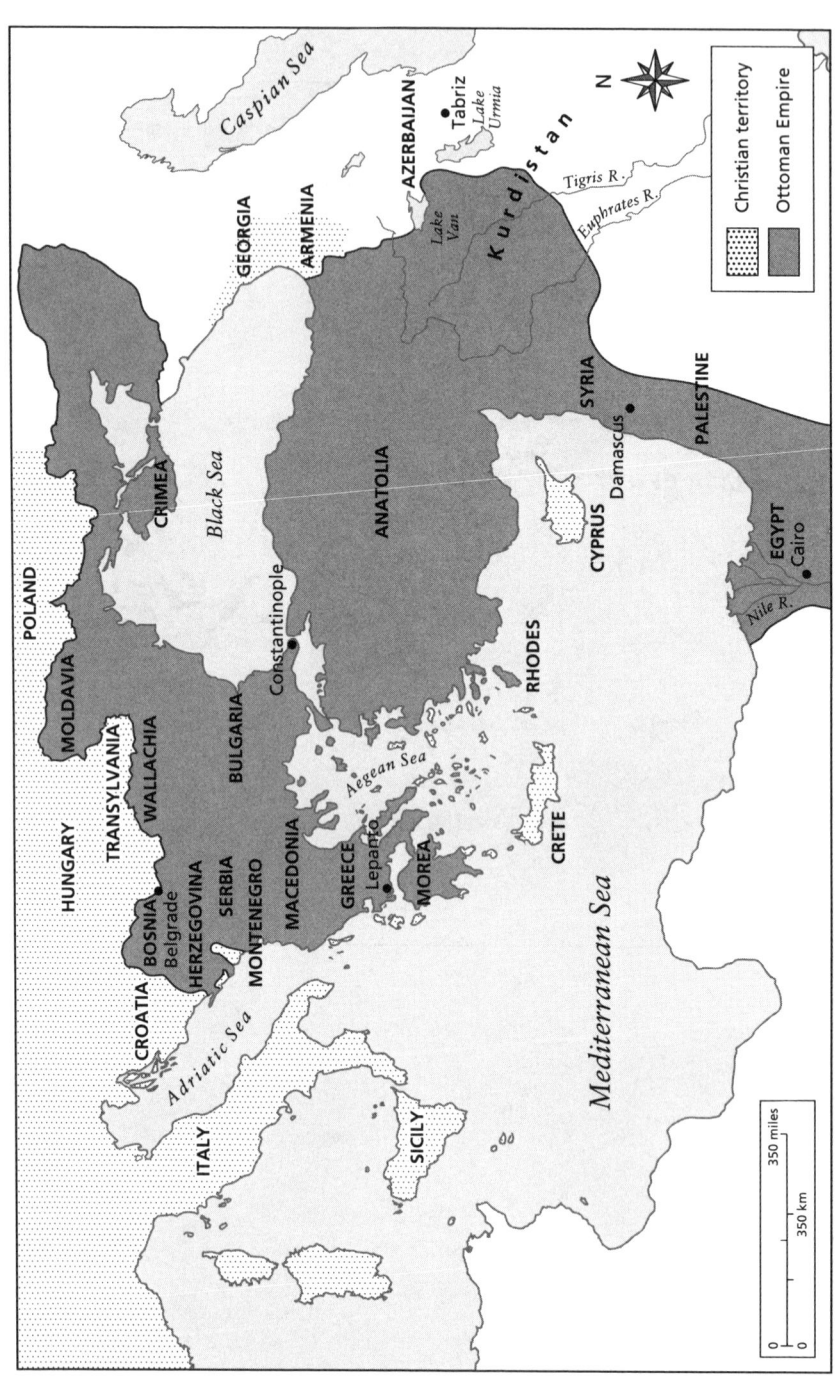

1.6 The Ottoman Empire, 1520

This map shows the extent of the Ottoman Empire in 1520, after a long period of expansion and during the first year of the reign of Suleyman I the Magnificent.

Facts and Figures

UNITED STATES
2.1 Religious Groups in the British Colonies, 1750

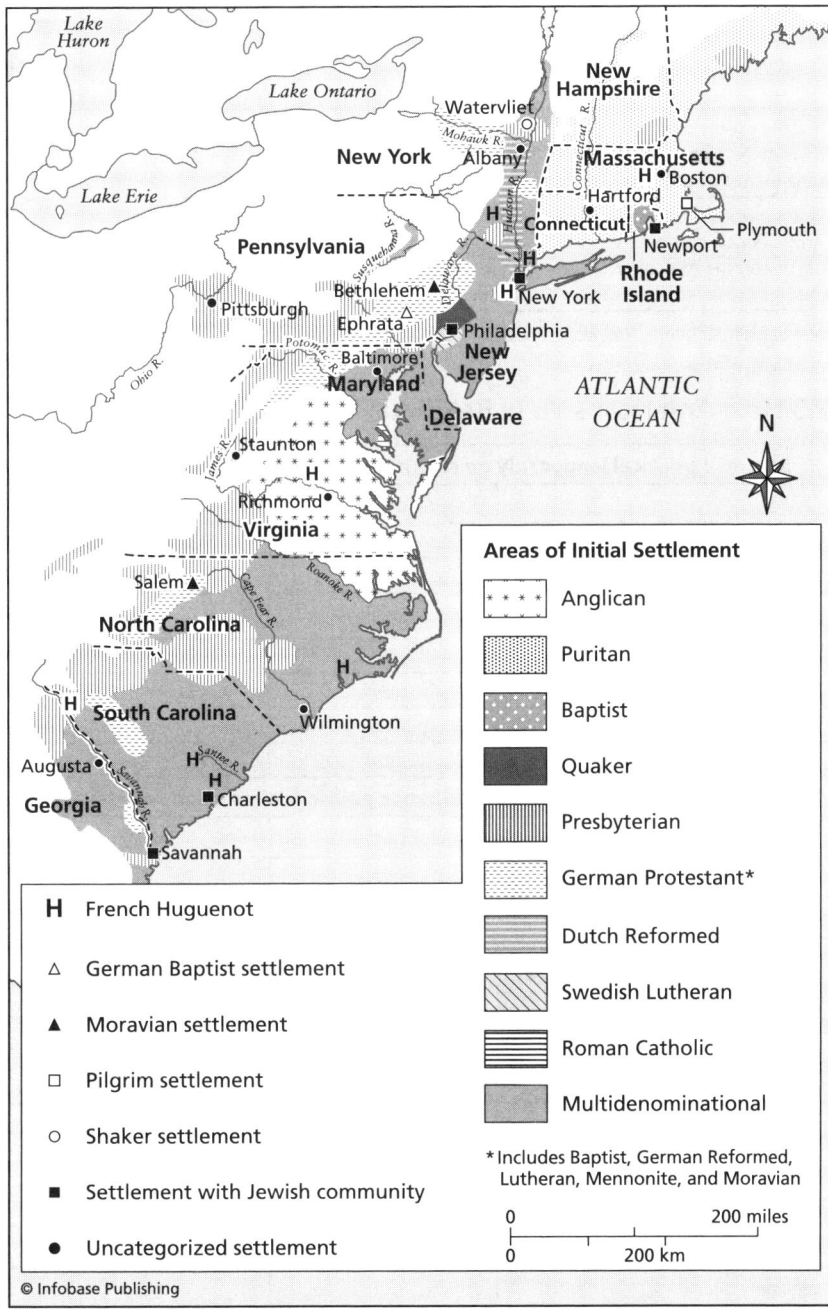

This map shows the distribution of different religious groups among settlers in the British colonies of North America in 1750.

2.2 Biblical Worldview of American Christians

Question	Responses
Is the Bible literally accurate?	National: Yes, 55% Evangelical Protestants: Yes, 83% Nonevangelical Protestants: Yes, 47% Catholics: Yes, 45%
Are these biblical events literally true?	Noah's Ark: Yes, 60% God's creation of Earth in six days: Yes, 61% God parting the Red Sea for Moses: Yes, 64%
Will the events described in the Book of Revelation occur sometime in the future or not?	All Christians: Yes, 59%; No, 33% Fundamentalists/evangelicals: Yes, 77%; No, 15%
Will the world end in an Armageddon battle between Christ and the Antichrist?	All Christians: Yes, 45%; No, 39% Evangelical Protestants: Yes, 71%; No, 18% Other Protestants: Yes, 28%; No 54% Catholics: Yes, 18%; No, 57%

Source: Philips, Kevin. *American Theocracy*. New York: Penguin Books, 2004, p. 102.

2.3 How Americans View Religious Influence on Government

Should a political leader rely on religion when making policy decisions?	Yes (%)	No (%)
Conservatives	63	32
Republicans	62	35
National Sample	40	55
Independents	38	59
Moderates	36	58
Democrats	27	65
Liberals	20	77
Should religious leaders try to influence politicians' positions on issues?	**Yes (%)**	**No (%)**
White conservative evangelicals	62	37
White churchgoing evangelicals	53	46
Conservatives	49	49
White evangelicals	46	53
Catholics	34	65
National Sample	35	64
Independents	32	67
Moderates	29	69
Democrats	28	71
Nonevangelical Protestants	27	70
Seculars	22	77

Source: Philips, Kevin. *American Theocracy*. New York: Penguin Books, 2004, pp. 196–197.

Facts and Figures

GLOBAL PERSPECTIVES
3.1 Modern Iran

This is a map of modern-day Iran, showing the country's major cities. It also shows the nations that border Iran.

3.2 Saudi Arabia: Ibn Saud's Campaigns of Conquest, 1902–1932

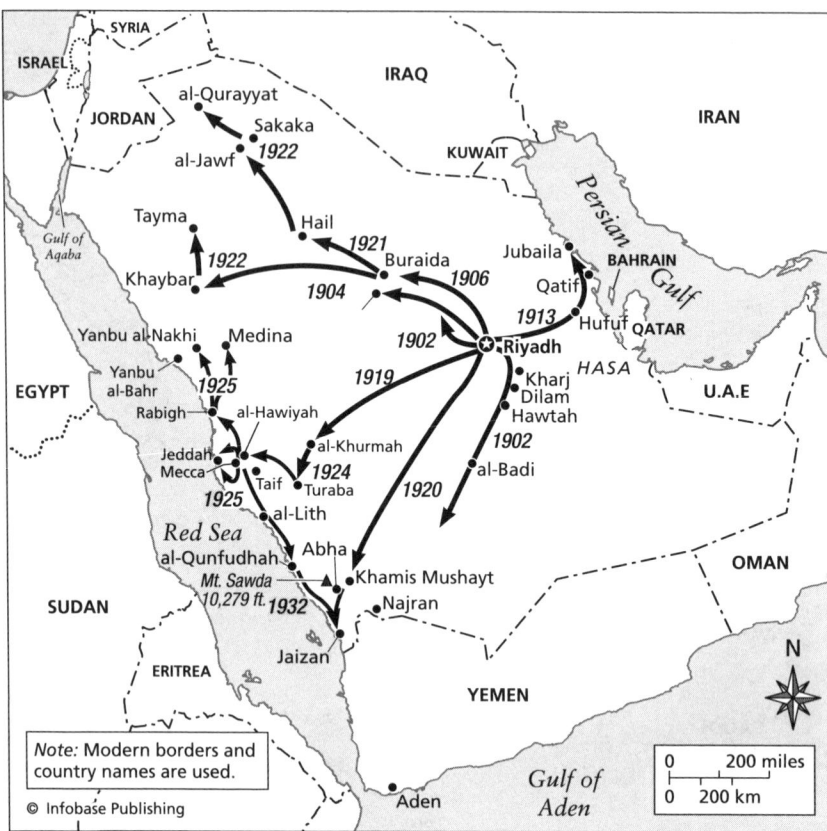

For three decades, starting with the capture of Riyadh in 1902, Ibn Saud fought to unify Arabia under his rule. His campaign culminated in the creation of the Kingdom of Saudi Arabia in 1932.

Facts and Figures

3.3 Tibet Autonomous Region and Historic Tibet

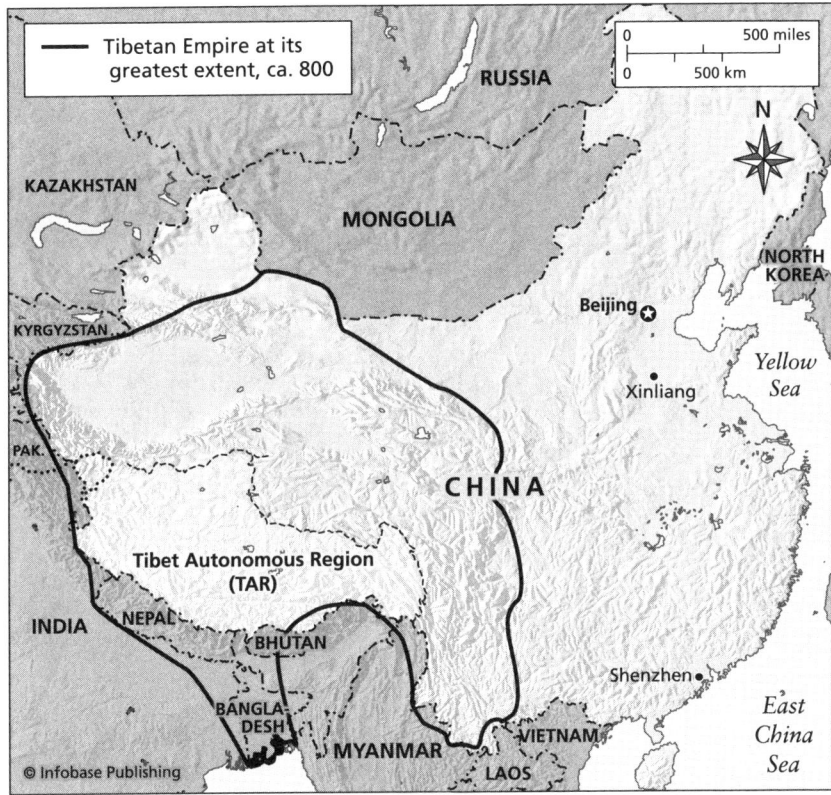

This map shows the location of the Tibet Autonomous Region in China and the boundary of the Tibetan Empire at its greatest extent, ca. 800.

RELIGION AND THE STATE

3.4 BJP Ruled States in India, 2009

This map shows the states that were ruled by the BJP or its National Democratic Alliance partners in early 2009.

Facts and Figures

3.5 Muslim Populations in Key European Countries and the United States

Country or Territory	Population (2007)	% Muslim	Total Number of Muslims
Turkey	76,805,524	99%	76,037,469
Kosovo	2,126,708	90%	1,914,037
Albania	3,619,778	65%–70%	2,533,845
Bosnia and Herzegovina	4,552,198	40%–45%	1,820,879–2,048,489
France	63,718,187	6.9%–10%	4,396,555–6,371,819
Netherlands	16,570,613	5.5%–6%	911,384–994,237
Germany	82,400,996	4.9%	4,413,639
Switzerland	7,554,661	4.3%	324,850
United Kingdom	60,776,238	2.7%–3.3%	1,640,958–2,000,000
Denmark	5,468,120	2%–3.7%	109,362–202,320
United States	301,139,947	0.8%	2,350,000

This table reveals the percentage of Muslims in the population in select European countries in 2007. Figures for the United States are given for comparison.

8

Key Players

MUHAMMAD IBN ABD AL-WAHHAB (1703?–1792?) A scholar and preacher of the rigidly orthodox Hanbali school of Islamic thought, Abd al-Wahhab traveled throughout Arabia denouncing behavior and belief that was not in strict accord with sharia law. In 1744, Abd al-Wahhab joined forces with the Saud family to forcibly impose rigid Islam on the peoples of Arabia. Abd al-Wahhab gave the House of Saud the religious legitimacy it needed to become absolute monarchs of the nation. Abd al-Wahhab's views of Islam (Wahhabism) continue to influence Muslims and inspire Islamic extremists.

MUHAMMAD ABDUH (1849–1905) Abduh, a student and follower of al-Afghani, was an Egyptian Muslim reformer. Though trained as a religious scholar, Abduh was radicalized by al-Afghani, though he never became the firebrand that his mentor was. Abduh wrote and lectured to encourage Muslims to rise up and overthrow the colonial powers that oppressed them and to shun the decadent lifestyle and values imperialists had brought with them. He advocated for a return to a more pure form of Islam, but, like al-Afghani, he believed that Islam could be reformed and even purified via reason.

ABU BAKR *(ABU BAKR AS-SIDDIQ)* (CA. 573–634) Abu Bakr was one of the earliest converts to Islam and one of the Prophet's closest and most trusted companions. After the Prophet's death, Abu Bakr became the first Rightly Guided Caliph, and was the only one who was not murdered. During his short caliphate, he fought Arabian tribes to bring them back into the fold of Islam, essentially uniting most of Arabia as an Islamic caliphate.

JAMAL AL-DIN AL-AFGHANI (1838–1897) Born in northwestern Iran, al-Afghani became a highly influential writer, speaker, and activist in the Muslim world, from the Middle East to Turkey, India, and even Western Europe. He railed against imperialism and urged Muslims to throw off the colonial yoke to realize their true strength and identity. His greatest influence came when he lived and lectured in Cairo during the 1870s. His lectures stressed the need for the application of reason and intellect in interpreting Islamic law. Al-Afghani remains one of the most respected thinkers in the Islamic world.

ALI IBN ABI TALIB (CA. 598–661) The Prophet's cousin and son-in-law, husband of his daughter Fatima. After being passed over in the early succession, Ali became the fourth and last Rightly Guided Caliph. His caliphate was tainted by rumors that he had killed the third caliph, Uthman, in order to gain the caliphate for himself. Despite constant pressure, he never investigated who had killed his predecessor. Ali was murdered by Kharijites who believed that his failure to bring Uthman's murderer to justice was an impious act that made Ali unfit to be caliph. Shiites view Ali as the First Imam, and his murder set the stage for the defection of Shia from mainstream Sunni Islam.

ATATÜRK *(Mustafa Kemal)* **(1881–1938)** A great Turkish leader, founder of the modern Turkish state, and the first president of Turkey. Ataturk's career began in the army, where he served with distinction. After the collapse of the Ottoman Empire, Atatürk and the Young Turks founded a political party that established a government in Ankara (in opposition to the Allied government in Constantinople). Determined to make Turkey a modern state, Atatürk booted the Europeans out of Turkey and proceeded to rule the nation for 15 years. He was, in fact, a dictator who imposed his will and his vision for Turkey upon the people. He instituted many reforms that largely Westernized the country. In 1924, he abolished the caliphate, essentially removing Islam's influence on government and policy.

HASSAN AL-BANNA (1906–1949) Al-Banna was an Egyptian religious and political leader and founder of the Muslim Brotherhood. The Brotherhood engaged in community service, such as creating schools that taught traditional Islamism. The Brotherhood became known for its assassinations of key government figures, first among the British colonialists and later among King Farouk's ministers. The group became increasingly militant and violent in the 1930s and '40s. Although he was never directly linked to any assassination, al-Banna was murdered in 1949, probably by agents of the state.

KARL BARTH (1886–1968) Barth was a Swiss Protestant theologian who became a professor in Germany (1921–35). In his theology, Barth sought to promote the principles of the Reformation; he saw the word of God and his revelation through Christ as central to Protestant Christianity. With the ascent of the Nazis, Barth led a group of Protestant clergy in writing the Barmen Declaration, which condemned National Socialist doctrine, actions, and religious perversion

RELIGION AND THE STATE

of Christianity through its Reich Church. Barth is considered one of the 20th century's greatest thinkers and theologians.

THOMAS BECKET (1118–1170)   A friend and adviser to the English king Henry II, Becket was appointed Archbishop of Canterbury in 1163 to promote the hegemony of the monarch over that of the church. Once ordained, however, he sided with the church against the king, who had him assassinated. His martyrdom led Becket to be canonized by the Catholic Church.

GEORGE W. BUSH (1946–   )   The 43rd U.S. president, Bush served from 2001 to 2009. When he was in his 40s, Bush became a born-again Christian. As president, he was a fervent supporter of religion, particularly the fundamentalist and evangelical religion of the Christian Right. His administration favored those "moral" and social policies espoused by the religious right. Bush created the Office of Faith-Based Initiatives to funnel federal funds to religious groups engaged in community and other types of service. Civil libertarians and others questioned the constitutionality of this initiative, which gave the public's tax dollars to overtly religious organizations, but Bush retained the support of the religious right and the courts.

JOHN CALVIN (1509–1564)   A renowned French Protestant and theologian during the Reformation, Calvin tried to impose his own strict version of Protestantism in Geneva, Switzerland, but he was at first persecuted and banished. While in exile, Calvin elucidated his religious ideas in his *Institutes of the Christian Religion* (1536), in which he rejected papal authority and stated that salvation came through faith alone. He also explicated his concept of predestination, the idea that God has determined beforehand which souls will be saved. Calvin insisted that the Bible was the sole source of God's law and the only guide for a just life. He also proclaimed that the only acceptable form of government was one in which all laws were based on the Bible. When he returned to Geneva, Calvin instituted a strict Protestant theocracy.

CHARLEMAGNE (742?–814)   Eldest son of Pepin the Short and grandson of Charles Martel, Charlemagne was heir to the throne of the Franks. Upon becoming king, Charlemagne annexed the lands ruled by his brother and continued to conquer territory for the Franks. He warred with the Saxons, massacred untold thousands, and took over their lands. He was crowned Holy Roman Emperor by the pope in 800. Thereafter, all his successful conquests ended with the forced conversion of conquered people to Christianity. Though he was reportedly more interested in hunting than governing, Charlemagne is credited with instituting effective administrative institutions to control his vast realm. The legends of his exploits and heroism are immortalized in the French classic *Chanson de Roland*.

Key Players A to Z

CONSTANTINE I (288?–337) He was the first Roman emperor to embrace Christianity as the official religion of the empire. After victory in a battle against his rival Licinus, Constantine ruled the western part of the Roman Empire until Licinus's death, after which Constantine was sole ruler. His rule was generally peaceful. In 325, he convened the Council of Nicea where the precepts of Christianity (even as known today), as well as the books of the New Testament, were determined. Constantine was baptized on his deathbed.

DALAI LAMA *(the 14th, Hlamo Döndrup)* **(1934–)** Found as a two-year-old boy to be the incarnation of the 13th Dalai Lama, the 14th Dalai Lama was taken from his home to Lhasa and trained to be the religious and political leader of Tibet. He was forced to assume his leadership role at 16 because of Communist Chinese attacks on Tibet. After attempts at negotiations failed to win Tibet even cultural sovereignty and fearing for his life, in 1959 the Dalai Lama fled Tibet and settled in northern India. From there, he has worked tirelessly to gain support for Tibetan cultural independence and to preserve Tibetan culture outside his native land, though the Chinese leadership has consistently rebuffed his overtures for talks. In 1989, he was awarded the Nobel Peace Prize for his efforts to negotiate peace between China and Tibet.

JAMES DOBSON (1936–) Trained as a pediatric psychologist, Dobson was a college professor and the author of several best-selling books, including the guide for parents *Dare to Discipline* (1970), in which he condemns excessive permissiveness in the family for social ills. As founder of the Family Research Council and a popular conservative Christian talk show host, Dobson has become a force for the Christian Right and a major player in Christian Republican politics; he was considered an insider and power broker in President George W. Bush's administration. Dobson's "pro-family" agenda includes outspoken condemnation of homosexuality and gay rights, especially same-sex marriage. After comparing stem cell research to Nazi medical experiments, Dobson resigned as head of Focus on the Family in 2009. The rumor that he condemned Spongebob Squarepants as a homosexual is not true.

DR. FADL *(Sayyid Imam al-Sharif)* **(1950–)** The man who took the name Dr. Fadl was born in Egypt where he studied medicine and became a skilled surgeon. At medical school, Fadl met Ayman al-Zawahiri, and together they discussed jihad against what they viewed as the corrupt Egyptian government. Fadl was already active in an extremist group. Later, Fadl became the chief adviser, or imam, to al-Qaeda. His extensive writings justified terrorism in the name of fundamentalist Islam. However, after being jailed for his extremist connections, Fadl had a change of heart. From jail he wrote *Rationalizing Jihad*, a vehement argument against terrorism and the killing of innocent civilians in the name of God. He also vilified al-Zawahiri as second rate and denounced both him and al-Qaeda.

JERRY FALWELL (1933–2007)   Falwell was the minister of the 24,000-member Thomas Road Baptist Church in his hometown of Lynchburg, Virginia. His radio show, the *Old Time Gospel Hour*, was so popular it was also broadcast on television. In 1971, Falwell founded the Moral Majority, a Religious Right political action organization, which he headed until 1987. At its peak, the group boasted more than 6.5 million members and raised $69 million for Christian Right causes. Also in 1971, Falwell founded Liberty University, where future leaders of the conservative Christian movement were educated and trained. For decades, Falwell was a vocal and recognizable proponent of conservative Christian values, including opposition to homosexuality and abortion. He gained some notoriety when he said the September 11 attacks were God's punishment for liberal U.S. policies. He later apologized for these remarks.

MOHANDAS K. GANDHI (1869–1948)   Born and educated in India, as a young man Gandhi practiced law in South Africa. The racism and oppression he found there impelled Gandhi to actively oppose the apartheid regime, though from the first he renounced violence and embraced ahimsa, or nonviolent protest. Returning to India in 1915, Gandhi became a leading figure in the Indian independence movement against Britain. He gave up Western customs and attire to live the simple life of a village Indian. The British jailed him several times, but his continued resistance earned him enormous moral authority among all sectors of Indian society. The effectiveness of his nonviolent protests, particularly the salt march, made him world famous and a revered figure in India. The Hindu-Muslim violence that followed independence deeply disturbed Gandhi, who vowed to fast unto death until the violence ended, which it did (at least temporarily). Gandhi's vision was one where people of all religions lived in spirit and harmony. His embrace of Muslims and Muslim equality led to his assassination by a Hindu nationalist extremist.

POPE GREGORY VII *(Hildebrand)* **(D. 1085)**   After spending several years as a monk and then as cardinal, Hildebrand became Pope Gregory VII in 1073. Hildebrand was born in Italy, but little is known of his early life. As pope, Gregory fiercely enforced papal supremacy and continually sought temporal power for the church. He also instituted reforms, such as prohibiting the clergy from marrying, condemned simony, and fought lay investiture. He sent legates throughout Europe to enforce his reforms. His strength and influence made him feared among many European monarchs of the time.

His demonstration of power over the humiliated King Henry IV at Canossa symbolized the uncompromising strength of the church. Gregory was later canonized; St. Gregory's feast day is May 25.

GEORG HEGEL (1770–1831) Hegel was born and educated in Germany. He became a university professor in 1805 and by 1812 a popular and respected lecturer in Berlin. Hegel's books of philosophy include the *Phenomenology of Mind* (1807), the *Science of Logic* (1812–16), and the *Philosophy of Right* (1821). Hegel's philosophy expounds an absolute idealism found in a world-soul that is realized through a dialectical logic. That is, every thesis has an opposite thesis. For example, the concept of *being* leads to the concept of *nonbeing*, but the two are connected via becoming. For Hegel, the absolute world process works through history and humans, who can bring about the ultimate world process through their worldly actions. Hegel's religious philosophy states that religion is a progression, with Christianity as its highest expression because the incarnate Christ united God and humans. Through religion, particularly Protestant Christianity, humanity can progress through history to create the ultimate absolute on Earth.

HENRY II (1133–1189) Henry Plantagenet, heir to the count of Anjou, gained the English throne in 1154, after marrying Eleanor of Aquitaine and gaining her vast lands in France and then invading England and taking the throne. He was a good king who restored peace and order to the realm and strengthened the power of the monarchy. His efforts in this latter pursuit put him in direct conflict with the church, so he named his friend and chancellor, Thomas Becket, as Archbishop of Canterbury. Becket did not give the king the support he had hoped for, and Henry had him assassinated for his disloyalty. Henry's Constitutions of Clarendon proclaimed the rights of the king over those of the church.

HENRY VIII (1491–1547) This powerful Tudor king of England is famous for his six wives, two of whom he had executed. After his first wife, Catharine of Aragon, bore him a daughter, she seemed incapable of producing the desired son. Henry took up with the young and fecund Anne Boleyn, but before he could marry her he had to divorce Catharine. Though Henry had earlier been a champion of the Catholic Church, the pope's repeated refusal to grant Henry's divorce infuriated the king beyond measure. He finally issued an Act of Supremacy, severing England's ties with the Catholic Church and establishing the Church of England, which he headed. The Anglican Church would soon become a bulwark of Protestantism.

THOMAS HOBBES (1588–1679) This English philosopher is one of the world's most famous pessimists. In his greatest work, *Leviathan* (1651),

RELIGION AND THE STATE

Hobbes presents his view of human life as "nasty, brutish, and short." He believed that fear of death and competition from others is the main motive behind people's willing submission to the state and to religion (the social contract), which they hope, vainly, will protect them, or at least relieve their perpetual anxiety. Hobbes championed the absolute power of the state over both people and the church. Hobbes's ideas continue to influence philosophers, historians, and statesmen. By changing the discussion of religion from theology to psychology (religion as a construct of the human mind), Hobbes opened the door to the eventual separation of church and state.

HUSAYN IBN ALI (626–680)   The son of Ali, the fourth Rightly Guided Caliph, Ali did not rise to prominence until Muawiya named his son Yazid to be his successor as caliph. Encouraged by Iraqi troops who promised to support him in overthrowing Muawiya, Husayn faced the caliph at the Battle of Karbala. Because the Iraqi troops never materialized, Husayn's small force was defeated. Approaching Muawiya's lines to negotiate a settlement, Husayn was killed. His body was mutilated, and his severed head was carried to Damascus and publicly displayed. Husayn's death solidified the Shiite movement. The anniversary of Husayn's martyrdom is a holy day of mourning still observed by Shia.

THOMAS JEFFERSON (1743–1826)   The third U.S. president, Jefferson was a Virginia landowner and intellectual who had enormous influence on the writing of the Constitution. Jefferson was a deist who argued tirelessly and with great eloquence for the separation of church and state; he coined the phrase "the wall of separation" to describe this. He championed this separation, as well as complete religious freedom and tolerance, for his native Virginia as well as for the nation.

IMMANUEL KANT (1724–1804)   A German philosopher, Kant is hailed as one of the West's greatest minds. Kant argued that the existence of God cannot be either confirmed or denied by man, though belief in God was, for him, essential to a moral life and society. Kant viewed humans as having an innate "radical evil" and consequent sense of guilt and shame that can only be overcome by one's will to pursue the highest good, which is attainable only through God and religion.

AYATOLLAH RUHOLLAH KHOMEINI (1900–1989)   An Iranian Shiite religious leader, Khomeini ruled Iran after its Islamic revolution, from 1979 until his death in 1989. Early on, he taught at a theological school in Qom, where he railed against the corruption of the shah's rule and was arrested for his extremist ideas. He fled to Turkey and Iraq before moving to Paris in 1978. His writing from exile inspired Iranians to overthrow the shah. After the shah was deposed by a popular uprising, Khomeini returned in triumph to Iran and declared the nation an Islamic republic. He exercised ultimate authority in Iran, instituting sharia law. His rule is noted for the taking of U.S. hostages (1979–1981) and for war with Iraq.

OSAMA BIN LADEN (1957?–) One of more than 50 children born to one of the wives of his enormously wealthy father, bin Laden was trained as a civil engineer in his native Saudi Arabia. He graduated from university in 1979, but when the Soviets invaded Afghanistan a year later, he moved to Pakistan to help finance the training and transport of Muslim fighters in the Afghan cause. In 1988, bin Laden founded al-Qaeda, an Islamic extremist organization for violent jihad against Western nations that it says oppressed Muslims, contaminated the holy land of Arabia, and/or supported the state of Israel. He violently opposed the Saudi monarchy, viewing it as infidel puppets of the Americans. After being linked to the attempted assassination of Egyptian president Hosni Mubarak in 1995, bin Laden settled first in Sudan and later in Afghanistan, where the Islamic fundamentalist Taliban gave him and al-Qaeda refuge and a base of operations. Bin Laden and others in al-Qaeda have claimed responsibility for the September 11, 2001, attacks on the United States, as well as for devastating bombing attacks in other parts of the world. When the U.S. military overthrew the Taliban in 2002, bin Laden and other al-Qaeda leaders took refuge in the mountainous border area between Afghanistan and Pakistan, where they are protected by a sympathetic populace and from where they may still be supporting (and are certainly inspiring) continued terrorist attacks.

JOHN LOCKE (1632–1704) Locke was a British philosopher and is hailed as one of the world's greatest champions of freedom and tolerance. Locke argued against Hobbes's notion of human nature, insisting that natural man is essentially good, reasonable, and tolerant. Thus, all people deserve equal rights to freedom and to "life, health, and liberty." He believed that society produced the evil in men's minds. Locke was the first to describe the system of checks and balances in government, which was adopted by the American founders. Overall, Locke's philosophy was probably the greatest influence on the shaping of the U.S. government. His *Letter Concerning Toleration* is a landmark of religious thought regarding the separation of church and state.

MARTIN LUTHER (1483–1546) This German monk and leader of the Reformation became disgusted by the laxity, corruption, greed, and lasciviousness of the Catholic clergy. His deep anxiety about the salvation of his soul led Luther to list ways that the Catholic Church should be reformed in order to make it a true vehicle for salvation. This list became the famous 95 Theses that Luther nailed to the church door in Wittenberg that instigated the Protestant Reformation. This led to the formation of a plethora of Prot-

RELIGION AND THE STATE

estant sects, many of which Luther found abhorrent. Lutheranism, a form of Protestantism that emphasizes baptism and communion, continues to be a major world religion.

JAMES MADISON (1751–1836) Fourth president of the United States, Madison was an impassioned champion of religious freedom, religious tolerance, and the separation of church and state. His ideas, most eloquently expressed in his *Memorial and Remonstrance*, were incorporated into the Constitution, as well as Virginia's constitution.

MOHAMMAD REZA SHAH PAHLAVI (1919–1980) The shah of Iran from 1941 to 1978, he was put in control of Iran after Western powers overthrew the democratically elected government of Mohammad Mossadeq in 1953. His rule was secular and was marked by his oppression of his people, his rightly feared secret police force (SAVAK), his corruption, and his cozy relationship with Western governments and corporations. His rule was bitterly opposed by religious Muslims, some of whom were tortured, executed, or "disappeared." This despot was removed after the Iranian Islamic revolution in 1979. The shah died in exile in Egypt.

MOHAMMAD MOSSADEQ (1880–1967) The democratically elected prime minister of Iran, Mossadeq led the militant nationalists who, after winning the election, nationalized their nation's oil industry. This seizure by Iranians of Iran's own resources so angered Western leaders and corporations that Western intelligence agencies organized the overthrow of the Mossadeq government in 1953; they then installed the shah. Mossadeq ended his life under house arrest.

MUAWIYA *(Mu'awiya ibn Abi Sufayn)* **(602–680)** A powerful figure in the Umayyad clan of Mecca who in early adulthood was a vehement opponent of the Prophet and Islam. After the defeat of his family and their entry into the *umma*, Muawiya reversed course and became a Companion of the Prophet. He later became caliph, ruling from Damascus. He waged perpetual war against Ali, who many thought the rightful successor to Muhammad. Ali's murder and Muawiya's son's subsequent disgraceful treatment of Ali's son Husayn led the Shia to break away from Sunni Islam. Today, Muawiya is viewed as having been such a despot and divisive figure that he is not only reviled by the Shia, but also no longer regarded as a Rightly Guided Caliph by most Sunni Muslims.

GAMAL ABDUL NASSER (1918–1970) The first president of Egypt after he and the Egyptian army deposed the despotic King Farouk. He nationalized the Suez Canal, leading to a brief war with Britain, and was a major player

Key Players A to Z

in the debacle of the Six-Day War with Israel in 1967. He is best known for the secular reforms he brought to Egyptian government and society. Most Egyptians of his time supported his forward-looking reforms, which did improve the Egyptian economy, but he also inspired a backlash from Islamic fundamentalists in Egypt.

SAYYID QUTB (1906–1966) Educated in both Islamic and Western subjects in his native Egypt, Qutb became a respected Islamic writer and philosopher among Islamic extremists. His writing provides the philosophical and theoretical foundation for Sunni Islamists. Qutb was radicalized by his revulsion at American culture during his sojourn in the United States (1948–50), and he used this experience to formulate his ideas about the need for strict adherence to Islamic law and for violent jihad against secularists. As a member of the Muslim Brotherhood, Qutb was arrested several times after the group attempted to assassinate Egyptian president Gamal Abdul Nasser. After being imprisoned following an assassination attempt, Qutb was executed in 1966. His writings on the obligation to wage violent jihad against infidels and his exaltation of martyrdom in this effort continue to strongly influence Islamic extremists.

RALPH REED (1961–) This political operative has been a powerful force in the Republican Party on behalf of the Religious Right. He has worked as an adviser and organizer on seven Republican presidential campaigns. While executive director of the Christian Coalition in the 1990s, Reed greatly expanded that group's reach and influence in U.S. politics. Newspapers and magazines have named him one of the top political operatives of his generation. He is also an author and columnist, television commentator, and lobbyist for the Christian Right. His carefully crafted image as a pure, moral Christian was tarnished when he was found to be implicated in the extortion racket run by Jack Abramoff.

PAT ROBERTSON (1930–) Born Marion Gordon Robertson in Lexington, Virginia, Pat Robertson became a Baptist minister, religious broadcaster, and prominent spokesperson for the Religious Right in the political arena. In 1960, he founded the Christian Broadcasting Network, where he hosted the popular "700 Club." As a Pentecostal, Robertson lost his bid for the Republican presidential nomination in 1988. He then founded the Christian Coalition and, with Ralph Reed, led it to become one of the most powerful and influential Christian Right organizations in the country. He resigned his presidency of the organization in 2001.

ROUSAS JOHN RUSHDOONY (1916–2001) Rushdoony was the leading proponent of Christian Resurrection theology in the United States. In 1965, he founded the Chalcedon Foundation and edited its monthly newsletter to proselytize his theological ideas. Born in New York City and educated at the University of California at Berkeley, where he majored in English, Rushdoony soon abandoned secular subjects to pursue and disseminate his religious ideas. He is the author of several books on Resurrectionism and, especially, on homeschooling, which he saw as the only way to shield children from the spiritually harmful effects of public education. In his most popular work, *Institutes of Biblical Law*, Rushdoony set out his notions of an American Christian theocracy. Though they have rejected Rushdoony's most extreme ideas, today's Christian dominionists have adopted his theocratic concepts.

VEER (VINAYAK DAMODER) SAVARKAR (1883–1966) A born rebel, Savarkar is known to have organized and led a gang of youths in his native village of Bhagur. His high school mentor, Bal Gangadhar Tilak, introduced Savarkar to Hindu nationalism. As a young man in Pune, Savarkar joined Tilak's Swaraj Party. The young Savarkar was known for his fiery speeches on nationalist themes and was also a well-known anti-British agitator. Yet in 1906, Savarkar went to London to become a barrister (lawyer), though in his spare time he founded the Free India Society, which organized Britain's Hindus against the British Raj. He supported armed rebellion against the British and openly supported the actions of assassins who attempted to kill high-ranking Britons. Savarkar was implicated in one political murder and in 1910 was sent to India to stand trial. He was convicted of illegal weapons trading and sedition and given a 50-year sentence. It was while serving time that he wrote his book *Hindutva*, which delineated his radical ideas for an Indian Hindu state. Savarkar was released from prison in 1924 on the condition that he not engage in politics. He ignored this stipulation and proceeded to organize Hindu nationalist political parties. His Hindu Mahasabha Party supported the creation of Pakistan to rid India of Muslims. Nathuram Ghose, Gandhi's assassin, was associated with both this party and its founder. Savarkar was again arrested for involvement in Gandhi's murder, but he was acquitted due to lack of evidence.

TAQI AL-DIN IBN TAYMIYYA (D. 1328) Ibn Taymiyya was born in Syria during the period of the Mongol conquests and the rise of Sufism. Educated in the rigidly orthodox Hanbali school of Islamic thought, his own mature work extended these orthodox ideas even further. Ibn Taymiyya's writing forcefully promoted adherence to the strictest form of sharia. He denied that reason was applicable to a strict interpretation of Islamic law and that the intellect must be subservient to the Sunna. For him, revelation via the Sunna was the one and only truth, and any form of *bida* made one an infidel. Ibn Taymiyya's work continues to have a profound influence on Islamic extremist thought and action.

A. B. (ATAL BIHARI) VAJPAYEE (1924–) Vajpayee was politically active as a teenager. As a young man, he was jailed briefly by British colonial authorities for his political anti-British activism. In 1957, Vajpayee was elected to the Indian parliament as a member of the Bharatiya Jana Sangh Party, a forerunner of the BJP. In the late 1970s, he served as foreign minister under a Congress Party government, while formally establishing and strengthening the nationalist BJP. Yet in 1992, his was perhaps the strongest voice speaking out against Hindu violence committed against Muslims and mosques. Vajpayee was elected India's prime minister in 1996, but, after failing to form a government (a needed coalition with other parties), his leadership collapsed after only 13 days. In 1998, he was again elected prime minister, this time as head of a strong BJP-led coalition. Many in the BJP were disappointed when he toned down his anti-Muslim rhetoric (and by his lack of anti-Muslim action) during his tenure as prime minister. The international community condemned his government when, in 1998, India tested its first nuclear weapons. However, despite international sanctions Vajpayee's policies improved India's economy. Ethnic violence led to a rejection of the BJP by the electorate, which defeated Vajpayee and his party in 2004.

ROGER WILLIAMS (C. 1603–1683) Williams was the founder of the state of Rhode Island. He was an American colonial clergyman who was banished from the Massachusetts Bay Colony by the Puritans for his unorthodox views and his criticism of their way of life and their treatment of native people. In his newfound state, Williams ensured religious tolerance, welcoming dissenters to settle there. He became a spokesman for freedom of religion, the separation of church and state, and respect for Native Americans.

9
Organizations and Agencies

The following list contains the name, contact information, and focus of a wide variety of groups that are concerned with religion as it applies to public life, culture, and politics. A few Web sites provide data or links to primary source materials. Most of the Web sites, however, present a point of view, provide news, or publish scholarly or informed studies about their topic of interest. Most agency and organization Web sites provide links that might be useful in finding additional information.

Alliance Defense Fund
URL: http://www.alliancedefensefund.org
15100 North 90 Street
Scottsdale, AZ 85260
Phone: 1-800-TELL-ADF
E-mail: ffs@telladf.org

The ADF was founded in 1993 by 30 of the most influential Christian fundamentalist leaders in the United States, including James Dobson. The ADF was formed to pool money to fund the Religious Right's court actions against legislation it perceived as too un-Christian. The group's Web site proclaims that its mission is to "reclaim the legal system for Jesus Christ." The ADF supports lawsuits brought by nonmembers, but it also files its own lawsuits to block legislation it does not support. Its Web site contains information on its litigation and in support of its values. Though it presents its legal function as a serious service to evangelicals, it has also promoted frivolous lawsuits, such as the "war on Christmas," which was intended to force governments and public agencies to stop substituting "holiday" or "season's greetings" for the more religious term. The ADF also has a facility for training lawyers in litigation in the religious arena.

Organizations and Agencies

American Buddhist Congress
URL: http://www.americanbuddhistcongress.org
3835 R E. Thousand Oaks Boulevard
Suite 450
Westlake Village, CA 91362
Phone: 1-877-7BUDDHA
E-mail: BuddhistCongress@adelphia.net

The American Buddhist Congress is an umbrella group of other U.S.-based Buddhist organizations. Its purpose is to promote the development and understanding of Buddhism in the United States, as well as to be an online meeting place and resource center for American Buddhists and others interested in Buddhism. The Web site contains information about Buddhism, the dharma, and similar resources. It also provides links to other resources and listings of Buddhist events in the United States.

American Center for Law and Justice
URL: http://www.aclj.org
PO Box 90555
Washington, DC 20090-0555
Phone: 800-296-4529
E-mail: online form

This organization's acronym—ACLJ—was intended to mimic that of the ACLU, though its focus is diametrically opposed to that organization's support of civil liberties. The main focus of the ACLJ is to mount legal challenges to Supreme Court and lower court rulings that uphold the separation of church and state, though it also focuses on other mainstream Religious Right issues, such as gay rights and abortion. The group's Web site provides information on the status of the many court cases it is monitoring and about its legal efforts in support of its viewpoint.

American Civil Liberties Union
URL: http://www.aclu.org
1400 20th Street NW
Suite 119
Washington, DC 20005
Phone: 202-457-0800

The American Civil Liberties Union (ACLU) is the nation's premier defender of civil and constitutional rights, including religious freedom and the separation of church and state as stated in the establishment clause of the Constitution. The ACLU helps individuals and groups litigate cases where limitations or abuses of civil liberties are alleged to have occurred. The organization supports the entire panoply of civil liberties as stated or implied in the Constitution, from criminal justice and the death penalty to the rights of the disabled, immigrants, and prisoners. It fights for reproductive rights, privacy rights, voting rights, and the right to religious freedom, among many others. The organization's Web site contains explanations and discussions of each of the liberties it defends. It also contains news and information about former and current court cases it is involved in, including cases before the Supreme Court. The group's Web site offers all of the above, as well as legislative updates on laws that touch upon civil liberties. From the Web site, anyone can access their state ACLU Web site and find information about how to contact their local office.

American Family Association
URL: http://afa.net
PO Box 2440
Tupelo, MS 38803
Phone: 662-844-5036

The AFA was founded by Donald Wildmon, a Methodist minister, in 1977. The organization's original name was the National Federation for Decency, whose stated goal was to prohibit antifamily programs on television and in other media. The group engages in boycotts of products that are advertised on objectionable programs. The organization has expanded to operate 176 radio stations in 34 states, which are used to promote its Religious Right agenda. A main focus of the organization is to undermine groups, such as the ACLU, that it sees as promoting the separation of church and state. The group's Web site contains articles with its point of view on a variety of topics, particularly the re-Christianization of the United States.

American Humanist Association
URL: http://www.americanhumanist.org
1777 T Street NW
Washington, DC 20009-7125
Phone: 202-238-9088
E-mail: online form

The American Humanist Association is dedicated to the separation of church and state. Its outlook and membership are primarily agnostic or atheistic. The group strongly counters the argument made by believers that people need God and religion in order to be good and act morally. The organization's logo is

Organizations and Agencies

"Be good for goodness's sake." The AHA publishes *Humanist* magazine, which contains numerous articles, essays, and other information in support of its point of view. The organization's Web site offers some articles from its magazine, as well as other essays and reports, news, a litigation watch, and information about humanist activities around the country and the world.

American Muslim Alliance
URL: http://wwwamaweb.org
39675 Cedar Boulevard
Suite 220E
Newark, CA 94560
Phone: 510-252-9858
E-mail: civilrightsforall@sbcglobal.net

The American Muslim Alliance is an organization that stresses the involvement of Muslim Americans in the political and social life of the United States. Its Web site offers information on political elections and candidates and the issues specifically relevant to the Muslim-American community. The organization offers news, an e-mail newsletter, community networking, and information about other Muslim-American organizations, as well as events, meetings, and seminars around the country of interest to Muslim-Americans.

Americans United for Separation of Church and State
URL: http://www.au.org/PageServer
518 C Street NE
Washington, DC 20002
Phone: 702-466-3234
E-mail: americansunited@au.org

As its name suggests, this organization promotes the absolute separation of church and state. It publishes the *Church and State* journal, many of whose articles can be accessed via the Web site, which contains historical, scholarly, and opinion articles supporting the separation of religion and politics. The Web site contains up-to-date news on attacks on the separation of church and state as well as victories in maintaining this separation. The group keeps a close eye on the Religious Right and reports news from that arena as well. The many articles it offers free on its Web site make this organization a good source of information from this point of view.

Center for Law and Religious Freedom: Christian Legal Society
URL: http://www.clsnet.org
8001 Braddock Road

Suite 300
Springfield, VA 22151
Phone: 703-642-1070
E-mail: clshq@clsnet.org

Founded in 1975, the center is a respected advocate for religious freedom in the United States, litigating cases that it deems a threat to the establishment clause of the First Amendment. It challenges laws that might limit religious freedom, though its conservative Christian bent also involves it in litigation promoting faith-based government initiatives, government support for religion-based education, and pro-life legislation.

Center for Progressive Christianity
URL: http://www.tcpc.org
4916 Pt. Fosdick Drive NW
148
Gig Harbor, WA 98335
Phone: 253-303-0022
E-mail: online form

The Center for Progressive Christianity's mission is to reach out to disenchanted evangelical Christians and others who have become alienated from conservative Christianity. The center embraces and promotes a faith community but educates and promulgates a Christianity that is founded on more socially and politically progressive ideas. The group's Web site has links to affiliate organizations around the country. It also offers extensive news, articles, analysis, links, and an events calendar.

Christian Century
URL: http://www.christiancentury.org
104 South Michigan Avenue
Suite 700
Chicago, IL 60603
Phone: 312-263-7520
E-mail: main@christiancentury.org

This organization primarily represents African-American conservative Christians. It works to combat inner-city poverty and advocates strong family values. It supports the closer integration of church and state and the concept of America as a Christian nation. The group's Web site offers articles about the Bible and Christian living, sermons, news, and other pertinent information, as well as videos, music, books, and other media about Christianity. The organization publishes the periodical *Christian Century,* which promotes its values and ideas.

Organizations and Agencies

Christian Coalition of America
URL: http://www.cc.org
PO Box 37030
Washington, DC 20013-7030
E-mail: online form

This group describes itself as a community for pro-family activism. It is highly political and actively seeks to influence legislation to bring it into line with the Bible and evangelical Christian beliefs. This group believes that the United States should be reformed to be the Christian nation the founders intended. In 2008, the Web site and the group offered extensive information and background to guide voters to support candidates who share its views. At its Web site, one can find numerous articles that support the organization's position, as well as information on how to combat more liberal actions currently in the news. There is also a blog where members can network and share their views and activism on various topics of interest to the Christian Right. The Reverend Pat Robertson, a founder of the group, withdrew from it in 2001 to found the Christian Broadcasting Network (CBN), one of the most powerful right-wing political voices in America today.

Congress of Secular Jewish Organizations
URL: http://www.csjo.org
320 Claymore Boulevard
Cleveland, OH 44143
Phone: 866-874-8608
E-mail: online form

The Congress of Secular Jewish Organizations is an umbrella group of independent Jewish organizations that promote the secular expression of Jewish heritage, with an emphasis on the culture and ethics found in Judaism. The organization promotes social justice and the separation of church and state, as well as all other tenets of humanism. It states as one of its main goals creating and promulgating a secular Jewish identity that is relevant to contemporary life and is committed to social justice, peace, and community. The organization supports the belief that humanism can serve to unite the Jewish people and help the Jewish community maintain its identity into the future. The group supports schools, educational programs for youths and adults in Jewish heritage, religion, and culture, including the revitalization of Yiddish. The group boasts a worldwide membership. The organization's Web site contains information about its programs, principles, and publications, as well as events, social actions, essays, and a newsletter of interest to its members and readers. Links to similar groups and a member lending library round out the Web site.

RELIGION AND THE STATE

Council for America's First Freedom
URL: http://www.firstfreedom.org
1321 East Main Street
Richmond, VA 23219-3629
Phone: 804-643-1786
E-mail: caff@firstfreedom.org

The Council for America's First Freedom, also called the First Freedom Center, seeks to educate the public to respect and tolerate freedom of religion in the United States and around the world. It promotes its core human values of freedom of thought, conscience, and belief. The organization is nondenominational and works to engender tolerance and the right to religious freedom for all people, but especially among Americans whose First Amendment constitutional rights guarantee a government free from religious influence. The organization's Web site provides information on the history of the establishment clause and the founder's concept of religious freedom, a question and answer section, and other information in support of freedom of religion and belief.

Council on American-Islamic Relations
URL: http://www.cair.com/Home.aspx
453 New Jersey Avenue SE
Washington, DC 20003
Phone: 202-488-8787
E-mail: info@cair.com

CAIR seeks to foster a better understanding and relationship between the U.S. Islamic community and other American religious and social groups, as well as the general public. Political action that fosters religious freedom and tolerance are one of its main focuses. The organization's Web site offers background information for non-Muslims about Islam, as well as discussions of civil rights, religion's role in government, and the importance of involvement in the political sphere. News and information on upcoming events, as well as topical articles, can also be found on the Web site.

Eagle Forum
URL: http://eagleforum.org
PO Box 618
Alton, IL 62002
Phone: 618-466-5415
E-mail: eagle@eagleforum.org

The Eagle Forum describes itself as the "leading pro-family movement" in the United States. Formed by Phyllis Schlafly in 1972, the organization supports

Organizations and Agencies

conservative family values, such as keeping women out of the workforce, homeschooling, and undermining public education, and is against abortion rights. It and its membership are active politically in promoting their agenda via government programs and laws. The organization's Web site provides a newsletter, articles, news, and other features related to its issues. It also offers a great deal of information about government and elections and about the need for political action to achieve its goals. The Web site also covers the courts and cases related to its interests. Visitors to the site can contact their congressional and state representatives and find out their representatives' "score" based on how closely they support the organization's conservative goals.

Family Research Council
URL: http://www.frc.org
801 G Street NW
Washington, DC 20001
Phone: 800-225-4008
E-mail: online form

The Family Research Council is an organization representing conservative Christians. The group was founded by James Dobson in 1983 and is now run by Tony Perkins, an antiabortion activist. The organization lobbies the government to get more Christian-oriented laws enacted or to prevent the passage of laws deemed too liberal for their views. It organizes "Justice Sundays," in which its members demonstrate in front of courthouses where "culture war" issues are being adjudicated. The organization Web site provides information on politics and elections, on member activism, and on books and periodicals and often has available for free viewing sermons or talks by leading Christian conservatives. There is also a blog where registered visitors can express their opinion and network with other members.

Focus on the Family
URL: http://www.family.org
Colorado Springs, CO 80995
Phone: 1-800-232-6459
E-mail: online form

This highly conservative organization was founded and is run by Dr. James C. Dobson, one of the formost spokesmen for the Religious Right in America. His organization boasts at least 5 million members in the United States. Through its publications, radio broadcasts, and Web site, the group promotes a highly conservative political stance with a laserlike focus on Christian values. It works toward transforming the United States into a Christian, Bible-based nation, and vehemently opposes choice, evolution, and gay rights. There are at least 32 state affiliates that monitor local and state legislation, lobby for a more Christian orientation, and pressure lawmakers to defeat what is deemed to be un-Christian legislation. In 2004, Dobson created Focus on the Family Action as the organization's more potent political arm, intended to push its agenda at the federal and state levels.

Free Muslims Coalition
URL: http://www.freemuslims.org
1050 17th Street NW
Suite 1000
Washington, DC 20036
Phone: 202-776-7190
E-mail: info@freemuslims.org

The Free Muslims Coalition is an organization that describes itself as "Muslims against terrorism and extremism." The group has attracted a large following of moderate Muslims in the United States, and it has chapters in several states around the country. The organization encourages political activism to promote social justice and religious freedom in opposition to the violent tactics of Muslim extremists. It works toward educating Muslims, and particularly Muslim youth in the West, to disabuse them of the notion that violence and terrorism are legitimate tools of Islam. The group's Web site offers valuable discussions of modern Islam, why Islam does not support terrorism, Islam's place in the modern world, and other vital and timely topics.

Free Tibet
URL: http://www.freetibet.org
28 Charles Street
London N1 6HT
United Kingdom
Phone: 044-020-7324-4605
E-mail: mail@freetibet.org

Free Tibet is an international organization working for religious freedom and autonomy for the people of Tibet. It supports activism of all kinds, including petitions and demonstrations, in support of autonomy for the Tibetan people. The organization's Web site offers information on its many campaigns and programs, articles about Tibet in the news and the media, news from or about Tibet, and a worldwide blog about the situation in Tibet. The group's main focus is political action and pressure on other nations to get China to loosen its control over the Tibetan people.

Organizations and Agencies

Government Is Not God
URL: http://www.govtnotgod.org
PO Box 77237
Washington, DC 20013
Phone: 202-554-2358
E-mail: online form

As its name suggests, this organization's main focus is to ensure that the U.S. government upholds a Christian, Bible-based view. Its members also fervently believe in the total separation of church and state. The Web site indicates the intense political focus of this organization. On it, one can find news, though only about the dangerous secularization of the nation, and some articles that promote its viewpoint. The organization also functions as a PAC (political action committee), or lobbying group, for the Christian Right.

Hindu American Foundation
URL: http://www.hinduamericanfoundation.org
E-mail: online form

The Hindu American Foundation is an advocacy group that provides a progressive voice for Hindu Americans. It is involved in educating the public about Hinduism and both domestic and global issues surrounding Hinduism. It also acts to fight discrimination against Hindus and for human rights and tolerance. The Web site provides a brochure that explains the organization's purposes and goals.

Hudson Institute's Center for Religious Freedom
URL: http://crf.hudson.org
1015 15th Street NW
Sixth Floor
Washington, DC 20005
Phone: 202-974-2400
E-mail: info@hudson.org

The Hudson Institute's Center for Religious Freedom seeks to promote freedom of religion and the separation of church and state in the United States. The center hosts events and seminars to foster in-depth and wide-ranging discussion of issues surrounding religious freedom. It also publishes books, reports, white papers, and other information on the issue. The organization's Web site contains news and commentary on current issues relating to freedom of religion. It also provides access to feature articles and essays by prominent thinkers in this field. Most important, the Web site provides access to expert testimony on religious freedom and the establishment clause given before Congress and other official bodies.

Institute for Humanist Studies
URL: http://www.humaniststudies.org
48 Howard Street
Albany, NY 12207
Phone: 518-432-7820
E-mail: online form

The Institute for Humanist Studies promotes the separation of church and state and a nonreligious approach to governance and social and political policy. As its name implies, it is a humanist organization focused on human rights, compassion for human suffering, and the role of reason as the prime mover of government and policy. The organization's Web site defines humanism as "a philosophy of life inspired by humanity and guided by reason . . . [that] embraces humanist values for fuller, more joyful lives without supernatural belief in gods, heaven, or hell." The atheistic, perhaps agnostic, IHS promotes ethics that are based on reason and secularism. The Web site offers background on the history of humanism, its role in governance, the importance of the separation of religion from politics, and other related issues. Secular humanism, as espoused by this organization, is the primary target of fundamentalists in the United States.

International Association for Religious Freedom
URL: http://www.iarf.net
Essex Hall
1-6 Essex Street
London WC2R 3H4
United Kingdom
E-mail: hq@iarf.net

The London-based International Association for Religious Freedom is a worldwide organization whose aim is to work for religious freedom in every nation in the world. The organization encourages interfaith dialogue and holds periodic seminars and conferences to promote religious tolerance among the followers of the world's religions. The group has 90 affiliates in more than 25 countries, representing a wide range of faiths, from Islam and Christianity to Sikhism and Shinto. The organization's Web site has links to descriptions of its projects, its congresses, and available publications.

Organizations and Agencies

International Campaign for Tibet
URL: http://www.savetibet.org
1825 Jefferson Place NW
Washington, DC 20036
Phone: 202-785-1515
E-mail: info@savetibet.org

The International Campaign for Tibet works to achieve religious freedom, if not total independence, for Tibet. The group provides speakers, gives testimony before Congress, and provides material support for Tibet, Tibetans in exile, and other groups sharing its mission. The organization's Web site provides extensive background on the issue of religious freedom and autonomy in Tibet. It also offers information about the Dalai Lama, Tibetan culture and environment, and background and news about human rights in Tibet, as well as resources for travel to Tibet. The Web site also offers articles, papers, reports, and testimony in support of Tibetan autonomy and religious freedom.

International Coalition for Religious Freedom
URL: http://www.religiousfreedom.com
7777 Leesburg Pike
Suite 404-N
Falls Church, VA 22043
Phone: 703-790-1500
E-mail: icrf@aol.com

The International Coalition for Religious Freedom seeks to promote this value in the United States and around the world. The organization monitors religious freedom in all countries and is active in promoting freedom of religion everywhere it is being curtailed. The organization's Web site contains a wealth of information on religious freedom, from articles and papers from its own and other conferences, to news articles, its Religious Freedom World Report, and an encyclopedia of features articles and information on all topics touching on religious freedom. The organization also publishes a newsletter for members and Web site visitors.

International Institute for Secular Humanistic Judaism
URL: http://www.iishj.org
28611 West Twelve Mile Road
Farmington Hills, NJ 48334
Phone: 248-476-9532
E-mail: info@iishj.org

RELIGION AND THE STATE

The IISHJ is a global organization of avowed Jews who also espouse humanistic principles, such as the separation of church and state and the universal right to religious freedom. The organization describes itself as an academic and intellectual center for a worldwide movement that appeals to cultural, secular, and humanistic Jews. The institute offers training for spokespeople, educators, leaders, and rabbis who wish to spread the teachings of Jewish humanism. The group's Web site offers news, articles, essays, and papers from its seminars and colloquia. A visitor to the Web site may also view or buy publications, sign up for educational tours, and read about the group's many programs and the resources it has available to the public and its membership.

International Institute of Islamic Thought
URL: http://www.iiit.org
500 Grove Street
Suite 200
Herndon, VA 20170
Phone: 703-471-1131
E-mail: iiit@iiit.org

The IIIT is an organization whose members include many of the most respected thinkers, writers, policy analysts, and intellectuals in the Muslim world, particularly those living in the West. The organization works toward reconciling the modern world with Islamic teaching and seeks to reform Islamic thought in the modern context. The organization and its Web site provide a forum for exploring the meaning of Islam in the modern world and the role of Islam in the pursuit of social justice and peace and functions as a counterweight to more extreme fundamentalist voices in the Islamic community. The group's Web site offers news about the Islamic community, a listing of events and conferences, and links to publications and resources of interest to the Islamic community and to its membership.

Islamic Circle of North America
URL: http://www.icna.com
166-26 89th Avenue
Jamaica, NY 11432
Phone: 718-658-1199

The Islamic Circle of North America describes itself as the largest grassroots Muslim organization in the United States, with chapters in several states. The ICNA offers social and religious assistance, via its organization and local chapters, to Muslims throughout the country. Its volunteers help run its outreach program, which includes brochures about its services, Islamic information,

Organizations and Agencies

mosque visits, and discussion forums. The group's Web site offers news of interest to the American Muslim community, articles, forums, and slideshows about its work, and information about the many outreach and online programs it offers. The organization encourages Muslim involvement in the political process and promotes religious freedom in the United States.

Islamic Society of Britain
URL: http://isb.org.uk
PO Box 42598
London E1 1WN
United Kingdom
Phone: 020-7247-8088
E-mail: info@isb.org.uk

The Islamic Society of Britain was founded to promote mutual assistance among British Muslims and to enhance understanding of Islam in Britain by encouraging the involvement of British Muslims in British society. The Web site describes the society's many social programs and activities conducted by its many branches throughout the United Kingdom. The site also provides links to additional information and resources.

Islamic Society of North America
URL: http://www.isna.net
PO Box 38
Plainfield, IN 46168
Phone: 317-839-8157
E-mail: online form

The ISNA is dedicated to educating the public, both Muslim and non-Muslim, about the Islamic religion and to promoting the legacy and values of Islam. The organization is deeply involved in interfaith efforts to promote understanding and tolerance of all religions. It also supports religious freedom and political action to maintain the separation of church and state, while respecting all religions equally. The organization's Web site offers news of recent events, recent and upcoming conferences, a blog for public interaction, and information on its youth program. A subscriber may also sign up to receive the organization's newsletter.

Liberty Council
URL: http://wwwlc.org
PO Box 540774
Orlando, FL 32854
Phone: 800-671-1776

RELIGION AND THE STATE

The Liberty Council was founded by the evangelical preacher Jerry Falwell and is just one of his Liberty institutions. The council encourages political activism in support of Christian Right doctrine and laws. The council's Web site has petitions in support of the Christian Right's positions on social and political issues that visitors to the site can sign online for forwarding to the appropriate governmental body. The Web site also offers news and information on perceived attacks on its positions and about its policy successes. From the Web site, one can use links to access other Falwell organizations, including the radio and television media he founded, prayer blogs and Web sites, the Liberty Center for Law and Policy, and Liberty University, including the university's law school.

Minaret of Freedom Institute
URL: http://www.minaret.org
4323 Rosedale Avenue
Bethesda, MD 20814
Phone: 301-907-0947
E-mail: mfi@minaret.org

The Minaret of Freedom sees its mission as countering stereotypes of Muslims in the West, and of demonstrating the harmony of Islam and the doctrines of democracy and freedom of religion. It seeks to show Muslim Americans, in particular, that one can live a devout Muslim life in accord with Islamic teachings while at the same time pursuing a fulfilling secular life in the United States. The group also focuses on the policy implications of sharia law in terms of its political and economic consequences for the Muslim community. The organization's Web site provides background on Islam and Islamic teachings, on Western education and Islam, on the role of women in Islam and in the West, on the importance of civil liberties for Muslims, and its repudiation of fundamentalist Islamic terrorism. The Web site also offers extensive news and analysis of events and laws pertinent to the Islamic community in the West. These include news and media items, essays, articles, letters, interviews, etc. The site also provides links to other Islamic organizations, including a launch pad to hundreds of Web sites addressing Islam and religious liberty.

Muslim Public Affairs Council
URL: http://www.mpac.org
110 Maryland Avenue NE
Washington, DC 20002
Phone: 202-547-7701
E-mail: mpac-contact@mpac.org

Organizations and Agencies

The Muslim Public Affairs Council seeks to enhance the voice of American Muslims in their communities and in government. The council promotes political activism, voting rights, and other civil rights for Muslims throughout America. The organization is also deeply engaged in promoting understanding of Islam and in helping Muslim Americans maintain their religious identity while being active participants in American life and democracy. The organization's Web site offers news, updates on pertinent legislation, and information about Islam via its publications. It also provides a calendar of events of interest to American Muslims and information on its many social and political programs.

Neturei Karta: Jews United Against Zionism
URL: www.nkusa.org
PO Box 1316
Monsey, NY 10952
E-mail: online form

Neturiei Karta is an organization of Orthodox Jews who oppose the establishment and existence of the state of Israel. The organization represents highly religious Jews in both the United States and Israel. The group was founded in Jerusalem in 1938 to fight Zionism. According to the organization's Web site, Jews in Israel "sold out to the Golden Calf," in direct violation of the Torah's teachings. Supporters of Neturei Karta believe that Israel is a heretical state because, as they see it, Judaism is violated when Jews use it to establish and maintain a secular state. The group's belief is therefore one of absolute separation of religion (Judaism) from all things political or secular; that anything secular necessarily pollutes the religion. The organization's Web site provides extensive background on the group's history and anti-Zionism. It also offers articles and essays on this subject that are available on the Web site in eight languages.

New Identity-Interfaith Alliance
URL: http://wwwtialliance.org
1212 New York Avenue NW
Seventh Floor
Washington, DC 20005
Phone: 202-238-3300
E-mail: info@interfaithalliance.org

New Identity-Interfaith Alliance is committed to acting as a counterbalance to the forces of the Religious Right in America. The organization works to protect faith and religion while ensuring the separation of church and state. It is especially involved in supporting religious faith at the same time that it seeks to ensure the integrity of U.S. democracy. The group's Web site contains reports and news about its work and the seminars it holds.

People for the American Way
URL: http://pfaw.org
2000 M Street NW
Suite 400
Washington, DC 20036
Phone: 202-467-4999
E-mail: online form

People for the American Way is dedicating to working for the equality and civil liberties of all Americans. It works for freedom of speech and freedom of religion, as well as the equal right of all to seek justice in a court of law. The organization helps build community support for equality, tolerance, and understanding in our multicultural nation. It also promotes fair and free elections and voting, progressive political policies, and accountability from government. The group's Web site describes its mission and projects, including its leadership program. Its blog allows users to become part of this liberal network and exchange ideas with others.

Prince Alwaleed Bin-Talal Center for Muslim-Christian Understanding
URL: http://cmcu.georgetown.edu/
Georgetown University
ICC 260
3700 O Street NW
Washington, DC 20057
Phone: 202-687-8375

The Prince Alwaleed Bin-Talal Center for Muslim-Christian Understanding seeks to enhance understanding and tolerance between the two major religions and to reconcile the teachings of Islam with modern Western thought. Featured articles on the organization's Web site address Western stereotypes of Muslims, the "clash of civilizations," and the compatibility of Islamic life and Western society. The role of Islam in politics and human rights is another major concern of the organization. The group's Web site offers news, a listing of academic and other events pertinent to its focus, and feature articles on its main research topics.

Roundtable on Religion and Social Welfare Policy
URL: http://www.religionandsocialpolicy.org/

Organizations and Agencies

411 State Street
Albany, NY 12203
Phone: 518-443-5014
E-mail: rndtbl@rockinst.org

The roundtable's mission is to promote faith-based government action and government support for faith-based community and social organizations. This is not an extreme Christian fundamentalist organization, as it is part of the Rockefeller Institute of Government at SUNY Albany. However, its work analyzes the effects of faith-based initiatives and promotes a positive role for religion and faith-based initiatives in government. The organization's Web site provides current news on such initiatives and government projects, as well as research in the field. It also offers articles and publications that provide background and facts on faith-based initiatives in the United States.

Rutherford Institute
URL: http://www.rutherford.org
PO Box 7482
Charlottesville, VA 22906-7482
Phone: 434-978-3888
E-mail: online form

The Rutherford Institute was founded in 1982 by John W. Whitehead, a noted constitutional lawyer and author. The institute's mission is to promote civil liberties, especially religious freedom via the establishment clause of the First Amendment. The organization also works to promote human rights nationally and globally. The institute's lawyers provide legal services to groups and individuals whose religious and civil liberties have been abused or curtailed. The group also has an extensive educational program about religious and civil freedoms in the United States. The institute's Web site offers background and information on a wide variety of civil liberties topics, including religion, separation of church and state, parents' rights, and the death penalty, among others.

Secular Philosophy
URL: http://secularphilosophy.com
E-mail: online form

Secular Philosophy is an atheist organization that promotes the total elimination of religion's influence on the state and on the making of public policy. The organization's Web site offers articles about its nonreligious philosophy and atheism written by some of the best-known secular humanists in the world. A subscriber may receive the group's newsletter and participate in the online blog.

Sojourners: Christians for Justice and Peace
URL: http://www.sojo.net/blog/godspolitics
3333 14th Street NW
Suite 200
Washington, DC 20010
Phone: 202-328-8842 or 800-714-7474
E-mail: sojourner@sojo.net

Sojourners is the magazine, Web site, and blog for Jim Wallis, a Christian conservative who has come to espouse more liberal views than most in this community. Neither Wallis nor any of the featured people or links subscribe to the extreme view that America is a Christian country and that the Bible should inform its laws. In fact, Wallis and the many Christians who believe as he does have embraced Jesus' teachings about caring for the poor, as well as caring for the Earth. Sojourners is therefore unique in that it provides a liberal Christian perspective on social justice, poverty reduction, and environmentalism. The group and its Web site feature articles, links, and news about their involvement in the political arena.

Thomas More Institute
URL: http://www.thomasmoreinstitute.org.uk
186 Netherhall Gardens
London NW3 5 TH
United Kingdom
E-mail: info@thomasmoreinstitute.org.uk

The Thomas More Institute is named after the English lawyer, scholar, author, and statesman. He gave his life to uphold the teachings of the church over the will of the king. The goal of the institute is to serve as a forum for civil discourse on public policy and social issues, particularly those that relate to religious freedom, rights of privacy, and the responsibilities of public officials. The organization's Web site offers background information on ethics in public policy, human rights, the role of religion in politics, and other pertinent issues. It also provides articles and academic studies and opinion on its primary topics of interest, as well as links to other Web sites that address similar issues. The institute organizes yearly seminars, and the speeches of main presenters are also found on the Web site.

Organizations and Agencies

Traditional Values Coalition
URL: http://traditionalvalues.org
139 C Street SE
Washington, DC 20003
Phone: 202-547-8570
E-mail: mail@traditionalvalues.org

Founded by the Reverend Louis P. Sheldon in 1980, this organization has broadened its scope from its original California base. Today it is a vocal and active critic of church-state separation and civil rights legislation. It also opposes public education and the powers of the federal judiciary. The group's Web site contains articles and calls to action regarding the issues and points of view it supports. Its tone is somewhat more shrill and provocative than other Christian sites.

Union des Organisations Islamiques de France
URL: http://www.uoif-online.com
20, rue de la Préôvté
93120 La Courneuve
France
Phone: 01-43-11-10-60
E-mail: contact@uoif-online.com

The Union de Organisations Islamiques de France encourages French Muslims to practice their religion and culture. It provides education for Muslims, while it also disseminates information about Islam to the general public. The organization helps in the building and maintenance of mosques and promotes Islamic culture, values, and the arts. It is engaged in representing and defending the interests of French Muslims among the public in general and the government in particular. The organization serves as a center for sustaining an open and cooperative dialogue between the French public and French Muslims, while promoting human rights and the dignity of all. Its Web site offers lots of information about Islam, Muslims in France, and the organization's programs, but this information is accessible only to those who can read French.

Unitarian Universalist Association of Congregations
URL: http://www.uua.org
25 Beacon Street
Boston, MA 02108
Phone: 617-742-2100
E-mail: info@uua.org

RELIGION AND THE STATE

The Unitarian Universalist Association is an umbrella group of more than 1,000 liberal Christian Protestant congregations that promotes and supports religious freedom and the separation of church and state. The organization's Web site provides information on the association's mission, its accomplishments, and its conferences and is a means to locate and contact any of its liberal congregations anywhere in the country.

10

Annotated Bibliography

The following annotated bibliography describes works that cover many aspects of the relationship between religion and state. Entries are grouped into the following categories:

Religion and the State: General Works
Christianity: General and Early History
Christianity and Politics
Religion and the State in Europe
Religion and the State in the United States
Religious Fundamentalism in the United States
Islam: General Works and Early History
Islam, Politics, and the State
Islam: Fundamentalism and Terrorism
Hinduism and Buddhism

Each category is subdivided into two section: Books, and Articles and Papers. A list of nonprint resources, such as films and videos, and of Web sites and documents closes the chapter.

RELIGION AND THE STATE: GENERAL WORKS
Books

Aldridge, Alan. *Religion in the Contemporary World: A Sociological Introduction.* Malden, Mass.: Blackwell Publishers, 1999. The author makes a strong argument for the relevance of religion in today's society and in the realm of public policy. Included is an examination of religious fundamentalism of all types.

Anderson, John, ed. *Religion, Democracy and Democratization.* London: Routledge, 2006. An examination of the role of religion within democracies and in those nations in the process of establishing democratic government.

RELIGION AND THE STATE

Aranoff, Myron J., ed. *Religion and Politics.* New Brunswick, N.J.: Transaction Publishers, 1984. An in-depth examination of the interaction of politics and religion.

Armour, Rollin, Sr. *Islam, Christianity, and the West: A Troubled History.* Maryknoll, N.Y.: Orbis Books, 2002. A close examination of the interactions and conflicts between the two great religions, from the time of Muhammad through the September 11 attacks in the United States.

Audi, Robert. *Religious Commitment and Secular Reason.* New York: Cambridge University Press, 2000. Examines the tension between holding to a religious faith and engaging in secular civic and political life.

Audi, Robert, and Nicholas Wolterstorff. *Religion in the Public Square: The Place of Religious Conviction in Political Debate.* Lanham, Md.: Rowman & Littlefield Publishers, 1997. An in-depth discussion of the value of religion in deciding public policy and state governance.

Berger, Peter L., ed. *The Desecularization of the World: Resurgent Religion and World Politics.* Grand Rapids, Mich.: Eerdmans, 1999. Essays on how peoples and states are adapting to the increasingly secular nature of government.

Berman, Harold J. *Faith and Order: The Reconciliation of Law and Religion.* Atlanta, Ga.: Scholars Press, 1993. An in-depth look at how religion has shaped Western law, the interactions and tensions between religion and jurisprudence, and the future of this interaction in a more secular state.

Bill, James A., and John A. Williams. *Roman Catholic and Shi'a Muslims: Prayer, Passion, and Politics.* Chapel Hill: University of North Carolina Press, 2003. Using insightful comparison, the author explicates the commonalities between two of the world's great religions, including their influence on law and governance.

Bruce, Steven. *Politics and Religion.* Malden, Mass.: Polity Press, 2003. An incisive evaluation of the role of religion in modern politics and governance.

Casanova, Jose. *Public Religions in the Modern World.* Chicago, Ill.: University of Chicago Press, 1994. Using case studies, the author examines whether secularization is as dominant in modern society as some thinkers believe.

Cochran, Clarke E. *Religion in Public and Private Life.* New York: Routledge, 1990. An interdisciplinary examination of political theory and its relationship to religion in terms of what is "public" and what is "private."

Davis, Creston, John Millbank, and Slavoj Zizek, eds. *Theology and the Political: The New Debate.* Durham, N.C.: Duke University Press, 2005. Essays revealing the new impact modern theology is having on politics and governments in the modern world.

Demerath, N. J. *Crossing the Gods: World Religions and Worldly Politics.* New Brunswick, N.J.: Rutgers University Press, 2001. This book recounts and dissects the growing tensions between religious believers and increasingly secular political systems.

Dorrien, Gary J. *Reconstructing the Common Good: Theology and the Social Order.* New York: Orbis Books, 1990. A classic study of the influence of the church on the development of Christian socialism, as well as on freedom and democracy.

Annotated Bibliography

These trends are contrasted to religion's impact on totalitarian and dictatorial political regimes.

Everett, William J. *God's Federal Republic: Reconstructing our Governing Symbol.* New York: Paulist Press, 1988. A classic work that compares religion's influence on both republican and federalist forms of government.

———. *Religion, Federalism, and the Struggle for Public Life: Cases from Germany, India, and America.* Oxford: Oxford University Press, 1997. A study of how different cultures incorporate religion into government and public life in a federalist society.

Forrester, Duncan B. *Beliefs, Values, and Policies: Conviction Politics in a Secular Age.* Oxford, England: Clarendon Press, 1989. The author argues that religion has a significant contribution to make to social values and public policies in our generally secular age.

Fox, Jonathan. *A World Survey of Religion and the State.* New York: Cambridge University Press, 2008. An up-to-date and very useful overview of the religions of the world and their impact on the state and governance.

Galston, William A. *Public Matters: Essays on Politics, Policy, and Religion.* Lanham, Md.: Rowman & Littlefield Publishers, 2005. Thoughtful and thought-provoking essays on politics, public policy, and religion.

Gauchet, Marcel. *The Disenchantment of the World: A Political History of Religion.* Princeton, N.J.: Princeton University Press, 1997. An in-depth discussion of the increasing secularization of the public sphere and politics; its effect on religion and religion's influence on politics.

Hauerwas, Stanley. *Dispatches from the Front: Theological Engagements with the Secular.* Durham, N.C.: Duke University Press, 1994. The author supports the view that religion, and Christianity in particular, has important contributions to make in the formation of public policy.

Hoetzl, Michael, and Graham Ward, eds. *Religion and Political Thought.* New York: Continuum, 2006. An examination of how religious belief influences politics and political theory.

Hurd, Elizabeth S. *The Politics of Secularism in International Relations.* Princeton, N.J.: Princeton University Press, 2007. Reveals how increasingly secular government in many parts of the world generates tension or conflict when confronted with or in relation to states whose government is more oriented to theology.

Johnson, Douglas, and Cynthia Sampson, eds. *Religion, the Missing Dimension of Statecraft.* New York: Oxford University Press, 1994. A collection of essays that support the view that public policy and governance would benefit from greater participation of religious institutions.

Juergensmeyer, Mark. *The New Cold War? Religious Nationalism Confronts the Secular State.* Berkeley: University of California Press, 1993. A thorough overview of the role of religion in the state, the rise of secularism, and its effects on society and governance.

Kepel, Gilles. *The Revenge of God: The Resurgence of Islam, Christianity, and Judaism in the Modern World.* University Park: Pennsylvania State University Press, 1995.

An expert on Islamic fundamentalism, Kepel analyzes the "societal malaise" that he feels is one contributing factor to Islamic extremism. He traces the roots of this fundamentalism to the Muslim Brotherhood, which formed before World War II to create an Islamic state in Egypt.

Maclear, I. F. *Church and State in the Modern Age: A Documentary History.* New York: Oxford University Press, 1995. A respected reference work on the relationship between church and state in modern Western history, from the post-Reformation to today.

Mews, Stuart, ed. *Religion in Politics: A World Guide.* Chicago, Ill.: St. James Press, 1989. A classic guide to the religious movements that have shaped national, and global, politics.

Moen, Matthew C., and Lowell S. Gustafson, eds. *The Religious Challenge to the State.* Philadelphia, Pa.: Temple University Press, 1992. The essays in this book cover the world's three major religions (Judaism, Christianity, Islam) and their interaction with and influence on 20th-century governments. Case studies illuminate each argument.

Moyser, George, ed. *Politics and Religion in the Modern World.* London: Routledge, 1991. A classic collection of essays that assesses religion's role in the politics of many modern nations.

Neusner, Jacob, ed. *God's Rule: The Politics of World Religions.* Washington, D.C.: Georgetown University Press, 2003. A fine examination of how many religions shaped the political landscape of their nations.

Norris, Pippa, and Ronald Inglehart. *Sacred and Secular: Religion and Politics Worldwide.* New York: Cambridge University Press, 2006. An explication of the tensions between the tendency toward secularity in the state and the religious beliefs of citizens in nations around the world.

Ramet, Sabrina P., and Donald W. Treadgold, eds. *Render unto Caesar: The Religious Sphere in World Politics.* Washington, D.C.: The American University Press, 1995. An in-depth examination of the role and effects of the separation of religion and the state in a global context.

Storey, John W., and Glenn H. Utter. *Religion and Politics: A Reference Handbook.* Baltimore, Md.: Johns Hopkins University Press, 2000. A useful guide to the relationship between religion and politics in the world.

Sweetman, Brendan. *Why Politics Needs Religion: The Place of Religious Arguments in the Public Square.* Downers Grove, Ill.: IVP Academic Press, 2006. An argument for the values that religion can and should contribute to political debate and civic discussion.

Wuthnow, Robert. *Encyclopedia of Politics and Religion. 2nd Edition.* Washington, D.C.: Congressional Quarterly, 2006. An updated, two-volume set of one of the most authoritative and complete overviews of religion and its effects on politics and global events. An invaluable resource on the subject.

———. *Producing the Sacred: An Essay on Public Religion.* Urbana: University of Illinois Press, 1994. A study into how different types of organizations that establish a form of community may influence public religious discourse and public policy.

Annotated Bibliography

Articles and Papers

Cochrane, James R. "The Boundaries of Hegemony: Configuring Public Space from the Margins." *Scriptura* 63 (1997): 451–466. Sets forth a strategy by which the church can participate usefully in the development of public policy by recognizing the boundaries of each.

Finke, Roger, and Amy Adamczyk. "Cross-National Moral Beliefs: The Influence of National Religious Context." *Sociological Quarterly* 49, no. 4 (2008): 617–652. This lengthy article examines how the moral codes embedded within the world's different religions affect the morality of the state and its policies.

Froese, Paul, and Christopher Bader. "Unraveling Religious Worldviews: The Relationship between Images of God and Political Ideology in a Cross-Cultural Analysis." *Sociological Quarterly* 29, no. 4 (2008): 689–718. This article uses data collected about many world religions to compare and reveal how different religion's views of God affect believers' views of authority and political ideology.

"Fundamentalism around the World." *Christian Century* 102, no. 25 (1985): 769–771. This articles examines the different forms of religious fundamentalism, contrasting these religious movements in the United States, Islamic nations, and other regions where fundamentalism is on the rise.

Lester, Toby. "Oh, Gods!" *Atlantic Monthly* 289, no. 2 (2002): 37–46. This article describes the evolution of religion through history. The author argues that though secularism seems ascendant in the 20th century, it is likely that religion will play a far greater part in social and political life around the world in the 21st century.

Siddiqi, Mona. "When Reconciliation Fails: Global Politics and the Study of Religion." *Journal of the American Academy of Religion* 73, no. 3 (2005): 1,141–1,153. This essay reveals how religious language and the tenets of religion have become key themes running through international politics. This situation makes it more difficult to find a common ground for reconciliation, solving conflicts, and peacemaking.

CHRISTIANITY: GENERAL AND EARLY HISTORY
Books

Barnes, Timothy D. *Athanasius and Constantius: Theology and Politics in the Constantinian Empire.* Cambridge, Mass.: Harvard University Press, 1993. An examination of Christianity's role during the reign of the first Christian emperor, Constantine.

Bible (any version that includes both the Old and New Testaments)

Chadwick, Henry. *The Early Church.* New York: Penguin, 1993. A classic history of the beginnings of the Christian church.

Digeser, Elizabeth D. *The Making of a Christian Empire.* Ithaca, N.Y.: Cornell University Press, 2000. A history of the rise of Christianity during the heyday of the Roman Empire.

Gonzalez, Justo. *The Story of Christianity.* 2 vols. San Francisco: HarperCollins, 1984. A thorough overview of Christian history and beliefs.

Hester, Joseph P. *The Ten Commandments: A Handbook of Religious, Legal, and Social Issues.* Jefferson, N.C.: McFarland & Co., 2003. An explication of how the Ten Commandments have influenced major issues regarding modern religion, law, and society.

Höpfl, Harro. *Luther and Calvin on Secular Authority.* New York: Cambridge University Press, 1991. An overview and explication of the views of these key Protestant thinkers on the relationship between Christianity and the secular state.

McGrath, Alister, E. *Christian Theology: An Introduction.* Boston: Blackwell, 2006. A well-written overview of the history of Christian belief and theology.

McManners, John. *The Oxford Illustrated History of Christianity.* New York: Oxford University Press, 2001. A fine study that covers the entire history of the Christian religion.

O'Donovan, Oliver, and Joan L. O'Donovan, eds. *From Irenaeus to Grotius: A Sourcebook in Christian Political Thought, 100–1625.* Grand Rapids, Mich.: Eerdmans, 1999. A valuable resource for understanding the development of Christian political thought during these crucial years in the development and advancement of Christianity.

O'Grady, Desmond. *Beyond the Empire: Rome and the Church from Constantine to Charlemagne.* New York: Crossroad Publishing, 2001. An investigation of the civic role of the church at the end and after the disintegration of the Roman Empire.

Pilgrim, Walter E. *Uneasy Neighbors: Church and State in the New Testament.* Minneapolis, Minn.: Fortress Press, 1999. An examination of what the New Testament reveals about the relationship of church and state.

Vidmar, John. *The Catholic Church through the Ages: A History.* Mahwah, N.J.: Paulist Press, 2005. A complete history of the Catholic Church, from its beginnings to today.

Articles and Papers

Jenkins, Philip. "Long-lost Christians." *Christian Century* 125, no. 22 (2008): 22–26. This article presents an overview of the development of Christianity during the Middle Ages, with a discussion of the nature of the religion's interaction with believers of other faiths, including Buddhism, Islam, and Taoism.

Kazen, Thomas. "The Christology of Early Christian Practice." *Journal of Biblical Literature* 127, no. 3 (2008): 591–614. This essay examines how early Christians viewed Jesus. It suggests that even in the religion's earliest days, Christ was viewed as an eschatological prophet, or one who prophesied the end days. This view has influenced the religion ever since.

Shaffern, Robert W. "Indulgences and Saintly Devotionalisms in the Middle Ages." *Catholic Historical Review* 84, no. 4 (1998): 643–661. This article examines the ideology and history of indulgences sold by the church and the effect of this activity on the church and the state.

Annotated Bibliography

CHRISTIANITY AND POLITICS
Books

Benne, Robert. *The Paradoxical Vision: A Public Theology in the Twenty-first Century.* Minneapolis, Minn.: Fortress Press, 1995. A discussion of how Christians and Christian theology can adapt to and influence public discourse and public policy in this secular century.

Bryan, Christopher. *Render to Caesar: Jesus, the Early Church, and the Roman Superpower.* New York: Oxford University Press, 2005. A discussion of how the early church adapted to, rebelled against, and influenced the Roman Empire during the time of Jesus and in the centuries immediately following.

Carter, Stephen L. *God's Name in Vain: The Wrongs and Rights of Religion in Politics.* New York: Basic Books, 2000. The author argues that Christians should not use the separation of church and state to disengage from politics, an arena where their faith can have a positive impact.

Cassidy, Richard J. *Jesus, Politics, and Society: A Study of Luke's Gospel.* Maryknoll, N.Y.: Orbis Books, 1978.

———. *Society and Politics in the Acts of the Apostles.* Maryknoll, N.Y.: Orbis Books, 1987. In both these volumes, Cassidy connects the teachings of the New Testament to current political systems and shows their relevance to politics and governance today.

Ferguson, Everett, ed. *Church and State in the Early Church.* New York: Garland, 1993. Essays that examine the relationship between the early Christian church and the states in which it was growing.

Gould, Andrew. *Origins of Liberal Dominance: State, Church, and Party in Nineteenth-Century Europe.* Ann Arbor: University of Michigan Press, 1999. A thorough examination of how the interaction of the church and state in Europe during this time period led to the development of the liberal democratic state.

Hart, D. G. *A Secular Faith: Why Christianity Favors the Separation of Church and State.* Chicago, Ill.: I. R. Dee, 2006. The author argues that true Christianity flourishes when church and state are separated.

Kimball, Charles. *When Religion Becomes Evil.* New York: HarperCollins, 2002. The author warns against overemphasizing some aspects of Christianity and ignoring others in order to further a political aim. He urges Christians to be true to all the principles of their faith and not exploit only those that suit a political point of view.

Lilla, Mark. *The Stillborn God: Religion, Politics, and the Modern West.* New York: Knopf, 2007. An important view of how the ambiguity in Christianity and the different philosophies of religion that grew out of that led to the growth of distinct governmental structures and public attitudes toward the state in Europe.

Maddox, Robert L. *Separation of Church and State: Guarantor of Religious Freedom.* New York: Crossroads Publishing, 1987. Using case studies from Europe and America, the author argues that the separation of church and state is vital in assuring and maintaining liberty.

Porter, J. M., ed. *Luther: Selected Political Writings.* Eugene, Ore.: Wipf & Stock Publishers, 2003. A discussion of Martin Luther's political thought and writing and their relevance today.

Sheldon, Garrett W., ed. *Religion and Politics: Major Thinkers on the Relation of Church and State.* New York: P. Lang Publishers, 1990. Essays about the views of important philosophers and theologians on the relationship between church and state.

Voegelin, Eric, and Manfred Nenningsen, eds. *Modernity without Restraint.* New York: Columbia University Press, 2000. The only one-volume compilation of Voegelin's major works on the relationship between church and state. Voegelin argues that secularization has cost the West its soul and its spiritual and religious foundation.

Wogaman, Philip J. *Christian Perspectives on Politics.* Louisville, Ky.: Westminster John Knox Press, 2000. An in-depth exploration of Christianity's contributions to the state, government, and society through history.

Wood, James Edward. *Church and State in Historical Perspective: A Critical Assessment and Annotated Bibliography.* Westport, Conn.: Praeger, 2005. An exhaustive study of the history of the relationship between the state and religion, with a voluminous annotated bibliography.

———. *Church and State in the Modern World: A Critical Assessment and Annotated Bibliography.* Westport, Conn.: Praeger, 2005. An exhaustive study of the relationship between the state and religion today, with an extensive annotated bibliography. Both volumes are invaluable resources.

Wuthnow, Robert. *Christianity and Civil Society: The Contemporary Debate.* Valley Forge, Penn.: Trinity Press International, 1996. A thoughtful and thorough explanation of the modern debate that swirls around Christianity's role in politics and public life and policy.

Articles and Papers

Aubin, Benoit. "End-Game." *Maclean's* 116, no. 44 (2003): 32–36. This article analyzes the role of the Catholic Church in relation to modern social change. It provides a historical overview of the interplay of church and state in the past and discusses how that role has changed today.

Caputo, John D., and Catherine Keller. "Theopoetic/Theopolitic." *Cross Currents* 56, no. 4 (2007): 105–111. The authors argue that religion, particularly Christianity, should have more, not less, influence on politics. They use a variety of examples to show how strongly religious belief and expression influence politics and government institutions.

Devine, Frank. "In Caesar's Pocket." *Quadrant Magazine* 52, no. 2 (2008), 64–66. This article examines the inseparability of the Christian church and the state, both historically and today. It examines arguments both for and against more involvement of the Christian church in politics and policy.

Nies, Gregory O. "A Secular Faith: Why Christianity Favors the Separation of Church and State." *Journal of Church and State* 49, no. 1 (2007): 152–153. This article reviews the history of Christianity and explains why it has led to and should continue to support the separation of church and state.

RELIGION AND THE STATE IN EUROPE
Books

Aston, Nigel. *Christianity and Revolutionary Europe: 1750–1830.* New York: Cambridge University Press, 2002. A historical view of the role of Christianity during this turbulent age.

Bernard, G. W., *The King's Reformation: Henry VIII and the Remaking of the English Church.* New Haven, Conn.: Yale University Press, 2007. A complete history of how England's Henry VIII broke with the Vatican to create the Anglican Church, or Church of England.

Besserman, Lawrence L., ed. *Sacred and Secular in Medieval and Early Modern Cultures: New Essays.* New York: Palgrave Macmillan, 2006. These essays explore the tensions between the church and the state during the Middle Ages and Renaissance periods.

Buchanan, Tom, and Martin Conway, eds. *Political Catholicism in Europe: 1918–1965.* New York: Oxford University Press, 1996. Historical essays cover the relationship between the Catholic Church and dictatorship, as well as the church's role in helping shape postwar Europe's society and politics.

Burleigh, Michael. *Earthly Powers: The Conflict between Religion and Politics from the French Revolution to the Great War.* London: Harper Perennial, 2006. Historical analysis of how tensions and conflict between the church and the state gave rise to the momentous events during this period of European history.

———. *Sacred Causes: The Clash of Religion and Politics, from the Great War to the War on Terror.* New York: HarperCollins, 2007. Building on his previous volume, this book is an in-depth and readable account of the role of religion, and its complicity or conflict with the state, in shaping modern history.

Burrell, S. A. *The Role of Religion in Modern European History.* New York: Macmillan, 1964. An in-depth look at how religion has shaped modern European society and politics.

Byrnes, Timothy, and Peter J. Katzenstein, eds. *Religion in an Expanding Europe.* New York: Cambridge University Press, 2006. The evolving role of religion as the European Union expands to take in nations with diverse religious beliefs and cultures.

Collinson, Patrick. *The Reformation: A History.* New York: Modern Library, 2006. A complete and readable history of Luther and the Protestant Reformation.

Ferrari, Silvio, et al., eds. *Law and Religion in Post-Communist Europe.* Leuven, Netherlands: Peeters, 2003. A collection of essays that explore religion and the law in Europe since the collapse of the Soviet Union in 1989.

Gorski, Philip S. *The Disciplinary Revolution: Calvinism and the Rise of the State in Early Modern Europe.* Chicago, Ill.: University of Chicago Press, 2003. An explication of how rigid Calvinist Protestantism affected governments and the state in Europe.

Hunter, Shireen T., ed. *Islam: Europe's Second Religion: The New Social, Cultural, and Political Landscape.* Westport, Conn.: Greenwood Press, 2002. A country-by-country survey of the impacts of Islamic populations on the nations of Europe.

Lewis, Bernard, and Dominique Schnapper. *Muslims in Europe.* London: Pinter Publishers, 1994. An overview of Muslims in Europe and their impact on society, the state, and religion, with particular emphasis on France, Germany, the Netherlands, and the United Kingdom.

Loades, David, ed. *Faith and Identity: Christian Political Experience.* New York: Blackwell, 1990. Essays that explore the relationship between religion and national identity in several European nations, with an extensive historical background.

Logan, Donald F. *A History of the Church in the Middle Ages.* London: Routledge, 2002. An in-depth history of the church during the medieval period.

MacColloch, Diarmaid. *The Reformation.* New York: Penguin, 2005. A thorough and readable history of the Protestant Reformation; its cause and impacts.

Michalski, Krzysztof, ed. *Religion in the New Europe.* New York: CEU Press, 2006. Essays that delve into the role of religion in today's secularist European states.

Monod, Paul K. *The Power of Kings: Monarchy and Religion in Europe, 1589–1715.* New Haven, Conn.: Yale University Press, 1999. A wide-ranging exploration of monarchical power in Europe at this time and its relationship to the church and religion. Most European countries are discussed.

Ratzinger, Joseph Cardinal. *Turning Point for Europe? The Church in the Modern World—Assessment and Forecast.* Harrison, N.Y.: Ignatius Press, 1994. The author, the current pope, argues that a greater emphasis on religion is a necessary counterpoint to the secularization of the state and to an overly materialistic culture.

Ravitch, Norman. *The Catholic Church and the French Nation, 1589–1989.* New York: Routledge, 1990. A thorough evaluation of the role the church played in France as it developed from a religion-centered to a modern secular state.

Rémond, René. *Religion and Society in Modern Europe.* Malden, Mass.: Blackwell Publishers, 1999. The author assesses the interaction between religion and the state over the last 200 years, with an emphasis on the evolution of political institutions.

Van Kley, Dale K. *The Religious Origins of the French Revolution: From Calvin to the Civil Constitution, 1560–1791.* New Haven, Conn.: Yale University Press, 1996. An in-depth analysis of how the changing role of Christianity and especially Protestantism in France led to the French Revolution.

Warner, Carolyn M. *The Catholic Church and Political Parties in Europe.* Princeton, N.J.: Princeton University Press, 2000. The author traces the influence of the Catholic Church on the development of religiously based political parties in modern Europe, including historical background. The emphasis is on France, Italy, and Germany.

Annotated Bibliography

Articles and Papers

Englund, Steven. "How Catholic Is France?" *Commonweal* 135, no. 19 (2008): 12–18. This article examines the strength and influence of Catholicism on France and its institutions.

Ferraro, Silvio. "Separation of Church and State in Contemporary European Society." *Journal of Church and State* 30 (Fall 1988): 533–548. The author examines the relevance of the 19th-century laws separating church and state and questions whether they should be renewed or changed for the modern era in Europe.

Geusau, Frans A. M. Alting von. "Europe: The New Christendom." *European Legacy* 3, no. 2 (1998): 1–6. This article focuses on the changes in religiosity in Europe as more eastern European nations enter the European Union. The authors also look at how greater Christian influence may affect EU governance, and they discuss potential areas of conflict between Christian and secular influences on policy.

Klausen, Jytte. "Europe's Muslim Political Elite." *World Policy Journal* 22, no. 3 (2005): 61–68. This article examines the underrepresentation of Muslims among the political elite in modern Europe and discusses ways that more Muslims can be brought into the political process.

Moro, Renato. "Religion and Politics in the Time of Secularization." *Totalitarian Movements and Political Religions* 6 (2005): 71–86. This article proved a thoughtful look at how secularization affects the beliefs and political attitudes of believers, as well as the political implications of their viewpoint.

Power, Carla, and Barbie Nadeau. "The New Crusade." *Newsweek* 144, no. 19 (2004): 24–27. This article focuses on the state of religion today in Europe, with a focus on the influence of religion on the state and policy, the tensions between the religious and secularists, as well as the interaction between Christians and Muslims.

RELIGION AND THE STATE IN THE UNITED STATES

Books

Ackerman, David M., and Kimberly D. Jones. *The Law of Church and State in the Supreme Court Revisited.* New York: Nova Publishers, 2006. The authors review how the view of the relationship between church and state has changed over time based on Supreme Court decisions.

Baldwin, Lewis V. *The Legacy of Martin Luther King, Jr.: The Boundaries of Law, Politics, and Religion.* Notre Dame, Ind.: University of Notre Dame Press, 2002. This volume analyzes the intersection of religion, politics, and the law in terms of Dr. King and the Civil Rights movement.

Balmer, Randall H. *God in the White House: A History: How Faith Shaped the Presidency from John F. Kennedy to George W. Bush.* New York: Harper San Francisco, 2006. An overview and analysis of the role of religion and faith in the chief executive and how it shaped U.S. policy.

RELIGION AND THE STATE

Buchholz, Rogene A. *America in Conflict: The Deepening Values Divide.* Lanham, Md.: Hamilton Books, 2007. An insightful overview of the seemingly unbridgeable divide between secular and religious Americans, and the effect on politics and policy.

Carter, Stephen L. *The Culture of Disbelief.* New York: Basic Books, 1993. The author supports the view that the United States is a Christian nation.

Church, F. Forrester. *So Help Me God: The Founding Fathers and the First Great Battle over Church and State.* Orlando, Fla.: Harcourt, 2007. The author reveals in great detail the disputes the founding fathers had over how to incorporate separation of church and state into the Constitution.

Curry, Thomas J. *The First Freedoms: Church and State in America to the Passage of the First Amendment.* New York: Oxford University Press, 1986. A historical overview of the principles, events, and viewpoints that went into the creation of the First Amendment.

Davis, Derek. *Religion and the Continental Congress: 1774–1789.* New York: Oxford University Press, 2000. A historical analysis of the debate swirling around religion and the writing of the Constitution.

Dionne, E. J., Jr., and John J. Diluliio, Jr., eds. *What's God Got to Do with the American Experiment?* Washington, D.C.: Brookings Institution, 2000. A collection of essays that express different points of view on the role of religion in government and the separation of church and state.

Dionne, E. J., Jr., et al., eds. *One Electorate under God? A Dialogue on Religion and American Politics.* Washington, D.C.: Brookings Institution, 2004. Essays presenting a wide range of viewpoints on the role of religion in American politics.

Djupe, Paul A., and Laura R. Olson. *Encyclopedia of American Religion and Politics.* New York: Facts On File, 2003. An extensive and valuable resource covering the role of religion in the United States and its effects on U.S. politics.

Dreisbach, Daniel L. *Thomas Jefferson and the Wall of Separation between Church and State.* New York: New York University Press, 2002. A historical examination of Jefferson's views on the separation of church and state and his role in crafting the First Amendment.

Eisgruber, Christopher L., and Lawrence G. Sager. *Religious Freedom and the Constitution.* Cambridge, Mass.: Harvard University Press, 2007. A historical analysis of the interpretation of religious freedom as contained in the Constitution.

Gaustad, Edwin S. *Proclaim Liberty throughout the Land: A History of Church and State in America.* New York: Oxford University Press, 2003. A historical overview of the effects of religious freedom on the United States and its citizens.

Gedicks, Frederick M. *The Rhetoric of Church and State: A Critical Analysis of Religion Clause Jurisprudence.* Durham, N.C.: Duke University Press, 1995. An examination of the interplay between religion and the law in the United States, including cases.

Gordon, Sarah B. *The Mormon Question: Polygamy and Constitutional Conflict in Nineteenth-Century America.* Chapel Hill: University of North Carolina Press, 2002. An analysis of the effect that Mormon beliefs and practices had during this

Annotated Bibliography

period, including their challenge to the 19th-century interpretations of religious freedom as set forth in the Constitution.

Al-Habri, Azizah Y. et al. *Religion in American Public Life: Living with Our Deepest Differences.* New York: W. W. Norton, 2001. A discussion of public life in America that argues that religion and religious morality are the foundation of the nation.

Hamburger, Philip. *Separation of Church and State.* Cambridge, Mass.: Harvard University Press, 2002. The author argues against Jefferson's "wall of separation" between church and state using historical examples.

Handy, Robert T. *Undermined Establishment: Church-State Relations in America, 1880–1920.* Princeton, N.J.: Princeton University Press, 1991. A close examination of the Constitution's establishment clause during this period.

Heclo, Hugh, and Wilfred M. McClay. *Religion Returns to the Public Square: Faith and Policy in America.* Baltimore, Md.: Johns Hopkins University Press, 2003. These essays generally support the view that the United States has always been a country in which religion has significantly informed government and public policy.

Hedges, Chris. *I Don't Believe in Atheists.* New York: Free Press, 2008. Perhaps as a counterpoint to his American Fascists, which excoriated the Religious Right, here Hedges explains why militant atheists are becoming as damaging to the U.S. body politic and culture as the fundamentalists they scorn. Hedges shows how rigid extremism and intolerance are polarizing and ultimately destructive.

Hitchcock, James. *Supreme Court and Religion in American Life.* Princeton, N.J.: Princeton University Press, 2004. How Supreme Court decisions on religion have affected the lives of a diversity of Americans.

Kramnick, Isaac, and R. Laurence Moore. *The Godless Constitution: A Moral Defense of the Secular State.* New York: W. W. Norton, 2005. As its title suggests, the authors defend the separation of church and state, contending that the Constitution does not permit religion to guide or control government or public policy.

Ledowitz, Bruce. *American Religious Democracy: Coming to Terms with the End of Secular Politics.* Westport, Conn.: Praeger Publishers, 2007. The author argues that religion will have an increasingly important role in American democracy and government.

Lynn, Barry, et al. *The Right to Religious Liberty: The Basic ACLU Guide to Religious Rights.* Carbondale: Southern Illinois University Press, 1995. In an easy-to-use question and answer format, the American Civil Liberties Union addresses numerous issues surrounding the right to religious liberty for U.S. citizens.

Noonan, John T., Jr. *The Luster of our Country: The American Experience of Religious Freedom.* Los Angeles: University of California Press, 1998. The author explains why he thinks that religious freedom is the greatest contribution the United States has given the world.

Thiemann, Ronald F. *Religion in Public Life: A Dilemma for Democracy.* Washington, D.C.: Georgetown University Press, 1996. The author examines the reemergence of religion as an important factor shaping modern public discourse and policy and analyzes religion's effect on democracy and democratic institutions.

Vowell, Sarah. *The Wordy Shipmates.* New York: Riverhead Hardcover, 2008. A highly informative and delightfully written history by a well-known radio personality and humorist. Despite her lack of formal historical training, this book is well-researched and packed with information about the Puritans, Massachusetts Bay Colony, and how early religious beliefs shaped the development of the United States. It is also a pleasure to read.

Wallis, James. *The Soul of Politics: Beyond 'Religious Right' and 'Secular Left.'"* San Diego, Calif.: Harvest Books, 1995. The author argues for a politics based on universal spirituality that transcends the extremes of religion and secularism in modern America.

Whitten, Mark W. *The Myth of Christian America: What You Need to Know about the Separation of Church and State.* Macon, Ga.: Smyth & Helwys, 1999. A readable argument about why the United States is not a Christian nation and how the Constitution protects religious freedom via the separation of church and state.

Wilson, John F., and Donald L. Drakeman, eds. *Church and State in American History: Key Documents, Decisions, and Commentary from the Past Three Centuries.* Boulder, Colo.: Westview Press, 2003. A comprehensive compilation of primary documents, court decisions, and expert essays about church-state separation throughout American history.

Witte, John. *Religion and the American Constitutional Experiment.* Boulder, Colo.: Westview Press, 2005. The author explicates the religious, civic, and philosophical bases for the constitutional separation of church and state. He then reviews and discusses recent debates on the subject, including key decisions of the Supreme Court.

Wood, James E., ed. *First Freedom: Religion and the Bill of Rights.* Waco, Texas: Dawson Institute of Church-State Studies, 1990. Essays derived from a symposium on church and state, including the religious foundations of the Bill of Rights.

———. *Religion and the State: Essays in Honor of Leo Pfeffer.* Waco, Texas: Baylor University Press, 1985. The essays in this book provide a useful, in-depth look at the role of religion in the United States, with an emphasis on legal interpretations of the establishment clause and freedom of religion.

Wood, Timothy L. *Agents of Wrath, Sowers of Discord: Authority and Dissent in Puritan Massachusetts, 1630–1655.* New York: Routledge, 2006. The author examines religious disagreements and power struggles among early Puritan settlers and discusses its implications for the influence of religion in U.S. political history.

Articles and Papers

Aronson, Ronald. "The New Atheists." *The Nation* 286 (6/7/07). Available online. URL: www.thenation.com/doc/20070625/aronson. This article provides an extensive explanation and analysis of the views of today's most militant atheists in the United States and Europe. While the author is sympathetic to the free choice to choose nonbelief, or atheism, he questions the vehemence of the new atheism and wonders to what extent it has itself become a type of rigid, fundamentalist religion.

Annotated Bibliography

Carter, Stephen, and Barbara Ehrenreich. "Roundtable on Religion in Politics." *Tikkun* 15, no. 6 (2000): 23–29. This article is a transcript of a discussion by prominent experts and writers regarding the role of religion in politics in the United States.

Demerath, N. J. "Religion, Politics, and the State, at Home and Abroad." *Sociology of Religion* 68, no. 1 (2007): 1–3. This article discusses religion and the state with particular emphasis on how religion affects politics and political campaigns today and conflicts regarding the teaching of science and history in schools.

Frykholm, Amy. "Discerning the Faith Factor." *Christian Century* 125, no. 21 (2008): 10–11. In an interview with pollster John Green, the author presents the relationship between religious belief and U.S. politics and policy.

Lazare, Daniel. "Among the Disbelievers." *The Nation* 286 (5/10/07). Available online. URL: http://www.thenation.com/doc/20070528/lazare/. This article presents a sharp critique of today's major exponents of atheism, particularly Richard Dawkins. The author argues that spokespeople for modern atheism are so scornful and contemptuous of religion, and so rigid in their attacks on it, they are fueling a religious backlash among believers and agnostics and are, in many ways, crafting an atheism that is as blinkered and fundamentalist as the religions they sneer at.

Peterson, Merrill D. "Jefferson and Religious Freedom." *Atlantic Monthly* 274, no. 6 (1994): 112–121. This article explores the religious views of Thomas Jefferson and relates them to his influence on the Constitution and the creation of the wall of separation between church and state.

Raskin, Jamie. "One Nation under the Constitution: Reason, Politics, and Morality in the New Century." *Humanist* 68, no. 6 (2008): 18–22. This article is an edited version of the speech given by Sen. Jamie Raskin after accepting a 2008 award from the American Humanist Association. His remarks emphasize the maintenance of a strict separation of church and state.

Stoll, Ira. "The Revolutionary Gospel According to Samuel Adams." *American History* 43, no. 5 (2008): 42–47. This article discusses the role the revolutionary and politician Samuel Adams had on the formation of the United States. The author explains how Adams's views on God and religion influenced leaders such as Franklin and Jefferson, and thus influenced the Constitution.

RELIGIOUS FUNDAMENTALISM IN THE UNITED STATES

Books

Boston, Rob. *Why the Religious Right Is Wrong about Separation of Church and State.* Amherst, N.Y.: Prometheus Books, 1993. A careful explanation revealing why the view of the Religious Right undermines the constitutional principle of the separation of church and state.

Colson, Charles W. *God and Government: An Insider's View on the Boundaries between Faith and Politics.* Grand Rapids, Mich.: Zondervan, 2007. A former Nixon aide and current exponent of the Religious Right explains why God and faith should play an important role in government and policy.

RELIGION AND THE STATE

Domke, David S., and Kevin M. Coe. *The God Strategy: How Religion Became a Political Weapon in America.* New York: Oxford University Press, 2006. The authors describe how the Religious Right has used faith as a means for influencing, even controlling, public policy.

Green, John C. et al. *The Christian Right in American Politics: Marching to the Millennium.* Washington, D.C.: Georgetown University Press, 2003. Case studies are used to present a history of how the Religious Right organized to become a force in American politics.

Hedges, Chris. *American Fascists: The Christian Right and the War on America.* New York: Free Press, 2008. In this book, Hedges, a respected and best-selling author, explores and explains how the Religious Right's beliefs, and its increasing power, are increasingly promoting, if not implementing, policies that the author argues are disturbingly fascistic.

Heineman, Kenneth J. *God Is a Conservative: Religion, Politics, and Morality in Contemporary America.* New York: New York University Press, 1998. The author explores the history of the Religious Right in the United States and shows how and why it has come to define American morality and to dominate politics.

Lerner, Michael. *The Left Hand of God: Taking Back Our Country from the Religious Right.* San Francisco, Calif.: Harper, 2006. A noted liberal rabbi describes how the Left can rescue the U.S. government from the excessive influence of the Religious Right.

Linker, Damon. *The Theocons: Secular America under Siege.* New York: Doubleday, 2006. How the fundamentalist drive for an American theocracy is undermining the U.S. secular state.

Long, Douglas. *Fundamentalists and Extremists.* New York: Facts On File, 2002. An overview of religious fundamentalism and the extreme views it promulgates.

Martin, William. *With God on Our Side: The Rise of the Religious Right in America.* New York: Broadway, 1996. In this book Martin analyzes the roles of all players in the rise of the Religious Right in America, from a compliant and/or sympathetic media, to corporations, to the White House.

Phillips, Kevin. *American Theocracy.* New York: Viking, 2006. The onetime spokesman for American conservatives turned outspoken critic of current right-wing doctrine, explains in detail how the Religious Right and its values are actually promoting, or are being co-opted to promote, the neoconservative agenda, including globalization, neoliberal capitalism, and U.S. imperial ambitions in pursuit of oil.

Reichley, James A. *Faith in Politics.* Washington, D.C.: Brookings Institution Press, 2002. An in-depth historical analysis of the separation of church and state in the United States, with a defense of faith-based influences on government and policy.

Whitten, Mark W. *The Myth of Christian America: What You Need to Know about the Separation of Church and State.* Macon, Ga.: Smyth & Helwys, 1999. The author argues that the founders never intended the United States to be a Christian country, but were more concerned with religious liberty and church-state separation.

Annotated Bibliography

Willis, Clint, and Nate Hardcastle, eds. *Jesus Is Not a Republican: The Religious Right's War on America*. New York: Thunder's Mouth Press, 2005. Essays discussing how the Religious Right has hijacked the Republican Party; its implications for governance and the state.

Articles and Papers

Antle, James W. "Purpose Driven Right." *American Conservative* 5, no. 18 (2006): 19–21. This articles focuses on the prominent role of the Christian Right in shaping the policies of the U.S. Republican Party. The article discusses the practices that have increased fundamentalists' influence in conservative politics.

Boston, Rob. "The Religious Right and American Freedom." *Church & State* 59, no. 6 (2006): 4–9. This article analyzes the Religious Right and the freedoms and influence it enjoys and compares that with its views and influence on guaranteed freedoms for others in the United States.

De Kedt, E. "Abusing Cultural Freedom: Coercion in the Name of God." *Journal of Human Development*, 6, no. 1 (2005): 55–74. An examination of how religious extremists resort to coercion, violence, or generating fear to realize their goals in the political policy sphere.

Douthat, Ross. "The God Vote." *Atlantic Monthly* 294, no. 2 (2004): 52–53. This article examines the relationship between religious belief and voting behavior in terms of U.S. demographics. The author shows that churchgoing is, increasingly, a valid predictor of voting behavior, particularly among Christian fundamentalists.

Green, Joshua. "God's Foreign Policy." *Washington Monthly* 33, no. 11 (2001): 26–34. The author examines the views of Christian fundamentalists on the causes of the September 11 attacks, as well as their view of how U.S. foreign policy should be formulated in response to those attacks.

———. "Second Coming." *Atlantic Monthly* 293, no. 3 (2004): 32–34. This article discusses the (former) Religious Right leader Ralph Reed and examines his role as a major voice in right-wing politics in the United States.

McAlister, Melani. "Prophecy, Politics, and the Popular: The 'Left Behind' Series and Christian Fundamentalism's New World Order." *South Atlantic Quarterly* 102, no. 4 (2003): 773–799. The author analyzes Christian fundamentalists' beliefs in the Antichrist, Armageddon, and the end times and how these beliefs influence their ideas about public policy and government. The article also examines the Left Behind series of fiction books by Tim LaHaye that describe the rapture of the believers and the doom of all others. This eschatology is related to U.S. policy, both domestic (environment) and foreign (Israel-Palestine conflict).

"Pulpit Politics Is Free Speech." Editorial. *U.S. News and World Report* 145, no. 11 (2008): 10. This editorial examines rules in the code of the Internal Revenue Service that prohibit the clergy from endorsing political candidates from the pulpit. The editorial argues that this is a violation of free speech.

Segady. T. W. "Traditional Religion, Fundamentalism, and Institutional Transition in the 20th Century." *The Social Science Journal* 43 (2006): 197–209. An in-depth, historical analysis of Christian fundamentalism in the 20th century, its origins and its influence on the state and civic institutions.

Stackhouse, John G., Jr. "A Variety of Evangelical Politics." *Christianity Today* 52, no. 11 (2008): 52–57. The author examines the American evangelical movement in terms of its political diversity, showing that it is not politically monolithic.

ISLAM: GENERAL WORKS AND EARLY HISTORY
Books

Armstrong, Karen. *Islam: A Short History.* New York: Modern Library, 2000. A brief and well-written description of the tenets of Islam by one of the best modern writers on religion.

———. *Muhammad: A Biography of the Prophet.* San Francisco: Harper, 1993. A thorough and readable account of the life of Muhammad, the prophet and founder of Islam.

Aslan, Reza. *No God but God: The Origins, Evolution, and Future of Islam.* New York: Random House, 2005. A highly interesting, provocative, and well-written best seller that explicates Islam and Islamic thought from its beginnings to today.

Egger, Vernon. *A History of the Muslim World: The Making of a Civilization, to 1405.* Upper Saddle Creek, N.J.: Pearson Prentice Hall, 2004. A complete history of the Muslim people to the early 15th century.

———. *A History of the Muslim World: A Global Community, 1260–Present.* Upper Saddle Creek, N.J.: Pearson Prentice Hall, 2007. This second volume reveals Muslim history to the present day.

Fletcher, Richard. *The Cross and the Crescent: Christianity and Islam from Muhammad to the Reformation.* London: Penguin Books, 2003. A brief but complete introduction to the history of the interaction between Christianity and Islam since the time of the Prophet.

Goddard, Hugh. *A History of Christian-Muslim Relations.* Chicago, Ill.: New Amsterdam Books, 2000. A comprehensive historical overview of the relationship between these two religions, from their earliest interactions to the present day.

Halliday, Fred. *Nation and Religion in the Middle East.* London: Lynne Reiner Publishers, 2000. An in-depth examination of how Islam has shaped the nations and the politics of the Middle East.

Hodgson, Marshall G. S. *The Venture of Islam: The Classical Age (Vol. 1); The Venture of Islam: The Expansion of Islam in the Middle Periods (Vol. 2); The Venture of Islam: The Gunpowder Empires and Modern Times (Vol. 3).* Chicago, Ill.: University of Chicago Press, 1977. A classic work on the history of Islam and Islamic civilizations, from the inception of the religion to the 20th century.

Lapidus, Ira. *A History of Islamic Societies.* Cambridge: Cambridge University Press, 2002. A thorough overview of Islamic societies around the world and throughout Islamic history, with particular attention paid to culture, identity, and political philosophy.

Annotated Bibliography

Nasr, Seyyed Hossein. *Islam: Religion, History, Civilization.* San Francisco, Calif.: HarperCollins, 2002. A short, readable introduction to Islamic beliefs, practices, and history, including its influence on the modern state.

Newman, N. A., ed. *The Early Christian-Muslim Dialogue: A Collection of Documents from the First Three Islamic Centuries (632–900 A.D.). Translations with Commentary.* Hatfield, Pa.: Interdisciplinary Biblical Research Institute, 1993. An illuminating volume of primary source materials in translation that reveal the initial relationships between Islam and Christianity.

Norman, Daniel. *Islam and the West: The Making of an Image.* Oxford, England: One World Publishers, 1993. A classic work that provides an in-depth analysis of the theology, philosophy, and practice of Islam and western Christianity, from the Middle Ages to the present. The author analyzes each group's view of the "other," and he shows how historical events and concepts have helped shape how practitioners of these two major religions view each other today.

Peters, F. E., ed. *A Reader on Classical Islam.* Princeton, N.J.: Princeton University Press, 1991. An excellent compilation of original classical Islamic texts in translation.

Ridgeon, Lloyd, ed. *Islamic Interpretations of Christianity.* New York: St. Martin's Press, 2001. Essays that explore and explain the diverse views of Muslims about Christianity and the West, based on the writings of Islamic scholars from ancient times to the present day.

Rippen, Andrew. *Muslims: Religious Beliefs and Practices: The Formative Period.* New York: Routledge, 2001. A detailed description and discussion of Islamic beliefs and practices in the first centuries after the religion's founding.

Yusuf Ali, Abdullah. *The Meaning of the Holy Qu'ran.* Beltsville, Md.: Amana Publications, 2004. This is judged to be one of the best translations, with commentary, of the Qu'ran, the holy book of Islam.

Articles and Papers

Brierley, Natalie, and Antonia Maqueda. "More Voices from the Muslim World." *New Statesman* 133, no. 4705 (2004): 26–27. This article contains short interviews with Muslims to elicit their feelings about changes taking place within the Islamic religion. Includes background and a discussion of modern Islamic fundamentalism and terrorism.

Dickens, Mark. "Islam's Sunni and Shia." *Calliope* 19, no. 3 (2008): 40–41. This article explains the historical background and theological reasons for the sectarian split within Islam.

"The Power of Islam." *Current Events* 101, no. 16 (2002): 1–5. An overview of the Islamic religion, including its history and beliefs, with a discussion of the impact of terrorist attacks.

Ryan, Patrick J. "The Roots of Muslim Anger." *America* 185, no. 17 (2001): 8–16. This article discusses the history of Islam and Islamic militancy, including Muslim anger resulting from less than optimal contacts with the Western world, and how these feelings continue in the Muslim world today. The author examines Muslim anger in terms of tensions between traditional religio-political governance and current trends toward democratization.

ISLAM, POLITICS, AND THE STATE
Books

About, El Fadi, et al. *Islam and the Challenge of Democracy.* Princeton, N.J.: Princeton University Press, 2004. The tension between traditional Islamic teachings and the desire for democratic government in Muslim nations.

Abu-Rabi, Ibrahim M. *Intellectual Origins of Islamic Resurgence in the Modern Arab World.* Albany: SUNY Press, 1996. The author traces the ideas of modern Islamists to the great thinkers and philosophers of Islam throughout history.

Akbarzadeh, Shahra, and Abdullah Saeed. *Islam and Political Legitimacy.* London: Routledge, 2003. An explication of the necessary role Islam plays in the development of a political system that is seen as legitimate by the Muslim population.

Ayoob, Mohammed. *The Many Faces of Political Islam: Religion and Politics in the Muslim World.* Ann Arbor: University of Michigan Press, 2007. A thorough examination of political Islam in all its forms and how the Islamic religion influences politics in Muslim countries.

Barber, Benjamin R. *Jihad vs. McWorld: Terrorism Challenges Democracy.* New York: Ballantine Books, 2001. A highly readable account of the Islamic culture clash with the West, its corporate representatives in the Muslim world, and the impetus to anti-Western jihad and terrorism.

Brown, L. Carl. *Religion and the State: The Muslim Approach to Politics.* New York: Columbia University Press, 2000. The author examines the history of Islam and how its relationship to politics has changed, from the earliest days of the religion to today's tensions between fundamentalist and moderate Muslims.

Butterworth, Charles E., et al., eds. *Between State and Islam.* Cambridge: Cambridge University Press, 2001. Essays that examine how Muslims interact with and feel about the different political systems in which they live, and their relationship with Islamic law.

Eickelman, D. F., and James Piscatori. *Muslim Politics.* Princeton, N.J.: Princeton University Press, 1996. An excellent overview of Muslim politics and the role of Islam in the political sphere.

Esposito, John L., ed. *Political Islam: Revolution, Radicalism, or Reform?* Boulder, Colo.: Rienner, 1997. These essays stress the diversity that exists within resurgent Islam and the impacts that globalization and the West may have on the shape of developing Islamic states.

Fatah, Tarek. *Chasing a Mirage: The Tragic Illusion of an Islamic State.* Hoboken, N.J.: Wiley & Sons, 2008. An analysis of the Islamic state as envisioned by traditional and fundamentalist Muslims, with an explication of why this Islamic ideal may never be realized.

Feldman, Noah. *After Jihad: America and the Struggle for Islamic Democracy.* New York: Farrar, Strauss, and Giroux, 2003. An in-depth look at how U.S. foreign policy, as well as other forms of influence, have affected the development, or stunting, of democracies in the Islamic world.

Annotated Bibliography

———. *The Fall and Rise of the Islamic State.* Princeton, N.J.: Princeton University Press, 2008. A detailed and insightful look at the history of the Islamic state, from its subjugation by the West to its current resurgence.

Fuller, Graham E. *The Use of Political Islam: The Future of Political Islam.* New York: Palgrave, 2003. The author explains how Islam's views of the world and politics not only reinforce the well-being and identity of Muslims, but also can sometimes be beneficially applied to Western social and political institutions.

Kamrava, Mehran. *The Modern Middle East: A Political History since the First World War.* Berkeley: University of California Press, 2005. A detailed history of the political forces that have shaped the Middle East and the political response and adaptation of the region's nations.

Khan, M. A. Muqtedar, ed. *Islamic Democratic Discourse: Theory, Debates, and Philosophical Perspectives.* Lanham, Md.: Lexington Books, 2006. These essays take different viewpoints on the prospects for democracy in Islamic nations, based on Islamic history, theology, and philosophy.

Lacy, Robert. *The Kingdom: Arabia and the House of Saud.* New York: Harcourt, Brace Jovanovich, 1981. In this best-selling book, the author traces the rise of the House of Saud and its capitulation to the fundamentalist Wahhabi sect. He narrates how this relationship has shaped the political and religious landscape of modern Saudi Arabia.

Mackey, Sandra. *The Iranians: Persia, Islam, and the Soul of a Nation.* New York: Dutton Books, 1996. This is a well-written and fascinating account of the history, culture, and religion of Iran. The book traces the development of Iranian religion and politics from ancient Zoroastrianism through the Iranian Revolution and beyond. Throughout, the author explains the relationship between religion and the culture, politics, and identity of the Iranian people. A must-read for anyone interested in the spirit and history of Iran.

Madelung, Wilferd. *The Succession to Muhammad: A Study of the Early Caliphate.* New York: Cambridge University Press, 1997. The author reexamines the historical conflict over finding a successor to Muhammad and suggests how these tensions shaped the rule of the first five caliphs; these ideological and theological concepts are also related to the development options in Islamic states today.

Majid, Anouar. *The Politics of Feminism in Islam.* Chicago, Ill.: University of Chicago Press, 2002. The author discusses the role of women in resurgent Islamic societies and rejects the idea that only in Western culture can women achieve rights and equality. However, the author argues that finding a path to democracy will improve the lives of women, and all of society, in Islamic states.

Mandaville, Peter. *Global Political Islam.* New York: Taylor and Francis, 2007. A worldwide overview of the political systems in Islamic states and their foundations, beliefs, and laws.

Marty, Martin E., and R. Scott Appleby, eds. *Fundamentalism and the State.* Chicago, Ill.: University of Chicago Press, 1993. An excellent compilation of essays that explore the various influences Islamic fundamentalism has on the state and society.

Mernisi, Fatima. *Islam and Democracy: Fear of the Modern World.* Cambridge, Mass.: Perseus Press, 2002. The author explains how modern secular democracy engenders a fear of a loss of faith and a corruption of Islam among many Muslims around the world.

an-Nairn, Abdullahi. *Islam and the Secular State: Negotiating the Future of Sharia.* Cambridge, Mass.: Harvard University Press, 2008. The author sets forth some possible approaches that might reconcile strict Islamic law (sharia) with the development of a secular state in Islamic nations.

Nasr, Seyyed Vali Reza. *Islamic Leviathan: Islam and the Making of State Power.* New York: Oxford University Press, 2001. An examination of the tenets of Islam and the views and practices of Muslims that tend toward the creation of an authoritarian state.

Roy, Olivier. *The Failure of Political Islam.* Cambridge, Mass.: Harvard University Press, 1994. This volume provides an in-depth look at why political systems based on Islamic law too often devolve into nondemocratic, totalitarian regimes.

———. *Globalized Islam: The Search for a New Ummah.* New York: Columbia University Press, 2006. A careful examination of the changes the Islamic community (*umma*) is undergoing as Muslim populations grow in Western countries and around the world.

Safi, Omid, ed. *Progressive Muslims: On Justice, Gender, and Pluralism.* Oxford, England: Oneworld Press, 2003. A study of the "other" side of Islam, in which progressive thinkers discuss the potential of Islamic states for developing political systems that embrace justice and human rights.

Shadid, Anthony. *Legacy of the Prophet: Despots, Democrats, and the New Politics of Islam.* Boulder, Colo.: Westview Press, 2002. The author traces the historical interpretations of Muhammad's teachings to show how they have variously given rise to different forms of government historically, though there is a movement today toward fundamentalism.

Takeyh, Ray, and Nikolas K. Gvosdev. *The Receding Shadow of the Prophet: The Rise and Fall of Radical Political Islam.* Westport, Conn.: Praeger, 2004. The authors contend that it is very likely that Muslim nations and peoples will increasingly abandon strict Islamic law and begin to adopt more secular political institutions.

Tibi, Bassam. *Islam between Culture and Politics.* London: Palgrave, 2002. The author reflects on the potential for retaining Islamic culture while developing a more secular form of democratic government in Islamic nations.

Vertovec, Steven, and Ceri Peach, eds. *Islam in Europe: The Politics of Religion and Community.* New York: St. Martin's Press, 1997. An examination of how European Muslims view and respond to Western xenophobia, nationalism, and secularism, as well as their efforts to maintain a Muslim identity and community within Europe.

Articles and Papers

Anderson, L. "Arab Democracy: Dismal Prospects." *World Policy Journal* 18 (Fall 2001): 53–60. The social, theological, economic, and political events and concepts that are making the march toward democracy increasingly remote in the Arab world.

Brown, N. J. "Shari'a and the State in the Modern Muslim Middle East." *International Journal of Middle East Studies* 29 (1997): 359–376. An in-depth look at how sharia law is increasingly affecting politics and governance in the nations of the Middle East.

Cantori, Louis J. "Civil Society, Liberalism, and the Corporatist Alternative in the Middle East." *Middle East Studies Association Bulletin* 31, no. 1 (1997): 34–41. The author explains in detail why the liberal, corporatist worldview of the West does not fit in with centralized powers found in the Middle East.

Chehabi, H. E. "Religion and Politics in Iran: How Theocratic Is the Islamic Republic?" *Deadalus* 120, no. 3 (1991): 69–92. This article analyzes how theocratic the Iranian state really is, discussing the power of the clergy on formulating public policy and the supposed role of democracy in Iran.

Fuller, Graham E. "The Future of Political Islam." *Foreign Affairs* 81, no. 2 (2002): 48–60. In this article, the author examines the impact of the September 11 attacks on the Muslim world. The article discusses the attacks in terms of how they might affect Muslim opinion about politics: Will Muslim politics be radicalized or democratized as a result of terrorism?

"Islam and Politics." *Third World Quarterly*. A special issue. 10, no. 2 (1988). The articles in this issue of the journal remain relevant, as they explicate the intricacies and problems found within Islam and the state.

Kramer, Martin. "Islam vs. Democracy." *Commentary* 95, no. 1 (1993): 35–43. This article takes an in-depth look at Islamic fundamentalism and evaluates its influence on potential democratization in Islamic states.

"The Law of Man or the Law of God?" *Economist* 368, no. 8341 (2003): 10–11. This article provides an extensive examination of the potential for democratic governance in Islamic nations.

McBeth, John. "The Case for Islamic Law." *Far Eastern Economic Review* 165, no 33 (2002): 12–15. This article presents arguments and evidence to show the many benefits, both political and economic, for a state whose politics are based on Islamic law.

Sinclair, Morgan. "The Two Sharias." *Weekly Standard* 11, no. 8 (2005): 35–37. This article compares the sharia law of traditional Islam and the far more extreme sharia that has emerged from the Islamic extremist community. The author relates extremist sharia more to ethnic traditions that the teachings of Islam.

ISLAM: FUNDAMENTALISM AND TERRORISM
Books

Ahmed, Rashid. *Taliban: Militant Islam, Oil and Fundamentalism in Central Asia.* New Haven, Conn.: Yale University Press, 2001. A deeply researched, insightful, and thorough explication of the history and policies that led to formation of the Taliban, al-Qaeda, and other Islamic fundamentalist movements and groups.

Allen, Charles. *God's Terrorists: The Wahhabi Cult and the Hidden Roots of Modern Jihad.* London: Abacus Press, 2006. This is the gripping story of how the obscure, fundamentalist Wahhabi cult rose from a small sect in the Arabian desert to become power brokers in Saudi Arabia and from there to being a major influence on fundamentalist Muslims in many Islamic nations.

Appleby, R. Scott, ed. *Spokesmen for the Despised: Fundamentalist Leaders of the Middle East.* Chicago, Ill.: University of Chicago Press, 1997. Revealing and fascinating interviews with many of the prime movers in the fundamentalist Islamic movements of this region.

Bergeson, Albert. *The Sayyid Qutb Reader.* London: Routledge, 2007. Primary source material from and about Sayyid Qutb, whose work inspired al-Qaeda and other fundamentalist and terrorist organizations, with explanation and commentary by the author.

Bergin, Peter L. *Holy War, Inc.: Inside the Secret World of Osama bin Laden.* New York: Free Press, 2001. A detailed look at how al-Qaeda functions, with a focus on bin Laden.

Bonney, Richard. *Jihad: From Qu'ran to Bin Laden.* New York: Palgrave: 2006. The author traces jihad from its original meaning as given in scripture to its many reinterpretations throughout history, up to and including its use by al-Qaeda.

Cook, David. *Martyrdom in Islam.* New York: Cambridge University Press, 2007. An in-depth historical and theological analysis of suicide in the name of Islam throughout history and in different contexts.

Gray, John. *Al Qaeda and What It Means to Be Modern.* London: New Press, 2005. In this volume, this well-known and prolific writer expands his critique of modern globalization and neoliberal capitalism to include the consumerism, materialism, and amorality of today's Western culture and how it influences and tends to motivate acts of violence against our culture.

Juergensmeyer, M. *Terror in the Mind of God: The Global Rise of Religious Violence.* Berkeley: University of California Press, 2000. An examination of how God is increasingly invoked to justify terrorist acts and other forms of violence in the name of religion. The author analyzes religious violence from all sources, from fundamentalist Christians to al-Qaeda.

Kepel, Gilles. *Jihad: The Trail of Political Islam.* Cambridge, Mass.: Harvard University Press, 2002. The author explains how significant segments of Muslim population in Islamic nations around the world have been disenfranchised by government policies and have turned to fundamentalist Islam or even to jihad.

Laqueur, Walter, ed. *Voices of Terror: Manifestoes, Writings, and Manuals of al Qaeda, Hamas, and other Terrorists from Around the World and Throughout the Ages.* New York: Reed Press, 2005. A fascinating compendium of primary sources on terrorism throughout history.

Marshall, Paul A. *Radical Islam's Rules: The Worldwide Spread of Extreme Sharia Law.* Lanham, Md.: Rowman and Littlefield, 2005. Analysis of sharia law and explanations of why it is becoming the primary goal of Islamic terrorists and fundamentalists who want to create political systems based on sharia.

Marty, M. E., and R. Scott Appleby, eds. *Fundamentalisms and the State.* Chicago, Ill.: University of Chicago Press, 1993. An invaluable collection of essays that analyze how various forms of religious fundamentalism have affected politics and the state.

Annotated Bibliography

Pape, Robert A. *Dying to Win: The Strategic Logic of Suicide Terrorism.* New York: Random House, 2005. An examination of the psychological, theological, and political motivations that lead to suicide terrorism as a strategy for attaining political goals.

Qureshi, Emran, and Michael A. Sells, eds. *The New Crusades: Constructing the Muslim Enemy.* New York: Columbia University Press, 2003. These essays describe how Western attitudes toward Muslims and Islamic states are actually creating the anger and hostility that manifests itself as Islamic terrorism.

Rashid, Ahmed. *Taliban.* New Haven, Conn.: Yale University Press, 2001. A best-selling history and analysis of how the Taliban came to power in Afghanistan, their beliefs and principles, and their impact on fundamentalist Islam in the region.

Tibi, B. *The Challenge of Fundamentalism: Political Islam and the New World Disorder.* Berkeley: University of California Press, 1998. How the West and moderate Islamic nations can address the growth of Islamic fundamentalism, help create more democratic states, and prevent social and political chaos arising from Islamist militants.

Wright, Robin. *Sacred Rage: The Wrath of Militant Islam.* New York: Simon and Schuster, 2001. A highly readable account of the causes of anger against the West among militant Islamists in the Islamic world.

Articles and Papers

Eickelman, Dale F. "Bin Laden, the Arab 'Street', and the Middle East's Democracy Deficit." *Current History* 101, no. 651 (2002): 36–40. The author suggests that lack of acceptable outlets for political expression in many Islamic nations has caused a "democracy deficit," which in turn has led to Islamic extremism and terrorism.

Euben, R. L. "Killing for Politics: Jihad, Martyrdom, and Political Action." *Political Theory* 30 (2002): 4–35. A provocative analysis of the politics that underlie and impel Islamic fundamentalist violence.

Sardar, Ziauddin. "The Struggle for Islam's Soul." *New Statesman* 134, no. 4749 (2005): 10–12. This article shows that while most Muslims reject violence and terrorism, the mindset of the terrorists has deep roots within Islam. This produces a conflict within the Muslim community that must be resolved.

Taylor, M., and J. Horgan. "The Psychological and Behavioral Bases of Islamic Fundamentalism." *Terrorism and Political Violence* 13 (2001): 37–71. An extensive study of the psychology that leads to supporting or joining fundamentalist Islamic groups.

Woltering, R. "The Roots of Islamist Popularity." *Third World Quarterly* 23 (2002): 1,133–1,143. A historical analysis that shows why many people in Muslim nations are attracted to and/or support fundamentalist Islam.

Wright, Lawrence. "The Rebellion Within." *The New Yorker* (6/2/08). Available online. URL: http://www.newyorker.com/reporting/2008/06/02/080602fa_fact_wright/. In this insightful and revealing article, Wright shows how the major religious philosopher who inspired and championed al-Qaeda came to condemn the group's violent tactics. The article offers an inside look at the political jockeying for leadership between this intellectual leader and Ayman al-Zawahiri, who has been the public face of al-Qaeda for years and who rejects nonviolent jihad.

HINDUISM AND BUDDHISM
Books

Dalai Lama XIV. *A Simple Path: Basic Buddhist Teachings*. London: Thorsons, 2000. The fundamental teachings of the Buddha are presented simply and related to everyday life. Written by a true expert in the field.

Goldstein, Melvin C. *The Snow Lion and the Dragon: China, Tibet, and the Dalai Lama*. Berkeley: University of California Press, 1998. This book provides a comprehensive overview of the conflict between the Chinese government and Tibet, whose spokesman is the Dalai Lama.

Khan, Yasmin. *The Great Partition: The Making of India and Pakistan*. New Haven, Conn.: Yale University Press, 2007. The immense significance of the partition of India, including its religious causes and effects on both countries.

Powers, John. *A Concise Introduction to Tibetan Buddhism*. Ithaca, N.Y.: Snow Lion Publications, 2008. A well-written overview of the history and basic tenets of Tibetan Buddhism.

Rosen, Steven. *Essential Hinduism*. Westport, Conn.: Praeger, 2006. A comprehensive and readable introduction to the beliefs and practices of Hinduism.

Smith, David. *Hinduism and Modernity*. Malden, Mass.: Blackwell Publishers, 2003. An important examination of how Hinduism and Hindus are adapting to the changes brought on by the modern world.

Smith, Huston. *Buddhism: A Concise Introduction*. New York: Harper, 2003. A good overview of the beliefs and practices of different types of Buddhism.

Weber, Max. *The Religions of China: Confucianism and Taoism*. Glencoe, Ill.: Free Press, 1964. A classic work that delves into the formative religions of the Chinese people.

Articles and Papers

Anand, Dibyesh. "Tibet Matters." *World Today* 65, no. 4 (2009): 31–34. A discussion of the relations between China and Tibet and why the problem seems so intractable.

———. "The Violence of Security: Hindu Nationalism and the Politics of Representing 'the Muslim' as a Danger." *The Round Table* 94, no. 379 (2005): 203–215. An in-depth examination of how the Hindu nationalist view of Muslims, and its violent tendencies, compromises India's national security.

Chorley, Aysa. "Tibetan Voices: Remembering the 1959 Uprising." *History Today* 59, no. 3 (March 2009): 46–53. A look back at the Tibetan uprising in 1959 that led to the exile of the Dalai Lama, viewed from a historical as well as a modern perspective.

Liu, Melinda, and Sudip Mazumdar. "Gods of Politics." *Newsweek* 144 (12/20/04): 56. An interview with the exiled Dalai Lama of Tibet that includes his thoughts on the relationship between religion and the state.

Annotated Bibliography

Shuja, Sharif. "Indian Secularism: Image and Reality." *Contemporary Review* 257, no. 1,674 (2005): 38–42. A thoughtful and insightful look at the rise of Hindutva in India and its consequences for the development of a modern, secular state.

Tamminen, Tapio. "Hindu Revivalism and the Hindutva Movement." *Temenos* 32 (1996): 221–238. A historical overview of the rise of Hindu nationalism in India and its effects on Indian culture and the state.

Thurman, Robert. "Fear and Nonviolence: China and Tibet." *Tikkun* 21, no. 5 (2008): 24–71. An extensive examination into the relations between the two countries, the plight of the Tibetans, and how the nation might achieve some autonomy.

NONPRINT RESOURCES

9/11 through Saudi Eyes. 53 min. Princeton, N.J.: Films for the Humanities and Sciences, 2003. DVD. Interviews with the families and neighbors of some of the 9/11 terrorists illuminate the motivation behind the act and the different ways Saudis view the event.

Al Qaeda 2.0. 46 min. Princeton, N.J.: Films for the Humanities and Sciences, 2003. DVD. A look at the terrorist organization after the attacks of September 2001.

Apocalypse. 60 min. Boston: PBS/WGBH Frontline, 1999. VHS. A clear-eyed view of apocalypticism in the United States, with an examination of its basis in Scripture (the Book of Revelation) and other writings, both ancient and modern, with a discussion of these beliefs and their influence on American society by religious and social scholars.

The Battle for Islam. 63 min. Princeton, N.J.: Films for the Humanities and Sciences, 2005. DVD. A far-reaching exploration of Islam post-9/11, with different views of the religion from interviews with Islamic scholars, and counterpoint from Muslim citizens in several Islamic nations.

The Battle for the Bible. 60 min. Princeton, N.J.: Films for the Humanities and Sciences, 2004. DVD. Efforts of the Southern Baptists to impose a literal interpretation of the Bible on American citizens via legislation and the courts.

The Birth of a New Religion: Christianity in the 1st and 2nd Centuries. 48 min. Princeton, N.J.: Films for the Humanities and Sciences, 1999. DVD. Historical overview of the development of Christianity during its first 200 years.

Bloody Cartoons: Freedom of Expression and the Clash of Cultures. 54 min. Princeton, N.J.: Films for the Humanities and Sciences, 2008. DVD. This film explores the violent Muslim reaction to the cartoons published in a Danish newspaper in 2005 that were interpreted as insulting the prophet Muhammad. Freedom of religion and speech are examined, as are the conflicts in interpretation of these freedoms by Western and Islamic cultures.

Buddha: The Path to Enlightenment. 43 min. Princeton, N.J.: Films for the Humanities and Sciences, 1999. DVD. An overview of the teachings of the Buddha and Buddhist beliefs and practice.

Buddhism. 57 min. Princeton, N.J.: Films for the Humanities and Sciences, 1999. DVD. The story of Buddha and Buddhism, with interviews with the Dalai Lama.

RELIGION AND THE STATE

Changing Christianity: From Schism to Ecumenism. 55 min. Princeton, N.J.: Films for the Humanities and Sciences, 1998. DVD. The effects of the French Revolution on the church and the state, especially in Europe.

Christian Zionism and the Rhetoric of Redemption. Bill Moyers's Journal. 58 min. New York: PBS/WNET, 2007. DVD. An interview with Pastor John Hagee, leader of Christians United for Israel, who describes why many Christian fundamentalists are strong supporters of Israel in order to fulfill a biblical prophecy regarding the "end of days."

Constantine's Sword. 95 min. Brooklyn, N.Y.: First Run Features, 2008. DVD. A dramatic look at the dark side of Christianity, when religion, politics, and military power converge to dreadful effect. Covers events from history to the present.

Contemporary Life vs. the Constitution. 60 min. Princeton, N.J.: Films for the Humanities and Sciences, 1987. DVD. The tensions between modern American life and the new freedoms it demands and the Constitution as it was written.

Crusaders and Schism in the East: Christianity in the 11th and 12th Centuries. 48 min. Princeton, N.J.: Films for the Humanities and Sciences, 1999. DVD. An examination of the Crusades and the Church during the late Middle Ages.

The Dark Ages and the Millennium: Christianity in the 9th and 10th Centuries. 48 min. Princeton, N.J.: Films for the Humanities and Sciences, 1999. DVD. A history of the Church and Christianity during the Dark Ages.

Edge of Islam. 25 min. Oley, Pa.: Bullfrog Films, 2008. A close look at the lives of three young Muslims facing a choice between their faith and accepting a secular future.

Essentials of Faith: Islam. 24 min. Princeton, N.J.: Films for the Humanities and Sciences, 2006. DVD. An explanation of the Five Pillars of Islam, and the religion's influence on society, culture, and politics.

Europe in the Middle Ages: A Way out of Darkness. 212 min. Princeton, N.J.: Films for the Humanities and Sciences, 2004. Four DVDs. An in-depth study of the medieval period in Europe, with emphasis on the role of religion and the church on all aspects of life at that time.

Examining Islam. 74 min, Princeton, N.J.: Films for the Humanities and Sciences, 2006. DVD. A compilation of PBS's *NewsHour* segments explaining the Islamic religion and beliefs.

Friends of God: The Evangelical Movement in America. 58 min. Princeton, N.J.: Films for the Humanities and Sciences, 2007. DVD. The rise and growth of the Christian evangelical movement in the United States is explored and analyzed.

Global Jihad. 22 min. Princeton, N.J.: Films for the Humanities and Sciences, 2004. DVD. From an ABC News special, this film examines terrorism and al Qaeda-style Islamic fundamentalists.

God and Politics. 270 min. Princeton, N.J.: Films for the Humanities and Sciences, 2005. Four DVDs. Four films that explore in-depth the way U.S. Christianity has changed, its diversity, and the influence of each type on society, the culture, and politics.

Hinduism. 57 min. Princeton, N.J.: Films for the Humanities and Sciences, 1999. DVD. An overview of the religious beliefs and practices of Hinduism.

Annotated Bibliography

Human Weapon. 55 min. Brooklyn, N.Y.: Icarus Films, 2002. DVD. A sociological and psychological analysis of suicide bombers, including interviews with experts.

Inside a Shari'a Court. 53 min. Princeton, N.J.: Films for the Humanities and Sciences, 2007. DVD. An unbiased documentary view of the proceedings in a sharia court hearing a variety of cases and handing down different decisions. These decisions are evaluated in light of Western ideas of justice and punishment.

Islam and Christianity. 105 min. Princeton, N.J.: Films for the Humanities and Sciences, 2004. Three DVDs. A thorough study of the differences and similarities between these two major religions.

Islam and Pluralism. 30 min. Princeton, N.J.: Films for the Humanities and Sciences, 1993. DVD. An examination of how different governments have reconciled societal pluralism with the tenets of Islam.

Islam: Empire of Faith. 160 min. New York: PBS/WNET, 2005. DVD. This three-part series, narrated by Ben Kingsley, presents a comprehensive overview of Islamic faith and beliefs, Muslim culture, and profiles of different Muslim believers from a variety of Muslim nations.

Islam: Facing East, Facing West: A NOW with Bill Moyers Special. 182 min. Princeton, N.J.: Films for the Humanities and Sciences, 2002. Four DVDs. This series offers an extensive examination of conflict between Christian and Muslim cultures, including how each religion influenced the society and politics in the West and in selected Muslim nations.

The Islamic State. 30 min. Princeton, N.J.: Films for the Humanities and Sciences, 1993. DVD. An exploration of Islam's influence on governance and the state.

Islam in America. 48 min. Princeton, N.J.: Films for the Humanities and Sciences, 2003. DVD. The film follows the daily lives of several Muslim Americans to highlight the tensions and problems they face.

Islam: There Is No God but God. 52 min. New York: TimeLife Films, 1978. An in-depth look at the beliefs and practices of Islam. A classic documentary.

Islam vs. Islamists: A NOW with Bill Moyers Special. 58 min. Princeton, N.J.: Films for the Humanities and Sciences, 2002. DVD. An in-depth discussion comparing moderate and extremist Islam.

Jesus Camp. 84 min. New York: A&E Indie Films, 2006. DVD. An unflinching look at the sometimes shocking indoctrination the children of fundamentalist Christians undergo at a religious summer camp.

Jesus Politics: The Bible and the Ballot. 90 min. Brooklyn, N.Y.: Icarus Films, 2008. DVD. This film examines the role of conservative Christian activists in the politics of the United States.

Jewish Law. 200 min. Princeton, N.J.: Films for the Humanities and Sciences, 2004. Four DVDs. This four-part series looks at Jewish law as it relates to the home, work, religious practice, and the community and politics.

Kundun. 134 min. Burbank, Calif.: Buena Vista Pictures, 1997. The story of the current Dalai Lama of Tibet, told and filmed brilliantly by director Martin Scorsese.

Mormons. 240 min. Boston: PBS/WGBH *Frontline,* 2006. DVD. This series takes a close look at the formation, development, and beliefs of American Mormons. It follows the religion from its founding, through its years of persecution, to its current politically influential role in the nation and its policies.

Muhammad: The Voice of God. 44 min. Princeton, N.J.: Films for the Humanities and Sciences, 1994. DVD. A film that explores and explains the life and teaching of the prophet Muhammad.

Muslims. 60 min. Boston: PBS/WGBH, 2002. An examination of Muslim identity in nations around the world, including Egypt, Nigeria, Turkey, and Iran.

Pat Robertson's University. Bill Moyers's Journal. 58 min. New York: PBS: WNET, 2007. DVD. An in-depth examination of the fundamentalist Christian university; its teaching, mission, and impact on U.S. public policy.

The Politics of Belief: Protestantism and the State. 60 min. Princeton, N.J.: Films for the Humanities and Sciences, 2006. DVD. An examination of Protestantism's influence on the state and politics from the time of Luther to modern Christian fundamentalists.

The Protestant Revolution. 240 min. Princeton, N.J.: Films for the Humanities and Sciences, 2006. Four DVDs. This series looks at key aspects of Protestantism, including its influence on the family, on the value of work, and on politics and the state.

Quest for Change: The Movement toward Democracy in the Middle East. 30 min. Brooklyn, N.Y.: Icarus Films, 1994. DVD. This film looks at the tensions between Islam and democratic institutions and shows how moderate Islam seeks and is working toward an Islamic form of democracy in the region.

Reinventing the Taliban. 48 min. Princeton, N.J.: Films for the Humanities and Sciences, 2003. DVD. The increasing influence of the Taliban in Pakistan and the problems it creates for political stability in this nation and in the region.

Return of Allah: Shiite Muslims in Iraq. 54 min. Princeton, N.J.: Films for the Humanities and Sciences, 2003. DVD. A religious and historical overview of Shia Islam, concentrating on centuries of suppression in Iraq, where many of its most holy sites are found.

Revolution of Conscience: The Life, Convictions, and Legacy of Martin Luther. 57 min. Princeton, N.J.: Films for the Humanities and Sciences, 2003. DVD. The events and thinking that led Luther to post his 95 Theses on the church door, and how this pivotal event led to the Reformation and dramatic changes in the state.

Shi'ism: Waiting for the Hidden Imam. 53 min. Brooklyn, N.Y.: Icarus Films, 2005. DVD. A clear explication of what Shia Islam is, its beliefs and practices, and its conflict with and differences from Sunni Islam.

Soul of India: Hindus and Muslims in Conflict. 58 min. Princeton, N.J.: Films for the Humanities and Sciences, 2002. DVD. An in-depth examination of the historical, political, and religious conflict between Muslims and Hindus in India.

Speaking to Power: A NOW with Bill Moyers Special Edition. 57 min. New York: PBS/WNET, 2003. An examination of the divisions among Christians on key social and political issues, such as social justice and living with political diversity.

Tibetan Buddhism: Politics, Power, and the Birth of the Dalai Lama. 46 min. Princeton, N.J.: Films for the Humanities and Sciences, 1999. DVD. The story of Tibetan Buddhism, its beliefs and tenets, with an emphasis on the current Dalai Lama.

Annotated Bibliography

Tibet: Cry of the Snow Lion. 103 min. Los Angeles: Earthworks Films, 2003. DVD. The history and country of Tibet, including the conflict between traditional Tibetan Buddhism and its suppression by China.

Tomorrow's Islam. 59 min. Princeton, N.J.: Films for the Humanities and Sciences, 2003. DVD. How Islam has changed from a formerly open and progressive religion to the fundamentalism that is becoming more widespread today and possible into the future.

Trials and Triumphs in Rome: Christianity in the 3rd and 4th Centuries. 48 min. Princeton, N.J.: Films for the Humanities and Sciences, 1999. DVD. The history of Christianity from persecution to the conversion of Constantine.

War and Peace. 136 min. Brooklyn, N.Y.: Icarus Films, 2002. DVD. An in-depth examination of religious fanaticism, extremism, and nationalism in India, Pakistan, Japan, and the United States. The film explores how religious extremism affects policy in these nations, particularly regarding issues of war and peace.

With God on Our Side: George W. Bush and the Rise of the Religious Right. 100 min. Brooklyn, N.Y.: Icarus Films, no date. DVD. An in-depth analysis of the role and influence of the Religious Right in the Bush administration and how the rise of the Right has affected politics and policy.

WEB SITES AND DOCUMENTS

The listing below is of Web sites that either contain documents that are important or pertinent to religion and the intersection of church and state, and that are only available online, or that maintain current news, background, or information and articles on relevant topics, or that have useful links to other Web sources of information on religion and/or religion and the state. Some Web sites maintain archives of previously published online information and/or articles. These may usually be found by clicking on Archives or a similar link within the Web site. Sometimes opening a current document will provide a list of articles on a similar topic archived on the Web site. When visiting a Web site, be aware of any bias it may have. This is especially important for Web sites run by particular religious denominations or those with a political viewpoint. Where possible, these points of view are stated in the Web site description.

Al-Islam. Available online. URL: http://www.al-islam.org/index.php. Accessed November 12, 2008. This fine Web site offers interesting information for Muslims and non-Muslims. Non-Muslims can learn about Islam's history and beliefs, explore the difference between Sunni and Shiite Muslims, read about the Haj, or browse through the site's extensive library that includes Islamic scriptures. The site also offers news and information for Muslims. Its most popular contents include a gallery of Islamic art online (including photos and calligraphy), an Islamic encyclopedia, and articles about Islam and the state, among other topics. A useful resource.

Answering Islam. Available online. URL: http://answering-islam.org/. Accessed November 13, 2008. This interesting Web site is devoted to the Christian argument against Islam and Islamic beliefs. It contains, for example, an ongoing dialogue about which religion "possesses" the "one true god" and publishes articles aimed at answering Muslims' objections to the notion of the Trinity. Links on the Web site reveal arguments and dialogues from Christians to Muslims on a wide variety of theological and social issues, including terrorism, Muhammad, etc. The site is obviously biased toward Christianity, but its point of view is nevertheless illustrative of one Christian position on Islam.

Azadpur, Mohammad. "Interpreting Political Violence in Islamic Philosophy." Available online. URL: http://etext.lib.virginia.edu/journals/ssr/issues/volume5/number1/ssr05_01_e04.html. Accessed November 12, 2008. This extensive article looks at Islamic philosophy and religion and shows that violence and terrorism are anathema to Islam.

Braden, Charles Samuel. *The Scriptures of Mankind: An Introduction*. Religion Online. Available online. URL: http://www.religion-online.org/showarticle.asp?title=704. Accessed November 13, 2008. The entirety of this classic book is available at this Web site. In 14 chapters, the renowned author and professor of literature and religion presents sacred literature and texts from preliterate societies to modern times. All religions are represented. The book contains descriptions and explanations of the primary source texts that make up most of the volume. This is an invaluable resource for basic primary source information on the scriptures and other religious texts that are the foundation of modern religions.

Brandon, James. "Koranic Duels Ease Terror." Available online. URL: http://www.csmonitor.com/2005/0204/p01s04-wome.htm. Accessed November 12, 2008. This article, from the *Christian Science Monitor*, explores the philosophical and theological changes occurring among some Islamic religious leaders. Where once many of these leaders supported, or tolerated, terrorism, many of them are now reinterpreting the Qu'ran as prohibiting the use of violence against civilians.

Brauer, Jerald C., ed. *Protestantism in America: A Narrative History*. Religion Online. Available online. URL: http://www.religion-online.org/showarticle.asp?title=1663. Accessed November 4, 2008. The entire 18-chapter volume is available at this Web site. The book covers the history of Protestantism in all its forms in America, from the early Puritans, through the Enlightenment, to recent times. Throughout, the author emphasizes the way the different forms of Protestantism affected governance and policy in the United States.

———. *Religion and the American Revolution*. Religion Online. Available online. URL: http://www.religion-online.org/showarticle.asp?title=1657. Accessed November 4, 2008. The entirety of this book is available online. The book contains three essays that examine in detail the influence of America's early religious beliefs and experiences on the American Revolution and its aftermath, as it progressed toward confirming the separation of church and state.

Braybrooke, Marcus. *What Can We Learn from Islam: The Struggle for True Religion*. Religion Online. Available online. URL: http://www.religion-online.org/show

Annotated Bibliography

article.asp?title=3269. Accessed November 14, 2008. The entire 11-chapter book written by Rev. Dr. Braybrooke is available at this Web site. The author first compares the tenets of Christianity and Islam, introduces Islam through its history and teachings, and then discusses the tensions between the "true" Islam and the trends toward Western secularization, even within Muslim nations. He also debunks the negative stereotypes some Westerners have about Muslims and describes the way in which the Muslim struggle to reconcile religious truth with modern materialism is relevant to our own societal problems.

Byassee, Jason. "What's Behind 'Left Behind?'" Religion Online. Available online. URL: http://www.religion-online.org/showarticle.asp?title=3045. Accessed November 5, 2008. In this fascinating article, the author reveals the theology, and the social values issues, that underpin the belief in the "Rapture" at the end times. The author explores why increasing numbers of fundamentalist Christians accept these concepts and believe in the imminence of the Second Coming and Armageddon.

Center for the Study of Law and Religion. Available online. URL: http://www.law.emory.edu/index.php?id=1570. Accessed October 21, 2008. This Web site contains articles about laws as they respond to or affect religion in the United States. It also offers news and a listing of events on this topic.

Chavanne, William Martin. "With God on Our Side: Reflections on the Religious Right." Religion Online. Available online. URL: http://www.religion-online.org/showarticle.asp?title=1658. Accessed November 3, 2008. The author, a professor of religion and public policy and a progressive Christian, explores the nature and beliefs of the Religious Right and discusses why contemporary American life may have generated the rise and popularity of fundamentalist and conservative Christianity in this country. The author maintains an unbiased view of this phenomenon, seeking to understand rather than judge.

Christopher Hitchens Online Directory. Available online. URL: http://www.buildupthatwall.com. Accessed November 10, 2008. The British writer, now a U.S. citizen, Christopher Hitchens is one of the most outspoken and eloquent proponents of the new atheism. His Web site contains links to numerous articles on disbelief and atheism, and why religion is no longer relevant or meaningful. One can also find his books (including the best-selling *God Is Not Great*), with excerpts, and a long list of links to his articles on atheism, interviews, and videos. Though one may not agree with him, Hitchens is one of the smartest and most eloquent writers on this topic today, and his works are worth reading.

Clarkson, Frederick. "Christian Reconstructionism: Theocratic Dominionism Gains Influence." Available online. URL: http://www.publiceye.org/magazine/v08n1/chrisre1.html. Accessed November 21, 2008. This article delves into the rising reconstructionist, or dominionist, Christian movement in America today. The author dissects the beliefs of reconstructionism (that the nation should be governed by biblical law) and why this movement is gaining strength among fundamentalist Christians.

Doland, Virginia M. "Totalitarian Evangelicalism." Religion Online. Available online. URL: http://www.religion-online.org/showarticle.asp?title=1668. Accessed

November 7, 2008. In this article the author explores the tendency of evangelical Christians to create and support strict hierarchical structures, from their churches to the state.

Falkowski, Lawrence. "Religion and Politics." Religion Online. Available online. URL: http: www.religion-online.org/showarticle.asp?title=1652. Accessed November 10, 2008. This article presents an historical overview of the interplay between church and state, or the influence religion and politics have on each other.

Islam. Available online. URL: http://uwacadweb.uwyo.edu/religionet/er/islam/index.htm. Accessed November 13, 2008. This Web site provides useful information about Islamic beliefs on many subjects, from the cosmos to worship and religious life. It also offers Islamic religious texts, as well as tales and stories from Islamic history and teachings. It has a very useful glossary of Islamic terms, and links to other Islamic Web sites.

Islam and Islamic Studies Resources. Available online. URL: http://uga.edu/islam/. Accessed November 13, 2008. This is an excellent Web site for learning about Islam and its history, its holy writings, the different forms of Islam, Islamic poetry and literature, Islamic theology and philosophy, jihad, terrorism, and a host of other topics. One can even find links to learning Arabic, Farsi (Persian), and other major Muslim languages. The Web site also offers numerous articles on a wide variety of topics relevant to Islam.

Islam Denounces Terrorism. Available online. URL: http://www.islamdenouncesterrorism.com/. Accessed November 12, 2008. This useful Web site provides access to numerous articles that show that terrorism and political violence are antithetical to the teachings of Islam. The Web site also offers books, some of which have chapters available online.

Islam for Today. Available online. URL: http://www.islamfortoday.com/. Accessed November 13, 2008. This Web site's mission is to be a guide to the religion of Islam. It offers articles about the Islamic religion from Islamic scholars and theologians as well as from Western converts. It also provides links to Islamic history and beliefs, and resources and information about many topics relevant to Islam, such as the contentious subject of Islam and women.

IslamiCity. Available online. URL: http://www.islamicity.com/. Accessed November 12, 2008. This is a Web site just stuffed with useful and interesting information about Islam, about what is going on in the Islamic community (both U.S. and abroad). It contains articles, papers, reviews, news and analysis, and videos of fascinating interviews with both Muslims and non-Muslims. One can even download Islamic television, radio, and other media from the site.

Kimball, Charles A. "Examining Islamic Militancy." Religion Online. Available online. URL: http://www.religion-online.org/showarticle.asp?title=2157. Accessed November 6, 2008. The author, a professor of religion and a Baptist minister, discusses militant Islam and its possible causes. He supports the view that, to a large extent, it has been U.S. foreign policy in Muslim nations—particularly U.S. support for despots and dictators, which undermines popular activism for a democratic state—that has triggered the intense resentment of the West that led to the attacks of 9/11 and continuing Islamic terrorism.

Latourette, Kenneth Scott. *Christianity through the Ages.* Religion Online. Available online. URL: http://www.religion-online.org/showarticle.asp?title=532. Accessed November 5, 2008. This 12-chapter online book covers the entire history of Christianity, from its earliest days to modern times. The author addresses Christianity's influence on the state, as both changed over time.

———. *The Unquenchable Light.* Religion Online. Available online. URL: http://www.religion-online.org/showarticle.asp?title=543. Accessed November 5, 2008. Originally written for the Noble lectures at Harvard University in 1966, this classic work is available in full at this Web site. The book details the origins and history of Christianity through what the author sees as its main periods of development and change. The book consists of nine chapters, each covering one time period in the history of the religion.

Lerner, Michael. "Why America Needs a Spiritual Left." Available online. URL: http://pubtheo.com/page.asp?pid=1517. Accessed November 21, 2008. This article, by a left-leaning and progressive rabbi, makes the case for a renewed sense of spirituality among those on the Left. The author argues persuasively that the rejection of all things spiritual, and especially religious, by progressives has created a damaging and ultimately unnecessary divide in the country and that the ability to speak of or accept spirituality will heal not only our politics but our society and culture.

Levenson, Jon D. "Do Christians and Muslims Worship the Same God?" Religion Online. Available online. URL: http://www.religion-online.org/showarticle.asp?title=3052. Accessed November 12, 2008. The first in a four-art article that reveals the similarities and differences in the way Christians and Muslims think of God and the way God is revealed in their holy books. The articles do not present a point of view but offer a fascinating contrast in the views of the two religions.

Marty, Martin E. "Religion and the Constitution: The Triumph of Practical Politics." Religion Online. Available online. URL: http://www.religion-online.org/showarticle.asp?title=182. Accessed November 11, 2008. In this article, the author explains the pragmatism, as well as the wisdom, of the writers of the U.S. Constitution. He focuses largely on the debate surrounding the wording and intent of the establishment clause.

Mishra, Pankaj. "Impasse in India." Religion Online. Available online. URL: http://www.religion-online.org/showarticle.asp?title=3382. Accessed November 3, 2008. Reprinted from the *New York Review of Books,* this article offers an in-depth look at two conflicts in India: that between tradition and rapid modernization and that between radical Hindu nationalists and the Muslim population.

Morgan, Kenneth W., ed. *Islam—The Straight Path: Islam Interpreted by Muslims.* Religion Online. Available online. URL: http://www.religion-online.org/showarticle.asp?title=1656. Accessed November 5, 2008. The entire volume is available online. Each of the 11 chapters in the book is written by a respected Muslim author on a specific aspect of Islam. Chapters include an explication of sharia law, the schism between Shia and Sunni Muslims, and Islamic culture and the state, among others.

Muslim Peace Fellowship. Available online. URL: http://mpf21.wordpress.com/. Accessed November 12, 2008. This Web site offers articles about the efforts of Muslims around the world to find peaceful solutions to some of the world's most intractable problems, such as the Israeli-Palestinian conflict. One can also read reports and papers about nonviolence in Islam, about Muslims working for peace, and about leaders in the Muslim peace movement.

Niebuhr, Reinhold. "Christian Faith and the World Crisis." Religion Online. Available online. URL: http://www.religion-online.org/showarticle.asp?title=381. Accessed November 10, 2008. The author, one of the most esteemed theologians of modern times, addresses the role of Christian faith and its relationship to world events. In this article, Niebuhr explores Christianity and Nazism, among other topics.

Novak, Michael. "Religion and Liberty: From Vision to Politics." Religion Online. Available online. URL: http: www.religion-online.org/showarticle.asp?title=955. Accessed November 13, 2008. In this article the author provides an extensive overview of how the idea of religious liberty was transformed into a cornerstone of modern democracies.

"The Other God: Lutheranism 101." Available online. URL: http://www.pubtheo.com/page.asp?pid=1338. Accessed November 11, 2008. This extensive article covers this story of Martin Luther, the beliefs of Lutherans, and Lutheranism's influence on attitudes, life, and the state today.

Peterson, Kurt W. "American Idol." Religion Online. Available online. URL: http://www.religion-online.org/showarticle.asp?title=3454. Accessed November 14, 2008. This article is an extensive study of the concept that the United States is a Christian nation that should be governed by Christian law. The article looks fairly at both sides of the issue.

Pierard, Richard V. "Standing the Founding Fathers on Their Heads." Religion Online. Available online. URL: http://www.religion-online.org/showarticle.asp?title=1682. Accessed November 12, 2008. The author, a professor of history, explores the impetus behind the creation of the "wall of separation between church and state" in the U.S. Constitution. He then goes on to show that this wall was originally intended to protect the majority Protestant sects and to prevent encroachment of Catholics on the body politic. The eventual, sometimes unintended, effects of this separation on its initial supporters is dissected.

Ramadan, Tariq. "A Struggle over Europe's Religious Identity." Available online. URL: http://www.iht.com/articles/2006/09/20/opinion/edramadan.php. Accessed November 18, 2008. This article, from the *International Herald Tribune*, is an insightful examination of the struggle of Muslims living in Europe to forge an identity that is both true to Islam and integrated into the secular society in which they live.

Religion and Law: International Document Database. Available online. URL: http://www.religlaw.org. Accessed November 5, 2008. This amazing Web site allows visitors to choose a nation, organization, or world region and explore the primary

Annotated Bibliography

source documents from that source that are related to religion and the law. It also offers news, information about events, and links to related Web sites. An interesting and useful site.

Religion and State Project. Available online. URL: http://www.biu.ac.il/soc/po/ras. Accessed November 5, 2008. This is the Web site for an Israeli group that conducts research into the relationship between religion and the state in countries around the world. It provides access to data for all the nations it has so far studied, revealing how citizens feel about religion and its role in politics, among other types of fascinating data.

Religion Online. Available online. URL: http://www.religion-online.org/. Accessed November 11, 2008. This wonderful Web site's home page offers numerous categories of links related to every aspect of religion. Click on a category to find numerous articles and sources of information on that topic. Truly an invaluable resource for anyone interested in religion and the issues of church and state.

Religious Freedom Page. Available online. URL: http://religiousfreedom.lib.virginia.edu. Accessed November 24, 2008. This Web site offers information about the importance of religion in life, but makes a cogent argument, through online data and papers, for the even more important separation of church and state in a democracy.

Religious Right Watch. Available online. URL: http://www.religiousrightwatch.com. Accessed November 9, 2008. This Web site offers news, information, and alerts about what is happening in the Religious Right community. The site is opposed to the efforts of the Religious Right to influence, if not take over, public policy. The site offers many links to articles, news, and information about the Religious Right and about those who oppose it.

Richard Dawkins Web page. Available online. URL: http://richarddawkins.net. Accessed November 9, 2008. This is the page for the scientist and outspoken British atheist Richard Dawkins. The Web site offers arguments in support of atheism from Dawkins and others who support his view. The first chapter of his book, *The God Delusion*, can be read free at this Web site.

RJ&L Religious Liberty Archive. Available online. URL: http://www.churchstatelaw.com/. Accessed November 12, 2008. This useful Web site describes itself as a repository of information and resources about state and federal laws pertaining to religious freedom in the United States. A free newspaper with articles on church and state is available free. The Web site links lead you to information about the history of religious freedom, historical materials, articles, and federal and state statutes on religion and the state. An excellent resource.

Separation of Church and State: The Constitutional Principle. Available online. URL: http://members.tripod.com/~cadnst/tnppage/tnpidx.htm. Accessed November 12, 2008. This Web site offers a wealth of information on the separation of church and state, including study guides, articles, information about relevant court cases, current news, and historical background on the issue.

Shinn, Roger. "The Old Question: Politics and Religion." Religion Online. Available online. URL: http://www.religion-online.org/showarticle.asp?title=388. Accessed

November 7, 2008. In this article, the author examines the role of the church in electoral politics, supporting the principle that churches, preachers, and priests do have an obligation to convey moral teachings but do not have the right to endorse or condemn particular candidates. That decision, the author argues, should be left to individual voters, who may or may not base their vote on the moral teachings of their church.

Shupe, Anson. "The Reconstructionist Movement on the New Christian Right." Religion Online. Available online. URL: http://www.religion-online.org/showarticle.asp?title=234. Accessed November 10, 2008. The author, an expert on the American Religious Right, examines the reconstructionist movement that is a growing part of conservative Christianity. Reconstructionism is the belief that the ideal state is modeled on Mosaic law and that the U.S. government should be rebuilt to uphold this ideal.

Siker, Jeffrey S. "The Bible and Public Policy." Religion Online. Available online. URL: http://www.religion-online.org/showarticle.asp?title=997. Accessed November 6, 2008. This thought-provoking article takes issue with the Christian fundamentalist idea that American foreign policy can be derived from the teachings of the Bible.

Sorkin, Madeleine. "Al-Qaeda's Defining Moment: The Prominence of the Scapegoat Strategy." Available online. URL: http://www.coloradocollege.edu/dept/RE/Sr Seminar04/Sorkinpaper.htm. Accessed November 12, 2008. This fascinating article examines the notion that al-Qaeda and similar terrorist groups are inspired to their acts of violence because they "scapegoat" the West as the cause of all the world's problems.

Todd, John M. *Luther: A Life*. Religion Online. Available online. URL: http://www.religion-online.org/showarticle.asp?title=801. Accessed November 10, 2008. This Web site offers the entire 17-chapter book by a noted historian of religion. The book details the life of Martin Luther, from his youth to his rebellion against the Catholic Church to the consequences of his actions: the development of Protestantism. The author also looks at how this new religion shaped states throughout Europe.

Wabash Center for Teaching and Learning in Theology and Religion. Available online. URL: http://www.wabashcenter.wabash.edu/resources/. Accessed October 25, 2008. This Web site is a virtual treasure trove of information, primarily Internet links, about all things relating to theology and religion, including religion and politics. If one clicks on Internet Guide, one gets a full page of topics; click on a topic and a list of numerous useful links and sources of information appear. This is truly an invaluable site for the study of religion, including religion and the state.

Wall, James M. "Religious Freedom: Tensions and Contentions." Religion Online. Available online. URL: http://www.religion-online.org/showarticle.asp?title=166. Accessed November 7, 2008. This article examines the history behind the crafting of the first ten amendments to the Constitution, the Bill of Rights, the history of their ratification by the states, and their interpretation in the courts over the last 200 years. He concentrates particularly on the establishment clause, and how it has been interpreted throughout U.S. history, and the rulings concerning the separation of church and state.

Westbrook, Robert. "Nullifiers and Insurrectionists: America's Antigovernment Tradition." Religion Online. Available online. URL: http://www.religion-online.org/showarticle.asp?title=2060. Accessed November 10, 2008. This article, a book review, delves into the cultural, political, and historical origins of Americans' distrust of government. The author examines the views of the founding fathers and explores how this uneasiness with powerful government found its way into the Constitution, the establishment clause, the wall of separation between church and state, and similar relevant issues.

Chronology

1000–961 B.C.E.

- Reign of King David, king of the Israelites; the golden age of biblical Israel

563 B.C.E.

- Birth of Siddhartha Gautama, the Buddha and founder of Buddhism

274–236 B.C.E.

- Reign of the Buddhist king Ashoka, of the Maurya Empire of India

164 B.C.E.

- Rule of the Maccabees over the Jews in Jerusalem

70 C.E.

- Roman destruction of the Temple in Jerusalem; start of Jewish Diaspora.

233

- Buddhism is introduced to Tibet.

325

- Constantine, emperor of the Western Roman Empire, adopts Christianity as the official religion.
- Officials, such as bishops, of the early Christian Church meet in Nicea, Greece, to formulate the definitive Christian Nicene Creed, which sets out official and acceptable Christian beliefs.

410–435

- Rome is sacked by invading "barbarians," including the Goths and the Vandals.

Chronology

610

- The "Night of Power and Excellence," when Muhammad first receives God's teachings from the Angel Gabriel.

622

- The *hijra*, when the prophet Muhammad and his followers travel to Medina, where the Prophet will be judge and ruler.

624

- Battle of Badr, in which Abu Bakr, the first Rightly Guided Caliph, defeats the Meccan army and establishes Islam throughout Arabia.

632–661

- Period when the *umma* was ruled by the four Rightly Guided Caliphs.

661–750

- Islamic Umayyad Empire

680

- ***October:*** Battle of Karbala in which Ali's son Husayn is killed; his body is mutilated and his head displayed by the Umayyads in Damascus. This marks the schism when the Shia, who support Ali and succession through the bloodline of the Prophet, break away from Sunni Islam.

719

- Muslims conquer Andalusia in Spain and rule there until 732, when they are defeated by Charles Martel.

750–1258

- Reign of the Islamic Abbasid Empire, whose capital was Baghdad and which fostered a rich culture and civilization.

751

- Frankish prince, Pepin the Short, is the first monarch to be anointed king by a Christian bishop.

800

- Pope Leo III crowns Charlemagne, a Frankish Christian, as Emperor of the West.
- Pope Nicholas II and his council decide that henceforth popes will be elected by cardinals.

RELIGION AND THE STATE

1075

- Pope Gregory VII issues his *Dictatus Papae*, returning investiture power to the church.

1095–1204

- Period of the four Christian crusades into the Holy Land to reclaim it for Christianity and the church.

1133–1189

- Reign of Henry II of England, who had Thomas Becket, Archbishop of Canterbury, murdered when he would not support the king against the power of the Roman church.

1258

- Abbasid Empire is destroyed by invading Mongols.

CA. 1300

- Period during which the orthodox, even radical, ibn Taymiyya wrote his influential works, which prescribed strict adherence to sharia as the true way of Islam.

1453–1919

- The Ottomans (Turks) of Anatolia establish and rule the vast Ottoman Empire, which falls only after World War I.

1501–1722

- The Islamic Safavid Empire rules Persia (Iran); it becomes influenced by Shiite rulers, and Shia Islam becomes the official religion of Persia.

1520–1566

- Reign of Suleyman the Magnificent, Ottoman emperor, at the height of Ottoman civilization

1565–1605

- Reign of Akbar, Islamic ruler of the Mughal Empire in India

1517

- *October 31:* Martin Luther nails his Ninety-five Theses to the door of a church in Wittenberg, Germany, thus initiating the Protestant Reformation.

Chronology

1522

- *August 24:* St. Bartholomew's Day Massacre in Paris; 2,000 Protestants are murdered by French Catholics.

1534

- England's King Henry VIII issues the Act of Supremacy, breaking with the Roman Church and creating the Church of England (the Anglican Church).

1571

- Battle of Lepanto, Greece, which halts the expansion of the Ottoman Empire

1618–1634

- Thirty Years' War in which Protestant German princes fought against the Holy Roman Empire

1619

- Legal establishment of the Anglican Church in the Virginia colony

1636

- Roger Williams banished from the Massachusetts Bay Colony by the intolerant Congregationalist (Puritan) community

1648

- Treaty of Westphalia ends the Thirty Years' War; gives equal rights to Protestants and Catholics.

1683

- Defeat of the Ottomans at the Siege of Vienna, blocking further Ottoman expansion in Europe

1730s–1740s

- First Great Awakening of evangelical revivalism in the American colonies

1744

- Al-Wahhab and ibn Saud join forces to convert Arabia to orthodox Islam and eventually to unite it into a single nation.

1776–1783

- American Revolution against British rule

1786

- Virginia passes Jefferson's Bill for Establishing Religious Freedom.

RELIGION AND THE STATE

1789

- States ratify U.S. Constitution

1789–1798

- French Revolution, in which the Roman church is severely curtailed and made subservient to the state. Attempts are made to outlaw church worship in France and replace it with a "revolutionary" religion worshipping Reason and a Supreme Being.

1791

- Ratification of the Bill of Rights, the first 10 amendments to the U.S. Constitution

1800s (EARLY)

- Second Great Awakening in the United States, accelerating the growth of dissident Protestant sects.

1804

- Napoléon Bonaparte has himself crowned emperor by Pope Pius VII.

1833

- Massachusetts is the last state to disestablish religion.

1854

- Know-Nothing Party is established to halt immigration of Catholics and to prevent U.S. Catholics from holding public office.

1860–1864

- U.S. Civil War; leads to decades in which southern white Protestants vote solidly Democratic, against the (Lincoln) Republicans who started the war.

1868

- Congress ratifies the Fourteenth Amendment to the Constitution.

1871

- German principalities are united into a German nation.

1879

- U.S. Supreme Court rules on the "Mormon case" *(Reynolds v. United States)*, stating that religious practice does not take precedence over civil law.

Chronology

1910–1915

- Publication in America of *The Fundamentals,* the reading of which leads to the terms *fundamentalist* and *fundamentalism.*

1914–1918

- World War I is fought primarily in Europe.

1915–1917

- The post–World War I Sykes-Picot Agreement carves up much of the Middle East, creating artificial states, colonies, and spheres of influence for Britain, Russia, France, and Italy.

1917

- The Bolshevik revolution in Russia overthrows the czar and establishes an atheistic communist state.

1919–1933

- Prohibition against selling and drinking alcoholic beverages in the United States; first established by the Nineteenth Amendment (1919) and ended by the Twenty-first Amendment (1933). Prohibition is an indication of the political influence of the Protestant pietist denominations.

1925

- Scopes trial in Tennessee, in which a high school teacher is convicted of violating a law prohibiting the teaching of evolution.

1928

- Egyptian Hassan al-Banna founds the Muslim Brotherhood, a radical Muslim organization, in Cairo.

1932

- *September 23:* The conversion and unification of Arabia is completed. The nation of Saudi Arabia is born.

1933

- Adolf Hitler is elected and becomes chancellor of Germany; his National Socialist (Nazi) Party gains control of the government. The Nazis institute the Reich Church in opposition to the German Protestant Church.

1939–1945

- World War II, primarily in Europe, in which the Allies fight against Nazi expansion

RELIGION AND THE STATE

1940

- U.S. Supreme Court applies the First Amendment's free exercise clause to the states.

1945

- U.S. Supreme Court applies the First Amendment's establishment clause to the states.

1948

- Creation of the state of Israel
- Assassination of Mohandas K. Gandhi, the great Indian independence leader, by a Hindu nationalist extremist

1949

- Communists take over the government of China; within months they attack and annex Tibet.

1951–1953

- Iran is led by the democratically elected Prime Minister Mossadeq. In 1953, he is overthrown in a CIA-run coup. The United States replaces him with the despotic Mohammad Reza Pahlavi, the shah of Iran.

1959

- *March 14:* The Dalai Lama is forced to flee Tibet after Chinese troops assault the Lhasa temple.

1960

- John F. Kennedy is elected as the first Catholic president of the United States.

1960s

- Europeans and European nations adopt more secular societies. Churches and religion no longer have significant input in politics.

1960–1962

- U.S. Supreme Court hears a number of cases involving prayer and Bible reading in public schools.

1964–1965

- Passage of the Civil Rights Act (1963) and the Voting Rights Act (1965), which alienated the South from the Democratic Party for decades.

Chronology

1966

- Sayyid Qutb, member of the Muslim Brotherhood and highly influential writer and thinker among Islamic extremists, is executed in Egypt after an assassination attempt on Egyptian president Gamal Abdul Nasser's life.

1967

- The Six-Day War in which Muslim powers in the Middle East attack Israel to regain control of Israeli-occupied lands. The Muslim nations are defeated by Israel, which defeat is experienced as a great humiliation by the Islamic nations and people.

1972

- U.S. Supreme Court exempts Amish teenagers from compulsory secondary education *(Wisconsin v. Yoder)*.

1973

- The U.S. Supreme Court decision in *Roe v. Wade* states that it is unconstitutional for the state to prevent a woman from terminating a pregnancy if she so chooses. The abortion issue becomes a lightning rod for Christian conservatives.

1977

- The nationalist Hindutva Bharatiya Janata Party forms in India.

1977–1980s

- Several important U.S. Christian evangelical organizations are founded, particularly the Moral Majority, the Christian Voice, the Christian Coalition, and the Family Research Council.

1979

- In Saudi Arabia, militant Sunnis take over the Grand Mosque; hundreds are killed in the battle to retake the mosque.
- The popular revolt of the Iranian people overthrows the shah and the Ayatollah Khomeini returns from exile to lead the Islamic Republic of Iran.

1981

- Assassins with ties to the Muslim Brotherhood assassinate President Anwar Sadat of Egypt.

1987

- U.S. Supreme Court addresses the teaching of creationism versus Darwinian evolution in public schools *(Edwards v. Aguillard)*.

RELIGION AND THE STATE

1989

- In France, the "affair of the headscarf" *(hijab)* begins and polarizes the nation over the issue of freedom of religious expression.

1990

- U.S. Supreme Court relaxes its "compelling interest" test for placing limitations on religious liberty *(Oregon Employment Division v. Smith)*.

1991

- Congress passes the Religious Freedom Restoration Act.

1997

- U.S. Supreme Court declares the Religious Freedom Restoration Act unconstitutional *(Boerne v. Flores)*.

2001

- **September 11:** Fundamentalist Muslim al-Qaeda operatives hijack jetliners in the United States and crash them into the World Trade Center and the Pentagon. One plane crashes in Pennsylvania.

2004

- The filmmaker Theo van Gogh is murdered in the Netherlands for making a film critical of the Muslim treatment of women.

2005

- Hurricane Katrina and the Terri Schiavo case cause many Americans to question the conservative Christian influence on the federal government.
- A Danish newspaper publishes cartoons lampooning the prophet Muhammad; riots ensue in Muslim countries and in Europe, and several people are killed.
- Many nights of rioting in French suburbs underscore the lack of employment and recognition of cultural diversity.

2008

- Barack Obama is elected U.S. president, carrying some formerly conservative Christian areas and states.

2009

- In India, the Congress Party wins a significant victory over the BJP in national elections and forms a government.

Glossary

Allah   the transcendent, monotheistic god of Islam.
Amish   a Christian faith dating to 16th-century Europe, which shuns modern ways of life and technology in favor of a simpler, nonmaterialistic life closer to God.
Anglicanism   the Church of England, originally much like the Catholic Church, but later highly Protestant, with a belief in the primacy of the Bible.
animism   belief that all or most things in the world are infused with spirit or a spirit, which can be propitiated or appeased for human benefit.
atheism   nonbelief in any type of god or deity.
Assemblies of God   the largest denomination of American Pentecostals.
ayatollah (pronounced eye uh toh' lah; Arabic: sign of God)   high-ranking Islamic cleric.
Baptists   Protestant Christian denomination that has no creed and whose sole authority stems from the Bible; the act of baptism is chosen freely by believers; baptism involves total immersion.
bourgeois   middle class, meaning acquisitive and materialistic.
caliph (Arabic: successor)   leader of the Muslim *umma;* the caliphate is ruled by the caliph.
Calvinism   a rigid Protestant denomination that demands strict adherence to the teachings in the Bible; founded by John Calvin.
Catholicism   Christian belief based on the teachings and guidance of the Roman church, the pope, and the clergy.
Christendom   refers to all the world's Christians and the lands they occupy; used primarily before nations arose.
communion   the Christian SACRAMENT in which consecrated bread and wine are taken as memorials of Christ's death or as symbols of the spiritual union between Christ and the communicant, or as the body and blood of Christ.
Congregationalist   See PURITAN.

RELIGION AND THE STATE

dar al-harb **(Arabic: House of War)**   concept in medieval Islamic legal thought to differentiate territories where the sharia is followed *(DAR AL-ISLAM)* from those where it is not followed.

dar al-Islam **(Arabic: House of Islam)**   concept in medieval Islamic legal thought to differentiate territories where the sharia is followed from those where it is not followed *(DAR AL-HARB)*.

deist   one who believes that the existence of God is found in reason and observation of the natural world; generally, deists reject the idea of divine revelation as the basis of truth.

dharma   in Buddhism, the "way" of living in harmony with the universe.

dhimmi   non-Muslims, such as Christians and Jews, who live under Muslim rule and have a regulated and protected status.

diaspora   dispersion (of a people).

dominionism   the extreme Protestant Christian belief that it is God's mandate that conservative Christians take control of, or have dominion over, all aspects of society, including government, which must be a theocracy.

ecclesiastical   relating to a church as an established institution.

emir   an Islamic leader or commander.

Episcopalian   a U.S. offshoot of the Episcopal Church, with worship based on the Book of Common Prayer and a modified Bible.

eschatology   beliefs surrounding the end-times or end of days, as contained in religious teachings.

evangelical   originally, referred to evangelizing or proselytizing a religious belief; later, someone who believes a Christian theology that stresses personal faith and the inerrant authority of the Bible.

fatwa (pronounced faht' wah)   an opinion of a mufti on an issue of canonical law.

fiefdom   refers to the small principalities ruled by petty kings during the Middle Ages.

fiqh **(pronounced feek; Arabic: understanding)**   term for Islamic law particularly as it is interpreted and implemented by legal experts from among the ulama.

fundamentalist   a conservative, right-wing Christian who believes in the end times, evangelism, and conversion via the Holy Spirit, and who has a literal belief in the inerrant Bible. Also, any ultraorthodox religious believer who believes in the literal truth of Scripture.

hadith (pronounced hah' dit)   the sayings of the prophet Muhammad; the body of exemplary words and actions of Muhammad is called the Hadith.

hajj   the pilgrimage to Mecca required of all Muslims once in their lifetime if they are able to do so.

haram **(pronounced hah rahm')**   in Islam, "expressly forbidden."

Glossary

heresy a religious opinion contrary to accepted church doctrine, or the denial of revealed truth; a heretic is one who believes in heresy.

Holiness churches Protestant denominations that emphasize personal experience of grace and the power of the Holy Spirit for salvation; there are numerous Holiness denominations and churches.

ijtihad **(pronounced ij tee hahd'; Arabic: striving)** a scholar's judgment in matters that are not explicitly addressed in the Quran and Sunna.

imam Sunni prayer or religious leader; in Shia Islam, an imam is a descendant of the Prophet who leads the *umma.*

immanence the presence of God or the divine in the world.

incarnation the divine taking a human form to live on Earth.

investiture in the Christian church, the power to appoint clergymen, at one time even bishops, cardinals, and popes.

Islam (Arabic: submission [to Allah]) religion based on the prophet Muhammad's teachings as set down in the Quran and Sunna.

jahiliyyah **(pronounced jah heel' yah; Arabic: era of ignorance)** the state of affairs before the rise of Islam. Lowercased, the term means "ignorance."

Jehovah's Witnesses U.S. Protestant sect founded by Charles T. Russell in the late 19th century; belief in the imminent Second Coming of Christ and the salvation of souls; do not believe in modern medicine, engagement with politics, or oaths to anything other than God.

jihad (pronounced jee hah'; Arabic: to strive, struggle) greater jihad is the inner struggle to live according to God's law; lesser jihad is the external struggle against those who threaten Muslims or the *umma.*

jizya **(Arabic: poll tax)** the tax that non-Muslims (DHIMMIS) living in a Muslim land have to pay to the state.

Kharijites (Arabic: those who go out) a group of ultraorthodox Muslims, mainly during the period of the Rightly Guided Caliphs, who believed nonorthodoxy made one an enemy of Islam and an apostate a true Muslim was obliged to kill to maintain the purity of the religion.

liturgy a religious ritual or ceremony, such as Christian communion, usually carried out by an ordained cleric.

Lutheranism Protestant Christianity based on the teachings of Martin Luther, in which faith is based on the Bible and is the only source of salvation.

messiah in the Jewish tradition, a fully human being who will appear on Earth to help the Jews realize God's Kingdom on Earth; in Christianity, the Son of God (Jesus) who is both God and man; in Shia Islam the Mahdi who will return at the end of time to restore Islam to its original perfection.

Methodist a revivalist Protestant sect founded by John Wesley that emphasizes the action of the Holy Spirit on individuals and on testifying for the faith.

RELIGION AND THE STATE

millennialism   belief in the end-times; in Christianity, the Second Coming of Christ; in Shia Islam, the return of the Hidden Imam, or Mahdi.

monotheism   the belief in one supreme God.

Mormonism (Church of Jesus Christ of Latter-day Saints)   founded by Joseph Smith in upstate New York in the 1820s; faith is based on the Bible as well as on the Book of Mormon, which contains Joseph Smith's revelations; the original followers (and some today) believed in polygamy, pure living, self-reliance, and proselytizing.

mufti   in Islam, one who presents the law to the people.

mujtahid **(pronounced mooj tah heed')**   interpreters of divine law in Shia Islam.

Muslim   those who follow ISLAM; literally "those who submit [to] Allah."

nirvana   in Buddhism, the blissful and transcendent experience of "non-self" and total immersion in the oneness of the universe.

Pentecostalism   church that grew out of the Holiness movement, which itself split from Methodism; beliefs include possession by the Holy Spirit, speaking in tongues, laying on of hands, the Second Coming, and the idea that the world can be perfected through Christian belief.

Pietism   Protestant sects that sought to purge the world of sin in order to usher in the Second Coming of Christ on Earth (MILLENNIALISM).

pluralism   the presence in a society of a variety of different religions, ethnic groups, cultures, etc.

polytheism   the belief in a pantheon of many gods, each controlling one aspect of life.

Presbyterianism   an outgrowth of CALVINISM in which clergy and lay members (presbyters) participate in courts and simple services.

Protestantism   Christian movement that arose out of the Reformation, which rejects the authority of the Roman Church and the pope and finds God in the Bible.

Puritan   a Protestant sect that opposed the ritual worship of God as against the teachings of the Bible and whose members lived under a severely rigid moral code.

Quakerism (Society of Friends)   founded by George Fox in England in the 17th century, Quakers believe religion is the inner light or voice of the Holy Spirit within each person; their meetings involve sitting in quiet meditation until one is moved to speak and share with others; members are often active in peace and social reform movements.

Quran (pronounced kuh rahn')   the Islamic holy book that contains the word of Allah, as God's teachings, as received by the prophet Muhammad.

Quraysh   tribe that dominated Mecca during the time of the prophet Muhammad.

Glossary

Ramadan (pronounced rah' mah dahn)   a monthlong fasting from sunup to sundown during the ninth month of the Islamic calendar.

Reformation   the movement, begun by Martin Luther, to reform the corrupt Catholic Church of the 16th century, which led to PROTESTANTISM.

Resurrectionism   the precursor to DOMINIONISM, the idea that the world should be ruled by a Christian theocracy; first expressed by R. J. Rushdoony.

revivalist   one who believes in conversion through the holding of revival meetings, as in the Great Awakenings; a Christian who evangelizes via religious revivals.

Salafi (pronounced sah lah' fee)   Sunni movement that militated for creating a society based on the pure model of early Islam, during the time of the Prophet.

sangha (pronounced sahn' gah)   the community of Buddhist monks and nuns.

secular   referring to worldly, nonreligious things; also "secular humanist," a person who places the importance of humans above that of God.

Seventh-Day Adventism   Protestant sect founded in the 19th century; belief that the Bible is the only creed; the Second Coming is awaited (though not necessarily imminent).

sharia (pronounced shah ree' uh)   in Islam, divine law as transmitted by Allah to the prophet Muhammad.

shayk   an honorific title often given to men over 40 years old; a Muslim who studies Islam and is knowledgeable about the Quran and Sunna.

Shia (pronounced shee' uh)   Islamic sect (about 15 percent of Muslims) that believes in the succession after Muhammad through his blood relatives, Ali and Husayn; Shiites believe the *umma* should be ruled by IMAMS, descendants of the Prophet.

shura **(pronounced shoor' uh)**   in Islam, "consultation."

state   a nation, or a national government; any government that rules over a distinct population.

Sufi (pronounced soo' fee)   a Muslim who practices Sufism, a mystical form of Islam in which the devotee seeks mystical union with Allah; some orthodox Islamic groups consider Sufis heretics.

sultan (Arabic: strength, authority)   a Muslim ruler; used especially in the Ottoman Empire.

Sunna (pronounced soo' nah)   the QURAN and HADITH, which together contain the teachings and law of Islam; also *sunna*, "example" of the holy Muslim life, as that lived by the prophet Muhammad.

Sunni (pronounced soo' nee)   the main group in ISLAM that accepts the lineage of the caliphate based on the four Rightly Guided Caliphs chosen by the *SHURA* after Muhammad's death.

taqlid   narrow legal interpretation of the QURAN or SUNNA.

RELIGION AND THE STATE

theocracy (Greek: government of god) form of government controlled by religious leaders regarded as divinely guided who impose religious law and belief on the populace.

theology study of religious belief, dogma, and practice.

ulama (pronounced oo lah' mah) Islamic religious scholars.

umma **(pronounced oo' mah)** the community of Muslims, locally, nationally, or globally.

zakat the tax, or tithe, paid by Muslims to help the poor, widows, and orphans.

Index

Note: Page numbers in **boldface** indicate major treatment of a subject. Page numbers followed by *c* indicate chronology entries. Page numbers followed by *f* indicate figures. Page numbers followed by *g* indicate glossary entries. Page numbers followed by *m* indicate maps.

A

Abbas, Shah (Safavid Persian ruler) 47, 105
Abbasid Empire **45–46,** 46–47, 104, 337*c*, 338*c*
Abd al-Aziz (king of Saudi Arabia) 116
Abd al-Wahhab, Muhammad ibn 114–116, 264*g*, 339*c*
Abduh, Muhammad 50, 51, 264*g*
Abdullah (king of Saudi Arabia) 118
Abingdon v. Schempp 71
abortion 91, 343*c*
Abraham (biblical patriarch) 12
Abu Bakr (father-in-law of the prophet Muhammad) 38, 43, 264*g*, 337*c*
academia xi
Act of Supremacy 27, 339*c*
"Advice to the Community to Reject the Fatwa of Sheikh Bin Baz Authorizing Parliamentary Representation" (al-Zawahiri, 2008) 232–236
Afghani, Jamal al-Din al- 50–51, 264*g*–265*g*
African-American churches **83–84**
afterlife 5
Ahmadinejad, Mahmoud 112
airports 3
Aisha (wife of the prophet Muhammad) 44
Akbar (Mughal emperor of India) 47, 338*c*
Alabama 73
Albania 263*f*
Alexander the Great (king of Macedonia) 14, 103
Algeria 137
Ali ibn Abi Talib 38, 43–44, 53, 105, 265*b*
Allah 41, 345*g*
Allegheny County v. ACLU 73
Alliance Defense Fund 276
Altan Khan (Mongol ruler) 122
American Buddhist Conference 277
American Center for Law and Justice 277
American Civil Liberties Union 69, 277–278
American Family Association 278
American Humanist Association 278–279
American Muslim Alliance 279
American Revolution 31, 339*c*
Americans United for Separation of Church and State 69, 279
Amish 76, 343*c*, 345*g*
Anglican Church, in U.S. 64–65, 79–80, 346*g*. *See also* Church of England

351

Anglicanism 345*g*
Anglo-Iranian Oil
  Company (AIOC)
  107
animism 5, 345*g*
Antiochus IV (Seleucid
  ruler) 14
antiwar movement 88
Arabia 39, 337*c*. *See also*
  Saudi Arabia
Arab League 117
Ashoka (Maurya
  emperor) **10–12**,
  184–187, 336*c*
assassinations 53, 55–57,
  342*c*, 343*c*
Assemblies of God 80,
  345*g*
asylum, in Britain
  136–137
Atatürk, Mustafa Kemal
  51, 265*b*
atheism 36, 37, **98**, 345*g*
Athens, ancient 6
Atisa (Buddhist monk)
  121
Augustine of Hippo
  (saint) 20
Augustus Caesar
  (emperor of Rome)
  15
Aurangzeb (Mughal
  emperor of India) 48
Australia 250*f*
authority 6, 8
automobiles 85
Avalokiteśvara
  (bodhisattva) 120,
  122
Avignon, France 24
ayatollah 45, 111, 345*g*.
  See also Khomeini,
  Ruhollah
Ayodhya mosque 131

B

Badr, Battle of 39, 337*c*
Banna, Hassan al-
  54–56, 265*b*, 341*c*
Baptists 79–80, 81,
  86–87, 345*g*
Barth, Karl 35, 36,
  265*b*–266*b*
  Theological
    Declaration of
    Barmen (1934) 36,
    212–214
Basic Law (Saudi Arabia,
  1992) 118
basijees 112
Becket, Thomas 23,
  266*b*, 338*c*
behavior v. values 88–89
Bhagavad Gita 7, 129
Bharatiya Janata Party
  (BJP) 130, 131–132,
  262*m*, 343*c*, 344*c*
Bible, literal
  interpretation of 85,
  86, 258*f*
bidaa 109, 115
bigamy 68–69
Bill of Rights (U.S.)
  66–67, 340*c*
bin Laden, Osama 57,
  271*b*
biofuels 119
biographies 264–275
birth rate 133
Bismarck, Otto von 35
Black, Hugo 70
Black Friday 109
Black Plague 24
black power 83–84
blowback 108
blue laws 68, 75–76
Bob Jones University 94
bodhisattvas, in Tibet
  121
Boerne v. Flores 344*c*
Bolkestein, Fritz 133

Bolshevik revolution 36,
  341*c*
Bön 120–121
Bonaparte, Napoléon
  (Napoléon I) 33–34,
  340*c*
Boniface VIII (pope) 24,
  194–196
Book of Jihad and
  Expedition, The (al-
  Hajjaj) 217, 219–220
Book on Government,
  The (al-Hajjaj) 217,
  220–223
Bosnia and Herzegovina
  263*f*
bourgeois 345*g*
Bouyeri, Mohammed
  135–136
Boykin, William 96
Brahma 7
Brahman 7, 8
Brahmins 7
Braunfeld v. Brown 75
British Petroleum 107
Brown, Janice Rogers 94
Bryan, William Jennings
  71, 83
Bryant, Anita 90
Buddha **8–9**, 10, 336*c*
Buddhism **8–12**. *See also*
  Tibet
  percentage of
    population 249*f*
  primary documents
    on 184–189
  in U.S. 98
Bull *Unam Sanctam*
  (Boniface VIII, 1302)
  24, 194–196
Burger, Warren 73, 76
burial 4–5
Bush, George W. 93–94,
  97, 266*b*
  "Remarks by the
    President in

Index

Announcement of the Faith-Based Initiative" (2001) 160–162
Buyids 46, 104

C

caliphs 41, **43–44,** 53, 337*c*, 345*g*
"Call to Renewal" Keynote Address (Obama, 2006) 166–172
Calvin, John 26, 95, 266*b*
Calvinism 26, 345*g*
Canada 250*f*
Capital (Marx) 36
capitalism 81
Carter, Jimmy 88
"cartoon jihad" 135, 344*c*
caste system 7, 129
Catholic(s)
   in Europe 133–134
   in U.S. 82–83, 84, 258*f*, 340*c*, 342*c*
Catholic Church
   courts of 23
   in French Revolution 32–33, 340*c*
   Great Schism of 24
   Henry II and 338*c*
   Inquisition of 23
   kings anointed by 20
   papal election in 338*c*
   in politics 19, 20–21, 22–23, 24
   simony in 22
   theology of 25
   in Thirty Years' War 339*c*
   in World War II 37
Catholicism 345*g*
Center for Law and Religious Freedom:

Christian Legal Society 279–280
Center for Progressive Christianity 280
Central Intelligence Agency (CIA) 107–108
charismatics 80
Charlemagne (emperor of the West) 20–21, 266*b*, 337*c*
Charles I (king of England) 29
Charter of Muslim Faith 139
China
   communism in 342*c*
   Olympics in 127
   and Tibet 120, 123–126, 342*c*
   traditional religions of 249*f*
Christendom 21, 28, 345*g*
Christian Century 280
Christian Coalition of America 93, 281, 343*c*
Christian Crusades **46–47,** 338*c*
Christian fundamentalism **85–88**
   backlash against 98
   biblical worldview of 258*f*
   in culture wars **88–90**
   definition of 85–86
   origin of term 341*c*
   prevalence of 96–97
Christianity **14–37.** *See also* Catholic Church; Protestantism
   during Dark Ages **20–24**
   early **15–20**

eschatology of 15–16, 21, 94
   in French Revolution 32–33
   Islam on 39
   kings anointed in 20, 337*c*
   in liberal theology 34
   medieval **20–24**
   Messiah in 15–16
   Nicene Creed of 336*c*
   percentage of population 249*f*
   political theology of **15–17,** 19, 20
   primary documents on 189–217
   in public schools 342*c*
   relationship with God in 16
   in Roman Empire 15
   salvation in 25
   state in 63, **77–99**
   in United States **77–99,** 258*f. See also* Christian Right
   after World War II 37
"Christian Reconstruction: A Call for Reformation and Revival" (Parsons, 2008) 176–182
Christian Reconstructionism 95, 96
Christian Right 89–90, **90–96,** 96–97, 343*c*, 344*c*. *See also* Christian fundamentalism
Christian Voice 91, 92, 343*c*
Christmas displays 72–73

353

Church History (Eusebius of Caesarea, ca. 326) 19
Church of England 27–28, 339c. *See also* Anglican Church; Episcopalian
Church of Jesus Christ of Latter-day Saints. *See* Mormonism
City of God, The (Augustine of Hippo, 410) 20
Civil Constitution of the Clergy 32–33
Civil Rights Act (1963) 88, 342c
Civil Rights movement 83–84, 87, 88, 342c
Civil War (U.S.) 86, 340c
Clawson, Patrick 106
Clement II (pope) 22
Clement V (pope) 24
clergy, Catholic 21, 22–23, 32–33
Clinton, Bill 92
cold war 74
college education 89
colonialism 49–50, 55
communion 345g
communism 36, 342c. *See also* Soviet Union
Communist Manifesto (Marx and Engels, 1848) 36
"compelling interest" test 344c
Concerned Women for America 93
Confessing Church 36
Congregationalists 79–80
Congress of Secular Jewish Organizations 281

Congress Party (India) 132, 344c
Connecticut Act of Toleration (1784) 65
Connecticut colony 65
Conservative Caucus 91
Constantine I (emperor of Rome) **17–20,** 267b, 336c
 Edict of Milan (313) 17, 189–190
Constitution (U.S.) **65–66**
 First Amendment. *See* establishment clause; free exercise clause
 Fourteenth Amendment 69, 340c
 Nineteenth Amendment 341c
 Twenty-first Amendment 341c
 Bill of Rights of **66–67,** 340c
 Locke's influence on 31, 63
 ratification of 66, 340c
Constitutional Revolution (Iran, 1905) 106
Constitutions of Clarendon, The (Henry II, 1164) 192–194
corruption 23, 52–53
Council on American-Islamic Relations 282
Council for America's First Freedom 282
Council of Guardians 110
Council of Nicea, First (325) 17–18
creation 5, 8, 12

creationism 71, 343c
Cromwell, Oliver 29
Crusades **46–47,** 338c
cynicism 36
Cyrus the Great (Persian ruler) 103

D

Dahmani, Areski 139
Dalai Lama, III 122
Dalai Lama, V 122
Dalai Lama, XIII 124
Dalai Lama, XIV 124–127, 267b, 342c
 Nobel Lecture of (1989) 187–189
Dalits 7
dar al-harb 346g
dar al-Islam 346g
Darrow, Clarence 71
David (king of Israel) 13, 336c
Dawkins, Richard 98
death 5
Debate on His Book *God Is Not Great* between the Author Christopher Hitchens and the Reverend Al Sharpton (2007) 172–176
Declaration of Independence 63
Declaration of the Rights of Man 32
deist 346g
deities, Hindu 7–8
democracy 52, **58–59,** 127
Democracy in America excerpt (Tocqueville, 1835/1840) 148–152
Democratic Party 82, 87, 340c, 342c
Denmark 263f
Desert Fathers 17

Index

dharma 8, 9, 11, 346*g*
dharma-raja 129
dhimmi 346*g*
diaspora 346*g*
Diaspora, Jewish 336*c*
Dictatus Papae (Gregory VII, 1075) 22, 190–192, 338*c*
dissenters 65
divine authority 6
Dobson, James 91, 267*b*
 "Judicial Tyranny" (2003) 162–166
dominionism 94–97, 346*g*
Douglas, William O. 75

E

Eagle Forum 282–283
Eastern Orthodox Church 18
ecclesiastical 346*g*
ecclesiastical courts 23
Edict of Milan (Constantine, 313) 17, 189–190
Edicts of Ashoka (ca. third century B.C.E.) 184–187
education. *See also* private schools; public schools
 college 89
 compulsory 76, 152–160, 343*c*
 in Islamic Reformation 51
 Supreme Court decisions on 69–72
Edwards v. Aguillard 71, 343*c*
Egypt 49, 51, 52, 55–57, 341*c*
Eightfold Path 9

Eisenhower, Dwight D. 107
Elizabeth I (queen of England) 27
emir 346*g*
Engels, Friedrich 36
Engel v. Vitale 70–71
English Civil Wars 29
enlightenment 8, 9
Episcopalian 346*g*
Epperson v. Arkansas 71
Equal Rights Amendment (ERA) 90
eschatology 15–16, 21, 45, 94, 346*g*
establishment clause **66–67, 69–74,** 74, 342*c*
Europe 133–136, 263*f*.
 See also specific nations
Eusebius of Caesarea 19
euthanasia 97
evangelical 346*g*
evangelical Christianity
 biblical worldview of 258*f*
 Democratic party and 82
 organizations 343*c*
 revivalism 79–81, 339*c*, 340*c*
Everson v. Board of Education 69–70
evolution, teaching 71, 341*c*, 343*c*
expression, free, and Muslims 133–136
extremism. *See* Hindu nationalism; Muslim extremism

F

Fadl, Dr. 57–58, 267*b*–268*b*
Fahd (king of Saudi Arabia) 117

Faisal (king of Saudi Arabia) 117
Falwell, Jerry 91–92, 94, 268*b*
family, in Islamic v. secular law 134
Family Research Council 93, 283, 343*c*
fanaticism 29–30
Fatimids 46
fatwa 54, 111, 134–135, 346*g*
Federation of Islamic Organisations in Europe (FIOE) 226–232
feudalism, Tibetan 123
fiefdom 346*g*
fiqh 346*g*
Fiqh Council, U.S. Muslims Issue Fatwa against Religious Extremism (2008) 224–226
First Amendment. *See* establishment clause; free exercise clause
Five Pillars of Islam 40–41
Focus on the Family 91, 283–284
Four Noble Truths 9
Fourteenth Amendment 69, 340*c*
France
 equality in 138
 Muslims in 137–140, 263*f*, 344*c*
 national religious associations of 138
 racism in 139–140
 religious influence on government 250*f*
 riots in (2005) 344*c*
 unification of 20

Frankfurter, Felix 74–75
free exercise clause **66–67**, 68–69, **74–77**, 342*c*
Free Muslims Coalition 284
Free Tibet 284
French Revolution **32–34**, 340*c*
fundamentalism
   Christian. *See* Christian fundamentalism
   Muslim, in Saudi Arabia 119
fundamentalist 346*g*
Fundamentals, The 85, 341*c*

G

Gabriel (angel) 38
Gallagher v. Crown Kosher Supermarket 75
Gandhi, Mohandas K. 127–128, 268*b*, 342*c*
   The "Quit India" Speech (1942) 183–184
Gaustad, Edwin S. 69
Germany
   Hitler as chancellor of 36–37, 341*c*
   Muslim population of 263*f*
   Protestantism in 24–26, 34–35
   religious influence on government 250*f*
   in Thirty Years' War 339*c*
   unification of 35, 340*c*
   in World War I 35
Ghose, Aurobindo 129
God 12, 18, 29, 74–75. *See also* Allah

Godan Khan 121–122, 123
Godse, Nathuram 128
Gogarten, Friedrich 36
government. *See* state
Government Is Not God 285
Grand Mosque (Mecca) 113–114, 117, 118–119, 343*c*
Grant, George 96
Grass, Günter 135
Great Awakenings 79–80, 339*c*, 340*c*
Great Britain
   India under 8, 129–130
   Iran and 106–107
   Muslims in 133, 135, 136–137, 263*f*
   religious influence on government 250*f*
Great Schism 24
Greece, ancient 6
Gregory VII (pope) 22–23, 268*b*–269*b*
   Dictatus Papae (1090) 22, 190–192, 338*c*

H

Hadith 39
hadith 346*g*
Hadith: *Sahih Muslim* (al-Hajjaj) 217, 219–223
hajj 39, 41, 346*g*
Hajjaj, Muslim ibn al-, *Sahih Muslim* (excerpts) 217, 219–223
Hamilton, Alexander 66
Hanbali school of Islam 115
haram 40, 346*g*

hard dominionism 95
Hare Krishnas 3
Hatch, Nathan O. 80
Hedges, Chris 96
Hegel, Georg 34, 269*b*
Henry, Patrick 64
Henry II (king of England) 23, 269*b*, 338*c*
   The Constitutions of Clarendon (1164) 192–194
Henry III (Holy Roman Emperor) 22
Henry IV (Holy Roman Emperor) 22–23
Henry VIII (king of England) 27, 269*b*, 339*c*
heresy 17, 23, 24, 347*g*
Hezbollah 110
hijab 138–139, 344*c*
hijra 38, 337*c*
Hindu American Foundation 285
Hinduism **7–8**, 47–48, 129, 130–131, 249*f*
   primary documents on 183–184
Hindu nationalism **127–132**, 342*c*
Hindutva 128, 129–130
Hitchens, Christopher 98
   Debate on His Book *God Is Not Great* between the Author Christopher Hitchens and the Reverend Al Sharpton (2007) 172–176
Hitler, Adolf 36–37, 341*c*
Hobbes, Thomas **28–30**, 269*b*–270*b*

Index

holiness churches 80, 81, 347*g*
Holy Roman Empire 20–21, 253*m*, 337*c*, 339*c*
Holy Spirit 18
homeschooling 95
homosexuals, discrimination against 90
Hudson Institute's Center for Religious Freedom 285–286
human existence, explanations for 5
Hus, Jan 24
Husayn ibn Ali 44–45, 270*b*, 337*c*
Hussein, Saddam 110
Hutchinson, John 13

I

Ibn Saud 260*m*
Ibn Saud, Muhammad 115–116, 339*c*
ijtihad 51, 105, 347*g*
Ikhwan 115–116
imam 45, 347*g*
Immaculate Conception of Mary 34
immanence 347*g*
immigration 69, 82–83, 87, 133, 137–138
incarnation 347*g*
India. *See also* Hinduism; Hindu nationalism
  BJP party of 130, 131–132, 262*m*, 343*c*, 344*c*
  British rule in 8, 129–130
  caste system of 7, 129
  Dalai Lama in 126
  independence of 128
  under Maurya Empire 11
  Mughal Empire of 129, 338*c*
  Muslim conquest of 8
  Muslim emigration from 133
indigenous religions 249*f*
indulgences 23
Innocent X (pope) 28–29
Inquisition 23
Institute for Humanist Studies 286
International Association for Religious Freedom 286
International Campaign for Tibet 287
International Coalition for Religious Freedom 287
International Institute for Secular Humanistic Judaism 287–288
International Institute of Islamic Thought 288
international primary documents 183–236
investiture 21, 22–23, 347*g*
Iran (Persia) **103–113**
  constitution of 110, 111
  empires of 103
  hostage crisis 110
  Iraq invasion of 110–111
  Islamic Revolution in **108–110,** 343*c*
  under Khomeini 110–111
  modern **105–113,** 259*m*
  under Mossadeq **107–108,** 342*c*
  nationalism in 106
  premodern **104–105**
  presidential election of 2009 112–113
  under Safavid Empire 338*c*
  shahs of 47, 106–107
  Westernization of 51
  after World War I 49
  youth of 112
Iraq 110–111
Islam **38–59.** *See also* Muslims
  under Abbasid Empire 45–47
  cartoon insult to 135, 344*c*
  Christian Reconstructionism and 96
  colonialism and 49–50
  Crusades against 46–47
  definition of 347*g*
  and democracy **58–59**
  early history 38–40, 337*c*
  in Europe 133
  extremism as contradiction of 54
  family in 134
  Five Pillars of 40–41
  Hanbali school of 115
  in India 128
  jihad in, Muhammad on 40
  law of. *See* sharia
  under Mughal Empire 47–48
  under Ottoman Empire 48

357

pan-Islam 50–51
percentage of
 population 249f
in Persia 105
political theology of
 40–45
primary documents
 on 217–236
under Rightly Guided
 Caliphs **43–44**
in Saudi Arabia
 113–119, 339c
under Safavid Empire
 47
secularism and 134
Shia. *See* Shia Islam
sovereignty in 58
spread of 38–39, 44,
 45–46, 254m–255m
state in
 Europe and 134
 ideal 39, **41–43**
 modern 50–53,
  58–59
 Muhammad on 40
 Quran as
  constitution 55
 Qutb on 56
 sharia in 41
 Sunni. *See* Sunni
  Islam
 Westernization of
  50–51
 after World War I 49
Islamic Circle of North
 America 288–289
Islamic extremism. *See*
 Muslim extremism
*Islamic Government:
 Regency of the Jurist*
 (Khomeini, 1970) 109
Islamic Reformation
 50–51
Islamic Revolution (Iran)
 108–110, 343c

Islamic Society of Britain
 289
Islamic Society of North
 America 289
Ismail 104, 105
Israel (biblical) 12, 336c.
 See also Jerusalem
Israel (modern) 14, 52,
 96, 342c, 343c
Israelites 12
Istanbul 48
Italy 250f. *See also* Rome

J

Jackson, Andrew 82
Jackson, Robert 75
Jacob 12
jahiliyya (ignorance) 56
Jahiliyyah (Age of
 Ignorance) 347g
Jana Sangh 130
Jefferson, Thomas 64,
 270b
 "The Virginia Act
  for Establishing
  Religious Freedom"
  (1786) 65, 145–147
 The "Wall of
  Separation Letter"
  (1802) 67, 147–148
Jehovah's Witnesses
 74–75, 81, 347g
Jenkins, Philip 140
Jerusalem 46–47, 336c.
 See also Israel; Temple
 in Jerusalem
Jesus 15, 18
Jewish Diaspora 336c
jihad 40, 53, 54, 57–58,
 347g
jizya 347g
Johnson, Lyndon B. 88
John XII (pope) 21–22
Jones, Bob, III 94
Jordan 52

Judaism **12–14**, 13, 15,
 16, 46, 75–76, 249f
"Judicial Tyranny"
 (Dobson, 2003)
 162–166

K

Kant, Immanuel 32,
 270b
Karbala, Battle of 44–45,
 337c
karma 8
Katrina, Hurricane 97,
 344c
Kemal, Mustafa. *See*
 Atatürk
Kennedy, D. James 95
Kennedy, John F. 87,
 342c
Khalid (king of Saudi
 Arabia) 117
Khamenei, Ali 110, 111,
 113
Kharijites **53–54**, 347g
Khatami, Mohammad
 111, 113
Khomeini, Ruhollah 103,
 106, 108–111,
 270b–271b, 343c
 The Uprising of
  Khurdad 15, 1979
  223–224
kingship 8, 10, 21, 22–23
Know-Nothing Party 83,
 340c
Korea 250f
Kosovo 263f
Kshatriyas 7, 129
Kublai Khan (Mongol
 emperor of China) 122

L

LaHaye, Tim 94
laïcité 138–139

Index

Lang Darma (king of Tibet) 121
Latter-day Saints. *See* Mormonism
law, Islamic. *See* sharia
law, Jewish 13, 16
law, secular. *See also* Supreme Court
   church law and 23, 37
   on family 134
   free exercise clause and 76–77
   Luther on 25–26
   Qutb on 56
   religious practice *v.* 68–69, 340*c*
Lazare, Daniel 98
Left Behind series (LaHaye) 94
Lemon test 74
Leo III (pope) 20, 337*c*
Lepanto, Battle of 48, 339*c*
Le Pen, Jean-Marie 139
Letter Concerning Toleration, A (Locke, 1689) 31, 202–211
Levy, Leonard W. 67
Lewis, Joseph 74
Lewis v. Allen 74
liberal theology **34–37**
liberty, worship of 33
Liberty Council 289–290
Liberty University 94
Lilla, Mark 34–35
liturgicals 82–83, 84–85
liturgy 347*g*
lobbying, Christian 93
Locke, John **30–32, 63–64,** 67, 271*b*
   A Letter Concerning Toleration (1689) 31, 202–211

"lost cause" theology 86
Louis XVI (king of France) 32–33
Luther, Martin **24–26,** 271*b*–272*b*
   The Ninety-five Theses (1517) 25, 196–202, 338*c*
Lutheranism 24–26, 347*g*
Lynch v. Donnelly 72–73

M

Maccabees 14, 336*c*
Madison, James 64–65, 67, 272*b*
Mahdi 45, 109
Mahfouz, Naguib 135
mail delivery, Sunday 68
majlis 106
Manchu 122
Marshall, Thurgood 72
Martel, Charles 20, 337*c*
Martin V (pope) 24
Marty, Martin 86
Marx, Karl 36
Mary, Queen of Scots 27
Mary I (queen of England) 27
Massachusetts 340*c*
Massachusetts Bay Colony 62–63, 339*c*
Maurya Empire 11
McCollum v. Board of Education 70
McCreary County v. ACLU 73–74
McKinley, William 83
Mecca 38, 39, 116. *See also* Grand Mosque
media, Christian 93
Medina 38, 116, 337*c*
meditation 9

megachurches 93
messiah 15, 36, 39, 45, 347*g*
Methodists 79–80, 81, 347*g*
Middle East 49, 52, 341*c*, 343*c*. *See also specific countries*
millennialism 96, 348*g*
Minaret of Freedom Institute 290
Minersville School District v. Gobitis 74–75
modernization 55, 86, 87, 117
Mohammad Reza Shah Pahlavi 107–108, 109, 110, 272*b*, 342*c*
moment of silence 71
Mongols 47, 54, 104, 105, 121–122, 123–124
monotheism 5, 348*g*. *See also* Christianity; Islam; Judaism
Moore, Roy 73
Moral Majority 91, 343*c*
moral relativism 90
Mormonism 68–69, 81, 348*g*
Morocco 137
Moses 12
Mossadeq, Mohammad **107–108,** 272*b*, 342*c*
Mousavi, Mir-Hussein 112–113
Muawiya 44, 272*b*
Mueller v. Allen 72
mufti 48, 348*g*
Mughal Empire 47–48, 129, 338*c*
Muhammad **38–40,** 41, 135, 337*c*, 344*c*
mujtahids 45, 109, 110
Murray v. Curlett 71

359

Muslim(s). *See also* Islam
　definition of 348*g*
　in Europe 133–137
　in France 137–140, 344*c*
　identity of 53
　in India 130, 131–132
　Indian conquest by 8
　populations of 263*f*
Muslim Brotherhood 55–57, 341*c*, 343*c*
Muslim extremism **53–58**
　in Britain 136–137
　as contradiction of Islam 54
　Kharijites **53–54**
　as minority 52–53
　Muslim Brotherhood **55–57**
　Nasser assassination attempt and 343*c*
　Qaeda, al- **57–58**
　in Sadat assassination 343*c*
　in Saudi Arabia 114
　ibn Taymiyya **54–55**
Muslim fundamentalism, in Saudi Arabia 119
Muslim Public Affairs Council 290–291
Muslims of Europe Charter (2008) 226–232
Muzaffar al-Din Shah 106

N

Nagata, Judith 85
Nasir al-Din Shah 105–106
Nasser, Gamal Abdul 51, 56–57, 272*b*–273*b*, 343*c*

National Christian Action Coalition 91
National Committee for the Survival of a Free Congress 91
National Conservative Political Action Committee 91
National Federation for Decency 91
National Front (Iran) 107
nationality, Qutb on 56
Nazi Party 36, 341*c*
Nehru, Jawaharlal 130
Netherlands 263*f*
Neturei Karta: Jews United Against Zionism 291
New Atheism **98**
New England Way 65
New Identity-Interfaith Alliance 291–292
Ngawang Losan Gyatso 122
Nicene Creed 17–18, 336*c*
Nicholas II (pope) 22, 337*c*
Niebuhr, H. Richard 35
Night of Power and Excellence 38, 337*c*
Nineteenth Amendment 341*c*
Ninety-five Theses (Luther, 1517) 25, 196–202, 338*c*
nirvana 9, 348*g*
Nixon, Richard 87
Nobel Lecture of the 14th Dalai Lama (1989) 187–189
North, Gary 95
North Africa 49, 133, 137–138

O

Obama, Barack 344*c*
　"Call to Renewal" Keynote Address (2006) 166–172
O'Connor, Sandra Day 71, 73–74
oil industry, in Iran 107
Old Testament, on Jewish state 14
Olympics, Beijing 127
order, search for 6
Oregon Employment Division v. Smith 76–77, 344*c*
Otto (Holy Roman Emperor) 21–22
Ottoman Empire **48,** 49, 256*m*, 338*c*, 339*c*

P

Padmasambhava 120–121
Pakistan, emigration from 133
pan-Islam 50–51
Parsons, Robert, "Christian Reconstruction: A Call for Reformation and Revival" (2008) 176–182
Parthian Empire 103
Pasqua, Charles 138
patriarchy, Jewish 12
Patt, David 124
Pawtucket 72–73
PEARL v. Nyquist 72
Penn, William 65
Pennsylvania 65, 73
Pentecostalism 80, 348*g*
People for the American Way 292
Pepin the Short 20, 337*c*
Persia. *See* Iran

Index

peyote 76–77
Philip II (king of Spain) 27
Phillips, Howard 91
pietism 82–83, 84–85, 341*c*, 348*g*
Pius VI (pope) 33
Pius VII (pope) 33–34, 340*c*
Pius IX (pope) 34
Pledge of Allegiance (U.S.) 74–75
pluralism 69, 79, 89, 130, 348*g*
political resistance, African-American 83
political theology 6
    Christian **15–17,** 19, 20, 28, 29–30
    of dominionism 94–95
    Islamic **40–45**
    liberal theology and 35
    Zoroastrian 104
politics and religion **6–7**
    Augustine on 20
    Barth on 36
    Calvin on 26
    Christendom's separation of 28
    of Christian fundamentalists 87–88
    Christian Right in **90–96**
    of dominionists 94–95
    interaction with xii–xiii
    in Islam 41, 42
    Luther on 26
    in Saudi Arabia 118
    in search for order 6
polytheism 5, 115, 348*g*

pope 19, 22, 34, 37, 337*c*. *See also specific popes*
postmillenialism 96
Powell, Lewis 72
prayer, in public schools 70–71, 342*c*
premillennialism 96
Presbyterianism 348*g*
primary documents
    international 183–236
    U.S. 145–182
primitivists 80, 81
Prince Alwaleed Bin-Talal Center for Muslim-Christian Understanding 292
printing press 25
private schools 69–70, 71–72, 84
pro-family 91–92, 93
Progressive Era **84–85**
Prohibition 81–82, 341*c*
Protestant(s)
    St. Bartholomew's Day massacre of 27–28, 339*c*
    in Thirty Years' War 339*c*
    in United States 84, 258*f*, 340*c*
Protestantism
    Church of England 27–28, 339*c*
    definition of 348*g*
    in Europe 133
    Hegel on 34
    liberal theology of **34–37**
    in U.S.
        dissident sects 340*c*
        evangelical revivalism 79–81, 339*c*, 340*c*
        evolution of 79–80

Progressive Era 84–85
Prohibition and 81–82, 341*c*
Puritanism 62–63, 77–78, 79, 348*g*
Quakerism 65, 79, 348*g*
Protestant Reformation **24–28,** 338*c*, 349*g*
public displays **72–74**
public schools
    in France 138–139
    in U.S.
        Bible reading in 342*c*
        Christian Right and 91
        creationism v. evolution in 71, 343*c*
        evolution taught in 71, 341*c*
        prayer in 70–71, 342*c*
        religious education in 70
        textbooks banned in 89
Puritanism 62–63, 77–78, 79, 348*g*

Q

qadis 41
Qaeda, al- **57–58,** 344*c*
Qajar dynasty 105–106
Quakerism 65, 79, 348*g*
"Quit India" Speech of Mahatma Gandhi, The (1942) 183–184
Quran 38, 53, 55, 118, 348*g*. *See also* Sunna
    Suras Relating to Governance 217–219

Quraysh 348*g*
Qutb, Sayyid 56–57, 273*b*, 343*c*

R

racism, in France 139–140
Rafsanjani, Akbar Hashemi 111, 113
Ramadan 40–41, 349*g*
Rama worship 130–131
Rapture 94–95
Rationalizing Jihad in Egypt and the World (Fadl, 2007) 57–58
Reagan, Ronald 92
reason 33, 41–42, 50–51
Reconstruction 86
Reconstructionist theology 95, 96
Reed, Ralph 93, 273*b*
reform, social 82, 84–85, 87
Reformation. *See* Protestant Reformation
Regent University 94
Rehnquist, William 72
Rehoboam (Israelite king) 13
Reich Church 36, 341*c*
Reign of Terror 33
reincarnation 7–8
Relbachen (king of Tibet) 121
religion
 in Europe 133
 and forms of government 251*f*–252*f*, 342*c*
 in French Revolution 32
 governance informed by 6, 9–10
 Hegel on 34
 Hobbes on 29–30

in human existence 4–5
Kant on 32
Locke on 31–32
Marx on 36
politics and. *See* politics and religion
purpose of **4–5**
in search for order 6
v. science 98
after World War II 37
Religion and Volkstum (Gogarten) 36
religious freedom
 absence of 4
 under Buddhist government 11
 evolution of 3–4
 in France 33, 138–139, 344*c*
 after Reformation 26–27
 as right 4
 as threat 4
 in U.S. 95, 339*c*, 344*c*. *See also* establishment clause; free exercise clause
 after World War II 37
Religious Freedom Restoration Act (1991) 77, 344*c*
Religious Roundtable 91
religious schools. *See* private schools
religious tolerance
 absence of 4
 in Britain 136–137
 Hobbes and 30
 in India 129–130
 Locke on 31
 Luther on 26

in Mughal Empire 47–48
 in Ottoman Empire 48
 in Roman Empire 14, 15
 in U.S. 3–4
 commitment to 99
 in Connecticut colony 65
 in Constitution **65–66**
 origins of **62–67**
 in Pennsylvania colony 65
 in Virginia colony 64–65
 in western society 3–4
 after World War II 37
Remarks by the President in Announcement of the Faith-Based Initiative" (Bush, 2001) 160–162
republican democracy, Buddha on 10
Republican Party 83, 87–88, 92–94
Restoration 29
Resurrectionism 349*g*
revelation, in authority 6
revivalism 79–81, 339*c*, 340*c*
revivalist 349*g*
Reynolds, George 68–69
Reynolds v. United States 68–69, 340*c*
Reza Shah Pahlavi 51, 106–107
Rhode Island 63, 72–73
Rightly Guided Caliphs **43–44**, 53, 337*c*

Index

riots, in France (2005) 139–140
ritual drug use 76–77
Robertson, Pat 93, 94, 273*b*
Robespierre, Maximilien 33
Roe v. Wade (1973) 91, 343*c*
Roman Empire 14–15, 17, 19–20, 336*c*
Rome 17, 336*c*
Roundtable on Religion and Social Welfare Policy 292–293
RSS (Rashitriya Swayamsevak Sangh) 128, 132
Rubin, Michael 106
rural conservatism 85
Rushdie, Salman 111, 134–135
Rushdoony, Rousas John 95, 273*b*–274*b*
Russia 36, 49, 106, 341*c*
Rutherford Institute 293

S

Sabbatarians 68
sabbath 75–76
Sadat, Anwar 57, 343*c*
Safavid Empire 47, 104, 105, 338*c*
Sahih Muslim (al-Hajjaj) 217, 219–223
St. Bartholomew's Day Massacre 27–28, 339*c*
Saladin 47
Salafi 51, 349*g*
Samuel (prophet) 13
sangha 10, 349*g*
Sarkozy, Nicolas 139
Sa-skya Pandit 121–122, 123

Sassanid Empire 103, 104
Satanic Verses, The (Rushdie) 111, 134–135
Sateer, Aatish 137
Saud (king of Saudi Arabia) 117
Saudi Arabia **113–119**
  history of **114–118**
  Islam in 113–119, 339*c*, 343*c*
  modern **116–118**
  politics in 118
  royal family of 116–117, 118, 119
  unification of 260*m*, 341*c*
Saul (Israelite king) 13
SAVAK 108
Savarkar, Veer (Vinayak Damoder) 128, 274*b*
Savonarola, Girolamo 24
Schiavo, Terri 97, 344*c*
Schlafly, Phyllis 90
Schleiermacher, Friedrich 34
schools. *See* private schools; public schools
science 87, 98
Scopes, John 71
Scopes trial 71, 341*c*
Secret Apparatus 55
secular 349*g*
secular humanism 37, 90
secularization xii, 55
Secular Philosophy 293–294
Seljuks 46
semantics, of Christian Right 92–93
separation of church and state
  Calvin on 26
  in early Christianity 16
  Hobbes and 30

  in Islam 41, 42, 58–59
  Locke on 31, 63–64
  Luther on 25–26
  in Ottoman Empire 48
  in U.S.
    Christian Right and 94
    under Jackson 82
    Jefferson on 64, 67
    Madison on 64–65
    in Massachusetts Bay Colony 62–63
    after World War II 37
September 11th terrorist attacks 94, 344*c*
Seventh-Day Adventism 75–76, 81, 349*g*
shah 47
sharia
  definition of 349*g*
  in Hanbali Islam 115
  and Islamic Reformation 50–51
  in Islamic state 41
  in Muslim extremism 54, 55
  reason and 41–42
  in Saudi politics 118
  in Sunna 40
  in Westernized states 52
Sharif, Sayyid Imam al-. *See* Fadl, Dr.
Sharpton, Al
  Debate on His Book *God Is Not Great* between the Author Christopher Hitchens and the Reverend Al Sharpton (2007) 172–176

363

shayk 349*g*
shayk-al-Islam 48
Sherbert, Adell 76
Sherbert v. Verner 76
Shia Islam
  break with Sunni 337*c*
  definition of 349*g*
  in Iran 110, 111
  origins of **44–45**
  in Persia 104, 105, 338*c*
  in Saudi Arabia 117
Shiva 7
Shiv Sena 130
Shudras 7
shura 43–44, 349*g*
Siddhartha Gautama. *See* Buddha
Siege of Vienna 339*c*
Sifaoui, Muhammed 136
simony 22
sin, in Islam 41
Singal, Ashok 132
Singh, Manmohan 132
Six-Day War 52, 343*c*
Smith, Alfred E. 84
social contract theory 30
social reform 82, 84–85, 87
social structure 7, 104–105, 129
society, fear in 30, 31
Society of Friends. *See* Quakerism
soft dominionism 95
Sojourners: Christians for Justice and Peace 294
Solomon (Israelite king) 13
Sönam Gyatso 122
Songtsen Gampo (king of Tibet) 120
Soroush, Abdulkarim 112

Southern Baptists 80, 86–87
sovereignty, in Islam 58
Soviet Union 36, 341*c*
Spain 250*f*, 337*c*
Spanish Armada 27
Sparta 6
speech, free, and Muslims 134–136
state
  Buddhist, Tibetan 122–127
  Calvin on 26
  Christian 63, **77–99**
  definition of 349*g*
  forms of 6, 251*f*–252*f*
  Luther on 25–26
  Muslim. *See also* Iran
    Europe and 134
    ideal 39, **41–43**
    Khomeini on 109
    modern 50–53, 58–59
    Muhammad on 40
    Quran as constitution 55
    Qutb on 56
    Saudi Arabia as 116–119
    sharia in 41
    religious influence on
      Buddhism 9–10
      in Europe 250*f*, 342*c*
      in United States 258*f*, 344*c*
    views by nationality 250*f*
  state religions **26–28**, 64–65
Submission (film) 135–136
suffering 9
Sufi 105, 349*g*
Suleyman the Magnificent 48, 338*c*

sultan 349*g*
Sunday mail delivery 68
Sunna 39, 349*g*. *See also* Hadith; Quran
sunna 39, 349*g*
Sunni Islam
  break with Shia **44–45,** 337*c*
  definition of 349*g*
  on innovation 109
  in Persia 103–104, 105
  in Saudi Arabia 113–114, 117, 118–119, 343*c*
Sun Yat-sen 123
Supreme Court **68–77**
  on abortion 91, 343*c*
  on bigamy 68–69, 340*c*
  "compelling interest" test of 76–77, 344*c*
  on compulsory education 76, 152–160, 343*c*
  on creationism in curricula 71, 343*c*
  establishment clause rulings 67, **69–74,** 342*c*
  free exercise clause rulings 67, **74–77,** 342*c*
  public display rulings **72–74**
  on religion in schools 69–72
  Religious Freedom Restoration Act ruling 77, 344*c*
  on separation of church and state 67
Switzerland 263*f*
Sykes-Picot Agreement 49, 341*c*
Syria 52

Index

T

Taj Mahal 48
Tamerlane 104, 105
taqlid 51, 349*g*
tax, for churches 65
Taymiyya, Raqi al-din ibn 54–55, 115, 274*b*–275*b*, 338*c*
Temple in Jerusalem 13–14, 336*c*
Ten Commandments 12, 73–74
Ten Precepts 9
Tenzin Gyatso. *See* Dalai Lama, XIV
terrorism 94, 110, 117, 119, 136–137, 344*c*
theocracies 81, 109, 122–125, 350*g*
Theocracy Watch 96
Theological Declaration of Barmen (Barth, 1934) 36, 212–214
theology 350*g*. *See also* political theology
Thirty Years' War 28, 339*c*
Thomas More Institute 294
Tibet **120–127**
   Buddhism introduced to 120–121, 336*c*
   China annexation of 123–126, 342*c*
   Dalai Lama's exile from 342*c*
   democracy in 127
   government of 11
   historic boundaries 261*m*
   history of 120–122
   under Mongols 121–122
   theocracy of 122–125
Tibet Autonomous Region 261*m*
Timurid Empire 105
Tobacco Protest 106
Tocqueville, Alexis de 80–81
   Democracy in America excerpt (1835/1840) 148–152
Traditional Values Center 295
Trinity 18
Trisong Detsen (ruler of Tibet) 120
Troeltsch, Ernst 34, 35
Truman, Harry S. 107
tuition vouchers 71–72
Tupden Gyatso 124
Turkey 51, 263*f*
Twenty-first Amendment 341*c*

U

ulama
   definition of 350*g*
   in Iran 106
   in Islamic state 41, 109
   in Ottoman Empire 48
   in Saudi Arabia 118
   in Westernized states 52
Umar (caliph) 43
Umayyad Empire 44–45, 103–104, 337*c*
umma 38, 42, 43, 350*g*
Unam Sanctam (Boniface VIII, 1302) 24, 194–196
Union des Organisations Islamiques de France 295
Unitarian Universalist Association of Congregations 295–296
United Kingdom. *See* Britain
United Nations Declaration on the Elimination of All Forms of Intolerance and of Discrimination Based on Religion or Belief (1981) 214–217
United States **62–102**, 257*m*, 339*c*
   African-American churches of **83–84**
   Anglican Church in 64–65, 79–80, 339*c*, 346*g*
   Bible reading in schools in 342*c*
   biblical worldview in 258*f*
   as Christian nation **77–99**
   Christians in. *See* Catholic(s), in U.S.; Christian fundamentalism; Christian Right; evangelical Christianity; Protestant(s), in U.S.; Protestantism, in U.S.
   Civil War of 86, 340*c*
   colonial 31, 79, 257*m*, 339*c*
   Constitution of. *See* Constitution
   frontier, Protestantism in 79–80

365

growth of religion in 98–99
Iran and 107–108, 110
Muslim population of 263*f*
Obama's election in 344*c*
Pledge of Allegiance of 74–75
political parties of 82–83, 87–88, 92–94, 340*c*, 342*c*
prayer in schools in 70–71, 342*c*
primary documents of 145–182
Prohibition in 81–82, 341*c*
religious evolution in **79–90**
religious freedom in 339*c*. *See also* establishment clause; free exercise clause; Supreme Court
religious influence on government 250*f*, 258*f*
religious tolerance in 3–4, **62–67**, 99
in Saudi Arabia 117
as secular nation **77–99**
separation of church and state in 62–63, 64–65, 67, 82, 94
terrorist attacks on 94, 344*c*
as theocracy **94–96**
Upanishads 7
Uprising of Khurdad 15, 1979, The (Khomeini) 223–224
Urban II (pope) 46
urbanization 86, 87
U.S. Muslims Issue Fatwa against Religious Extremism (Fiqh Council, 2008) 224–226
Uthman 43

V

Vaishyas 7
Vajjian government 10
Vajpayee, A. B. (Atal Bihari) 131, 132, 275*b*
values 88–89
Van Gogh, Theo 135–136, 344*c*
Vegas 7
velayat i-faqih 109, 110
Vienna, siege of 48
Viguerie, Richard 91
"Virginia Act for Establishing Religious Freedom, The" (Jefferson, 1786) 65, 145–147
Virginia colony 64–65
Vishnu 7
Vivekananda, Swami 129
Voting Rights Act (1965) 88, 342*c*

W

Wallace v. Jaffree 71
Wallis, Jim 97
"Wall of Separation Letter," The (Jefferson, 1802) 67, 147–148
war 30, 31
Warren, Earl 75
Wars of Apostasy 43
Wedgwood, Veronica C. 28
weekends, court rulings on 75–76
West Africa 137–138
Westernization **50–51**, 55
Westphalia, Treaty of 28–29, 339*c*
West Virginia State Board of Education v. Barnett 75
Weyrich, Paul 91
Whig party 82–83
Wilhelm I (emperor of Germany) 35
Williams, Roger 62–63, 275*b*, 339*c*
Williams, Rowan 37
Wills, David W. 83
Winthrop, John 63
Wisconsin v. Yoder Supreme Court decision (1972) 76, 152–160, 342*c*
World Hindu Council 132
World War I 35, 49, 341*c*
World War II 37, 133, 341*c*
worship 5, 7–8, 12
Wright, Robin 110
Wuthnow, Robert 88
Wycliffe, John 24

Y

Yarlung dyansty 120
Yazdi, Ebrahim 108
Yazid 44
yoga 8
Young, Brigham 81

Index

Z

Zakaria, Fareed 113
zakat 40, 350g
Zawahiri, Ayman al- 57
  "Advice to the
    Community to
    Reject the Fatwa
    of Sheikh Bin
    Baz Authorizing
    Parliamentary
    Representation"
    (2008) 232–236

Zorach v. Clausen 70
Zoroaster 104
Zoroastrianism 104,
  105